TRAVELS

IN THE

ATLAS AND SOUTHERN MOROCCO.

TANGIER.

TRAVELS

IN THE

ATLAS AND SOUTHERN MOROCCO

A NARRATIVE OF EXPLORATION

BY

JOSEPH THOMSON, F.R.G.S.

GOLD MEDALIST OF THE ROYAL GEOGRAPHICAL SOCIETY
HON. MEMBER OF THE ROYAL SCOTTISH, THE MANCHESTER, ITALIAN, AND
NETHERLANDS GEOGRAPHICAL SOCIETIES

Author of "Through Masai-land," &c.

LONDON
GEORGE PHILIP & SON, 32 FLEET STREET, E.C.
LIVERPOOL: 45 TO 51 SOUTH CASTLE STREET

1889

TO

MY VERY DEAR FRIENDS

Dr. and Mrs. HUGH LOGAN CALDER

This Book

IS DEDICATED

BY

THE AUTHOR.

PREFACE.

In introducing this book to the reader, little need be said. It is nothing more than what it pretends to be —a Personal Narrative of Exploration. It does not claim to be a book on Morocco, and consequently may appear in many respects to be very defective. To write such a book was originally my ambition when I turned my attention to that remarkable country, but the abrupt and premature conclusion of my travels has made me perforce alter my intention, and devote myself to recording only something of what we saw and experienced in the parts in which we travelled. It has, moreover, been as much my object to sketch pictures as to chronicle facts. For the same reason this book has been made a personal narrative, with its inevitable frequent use of the first person singular or plural.

To preserve the popular and handy character of the volume, much of general and scientific interest has been omitted, which will see the light through more appropriate channels.

Treatises on the geography, geology, and botany of

the Atlas would be as much out of place in a popular work, as would be the military notes of the energetic young officer who accompanied me, and, therefore, on such topics, except in a superficial manner, I am silent.

It only remains for me to add that the illustrations of this book are from photographs taken by myself, with the exception of half-a-dozen kindly supplied to me by Mr. White, H.M. Consul at Tangier, and three others by unknown photographers, to whom I now beg to offer my apologies for making unauthorised use of their productions.

It may be well to state that in the spelling of new proper names I have adopted the Italian vowel sounds.

EDINBURGH, *April* 1889.

CONTENTS.

CHAPTER I.

GIBRALTAR TO TANGIER 1-9

Departure from Europe—Arrival in Tangier—A night-ramble through the town—Condition of the streets—A Moorish café—A Jew's wedding.

CHAPTER II.

MORNING IN TANGIER 10-17

How I came to visit Morocco—Past history and present condition of the country—My companion, Lieutenant Harold Crichton-Browne—View of Tangier—A native school—Visit to the British Ambassador, Sir William Kirby Green.

CHAPTER III.

A STROLL THROUGH TANGIER 18-30

The inhabitants—The shops—The market-place—The Kasbah—A wedding-procession—A funeral—Residence of the Governor—Moorish decoration—View from the Marshan.

CHAPTER IV.

TANGIER TO AZAMOR 31-43

Letter from the Sultan—Departure from Tangier—A stormy passage—Arrival at Casablanca—Departure for Azamor—Our soldier-guide—Fertility of the country—Kubas—Profusion of flowers—Camp near an Arab *duar*.

x   CONTENTS.

CHAPTER V.

AZAMOR TO MOGADOR 44–64

Native wells and water-wheels—Portuguese fortifications at Azamor—Mazagan—Portuguese remains—Kasbah of Northern Dukalla—Geological features of the country—Kasbah of Southern Dukalla—Mona-Metamores and mitfires—Reception at Kasbah of Aissa—*Kuskussu* and *Tajen*—Night in the Kasbah—Departure for Saffi—Nearing the town—Mr. George Hunot, British Vice-Consul—Hawking—Departure for Mogador—Physical features of Shiedma—Akermut—First view of the Atlas—Mogador.

CHAPTER VI.

MOGADOR 65–78

Delays—Kindness of Mr. Payton, British Consul, and of Mr. J. Louis Ratto—Climate of Mogador—The town—Its sewage system—The Mellah—The Mogador Jew—Procession in honour of Sidi Hamadsha—Moorish fanaticism.

CHAPTER VII.

THE BOAR-HUNT 79–87

On the way to the hunting-ground—The Palm-tree House—Concert by the beaters—The hunting-party—On the scent—A false alarm—At bay—A disappointment—On the scent again—The *coup de grace*—The return home.

CHAPTER VIII.

THROUGH SHIEDMA TO SAFFI 88–111

A trial trip—Moorish adieux—Sand-dunes—Aspect of the country—Beginning of our troubles with our men—Their rapacity—Visit to the Kaid of Shiedma—Camp at Jebel Hadid—Ascent of the Iron Mountains—An evening with the Sheik of Takat—Exploration of disused iron-mines—Geological features—*Zawias*—Fording the Tensift—A blow for the mastery.

CONTENTS.

CHAPTER IX.

SAFFI TO THE CITY OF MOROCCO 112-126

Rearrangement of our escort—The town of Saffi—The palace—The climate—Start for the interior—Province of Abda—Province of Bled Hummel—Fertility of the land—Poverty of the people—Panoramic view of the Atlas and the city of Morocco—Approach to the city—Arrival, and reception by the Governor.

CHAPTER X.

MARAKSH, OR CITY OF MOROCCO 127-139

A levée—A stroll through the city—First impressions—Arrival of a guide—Desertion of one of our men—Departure from the city—Route to Sidi Rehal—Irrigation channels—View of the Plain of Morocco and the Atlas Mountains.

CHAPTER XI.

SIDI REHAL TO DEMNAT. 140-153

Departure from Sidi Rehal—Tezert—The Wad Tessaout—The province of Srarna—Approach to Demnat—Reception—We array ourselves in Moorish costume—Interview with the Kaid—The Kaid's garden.

CHAPTER XII.

TOWN AND VALLEY OF DEMNAT 154-173

The inhabitants—The Berbers or Shellach—Dress of the women—The Mellah—Prevalence of ophthalmic diseases—Visit to Iminifiri, "the big cave"—Geological features of the valley of Demnat—Remains of the Rum or early Christians—Ascent of Irghalnsor—Elevation of the Atlas at this point.

CONTENTS.

CHAPTER XIII.

TASIMSET 174–190

Visit to Tasimset proposed—Objections of the Kaid—A row among our men—Features of the road to Tasimset—Waterfall and caves at Tasimset—Jewish method of baking bread—A Jewish interior—Berber villages—Ascent of Tazaroch.

CHAPTER XIV.

THE GLEN OF THE WAD GADAT 191–203

Reception at Tezert—Enzel and the Wad el Mulha—Ascent of the Gadat glen—Difficulties of the pathway—Camp at Zarktan.

CHAPTER XV.

ACROSS THE TIZI-N-TELUET 204–222

Desolation of mountain scenery—Jebel Glauwi—Ascent of the pass—Sure-footedness of the mules—The mountaineers—Titula—Evidences of glacial action—View from head of the pass—Geological features—Valley and Kasbah of Teluet—A mountain welcome—The Kaid of Glauwa—We present the Sultan's letter.

CHAPTER XVI.

THE KASBAH OF TELUET 223–240

Machinations of our men—Moorish immorality—The Kaid's attendants and *ménage*—Life at the Kasbah—Elevation and climate of Teluet—The "Anti-Atlas"—Caves of the Rum—Tabugumt—Fight among our men.

CONTENTS.

CHAPTER XVII.

ASCENT OF TAURIRT 241–254

Geological and other features of the route—Elevation of the peak and of the Atlas—A *malade imaginaire*—Atlas Jews—"Protection"—Costume of mountain Jews—Child-wives.

CHAPTER XVIII.

INCIDENTS OF LIFE AT TELUET 255–273

A Moorish holiday—A native dance—The onlookers—We prepare to leave Teluet—Obstacles to exploration—Our men again to blame—Attacked by religious fanatics—A Moorish feast.

CHAPTER XIX.

TELUET TO AMSMIZ 274–284

Return to the Plain—Traces of glacial action—Other geological peculiarities—Iminzet to Amsmiz—Situation and population of Amsmiz—Experiments with aneroid and boiling-point thermometer—The Jews of Amsmiz—Child-marriages.

CHAPTER XX.

GLEN OF THE WAD AMSMIZ 285–299

Ascent of the glen—Our camp—More remains of the Rum—Blue daisies—Imintella—Performance by snake-charmers.

CHAPTER XXI.

GINDAFY 300–319

Second crossing of the Atlas—Geological features—Jebel Tezah—Ascent of the Tizi Nemiri—View from the pass—Elevation—Mountains of Wishdan—Red sandstone—Descent on Gindafy—Cold reception by the Kaid—Crichton-Browne stung by a scorpion—Good workmanship and its reward—Glen of the Wad Agandice—Mountain ascent—Glen of the Wad Nyfis—Return to Amsmiz.

CHAPTER XXII.

MAROSSA AND THE ASIF EL MEL 320–327

Amsmiz to the Asif el Mel—Development of cretaceous rocks at Marossa—A bad night—Glen of the Wad Erght—A terminal moraine—Camp by the Wad Erduz.

CHAPTER XXIII.

THE ASCENT OF JEBEL OGDIMT 328–345

Protestations of escort—The ascent commenced—Above the clouds—The Tizi Nslit—The landscape—Berber villages—Camp by the Wad Nyfis—Attitude of the mountaineers—A difficult climb—View of the Sus valley and the glen of the Nyfis—Robbers in the path—Other obstacles—The summit reached—View of the Atlas and the Sus valley—Elevation—Return to Amsmiz—Wrath of the Governor.

CHAPTER XXIV.

MARAKSH 346–369

Return to the city—View from the house-tops—The houses—The minarets—The Kutubia—The walls—Population—The Kasbah, Medinah, and Mellah—Ruined buildings—Mosque of the Kutubia—Mosque of Abdul Aziz—The gateways—The palace—Difficulties in obtaining photographs—The fountains—The business quarter—The bazaars—The workshops—The fundaks—The Kaseria—The markets—Native entertainments in the market-place.

CHAPTER XXV.

LIFE IN MARAKSH 370–392

The excessive heat—Cost of living—A Moorish house—The harem—House decoration and furniture—Degeneracy of modern Moorish art and its causes—Social position of women—Itinerant musicians—A Moorish interior—Moorish women at home—Their dress and appearance—The Hammum—Shampooing a Jew—Moorish dancing-women.

CHAPTER XXVI.

THE AID-EL-KEBIR 393–413

Gathering of Kaids to do homage to the Sultan—Maraksh *en fête*—The scene outside the walls—The Viceroy—The religious ceremony—The sacrifices—The state function—Reception of the Kaids—A fanatical crowd—Stoning the Christians—Lab el Barud or powder-play—Feats on horseback—An example of Moorish justice.

CHAPTER XXVII.

THE JEWS 414–428

Reputed galling restrictions under which they live—Their actual comparative exemption from such—Their usury—Their mercantile spirit—Their dwellings—Over-crowding—Jewish hospitality—Religion—Former persecutions.

CHAPTER XXVIII.

THE HOUSE-TOPS 429–443

View of the Atlas—Night in Maraksh—Domestic discord—"A piece of her mind"—The call to prayers—Mohammedanism in Morocco—Moorish system of government—Sale of "protections"—Europeans in Morocco—Prospects of the Empire.

CHAPTER XXIX.

URIKA 444–455

Another *malade imaginaire*—Final departure from Maraksh—Arrival at Achliz—Ascent of the Urika glen—Meeting with the Kaid—"To arms"—An effectual barrier—We beat a retreat—A lavish bill of fare—Return to Achliz—Glen of the Wad Reraya.

CHAPTER XXX.

THE ASCENT OF THE TIZI LIKUMPT 456–467

Glen of the Wad Iminnen—Its desolation—Its inhabitants—Tashdirt—Ascent of the mountain—We reach our highest point in the Atlas—The Tizi-n-Tamjurt—Mountain tarn of Ifri—A native superstition—Boycotted—Return to Asni—Asni to Imintanut—A slave caravan—Winnowing corn.

CHAPTER XXXI.

THROUGH SUS TO THE COAST 468–484

We set out for Sus—Anarchy in the province of Mtuga—A scene with our men—The Wad Isserato—Sok in the glen of Msira—The end of the Atlas range—The "Burj Anserrani"—Mountains of Ida Uziki and Ida Mhamud—The province of Sus—The Howara in revolt—Reception at the Kasbah of Msgina—Agadir—Agadir to Casablanca—Departure for England.

INDEX 485–488

LIST OF ILLUSTRATIONS.

Full Page Illustrations.

1. Tangier		*Frontispiece*
2. Street Scene, Tangier		*facing page* 4
3. A Sok or Market	,,	,, 21
4. Saffi from the North	,,	,, 58
5. Street in Kasbah, Mogador	,,	,, 68
6. Mogador from the South	,,	,, 80
7. Group, Top of Jebel Hadid	,,	,, 106
8. Sultan's Palace, Saffi	,,	,, 114
9. Street in Maraksh	,,	,, 129
10. Fountain in Morocco	,,	,, 131
11. Demnat	,,	,, 161
12. Camp in Olive Grove	,,	,, 189
13. Adrar-n-Iri and Glen leading to Tizi-n-Teluet	,,	,, 205
14. Kasbah, Teluet	,,	,, 215
15. "Dinner Ready"	,,	,, 268
16. Amsmiz	,,	,, 282
17. Jewish Child-Wives, Amsmiz	,,	,, 284
18. Wad Nyfis, East of Camp, Gindafy	,,	,, 318
19. Jebel Ogdimt from the Tizi Nslit	,,	,, 332
20. View of Morocco from the Housetop	,,	,, 347
21. Mosque of the Kutubia	,,	,, 353
22. Entrance to One of the Business Quarters, Maraksh	,,	,, 361
23. Our Quarters, Maraksh	,,	,, 373
24. Women at the Door of the Harem	,,	,, 374
25. David Assor, Shalum, and Jews of Maraksh	,,	,, 417
26. Jewesses, Maraksh	,,	,, 420
27. Mouth of the Wad, Urika Glen	,,	,, 446
28. Village in Urika Glen	,,	,, 448
29. Tashdirt, Wad Iminnen	,,	,, 461
30. Jews, Asni	,,	,, 465
31. Moorish Guns, Daggers, and Powder-Horns	,,	,, 484

xviii LIST OF ILLUSTRATIONS.

Small Illustrations in Text.

	PAGE		PAGE
Boy and Beggar	30	Waiting for Dinner	269
Our Soldier-Guide	34	Kasbah, Gindafy	308
Water Wheel	45	The Cloud Scene, Tizi Nslit	330
Market-Place, Azamor	47	The Walls of Morocco	349
Jew of Mogador	69	Entrance to Palace Court	355
Woman, Out-Door Costume	74	A Potter's Shop	359
Brass Tray, Mogador	87	A Moorish Audience	368
Camp in Olive Grove	98	Leather Tea-Tray Mat	369
Court in Palace, Saffi	115	Itinerant Musician	379
H. Crichton-Browne	121	In Disguise	387
Moorish Girl	132	Water Carrier	394
C.-B. in Moorish Dress	149	Faces in the Crowd	403
Garden in Kaid's House	151	Powder-Play	408
Mellah	158	The Kutubia	413
Mountain Village	186	Among the Gardens, Maraksh	443
Daggers, Powder-Horn, and Ornaments	190	Powder-Horn and Bullet-Pouches	455
Zarktan	202	Village in the Glen of the Wad Iminnen	459
Daggers and Powder-Horn	240		
Atlas Jews	249	Winnowing Corn	466

Maps.

1. PHYSICAL MAP OF SOUTH-WESTERN MOROCCO, SHOWING AUTHOR'S ROUTE . . . *facing page* 1
2. GEOLOGICAL MAP OF SOUTH-WESTERN MOROCCO „ „ 488
3. STRAIT OF GIBRALTAR . . . . . *page* 2
4. ROUTE FROM RABAT TO SAFFI . . . „ 36
5. ROUTES IN THE CENTRAL ATLAS . . . „ 287
6. PLAN OF MOROCCO . . . . . „ 351

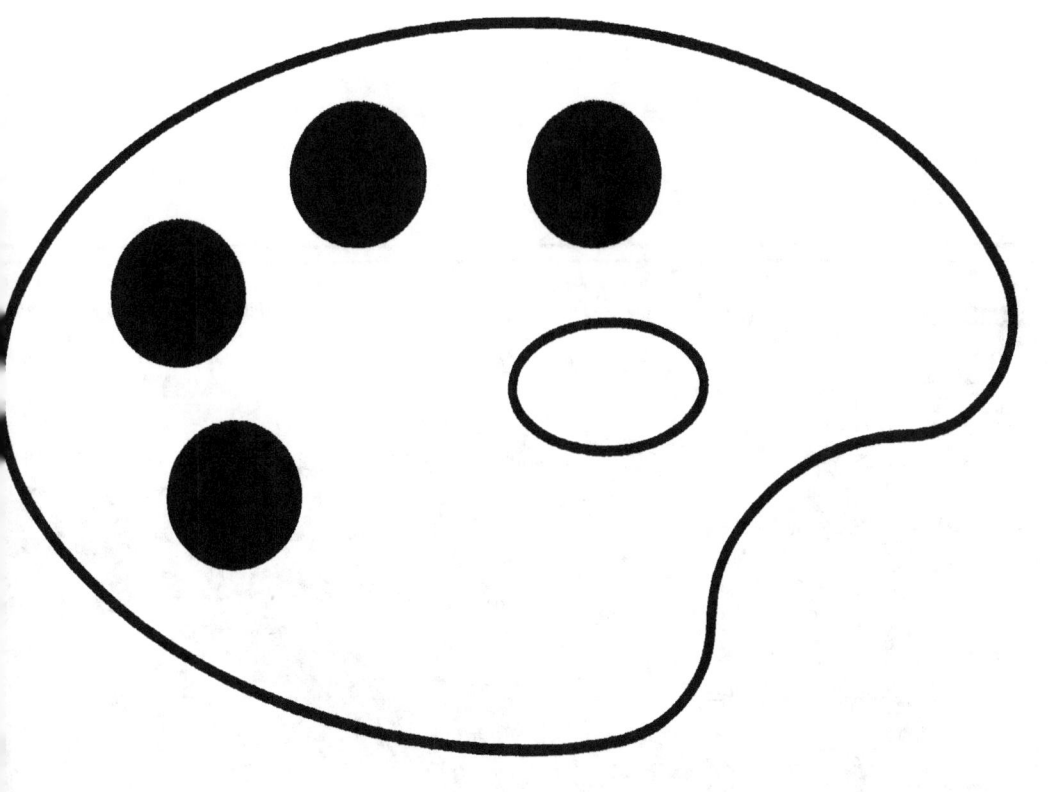

Original en couleur
NF Z 43-120-8

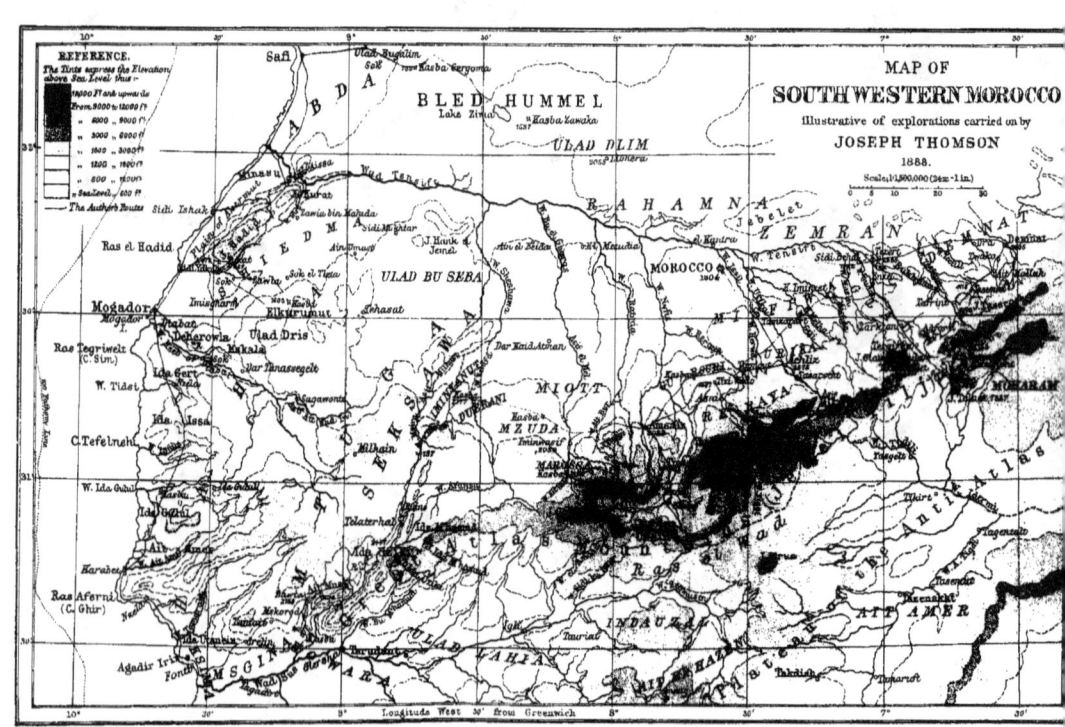

MOROCCO.

CHAPTER I.

GIBRALTAR TO TANGIER.

At mid-day, on the 17th of March 1888, we were still in Gibraltar, still on the threshold of Europe. We were wandering through lanes and streets whose English names seemed as much out of place as did the blue-costumed policemen and red-coated soldiers among the swarthy Gibraltarians and black-eyed Spanish girls. At every step we could not but be aware that we were still under the British flag. We saw much to interest and delight us—much to instruct; but we could not feel at rest while the current-swept Straits lay between us and our more immediate goal, Morocco.

As the sun began to decline towards the west, we found ourselves on the turbulent stretch of blue waters. Europe was now behind us, and Africa, with all its promised joys, in front. Once fairly clear of the protecting headlands, there was a short period of "tremendous motion" and "rueful throes," and then Africa received us in her sheltering arms.

The sun was nearing the horizon as we steamed into the little Bay of Tangier.

The town, however, we could not see, strain as we might; for just beyond it hung the sun, shedding a dazzling flood of light like a marvellous aureole over its every feature, and effectually hiding it from our

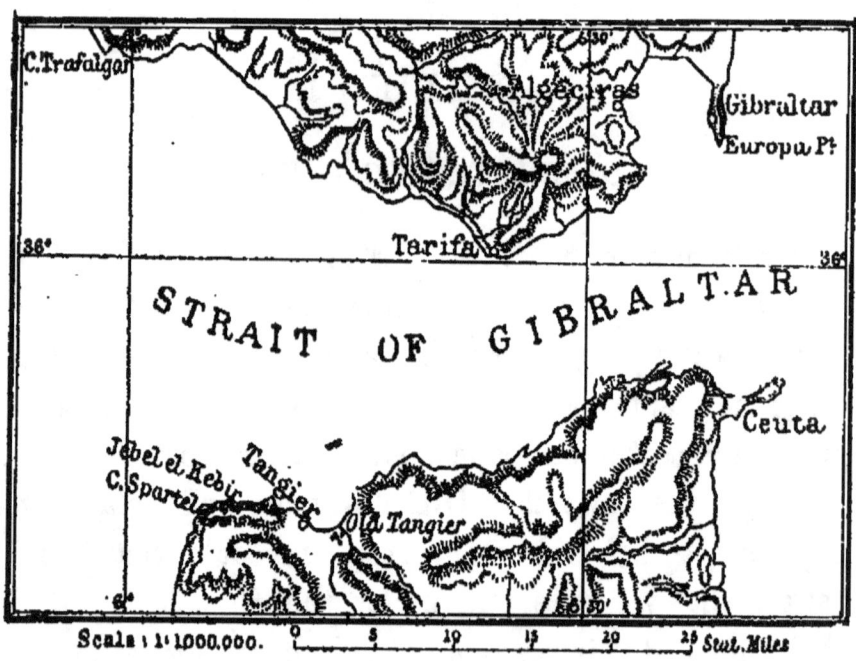

infidel gaze. Only for a few moments, however; for speedily we steamed into the shadow of the hills, and, as if by enchantment, the town sprang into view, cradled in a niche of the hillside which bounds the western aspect of the little bay. There indeed it lay, a thing of beauty to us, in all the glamour of its Oriental architecture; its otherwise dazzling white-washed walls toned down by the soft evening shadows, though every detail of house or mosque stood out sharp and clear in the pure atmosphere.

We had barely time to review the general impression conveyed by the scene when we became aware that the little steamer had stopped, and the rattling of the anchor-chains brought us back to the more practical necessities of the moment.

Scarcely had we taken up a watchful attitude beside our baggage before the steamer was surrounded by boats, and in a twinkling Negro, Berber, Moor, and Spaniard were scrambling on board, bent on taking possession of the persons and *impedimenta* of passengers.

For a moment I allowed myself to be entranced by the (to me) not unpleasant gabble and scramble. The Arab gutturals and pigeon-English brought back many memories of East and West Africa, and the constantly recurring name of "Allah" sounded sweet and musical, and altogether seemly, after the sharp significance of its English equivalent, as we are accustomed to hear it under similar circumstances. But while I stood and dreamed I was not asleep. On seeing some friendly Moors put unauthorised hands upon our belongings, the old spirit of command (which had been developed in me as leader of several African caravans) instinctively leapt up, and with wild whoop I sprang among the noisy crew and drove them forth till I saw it necessary to utilise their services.

A few minutes later we were landed on the shore of Africa—not, however, Africa as I had known it elsewhere, black, barbarous, and breechless, but Africa Orientalised, in which the Negro and the European alike seemed extraneous elements.

A slight inspection sufficed to pass our baggage before the grave and dignified Moors who sat as customs-inspectors at the water-gate of the town, and then, with eyes now watchfully directed towards our little caravan of porters, anon taking note of passing Moor, Jew, and Gentile, we wended our way up a rising winding lane, till we found ourselves at the doorway of the Continental Hotel, and passing in, were once more in Europe, with all that phrase implies in regard to the good things of this life which minister to the body.

A couple of hours later we were sitting in the cool corridor sipping our coffee in the most approved civilised fashion, watching the movements of visitors, and catching now and then a glint of local colour in the shape of picturesquely-dressed native waiters, an impudent little Jew guide in Tunisian costume, and the amply dressed and portly form of his Moorish companion.

But we did not feel contented. What came we out for to see? we asked each other. Not this certainly. We felt we could not possibly sleep that night in peace unless we had sought out some adventure or seen something thoroughly Moorish to dream about.

Visitors had been seen to leave the hotel mysteriously, headed by a guide and a lantern. Here was something to go upon. We also called for a guide

STREET SCENE, TANGIER.

Page 4.

and a lantern, and sallied forth into the unlighted streets of Tangier.

We soon learned that the lantern was an important adjunct to night-rambles in a Moorish town, lessening the risk of unpleasant shocks to head or feet, or unwished-for contact with disagreeable sewage-scented puddles and dead dogs and cats. These, however, in our fresh enthusiasm, were considered so thoroughly Eastern and in harmony with things Moorish, that we raised not our voices against them. Indeed, I verily believe we should have complained had we found the streets thoroughly clean, and had not occasionally stumbled against some malodorous dead animal. Be that as it may, there was no doubt as to what was the real thing in Moorish street amenities, and we found ourselves kept continually on the alert, looking after head and feet.

When we sallied forth, it was yet too early in the evening to find adventures. There were too many people in the streets, too many glowworm-like lanterns lighting up the darkness. We therefore made for a Moorish café, which, as a rule, is the first, and not uncommonly the last glimpse that European visitors get of Moorish life.

The café we found to be a very poor place, decorated with gaudily-coloured brackets and some cheap mirrors and prints. We felt quite insulted on being offered chairs to sit upon, and waved them haughtily away with "*Baraka! baraka!*" which we had been told was the right way to decline with thanks. The coffee-grounds and warm water put us into better humour. We tried hard to enjoy the terrific din raised by a band of musicians, who, with an accompaniment of tomtoms, violins, pipes, and hand-clapping, howled out a song which apparently required many contortions of the face and much raising of the eyes to heaven to bring out the due effect. That we did not altogether succeed may have been due to a presentiment that this was not the genuine article—as neither it was—the music being Jewish and Spanish. As a rule, however, everybody goes away from such an entertainment immensely delighted, satisfied that he or she knows now what Moorish music is like.

After an interval sufficiently long to enable us to take in the situation, we felt that the time had come to seek something more stirring, and muffling our forms in imaginary cloaks, we left the café.

The lanes were now nearly deserted. Only here and there a light appeared glimmering in the distance, dancing about like a will-o'-the-wisp. On nearer approach, a figure in sepulchral cerements becomes vaguely outlined behind the light, looking like a ghost in search of his tomb—so slow and measured the step, so weird the effect of the white dress and draping. Anxious to be friendly, while improving our Arabic, we saluted such passers with "Peace be with you," but hearing no reply, concluded that our Arabic was not, as yet, "as she is spoke."

At various places we heard sounds of mirth and music, and stopped to listen and watch for whatever might turn up. But no black-faced slave accosted us in mysterious fashion and invited us to follow him to—well, anywhere. One mustn't ask questions when on the search for adventures.

We were fast becoming rather tired of our wanderings, and, in the absence of anything to excite the fancy or quicken the pulses, we were inclined to vote the whole thing "slow," when suddenly a pronounced sound of revelry struck refreshingly on our ears. We at once held a council of war with our guide, from whom we learned that a Jewish wedding was being celebrated, and that the parties would feel honoured by our presence. Being assured that our appearance would not be considered an unwarrantable intrusion, we passed the word, "Bismillah!" and moved forward.

Traversing a narrow passage, we boldly pushed our way, till suddenly we found ourselves in a small *patio* or court in the centre of the house, round which ran galleries giving entrance to the various rooms, thus securing both ventilation and privacy. The *patio* on this occasion was brilliantly lighted up with lamp and candle, displaying a crowd of young Spanish Jews smoking the eternal cigarette, while an open door revealed an interesting bevy of black-eyed women.

Our unannounced appearance was greeted by a sudden cessation of the conversation, and for a moment tobacco-smoke ceased to curl upwards. All eyes were turned upon us. An awkward moment ensued. We began to think our guide had deceived us, and were about to retire with apologies, when a young lady, apparently an attendant spirit of the house, hurried up, and with engaging frankness saluted us with "*Bon jour.*"

We replied with extreme cordiality, and, nothing loath, allowed ourselves to be led into the room beyond, where my young friend was soon blushing happily among the bright faces and scintillating eyes of the circle of damsels who massed themselves around us. We speedily felt quite at our ease—my friend the cynosure of every black eye, and I myself, in the *rôle* of a philosophical observer of mature years, finding amusement in watching the disgusted faces of the young Jews and the animated manners and ample charms of the Jewesses.

Unable to resist our tempters, we drank cup after cup of highly sweetened tea. Our conversation was of an embarrassingly polyglot character, French, Spanish, and English phrases being used with a delightful disregard of their meaning. But what did it matter while smiles, laughter, and bright glances kept everybody happy—except, of course, the young men out in the cold of the *patio*.

At length, across the pleasant din sounded the twanging notes of a guitar, and a general movement showed that these were the signal for a dance.

Forgetting my character as merely "a chiel amang them takin' notes," oblivious also of the mature years I have alluded to, I was on my feet in an instant, and bending in respectful salutation to the ground before a plump maiden. Ere my astonished companion recovered his surprise, or the lady's countrymen their breath, I was whirling round in a waltz. Polkas followed, and everything went as merrily and decorously as could be desired. We did not, however, stop there. In the interval of a dance my friend proposed that we should go through the steps of a reel, "just to show them a thing or two, you know." At first I made a feeble attempt at remonstrance, but at that moment the guitarist struck up something which had a distant resemblance to a Scotch tune, and almost before I knew, I was facing C.-B. and throwing my legs about in all the *abandon* of the dance, not forgetting to give character and life to it by the inspiring " hooch" that helps to stir the blood of Scottish lads and lasses.

Needless to say our terpsichorean efforts were received with applause and undisguised admiration, and we retired to our seats in blushing triumph, amidst which, resuming the grave character which sat more naturally upon me, I wondered at the fortuitous concourse of circumstances which had landed us at a Jew's wedding in Africa to dance a reel.

CHAPTER II.

MORNING IN TANGIER.

When I awoke next morning it was still dark. Through the latticed shutters and open window of my bedroom a delicious breeze found its way.

While I lay trying to realise where I was and gather my scattered thoughts back from their dream-wanderings, my attention was arrested by certain sounds which suddenly burst upon the stillness of the morning, and came to my ears in rich Arabic gutturals and long-drawn musical cadence.

My knowledge of Arabic was of the slightest, but I had not travelled in Mohammedan countries without picking up some knowledge of their ways and customs, and I knew at once that I was listening to the Mueddin calling the faithful to their morning spiritual duty. "Prayer is better than sleep! Prayer is better than sleep! Come to prayers! Come to prayers!" Such was the burthen of the soul-stirring cry, which, emanating from the minaret of the neighbouring mosque, vibrated over "the city protected by the Lord," and rang in my ears with an overpowering attraction and impressiveness.

As I lay and listened to the long-drawn syllables of the summons, I could not but recall the time when I last heard them. It was in the Central Sudan and the very heart of Africa. Negro races surrounded me, and the land lay parched and desolate under the burning brilliancy of a tropical sun. To that far-off region Islam had penetrated, and finding suitable fuel, had caught fire and blazed with all the vigour of its early days in the deserts of Arabia, bringing in its wake new life and energy, and the seeds of civilisation. There also it was that the desire to visit Morocco first took root in my heart. On all sides I had remarked the impress of Moorish ideas, in manners and customs, and in the character of arts and industries. I knew that for centuries traders from Morocco had continued to cross the desert, braving all its unparalleled hardships and terrors, to carry to the natives of the Sudan such good things of this world as they themselves possessed, and spread before them promises of the infinitely greater and more glorious things of another if they would but acknowledge the One God and His Prophet, at the same time threatening them with all the terrors of Gehenna if they turned not from their evil ways.

The result of that commercial intercourse and religious teaching I had seen with admiration. It had awakened within me for the first time a belief in the improvability of the African race. And now I had come to one of the parent sources to see what Moorish art was, and what the secret of the wonderful power of Islam.

Morocco, moreover, spread before me other and no less potent attractions. For centuries it had been more or less the scene of European warlike or commercial enterprise. The Romans had held sway over a considerable area in the north. Some centuries later the Portuguese had laid an iron hand upon its western littoral, and there left striking monuments of their former greatness and commercial vigour. The British too had had a footing in the north, and our national flag had waved over the very town in which I lay.

Nor had the Spaniards been without a finger in the pie—a finger too which, unlike Britain and Portugal, they mean to retain there, pending the hour when they shall endeavour to push in the whole hand and arm, and, in grasping hold of the inheritance of the Moor, wipe out the stain of the Moorish domination in Spain, the memory of which still rankles deep in their hearts.

In spite, however, of all these conquests and settlements, as well as of the more widely spread ramifications of commercial enterprise, Morocco, though at the very gate of Europe, remains one of the most impenetrable of countries. Till this day large areas remain as completely unknown as many parts in the very heart of the continent. Religious fanaticism has had much to do with the continuance of this state of things, making everything which had not the stamp of Islam an abomination; but a not unimportant factor also has been the growing fear of the Christian nations they despise, who, though "rebels against God," have been given the arts of war wherewith to scourge the Faithful. The Moors know too well that the Nazarenes only await their opportunity to pounce upon them. As for the result, well, "God will show." Meanwhile their policy is passive resistance and complete isolation. Keep the Christians quarrelling among themselves, and let us not rouse their cupidity by the fertile lands, the mineral riches, and the living streams of this the heritage of the true believers.

To penetrate this barrier of religious fanaticism, hatred, fear, and official obstruction; to strike away from the oft-traversed tourist routes and penetrate the unknown provinces; but more especially to explore the little known and reputedly dangerous Atlas Mountains, which throughout the centuries had almost defied the curiosity of a host of travellers, was the congenial task I had now set myself. In carrying out my geographical programme, I did not doubt but that I should also satisfy the original desires which had turned my thoughts to Morocco, and learn something of the Moor himself, his social condition, his religion, his mode of government, as well as his arts and industries.

At home my scheme had met at first with but scant encouragement from those who knew, as well as those who thought they knew, something about Morocco and the Moors. It was represented that any attempt to penetrate the Atlas Mountains in the present condition of the country could only end in disaster, and probably death—so effective was the official obstruction, so dangerous and fanatical the ways of the mountaineers.

The comments of my geographical friends, however, had failed to discourage me. I had never been accustomed to shape my course by second-hand reports, and having once made up my mind to go to the Atlas Mountains, I was determined that I would see for myself what was possible and what impossible before I altered my plans.

Once it was seen that I was not to be dissuaded, my friends had shown a most gratifying alacrity in doing everything in their power to assist me. The Royal and the Royal Geographical Societies, Lord Salisbury as Foreign Secretary, and Sir Joseph Hooker —whose hints and advice were invaluable—all had vied with each other in putting me in the most favourable position possible to do good work—making me feel (if they did nothing else) that it would be a terrible disgrace if I did not fulfil to some extent the trust they placed in me—a healthier inspiration undoubtedly than that arising from the determination to succeed because failure had been predicted.

On previous African journeys I had travelled alone, in weary isolation from all civilised intercourse. In this trip circumstances had led me to try a companion. An enthusiastic young friend—henceforth in these pages to be known as C.-B. (Lieutenant Harold Crichton-Browne, 2nd Batt. King's Own Scottish Borderers)— anxious to see something of African travelling and widen his experience of life, had volunteered to accompany me, and share my hardships, dangers, and expenses, and I had agreed at once to the proposal.

Once everything was arranged we had soon completed our preparations, and left England on the 9th of March, arriving at Tangier, as I have already described, on the 17th of the same month.

By the time I had finished my retrospect of the chain of events which had led to my being where I was, the day had not only dawned, but the sun had risen.

Getting up myself, and eager to commence my exploration of the town, my first care was to visit the neighbouring bedroom. There, oblivious of Mueddins and everything else, lay C.-B. sound asleep.

"What! not up yet? Look here!" I cried, as, drawing back the curtains from the window and pushing open the venetian shutters, a glorious flood of light filled the room and dazzled the half-opened eyes of my friend.

Before us a succession of whitewashed houses rose tier above tier, reflecting back the rays of the morning sun with blinding power.

Minaret and dome rising from mosques relieved the somewhat monotonous aspect of the house-terraced slope, while the battlemented walls and frowning ramparts of the Kasbah or citadel, which overlooks the town, formed a broken outline projected sharply against the marvellously deep blue of the sky.

In opening that window we have transported ourselves from Europe to Africa. Right beneath our window, on the other side of the four-feet broad street, we peep into a native school, and see small boys squatting on the floor round a venerable be-turbaned *Taleb* or teacher, while, with blatant discord and much swaying of bodies, they repeat vociferously texts from the Koran inscribed on wooden boards, thus learning at once the precepts of their faith and a smattering of classic Arabic.

Farther off we hear some wildly attractive though barbaric music, with shouting, singing, and firing of guns, which we conclude must proceed from a wedding-procession.

Tantalising we find it in the extreme to crane our necks and look down on the *haik*-draped Moors or blanket-shrouded females of the race. We are too high up to see their gazelle-like eyes, and can only feel in imagination their irresistible glances.

As we bathe in the wealth of morning light, see overhead the clear blue sky, and feel our faces fanned by the fresh breeze, we cannot but picture the environment of our friends at home, who are beginning to struggle reluctantly out of bed, and shiver in their cold rooms, while they curse the sleet, the rain, the east winds, the fog, and their luck generally. We generously wish we could send them some Moorish weather, or mix for them a pot of our local colour.

Our first duty after breakfast was to call upon His Excellency Sir William Kirby Green, our Minister to the Court of Morocco. Bent on business, we shut our eyes to everything that would have detained or led us astray from the road to the Legation.

This centre of British influence was found to be modestly hidden, well out of the way. With due formality we were ushered into the presence of His Excellency, wondering what was to be his attitude to our enterprise. We were soon put at our ease in that respect. We found ourselves before the most genial and good-natured of men, who gave us more courage by the cheering way in which he spoke of our prospects. He had already taken steps to obtain a letter or firman for us from the Sultan, which would be of use to us in places, but which he was careful to explain would be an obstruction to us in the most important parts if we were not judicious in showing or suppressing it as circumstances demanded.

We left the Legation in a most hopeful spirit, feeling that, socially at least, our country could have no better representative. Later on we also learned that, diplomatically, we had the right man in the right place. Our policy previous to his arrival had threatened to get into grooves which were not only detrimental to our own but also to Morocco's best interests; but happily Sir William had arrived in time to strike out in new and better lines before much mischief had been done.

CHAPTER III.

A STROLL THROUGH TANGIER.

WE were fated to commence our trip with the characteristic experience of the traveller in Oriental lands. For nearly three weeks we waited patiently the arrival of the Sultan's letter, and had abundant opportunities to improve our acquaintance with Tangier.

To one who had seen a few of the less adulterated cities of the shining Orient, "the city protected of the Lord" was something of a disappointment, and by no means fulfilled the expectations aroused by our first glimpses of it when bathed in all the glory and the glamour of the setting and rising sun.

Let us take a haphazard ramble and note its characteristic sights and scenes. We are soon mounted, and giving our animals their heads, we commit ourselves to the guidance of Allah. Our road, it seems, leads back towards the gate of the Customs, from which we once more diverge up a comparatively straight, badly-paved street.

We speedily call a halt to admire the fine horseshoe-shaped doorway of the principal mosque of Tangier. Graceful arabesques in stucco, and tile-work in geometrical patterns ornament its fine curves, while effective deep mouldings form a species of eaves overhead. While we crane our necks to peep inside, and with truly infidel curiosity long to explore its cool courts and sacred precincts, the Mueddin far up in the tower, with face turned to the holy East, commences to call the Mussulmans to prayer. But alas! looking around, we see more listeners among Jews and Gentiles than among those who are destined to enjoy the pleasures of Paradise. It is easy to understand how bitter must be the feelings of the pious Moor who on his way to the mosque has to pass the tobacco and drink shops, the post and telegraph offices, and other infidel abominations which have sprung up under the very shadow of the sacred structure.

Our restive horses, however, will not permit us to moralise in comfort, and we pass on.

There being nothing else of an architectural character to stay our wandering eyes, we commence our search for the grave and dignified as well as superbly dressed Moor of our dreams. On all sides, however, we are confronted by grizzly-faced scarecrows from the other side of the Straits, who have apparently left their country for their country's good. Our eager outlook for the gazelle-eyed and veiled Moorish beauties of whom we had had daily visions on our way hither is equally fruitless. Only black-eyed Spanish and Jewish damsels meet us at every turn, displaying on their persons the latest reputed Parisian costume and newest fashion in dress-improvers.

Nothing daunted, though disappointed, we mount the street intently on the watch for the genuine article. We peep into box-like erections which do duty for shops, in the expectation of discovering placid Moors, cross-legged, picturesquely enveloped, and almost lost in huge turbans, while, more bent on laying up treasure in heaven than on earth, they repeat as they count their beads the sacred titles of Allah. But no! Only hawk-nosed Jews, with greedy eyes burning with the hope of prey, jump to their feet, and, clawing the air with their fingers, invite us in broken English or French to inspect their wares. As we hurry on, we wonder what special curses the Moors have in their rich *repertoire* to hurl at the sons of Judah, that we might learn them for our own future use.

It is almost with a sigh of relief that, nearing the head of the street and the inner gateway of the town, we come at last upon something genuinely Moorish. Here a number of women sit huddled together, showing, however, a shocking disregard to native notions of decency by having their withered faces exposed while they wait the will of Allah and the arrival of purchasers of their small stock of eggs, butter, fowls, &c. Age, ugliness, dirt, rags, and poverty are their portion; but nevertheless we look upon them with more interest and pleasure, though not without a touch of melancholy, than upon the European lady-tourists who ride past us at the moment on what we guess to be diminutive asses, from the prominence and shape of the huge ears and the irrepres-

A SOK OR MARKET.

sible wag of the tails, which project from beneath the voluminous skirts of their riders.

The disappointment which we have experienced so far somewhat disappears as we pass through the small market-places, the surrounding walls of which form a series of inner fortifications.

Passing through the outer gateway, we emerge upon the market-place proper, and are suddenly confronted with a seething mass of white-robed people, all in an excited tremor and movement, and all talking and shouting—nobody apparently listening.

The idea is irresistibly suggested that here is a vision of what a graveyard would look like at the last day, before the newly-risen had fully realised their position or had time to divest themselves of their grave-clothes, while eagerly demanding of each other where they were and what was going on.

But while, from our point of vantage on horseback, we cannot but sit and admire the general effect of the striking spectacle—becowled Moors of the town, blanket-draped women, bareheaded wild-looking Berbers from the Riff Mountains, weather-beaten and poorly-dressed Arabs from the country, and caftan or blue *jellabia*-clad Jews mingling in the most quaint and bizarre fashion—we are not oblivious to the rich odour arising from the indescribable filth, which turns the market-place in the rainy season into a veritable dunghill of the most offensive description. Doubtless we had all anticipated the romantic pleasure of tasting salt with the Arabs and living in a *duar* or tent-village; but we were not disposed, from what we saw, to test their proverbial hospitality. To have passed the night in any of the gunny-bag and rag-made tents which we saw pitched at one corner of the sloping ground, in close proximity to a dead donkey and camel, which had met their fate overnight, would have been a proceeding more romantic than pleasing. Nevertheless the *sok* or market is a perfectly inexhaustible mine of subjects to the artist. Without going farther afield, he may there sketch for himself almost everything that is most interesting and characteristic of Moorish life.

It is in the Kasbah, however, that we shall find most delight, undisturbed by the incongruous elements that so far have dogged our every movement. The Kasbah is a quarter of the city where the Moor has so far been able to keep out Nazarene abominations, and reserved solely for the abode of those who acknowledge the one God and his Prophet.

Passing through the gateway near our hotel, we enter this interesting region. Our first impression is disappointing. We have been buoying ourselves up with the expectation of meeting something more attractive in Moorish architecture than the low and mean buildings we have so far seen. But here, as elsewhere, we find few touches of the artistic genius and graceful fancy we have been accustomed to attribute to the Moors. We look in vain along the monotonous expanse of whitewashed walls for a projecting latticed window, such as we had been accustomed to see in the East, and which suggest to the romantic imagination of untravelled travellers all that is meant by the word " harem."

We thread tortuous narrow lanes, alive with small Mussulmans with bright eyes and heads close shaved, except where a lock is left for the convenience of the angel who has in due time to hoist them into heaven. They are generally in their dress quaint counterparts of their parents, except that bright colours are more commonly worn. We listen with delight, as we pass groups of them, to their shrill piping voices consigning the bones of our ancestors to a fiery fate, plainly showing that even in Tangier there are pious parents who bring up their children in the way they should go.

We remark also that here the men walk about with a different air. Dignity and ease are in their step, and a holy assurance of heaven in their countenance. Their *haiks* embrace their ample persons in creamy, gauzy folds, and with an artistic grace unseen in other parts of the town. Even their turbans have taken to themselves added fulness, and overhang their tanned and bearded faces like wreathed masses of snow.

Nor are we long in discovering that in the Kasbah we have glimpses of something far different from the rheumy-eyed and shrivelled women of the market-place. Animated bundles of clothes glide down the street; and as we pass their jealously-veiled charms, we are only permitted a glint of a pair of laughing brown eyes, which from their encircling veil peep like twin stars from a rift in a fleecy cloud.

At places we have to stand aside while a wedding procession passes; the bridegroom, with face covered, riding on horseback, surrounded by his friends, who shout, sing, dance, and fire their guns, while pipes and drums keep up a continuous din.

Of no less interest, though of a more melancholy nature, is a funeral procession of some one who has paid the debt of nature, and wrapped in his shroud, is being hurried off on an open bier to his last resting-place. His friends are also about him, but not dancing and firing guns, only incessantly chanting with mournful voices and monotonous iteration the central doctrine of the Moslim faith, "There is no God but God, and Mohammed is his Prophet."

Through such scenes we slowly and lingeringly pass, till, making a sharp ascent of some twenty feet, we find ourselves at the gateway of the Kasbah proper. This is the residence of the governor, and is strongly fortified, not only to protect itself from and overawe the town, but also as a special place of strength in case of outside attack. At this point we cannot but halt to take a look over the town we have left lying in its sheltering niche, like a snowdrift nestling on a green hillside. From no point of view, to my mind, does Tangier look so beautiful and virginal, especially towards sunset, as from this particular gateway of the Kasbah.

Entering the military precincts, we cross some puddles, wind round a few dunghills, and then stop to view a graceful colonnade with marble pillars and

Corinthian capitals, resembling a cool, airy Italian loggia. On the right, and facing the entrance, a flight of steps leads up to another open colonnade of distinctly Moorish character, with horseshoe-shaped arches and slender pillars. Seen by moonlight, Tangier presents no more beautiful and romantic sight than this.

Morocco is a land of strong contrasts. Our guide calls us from the contemplation of these graceful triumphs of architecture, and draws our attention to what looks like a peep-hole in a door. On nearer approach, a sickening odour assails our sense of smell, and nearly drives us back. Mustering up courage, we peep in, and see before us a dungeon plunged in semi-night, in which lie numbers of chained and half-starved criminals. Turning from the disgusting scene, we proceed to the left, pass an open door, which gives us a view of the governor of the town in full divan, administering justice as it has been administered for centuries. Next we traverse a narrow lane, till, reaching a battered door, we are led into a dark and dirty passage, such as one might expect to lead to the deserted stable of an old farmhouse. Passing through this and round one or two corners, we suddenly emerge upon a court with tesselated floor, flooded by the light of the afternoon sun, made almost blinding by the reflection from the newly whitewashed walls. In the centre of the court bubbles a fountain in a marble basin, and around it runs a cool, sheltering colonnade of marble pillars.

From each side of this tesselated and pillared court handsomely carved and painted doors give entrance to corresponding windowless apartments. These are the rooms which are being prepared in expectation of the arrival of the Sultan.

We can hardly believe our eyes on seeing the rich ornamentation in stucco, tile, and painted arabesque which cover their walls. A dado of tiles arranged in the most intricate of geometrical patterns runs round the room, having an upper row with glazed scroll-work, or equally beautiful texts from the Koran, so that the sacred words shall always be before the believer in Islam. What appears to us quaintest and most beautiful is a deep recess or niche forming a half dome in sculptured and painted stalactitic woodwork, the graceful pendants gleaming with bright gold, set off by more subdued tints of red and black. From the niche we accidentally turn our eyes upward, to be further delighted by the wonderful arrangement of polygonal and circular domes which form the ceiling, and are likewise painted in the remarkable geometrical patterns which are the special delight of the Moorish artist, piously bent on seeking the beautiful without attempting to portray the works of Allah either in flower, fruit, or animal.

The beautiful stucco-work which surrounds the niches and adorns the walls over the doorway gives us new pleasure, and forms a striking example of the inventiveness and artistic genius, as well as the executive skill, of the workmen of former days.

We leave this charming artistic oasis in the wide waste of dirt and ugliness, and continue our way through the precincts of the Kasbah, till, passing through a massive gateway, we find ourselves outside the town.

We saunter along a narrow lane walled in by giant grasses, through which aloes and prickly pears push their huge stiff spines or prickly bulbous stumps, giving support to bramble, convolvulus, and periwinkle, and a profusion of geraniums, lilies, and irises.

From this delightful tangle of vegetation we emerge upon a breezy and grassy expanse called the Marshan. From this height we are able to take in at a glance all the more striking aspects of Tangier and its surroundings.

And a glorious and impressive sight it is. Beneath us lies the town in all its snow-white loveliness. Its margin is bathed by the blue waters of the little bay. Glittering sands are heaped in soft rounded masses to the south, while east and north undulating grass and grove-clad heights form a cradle in which the town snugly reclines.

Looking across the bay in a wider survey, our eyes first rest upon some rounded hills whose palmetto-clad slopes have a forcible resemblance to heathery hillsides. Beyond we see the dark picturesque mass of the southern Pillar of Hercules, now less imaginatively termed the Ape's Hill. From this prominent height our gaze is drawn southward along the Andjera range till it rests on the magnificent masses of the Riff

Mountains, prominent among which rises Beni Hosmar, at whose foot lies the interesting town of Tetuan.

Turning gradually round, we glance along a magnificent stretch of undulating ridges, rising from fertile hollows and ending in mountain masses, till, eastward, our eyes rest on the cistus-clad heights of Jebel Kebir, whose sandstone and limestone rocks form Cape Spartel. The lower slopes have become the heritage of the Nazarene, and from cedar or eucalyptus groves, or among sunny rose-scented gardens, rise the houses of many Europeans, who, attracted by the balmy air, blue skies, and bright sunshine, have forsaken their own countries and commenced a new life here. They may well call their houses by such names as Bella Vista, for that is by no means a too good title for the fair prospect of hill and sea on which they look down from their airy heights.

Our survey of Tangier and its surroundings is complete when, looking north over the disturbed Straits, we remark the yellow sand-dunes of Tarifa, where the Moors first set foot on Spanish soil, and the dark sierras which close the view behind. Not least, however, is the interest with which we follow the Spanish coast-line eastward till we descry in the dimming haze of distance a grey rock, and know that there floats the British flag. As we recall the sights and scenes we have just passed through on our way to the Marshan—see before us, in fact, that curious Oriental town—and consider that at the proper hour we may hear the morning and evening guns from the British garrison across the narrow Straits, we are irresistibly drawn into making certain edifying reflections.

The passing traveller of course has no means of penetrating the armour of reserve in which the Moor clothes himself, and therefore can form no idea of the inner workings of his mind; but an observant person cannot pass a few days knocking about the town without being struck by a very remarkable fact.

Here we have a town almost in touch with Europe, inhabited by a people of no small intelligence, and who daily come in contact with Europeans politically, commercially, even to a certain extent socially, and who yet seem to be absolutely unaffected by the influences that are thus brought to bear on them. Unlike almost all other peoples on the face of the earth, the traveller will not see on the most abject beggar the trace of a cast-off coat of a European. It is the same with all classes. Nowhere can one see the slightest evidence that the Moor's dress, his manners and customs, his ideas, religious or secular, or any other aspect of his life, have been modified in the slightest degree. He might be the inhabitant of another planet, whose mental and physical constitution rendered it absolutely impossible to make his ways our ways. He carries about with him an impenetrable barrier, which so far has only permitted the passage among the more reckless and depraved of such pleasing European influences as cigarette-smoking and brandy-drinking, and the adding to his already rich *repertoire* of profane phrases of a few choice forms drawn from Spanish criminals and British sailors. That, I think, may safely be said to be the sum-total of what the Moor has gained from the Christian during the centuries he has been more or less in intercourse with him.

BOY AND BEGGAR.

CHAPTER IV.

TANGIER TO AZAMOR.

On the 3rd of April the long-expected letter from the Sultan arrived at Tangier. Its opening quotation from the Koran, "There is no help nor strength but in God," sufficiently indicated its contents (see Appendix A.), for it clearly stated that we were to receive no protection from the "Sharifian Umbrella," nor help from the Government authorities, except in the frequented routes and cities of the Sultan's "happy dominions." The mountains and reputedly dangerous parts were expressly interdicted to us; and as these were the very places where we desired to intrude our infidel foot, the prospect was by no means encouraging. It seemed, indeed, as if our sole chance of seeing the Atlas Mountains would be "as prisoners to the mountaineers," as the personage who had the character of knowing Morocco better than anybody else cheeringly suggested.

To all discouragements, however, there could be but one answer. We must go and see for ourselves what could and what could not be done.

At mid-day on the 5th we left Tangier on board

the *Empusa*, the interest of our departure quite overshadowed by the attempted arrest by the British Consular authorities of a Mogador Jew who had made himself notorious in some recent English theatrical scandals. The wily Jew was too sharp for them, however, and before the steamer left the harbour he was on board bound for his native place.

Ere we rounded Cape Spartel we were sadly gazing into the pitiless sea, though we did our best to turn our lack-lustre eyes on the interesting shore, and develop a classic rapture over the Caves of Hercules, which we knew to be there.

Once round the sheltering cape, matters became worse. The south-west winds were blowing their hardest, driving before them the long heavy rollers from the Atlantic, and hurling them upon the shore, only to surge back with a nasty choppy movement, which tumbles the passing ship about and upsets even seasoned sea-goers.

We found ourselves unable to communicate with El Araishe or Rabat, and we were not in a fit condition to take much note of the distant views they presented.

On the 8th we arrived off Casablanca, at which we were able to land cargo. Here we suddenly made up our minds to leave the steamer and travel overland to Mogador, which was to be the real starting-point of our trip. It occurred to us that we might not have another opportunity of seeing the coast provinces, and we wondered that we had not thought of it before. Our enemies have insinuated that the state of the sea had stimulated or originated our sudden change of purpose; but those who know us will also know how to treat such invidious suggestions.

Our minds made up, we did not take long to throw a few travelling necessaries together, and soon we found ourselves established in a small inn kept by one Arturo Pitto. We had a glorious lunch after our privation of the past three days. Afterwards we took a stroll through the town, returning with these notes towards the evening. Casablanca occupies a flat, low-lying piece of ground close to the sea; the houses have not a single feature worth remarking; the principal street is a running sewer of filth, largely due to the late rains and the enormous herds of cattle which pass along it morning and evening; the people are more ugly and dirty, the donkeys worse treated and more mangy, the dogs more numerous and repulsive, and the beggars in greater numbers and decidedly more importunate and loathsome, than in any of the other places we had yet seen. The country around is flat, treeless, and uninteresting, but decidedly fertile. During the summer there is a considerable trade in wool, and in the autumn a still greater traffic in grain.

On the 10th the sonorous voices of the various Mueddins calling the Sālat el Fejir (prayers at dawn) were sufficient to wake us to our practical duties, and before sunrise we had cheerfully paid Arturo's modest bill, and suitably acknowledged the "God speeds" of such dependants on the good providence of Allah as had gathered to see us off and give us an opportunity

34   MOROCCO.

of exercising the cardinal virtue of charity ere we left the town. A handsome soldier, with military peaked fez, and the snow-white burnous, and voluminous *haik* which showed that he was a *kaid* or officer, bestrode a well-caparisoned grey horse, and acted as our guide and escort, the living symbol that we travelled under the special protection of the Sultan.

A long flint-lock gun lying across the pommel of

OUR SOLDIER-GUIDE.

his saddle or resting on his knee warned all passers-by of the deadly danger of molesting its owner or those under his charge. A long sword swung in un-military fashion at his side as a recourse when the gun failed him, while a curved dagger hidden in the ample folds of his dress was still a third weapon to carry out the will of Allah and the behests of his lord.

It was much to have such an one as Kaid bin Mahedi to give an air of distinction and pomp to our party, but it was of more practical importance to be the possessors of El Hadj Hamad, who followed behind him on a mule heaped with all the *impedimenta* we required on the way. He was at once interpreter, valet, cook, groom, and muleteer, who spoke a fair amount of French, English, and Spanish, and placed all his varied acquirements at the disposal of such Nazarenes as ourselves—never ceasing to ask the pardon of Allah—for the small sum of 1s. 8d. a day.

Following Hamad rode C.-B., feeling decidedly out of harmony with the sober mule he bestrode in riding-boots, spurs, and breeches, military helmet, and all the warlike glory of revolver and hunting-knife. This humble mount did not quite agree with his idea of the romance of travel, and he was apt in consequence to forget that the mule was in no wise to blame for the fact that he could not buy or hire a suitable horse.

I myself brought up the rear on a delightful little barb, which I had bought and christened "Toby." As I ambled easily along, I could afford to compassionate the unavailing efforts of my companion to get into accord with the unwonted and exasperatingly irregular movements of his charger.

Leaving Casablanca—the Dar el Baida of the Arabs—we set our faces southwards.

Passing through a series of rich vegetable-gardens, we found ourselves on a breezy and grassy expanse which stretched away south in undulating treeless monotony. A few herds and flocks grazing to right and left, and a varied succession of country-people on donkeys or trudging along behind camels, alone attracted our attention.

Gradually the plain rose into a palmetto-clad and boulder-strewn ridge, from the top of which we took our last view of Casablanca. Turning to the south, we

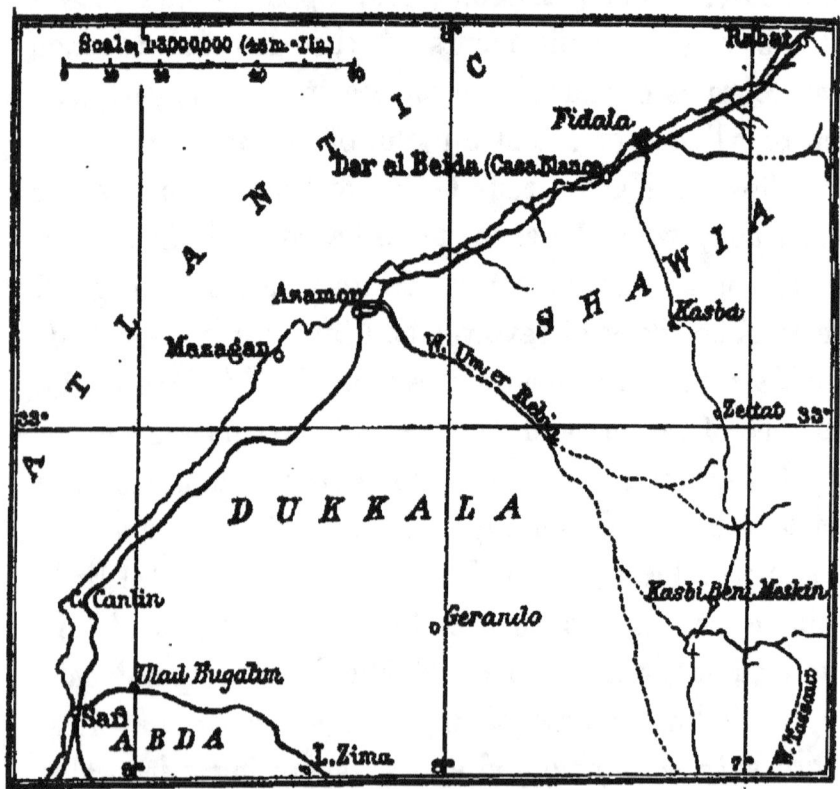

saw little to promise an interesting ride. As far as the eye could reach, the country spread itself out in low grassy undulations, unrelieved by rock or tree, by hill or valley. The sole conspicuous objects were the glaring whitewashed cupola-covered tombs of saints, called *kubas*, which everywhere reminded the traveller of the good Mussulmans who had died, but whose influence still lived for good to those who resorted to their shrines to pray. The view was not lacking in charm, however, wherever we could see the irregular coast-line and the green headlands running into the deep blue ocean. And if the surroundings were not specially attractive, we could at least hear the impressive roar of the breaking rollers and inhale the fresh sea-breeze.

Full of joyous spirits and the exhilarating sense of freedom from conventional trammels, we dubbed the "Pilgrim" (*El Hadj*) our *Tuleb* (teacher), and demanded of him instruction in the pious conventional phrases in which the heart of the Moor rejoices, as well as a few of the more choice expletives without which the life of the good Moslim would be stale, flat, and unprofitable. With a sufficient fluency in blessing and cursing one may go anywhere in Morocco without further need of the Arabic language. To fix at least the blessings in our mind, we practised upon such of the wayfarers as seemed peaceful and humble-minded, and tried not to look discouraged when, saluting them with "Peace be unto you," we were answered by "Peace be unto *the true believers*," which plainly indicated that there could be no peace for such rebels against God as we were. More than once we were savagely consigned to sulphurous flames and eternal punishment, to the barely suppressed delight of our attendant, who doubtless added an "Amen" in his sleeve.

Any temporary lowering of our spirits was soon

forgotten, however, on turning our attention to the floral displays which everywhere presented themselves. The whole country seemed a glorious natural flower-garden. Nowhere in field or conservatory have I seen anything so rich and profuse, and withal so extensive, as the exhibition of wild flowers presented by these fertile undulating plains of Shawia. Poppy, marguerite, and marigold, and fifty other familiar and unfamiliar flowers, vied in glory of bloom, producing exquisite kaleidoscopic combinations of rich colours on the green sward. Acres of the bright yellow marigold contrasted with acres of the crimson-flushed poppy. More commonly they were intermingled and sprinkled with the added hues of white and pink and blue, revealing in their gorgeous and striking combinations the source from which the Moorish artist in wool derives the ideas expressed in his wonderful *zerubias* or carpets.

Through miles of this exquisite flower-land we jogged along, finding continually a new species or fresh touch of colour to notice on some tract apparently more richly covered than anything we had yet seen. The Arab tents, which we observed rising here and there from the fields, looked Arcadian and ideal in the extreme, with their frisking goats, playing children, and barking dogs.

Farther off, shepherds tended their flocks, not uncommonly beguiling the time with such simple harmony as they could draw from reed-made pipes. We thought then what a happy, free, and careless life these Arab wanderers led. Afterwards we knew that other things skipped and played about their tents besides goats and children, and that a more oppressed and miserable race does not exist.

At mid-day we halted for a short rest and lunch. There was no need to spread our carpets, for a more beautiful one was already laid. On this we threw ourselves, to be almost hidden among nodding marguerites and marigolds, while the air was charged with the fragrance we crushed out of the flowers we lay upon.

We thoroughly enjoyed our roast-chicken and hard-boiled eggs after our six hours' ride, and did not forget the thoughtful Arturo as we washed them down with good Valdepenas. We thought ourselves the most favoured of mortals when we sniffed and sipped the steaming cup of coffee which the "Pilgrim" afterwards placed in our hands, and with a *Hamdulillah* (Praise be to Allah) we laid ourselves back on our flowery carpet in a delicious *dolce far niente* mood.

A little later we resumed our march, and ambled cheerily and rapidly along the footpath which curved and winded through a more bush-clad country, where the friendly rivalry of arbutus, myrtle, and flowers only served to heighten each other's beauties.

Towards four in the afternoon we left behind the almost uninhabited grazing-grounds and bush tracts, and entered a well-cultivated district, rich with fine crops of fast-ripening barley, which waved with silky lustre under the passing breeze. Whitewashed houses, not unlike Irish cabins, though more clean and comfortable-looking, stood here and there among the fertile fields. On our left rose the extensive ruins of the Kasbah or castle of a former Kaid or governor of the province, who, being suspected of having laid up treasure on this earth, was cast into prison till his wealth found a resting-place in the coffers of the Sultan and his ministers, while his dwelling was laid waste in search of hidden wealth.

The full significance of this story we did not then divine, but as time went on we found that almost every square mile of Morocco told the same tale with a terrible persistence and an appalling resemblance in all the main details; and we came to know that the life of the Moorish governor is no more desirable than is that of the humblest and most down-trodden of those whom he for a brief period tyrannises over.

Towards sunset our soldier left the main track, and guided us to a plain quadrangular group of buildings, which he informed us was the *fundak* or Government caravanserai for the protection of travellers. The very thought of spending a night in anything like an Eastern caravanserai was sufficient to fire our imaginations, and we made our animals move along more cheerfully with extra touches of the spur. A look inside was quite sufficient to dissipate all these pleasing illusions. An ordinary farm dunghill would have been simply heavenly beside the cesspool we were asked to pitch our tent in. We showed that we were apt pupils as we turned indignantly upon our soldier-guide. "Allah!" we cried. "Are we sons of dogs—are we of the vile race of pigs, that you ask us to camp here? No! By the beards of our ancestors, we will do no such thing!" As we marched out again the soldier stormed and pleaded that we should remain inside the *fundak*, otherwise (he protested) we should be murdered; we should have everything stolen by thieves, and he, one of God's chosen, would end his life miserably in prison, and all on account of a couple of infidels! Allah forbid!

For answer we laughed derisively at the picture he drew; and in his own manner vowed that we would see the bones of his great-great-grandmother consigned to Gehenna before we would consent to remain in such a beastly place.

Finding all his alarms and entreaties in vain, he at last consented to pass on a little farther, and camp near a *duar* or tent-village. Here at sunset we pitched our little tent and spread our waterproof sheets, and ere the twilight gave place to darkness and the twinkling stars, we were demolishing with immense gusto the remainder of the cold meats provided by our friend Arturo Pitto, too hungry to wait on such good things as El Hadj Hamad hastened to prepare. After the oranges, however, the coffee once more came with welcome incense; and feeling expansive and unselfish under its grateful influence, we commiserated our poor friends at home, who had to go through the same terrible round of irksome and uninteresting duties, knowing nothing of the pleasures of camp-life in Morocco.

For a little time we sat and talked. Then I began to observe that, in spite of the stoicism of my friend, he betrayed signs of weariness. Of course he thought it unworthy of a traveller to admit the impeachment, but, as we wrapped ourselves in our ulsters and stretched ourselves out—a change of clothes for pillows—I heard a soft sigh of intense relief, which spoke volumes.

Although we thought we had a right to expect a good night's sleep after our fifty miles' ride, we were doomed to disappointment. At first Morpheus coquetted with us and spread the allurements of semi-unconsciousness over our senses; but just as we seemed to be on the point of sinking into sweet and blissful slumber, we were time after time ruthlessly hauled back into hated wakefulness. Scores of dogs from our own and the neighbouring *duars*, attracted by the presence of strangers and the unwonted rich scents which emanated from our Pilgrim's stewpan, gathered in hostile and hungry eagerness around our tents. Having conflicting interests and deeply-rooted hates, they ever and anon set upon each other with savage yells and howls, making night truly hideous. Their wild hyena-like clamour rose and fell, came and went, in the most exasperating manner. Now and then amid the fearful din the strident voice of El Hadj could be heard hurling fearful expletives at them, accompanied by stones, and, if I mistake not, the stewpan, when, attracted by the appetising odours, they had ventured too near his belongings.

The dogs, however, were not the only element of riot

and disorder. Our horses, picketed close to the tent, after a little rest, developed decidedly combative feelings, and manifested an irritating desire to get within fighting distance. Neither ropes nor hobbles were sufficient to restrain their impulses, and more than once they broke loose and rushed at each other with fierce screams, kicking and biting furiously, to the imminent danger of our tents and of ourselves inside. Then was heard the full vituperative power of the Arabic language as our men rushed to separate the infuriated brutes; then disappeared the cold chicken from the kitchen, borne off in the ravenous jaws of a wretched dog; and then I discovered that even Moorish travelling has its drawbacks, and that life at home has at least some advantages.

CHAPTER V.

AZAMOR TO MOGADOR.

TOWARDS daybreak the dogs quietened down, the horses renounced their fighting attitude, and the guards fell sound asleep, unable to keep awake even while proclaiming the greatness of Allah, the worthiness of his Prophet, and the virtues of all the saints in the Moorish calendar. As I myself began to feel my senses dulled, the cracked voice of some one in the *duar* quavered out that "Prayer was better than sleep," a statement which on this occasion I felt inclined to question, though I reluctantly pulled myself together and set about the task of waking C.-B.

Ere the sun rose we were in the saddle. I myself felt somewhat stiff, while my companion was grievously aware that fifty miles cannot be accomplished on a fractious mule without painful results. The consequence was that I missed the erect carriage and easy seat which I had previously admired in him.

The country over which we passed still presented the same monotonous physical features, only that cultivated fields now took the place of the bush-land and flowery grazing-grounds. Everywhere also stone

AZAMOR TO MOGADOR.

cabins or wretchedly-made thatched huts replaced the goat's or camel's-hair tents of the more pastoral and migratory Arabs.

What chiefly attracted our attention, however, were the picturesque scenes presented by the numerous wells, which here dot the landscape and supply the inhabitants with brackish water, there being no running streams or springs.

WATER WHEEL.

These wells in the porous consolidated shell-sand are frequently of great depth, and the water has to be drawn by means of camels. These work a horizontal wheel, which again revolves a vertical one overhanging the well. From this a double rope of the necessary length, and having earthenware pots attached at intervals, descends into the water. As the wheel revolves the pots are drawn up full and their contents tipped into a trough placed ready for the purpose, exactly as the mud hauled up by a dredger from the sea-bottom is tipped from the buckets into the required receptacle. Few more interesting sights can be seen in Morocco than these clumsily made wheels, the patient camel walking round and round, the groups of men and women filling their water-pots, and the donkeys or cattle waiting to be watered, while perhaps a little way off a flock of goats or sheep are approaching for the same purpose.

As we continued our way south in the fresh crisp morning air, we remarked that houses and villages became more and more common, with a corresponding addition to the traffic on the road. Finally, after a ride of nearly four hours, we descried the dazzling white mass of Azamor.

Another half-hour and we tumbled our horses and mules into a large ferryboat and crossed the Wad Um er Rebia, on the overhanging ridge of which Azamor is picturesquely situated, looking undoubtedly the most striking town on the coast, though having no buildings worth individual attention.

We halted in the market-place to have a mule shod, regaling ourselves the while on walnuts and Moorish coffee. Finding nothing more interesting than the old Portuguese fortifications to detain us, we resumed our march at mid-day. Two and a half hours later we entered the interesting little town of Mazagan, which in its snowy whiteness we had seen all the way from Azamor in the most irritating apparent proximity.

We rode at once to our Vice-Consul, for whom I was charged with a letter of introduction from Sir Kirby Green. He showed at once a gratifying alacrity in giving us information about the only inn in the place, and even had the goodness to send a servant to show us the way.

MARKET-PLACE, AZAMOR.

In the evening we strolled through the town, and admired the substantial nature of the work left behind by the Portuguese in the old days when they were masters of the entire western littoral of Morocco.

Among other examples of their enterprise which remain is a good boat-harbour, the only one on the coast; but indeed Mazagan, of all the towns, possesses the most striking remains of Portuguese workmanship.

Being well provided with letters of introduction to the various merchants, we thought we could not do better than see what they were like and what they thought about things Moorish. Calling upon the principal one, we found him out, but shortly after, meeting him in the street, we introduced ourselves. He made us feel at once that he guessed we had an idea of writing a book, and had in consequence become fit objects for his veiled sarcasm. Our hopes of getting a cup of tea vanished as he commenced a dissertation on the silliness of all English books on Morocco, and on the shallow knowledge and plentiful lack of wit of their authors; while by inference he gave us to understand what a good book he could write if he would only take the trouble. One late traveller he held up to scorn for having called a bird *Tabib* instead of *Tabibt*. He smiled with a mixture of amusement and profound commiseration when we timidly hinted our hope of getting into the Atlas Mountains. "*He* had never got there," he crushingly told us. To show, however, that he was actuated by the most friendly spirit in putting us on the right track, and that the duties of hospitality rose above all other considerations, he was so good as to ask us to call upon him on our return from the interior.

We did not present any more of our letters of introduction.

A good night's sleep brought back our naturally

sanguine spirits to the normal level after the crushing of the previous evening, and we rode gaily out of Mazagan with the rising sun.

The disadvantages of being under the special shadow of the Sharifian Umbrella were brought forcibly home to us during the day's ride. We found we were not free agents to go where we pleased or camp wheresoever it seemed good to us. We had to be passed on from governor to governor like a piece of goods specially invoiced, and concerning which acknowledgments of safe delivery were required. We should doubtless have energetically rebelled against these restrictions upon our movements, but that at the moment it did not much matter what direction we took, so that we reached Mogador with reasonable speed.

The first soldier only took us two hours' journey to the Kasbah of Northern Dukalla, where the responsibility of the governor of Mazagan ceased. The Kaid was most energetic in his attempts to get us to stop to breakfast, but we would not listen to his hospitable entreaties, and insisted upon going forward without delay.

We still passed over the same treeless, monotonous undulations, cultivated fields alternating with palmetto scrub, or acres aglow with poppies and variegated with dark-green patches of arbutus and myrtle. There was hardly a village to give an inhabited air to the landscape. One might have imagined that the natives were all dead and had all been saints, so numerous and conspicuous were the white *kubas* on every ridge and hill-top.

Here and there, however, the rich dark loam was being turned over by primitive wooden ploughs drawn by an ox and an ass or by mangy horses, and guided by bare-legged and shirt-clad labourers, while boys tending scattered flocks of goats or sheep stood and gazed upon us, practising at a safe distance the curses their careful parents had taught them.

But while our eyes roamed over the wide landscape in search of the new and the interesting, we were not oblivious to other and deeper things. Fired with a scientific ardour, and feeling it incumbent on me to improve the mind of my companion, whose studies had not been geological, I now and then drew his attention to the minor significance of certain surface features. I pointed out how these features were clearly not such as would result from subaërial denudation—that is, the action of rain and running water. Those hummocky ridges and irregular hollows could only have been formed in the bed of the sea, and consequently we were then travelling on an upraised sea-bottom—a late Tertiary sea-bottom, I was careful to point out, which had been able to retain its original features because the porous character of its shell-sands had permitted the rapid absorption of the rainfall, so that streams had not formed to denude and alter the aspect of the land. To all my geological disquisition, however, C.-B. gave but sparing attention, for his mind was more taken up with questions about routes and supplies, and other things relating to military operations.

It was sunset when we reached our camping-place for the night under the walls of the Kasbah of Bin Busheib, governor of Southern Dukkala. We had just time to get our tent pitched after our forty-five miles' ride when darkness fell and rain began to pour down upon us. We had not to wait long before the Kaid sent us our *mona*, or supplies given to strangers travelling with a letter from the Sultan—although in a wider sense *mona* means provisions given and not sold.

Our next day's march was made in much discomfort. Storms of rain and thunder broke overhead time after time, drenching us to the skin, and rendering the black mud of the footpath either excessively slippery or painfully the reverse.

Our attention was on this day first drawn to the manner in which the country Arabs store not only their food, but their water supplies. Pits having the shape of champagne bottles are dug in the easily-worked shell-sand, and then cemented inside to keep out the damp when filled with grain, or to keep in the water when filled with water, the former being called *metamores* and the latter *mitfires*.

A curious surface feature materially aids in the construction and adds to the stability of these granaries and reservoirs. Enormous areas are covered with a slag-like crust of adamantine hardness, which does not permit the permeation of the rain, while forming a splendid roofing material. The rain thus compelled to run off the surface naturally falls into such ruts as the footpaths usually are, and is thence led into the *mitfires*, with all the dirt and refuse it carries in the current. The condition of the water thus stored after a couple of months may be imagined, though over large areas no other is obtainable during the summer. This hard slaggy crust is formed by the evaporation of the surface-water containing lime in solution, which is thus precipitated and forms a cementing substance to the sand, and in time a thin scaly deposit such as is seen near calcareous springs.

Besides being convenient granaries, these *metamores* serve the purpose of hiding the food supplies of the poor country-people—a matter of great importance in a country where the Sultan every now and then passes with his army like an invasion of locusts, and literally and figuratively "eats up the land."

In parts the whole country is honeycombed with these pits, which become in the deserted districts sources of no small danger to the unwary traveller, especially when half-hidden by scrub and bush, as they usually are.

While much of the soil of Southern Dukkala is practically sealed up by the stony crust above referred to, there are also wide plains of the richest arable loam covered with magnificent crops of barley, wheat, and beans; the extent of the fields, the plentifulness of the yield, and the striking scantiness of the population being matters of constant remark and wonderment to us.

Towards sunset we reached the Kasbah of Aissa, Kaid of Northern Abda. This appeared from the outside like a huge quadrangle with plain whitewashed walls, such as people surround their gardens with in England.

It here occurred to us that we might do worse than see what was the effect of the Sultan's letter, and what the character of Moorish hospitality when exercised by a powerful governor. Passing inside the quadrangle, we found that it was simply an enclosure in the centre of which stood the Kasbah buildings, so arranged as to form an inner court.

We dispatched the Sultan's letter to the Kaid, and after a time a message arrived overflowing with the "*Marhababikums*" (welcomes) of his lord Kaid Aissa. Numbers of portly Moors and wild-looking soldiers were massed to receive and see us at the gate of the inner buildings. Under these circumstances I felt it incumbent on me to ride in with becoming dignity. I therefore proceeded to remount the mule I had been riding for the last two hours to ease the bones of "Toby." In swinging myself into the saddle with becoming grace and ease—though I was a trifle stiff—I somehow unwittingly drove one of my spurs into the brute's side. To my horror and disgust, before I could gather up the reins, the hitherto spiritless creature bolted with me and skipped and bucked with all the liveliness of a kid. Not having got my off foot into the stirrup, it was necessary for me to embrace the mule with my legs, if I did not want to kiss the dust. In consequence each new caracole sent the spurs deeper into its sides and stimulated it to more fiery evolutions. The Moors, meanwhile, though scattered by the onslaught, were delighted beyond description to see a Nazarene thus tossed and shaken by a mule. The only thing wanted to complete their happiness would have been to see me get my neck broken. Happily I retained my seat, and at last got command of my legs, the reins, and the mule. Flushed and annoyed with the undignified struggle, I then assumed as haughty an air as circumstances would permit, and rode through the now courteous throng of retainers, C.-B., still chuckling with amusement, following behind.

The inner court presented an animated spectacle, which at another moment I would have viewed appreciatively. Some fifty or sixty magnificent barbs stood there hobbled, the stir of our arrival causing them to quiver with eager fiery life, and show themselves to the best advantage, as, with expanded nostrils, erect ears, and curved neck, they plunged about, trying to free themselves from their bonds. A line of mules of the best breed fed a little way off, while numbers of donkeys strolled about picking up any kinds of odds and ends, and ready to add a lusty bray of welcome whenever any of their kind appeared on the scene. What with the commotion among the horses, the braying of the donkeys, and the barking of dogs, the hurry-skurry of slaves and soldiers, the frightened flight of poultry, and the stampede of some cattle, our entrance to the inner court of the Kasbah of Kaid Aissa was a noteworthy one.

With all due ceremony a chamberlain conducted us to a well-carpeted guest-chamber, hastily prepared for our reception, and where we found green tea ready for our refreshment after our arduous ride.

After a wash and brush-up, we eyed El Hadj somewhat wistfully, dying to demand something from him, even though it should be but a tin of sardines, to take the edge off our ravenous appetites. We heroically forbore, however, determined, since we were under a Moorish roof, to do everything in harmony with our surroundings. Pending, therefore, the arrival of our *mona* we practised sitting cross-legged on the carpet.

After a time two huge candles, two loaves of sugar, and half a pound of green tea were brought, along with four loaves of bread, and about a dozen pounds of butter. This was rather disappointing, but, encouraged by the knowing Hadj, we restrained ourselves. At length a knock came to the door. "In the name of Allah, enter," cried Hadj. We sat expectant. The door creaked and groaned on its hinges, pushed wide beyond its usual limits. As we grasped the full significance of this fact our mouths became moist, and but that we were not demonstrative, we should have clasped each other's hands in the emotion of the moment. A few more seconds, and in the dimly-lighted room we descried something resembling a large beehive carried on the upturned lid of a big barrel, and borne by one of the Kaid's retainers. Behind came a second and a third. A dimly-lighted room, two hungry Europeans seated tailor-fashion on a carpet, three beehives before them, three dark-complexioned *jelab*-clad servants standing over the beehives, and in the background the lithe form and eager grinning face of Hadj, formed the chief elements of the picture. The retainers volubly declared for the hundredth time that we were welcome, that we had but to speak and whatever we desired should be ours. Again we thanked them for the welcome, and hoped that Allah would long protect the life of their lord, &c., &c. Compliments thus interchanged and Moorish ideas of courtesy satisfied, the three beehives were suddenly lifted from their lid-like tables, and an appetising cloud of steam assailed our nostrils, rising from three huge glazed earthenware basins. With difficulty we preserved our equanimity and dignity while some silver changed owners. At last we were left alone. Then did we bend eagerly over the huge piles of food, our heads in close contact with that of Hadj, who, as hungry and eager as ourselves, forgot his proper distance as he pointed out that this was "*Kuskussu*" and that "*Tajen*"—the former being granulated wheat strained over a dish of fowls or meat; while of the other two one was mutton stewed in butter with potatoes, onions, and raisins, and the other beef similarly cooked, and served with carrots and raisins.

On seeing this abundant spread in the wilderness we apostrophised the stars, and forgetting our intentions of doing the thing properly, called for spoons, knives, and forks. "First-class!" was our decision after the first essay; but gradually we became aware of the flavour of rancid butter; the alteration in our expression being noted with delight by Hadj, who had seen our early eagerness with dismay.

Soon after we wrapped ourselves in our rugs and stretched ourselves out to sleep. I had nearly succeeded, when I became restless under the influence of some unwonted irritant. Half-asleep and half-awake, I fidgetted about till something more marked than before made me sit up.

"What's wrong?" demanded C.-B., as wakeful as myself.

"*Pulex irritans*," I groaned.

"What?"

"Well, then, *fleas*. Confound them!" I added irritably, as I turned over to try to sleep once more. Little use, however. There were other things to make the night hateful and hideous. My horse broke loose, and had a lively time of it fighting all round till we caught him. Donkeys brayed incessantly with astounding lung-power. Pigs squealed and rioted round and round the court. The Kasbah guards wiled away the long hours by stoning to death a wretched pariah dog, which they held by a string, its heart-rending yells horrible to hear.

With lively imagination they derived additional delight from its tortures by assuming the poor brute now to be a Jew, now a Christian. Rats, too, held high holiday, and evidently enjoyed themselves immensely, scuttling about or gleefully running over us. So much was I taken up with all these novel or unwonted experiences and sensations, that I was careful not to lose one of them by falling asleep, and long before dawn. I was stirring up Hadj and tugging at my companion. Ere the sun was up we had drunk our morning's coffee and were *en route* for Saffi.

The approach to the ancient coast-town of Saffi seemed to us quite picturesque and beautiful after our 150 miles' ride through Shawia, Dukkala, and Abda. So far we had not seen a single tree worthy of the name, nor had we crossed a single stream or rivulet, with the exception of the Azamor river. Neither had we ascended a hill, nor even seen one, nor had we found occasion to halt and admire the slightest approach to a picturesque landscape. We had, in fact, seen nothing but rounded low ridges, or even more monotonous flat expanses, varied only by waving corn, dark-green bush tracts, or gorgeous flower reaches.

Now, however, we descended a narrow defile, along which trickled a small muddy streamlet shaded by olive and fig. Farther down, the narrow defile opened somewhat, and enclosed a series of pleasant little gardens shaded by pomegranate and orange, fig and olive, date and banana, and beautified by an abundance of geraniums and lilies, and numerous other familiar and unfamiliar flowers.

At length we reached the seaward mouth of the glen, and Saffi, all white and gleaming, lay between us and the turbulent sea.

On our right were now the numerous *kubas* of the saints of Saffi, and on our left the huge barrack or

SAFED FROM THE NORTH

rather prison-like palace of the Sultans dominated the town. A fine Portuguese gateway gave entrance through the well-built crenelated walls which girdle the compact mass of houses.

Nearer approach, as usual, belied the promise of the distance, and we passed along repulsive lanes, hemmed in by mean buildings, and finally reached the residence of Mr. George Hunot, British Vice-Consul.

Here we got a hearty welcome, and were soon made aware that we had not only discovered a generous host, but an unrivalled adviser on all matters pertaining to Moorish travel. I do not know if there is another European in Morocco who in any way approaches Mr. Hunot in his knowledge of the Moor and his language, as well as of many of the southern provinces of the Empire.

As our horses and mules were showing signs of fatigue, we remained at Saffi on the following day, not by any means unprofitably, and certainly not unpleasantly. During the day we experienced the excitement of hawking in Morocco. The lesser bustard was our quarry, and the following was the method of procedure. As soon as the whereabouts of a bustard is discovered, the falconer lets loose his bird and runs forward, directing it by his cries and gestures. At first the hawk flies at a low level over the fields, as if in search of its prey, till, rising higher and higher, it sweeps round in graceful circles. The bustard, knowing its danger, and that the hawk can only strike during flight, keeps close, though in deadly terror. Now is our time to rush in. Spreading out in a line, we give our horses the rein and gallop forward helter-skelter over rocks and through bushes, ever in danger of a nasty fall over hidden obstacles or from disused *metamores*. We shout and halloo till the welkin rings, to cause the bustard to rise. Once up, the excitement redoubles. We now scream and yell our loudest, chiefly to direct the hawk. There is a moment of wild uncertainty, till the wheeling of the hawk stops, and down like a stone it sinks, and with one fell blow strikes its victim to the ground.

We would willingly have stayed longer at Saffi, but we were anxious to hurry on to our destination, where our goods awaited us, and where our little caravan had to be organised.

On Monday the 16th we resumed our march, following the sea-shore as far as the river Tensift. The heavy rains had made the Tensift unfordable near its mouth, and there was nothing for it but to ascend some distance. With the assistance of the natives of the place we were at last landed safely on the other side. Ere this was accomplished the sun had set, and we were compelled to ride along in the dark for a couple of hours to the Sanctuary of Sidi Aissi, near which we pitched our tent in no very good humour, for we were not only hungry, but annoyed at having been brought a different road from what we wanted. It was ten o'clock before Hadj served up to us a savoury stew, and appeased our appetites and wrath at one and the same time.

In crossing the Tensift we had entered a widely different country from that we had so far traversed. We had left behind us the monotonous upraised sea-bottom of Abda and Dukalla, and were now riding through the more varied scenery characteristic of the province of Shiedma.

Red sandstones, and shales, and compact white limestones replaced the friable and crust-bound shell-sands, and showed themselves in a refreshing variety of surface features, making our riding less easy but infinitely more delightful. The country also was no longer treeless, for everywhere the remarkable oil-bearing argan tree enhanced by its gnarled branches and dark-green foliage the picturesque irregularities of hill and dale through which we rode. To this landscape the long irregular range of Jebel Hadid or the Iron Mountains, the western foot of which we followed, gave an air of dignity, and even grandeur.

About mid-day we entered the curious depression known as Akermut, and three hours later we were ascending the low ridge which encloses it on the south and west, and passing by an irregular pathway through gum cistus bush and resin-scented tracts of small conifers, known by the natives as *arar*; and by the learned as *Calitris*.

At the top, as we halted for a time to give our animals breath as well as to enjoy the cool sea-breeze after the sweltering heat of Akermut, we naturally sought eagerly for our goal. Beneath us, on the seaward front, and at the base of the ridge which formed our coign of vantage, lay the Sanctuary of Sidi Buzarktan, and from it a golden strip of sand ran southward in a winding line of demarcation between the ocean and the land. In the mid-distance, half shrouded in a sea-woven veil of grey mist, lay Mogador on its jutting spit of sand like some white gigantic sea-bird resting after an ocean-flight, its feet laved by the murmuring wavelets, to which the savage strength of the Atlantic rollers is subdued by the sheltering island outside.

From Mogador our eyes roam eastward over the sand-dunes which mass themselves on the sloping face of the coast-hills and pass swiftly over the featureless dark-green arar and argan-clad plateau. Suddenly an exclamation of delight bursts from us as our gaze is riveted by an altogether unexpected sight. There in the far east we descry a snowy peak sharply projected against the deep azure of the cloudless sky, gleaming with unspeakable whiteness under the rays of the declining sun. At once we realise that we are looking for the first time on one of the higher elevations of the great range of mountains we had come to explore; all unexpectedly one of its peaks stands revealed to us like a beautiful vision, to lure us on and fire our eager enthusiasm to be among its rocky heights and snowy recesses.

But while we lingeringly stand and gaze on what for the moment is our *kubla* or point of adoration, an altogether different direction is given to our thoughts as Hadj startles us with the cry of "Steamer! steamer!" As we turn with quick expectancy, he points to a mere dark speck on the glistening sea, and true enough a steamer it is, smoothly gliding south towards Mogador.

All the allurements of the Atlas snowy peak are in an instant forgotten in the thought that letters from home are there. Before hurrying on, we turn but to look at and fix on the tablets of our memory the grey and dark-green mass of Jebel Hadid, where, perched on its highest summit, is a tiny but conspicuous point of white, like a patch of snow or a huge quartz rock, telling that such a one as Sidi Yakub has lived and died, and is now one of the glorious phalanx who surround our Lord Mohammed, standing ready to give a lift to such of the faithful as are eager to inherit the joys of Paradise.

Under the special protection of Sidi Yakub, and fertilised by the springs from Jebel Hadid, lies the lemon-coloured plains of Akermut, mottled by green fields and olive groves, and clothed with isolated argan trees, among which may be descried mosque and tomb, and, less conspicuously, inhabited houses and ruined dwellings.

Satisfied that we had seen all that was most noteworthy between us and the four points of the horizon, we now started for Mogador with all speed possible. We cheerfully stimulated and encouraged our fagged Rozinantes with voice and spur, and through arar and argan groves, into a dense tangle of myrtle and arbutus, over dangerous boulder-strewn slopes, we impatiently hurried, till, reaching the sandy beach south of Sidi Buzarktan, our progress became easy and rapid.

As the sun set in the west we neared the northern gate of Mogador. Rounding a jagged rock, we were suddenly confronted by a European lying in wait for us, apprised from his house-top of our coming by telltale glass.

Happily the conventional forms of society were not violated when we greeted each other right heartily, for already our postal system had acted as a medium of introduction between ourselves and our right good friend, Mr. Payton, H.M. Consul at Mogador.

Ere darkness set in we were comfortably installed in one of the inns which give food and shelter to European wayfarers. Grizzly and sunburnt, with all the outside polish of Piccadilly rubbed off, we felt that we were now well broken in by our ride from Casablanca, and fit for any hardship that might be in store for us.

CHAPTER VI.

MOGADOR.

The irritating delays which had marked our stay at Tangier were fated to be similarly our portion at Mogador. No matter how boundless our energy might be, or how determined and anxious we were to hurry forward our preparations, we were bound hand and foot by the inexorable laws of procrastination and inaction which rule all things Moorish. Servants had to be hired, mules and horses bought, and information generally picked up, and all had to be done with a truly exasperating degree of deliberation.

We heartily longed to hear the sharp decisive "Very well—that's settled!" or "Done!" as daily we were put off till "To-morrow," or were brought to the verge of profane language by the pious phrase "Inshallah!" ("If it please God").

None of my previous experiences of travel in East or West Africa were of the slightest use to me here; and not being able to do anything but bless and curse in the native language, I was at a disadvantage in trying to strike a bargain. I was fain, therefore, to leave everything in the hands of our friends, chief among whom were Mr. Payton and Mr. J. Louis Ratto, whose desire to assist us, like their good nature and their hospitality, was boundless. Finding that interference in our own affairs was productive of no good, there was nothing for it but to seek refuge and consolation in the latest acquisition to my phrase vocabulary and sigh out "Kismet! Who can avoid the decrees of Allah?"

Under these depressing circumstances, we tried to make the best of the situation, and let off our surplus energies in such ways as "Allah would show." If the Atlas Mountains had not always loomed so largely in our imagination, this would have been no very difficult or irksome matter for a week or two in a land of perennial summer, and where, according to Mr. Payton, "There is no weather;" where the movements of the thermometer are restricted between 62° and 75° F., and the rain-gauge rarely shows a fall of over twelve inches in the year. The tendency which such a condition of things produces to let things slide is further assisted by the languorous and soporific quality of the atmosphere, which, saturated with the damp developed by an ocean-current striking the land, represses over exuberant energies. While we tried with such patience as we could command to conform to the advice of our friends, we naturally did our best to fight against the do-nothing tendency of the place by looking round and making ourselves acquainted with Mogador and its vicinity. We did not discover much that needs be recounted here, or cannot be more conveniently or appropriately left to later chapters, but a hasty glimpse of the town may not altogether be out of place.

Mogador rejoices in being the best-built and cleanest-kept place in Morocco. This is largely due to its also being the most modern, having been built in 1760 by Mulai Ishmael. The applicability of its native name of Suerah (the beautiful) is not so easily understood by men of prosaic souls, who, going outside, remark its familiar architectural features and the heaped-up masses of sand which shut in the view to the east. Others, however, capable of higher flights, standing upon the arar-topped hills and looking down upon the mist-veiled town, a glowing sun overhead and yellow sands around, will see in Mogador a delicately-tinted opal set in a rich yellow topaz.

One of the unique distinctions of Mogador—to come back to prose—is its possession of a partial sewage system, which means that instead of the good old Moorish plan of having the sewage deodorised and rendered innoxious in the open air, and occasionally washed away by rain or carried off by scavengers, it is now collected for a whole year in typhoid-breeding drains along the streets, from which it is extracted once a year.

On these occasions the Europeans fly to the country or the island outside the harbour, where, amid healthy breezes, they may turn over in their mind whether or not "the good old rule, the simple plan," of chucking your household refuse into the street, is not better than attempting to introduce the sanitary arrangements of their infidel land to a country where man attempts not to fight against that which is written.

The citadel of Mogador is a specially well-built quarter, with spacious houses, clean squares, and straight streets. Through the Medinah or Moorish quarter also a broad street forms a continuous market-place, full of interest to the stranger.

A network of walls divides Mogador, as is usual in Moorish towns, into the Kasbah or quarter of the Government officials, the Medinah or Moorish quarter, and the Mellah or Jews' town. In the Kasbah Europeans and European-Jews reside.

Though the town presents few noteworthy points of interest in respect of its architecture, in other ways, like all Oriental towns, it is replete with little pictures and glimpses of life which cannot fail to delight the traveller. One can never tire strolling about, peeping into the little workshops, and seeing the artisans working away in the quaint primitive fashion which has existed unchanged for centuries. The markets, too, form an animated panorama of scenes of inexhaustible variety, whether it be during the day, when buyer and seller eagerly haggle over the various articles exposed for sale, or towards evening, when the finer splendour of the sun is softened in the west, and strolling musicians, storytellers, snake-charmers, or readers of the sacred book gather round them attentive circles of listeners or onlookers.

Less agreeable are the impressions conveyed by a

STREET IN KASBAH, MOGADOR.

visit to the Mellah. Led by an ordinary feeling of curiosity, or impelled by a sense of duty, the European traveller strolls through the gate which gives entrance to a narrow street leading evidently into the heart of

JEW OF MOGADOR.

the quarter, and which branches into a puzzling network of blind alleys and lanes.

A little of the Mellah suffices; but the traveller, if unaccompanied by a guide, is speedily lost in the labyrinth, and gets ever deeper in the loathsome continuous dunghill, over which he must tramp or wade. Unacoustomed to the sight of a European stranger in their quarter, the news spreads like wildfire among the inhabitants, and his movements are watched with eager curiosity. He is stared at from every house-top and window by dirty fat women, the grossest of their sex; the doorways and corners of the streets are crowded by mean and miserable-looking men, all of whom either squint or are blind, or are otherwise marked by some disease, and look the beau-ideal of cowardly villany or miserly greed, as they canvass with low voice the why and wherefore of the stranger's presence. A more forward and obtrusive phalanx of impudent boys and idlers dog his footsteps or rush past him to watch his next move. Jewish curs, frightened at the unwonted presence, fly howling, with tails firmly pressed between their legs, while an occasional cow coming suddenly round a corner, stands for a moment paralysed, then turns and rushes amuck through the streets, knocking down all who stand in its terror-winged path.

From this horrid cesspool, where human beings batten and grow up repulsive and cancerous, strangers to all that is bright and wholesome and beautiful in God's creation, the visitor at last escapes with a nasty taste in the mouth, a sense of being saturated with foul odours, and an unpleasant sensation about the stomach, to breathe with a new delight the fresh breeze outside the town, and drive away as far as possible the nightmarish feeling which has taken possession of him.

Between the Moorish Jews in the Mellah and the European Jews in the Kasbah there is nothing in common except their religion and their thirst for gold. Under the protection of their respective nations, the latter enjoy all the immunities and advantages of the Europeans, and are able to emulate their brethren in Egypt, and pay off old scores by despoiling of their gold the former oppressors of their race. Almost the entire trade of Mogador is in Israelitish hands, and loud is the outcry of Moor and European alike against the position they have acquired for themselves.

Attired in silk hats and other characteristic European articles of apparel, the Jew of the Kasbah struts about the streets and eyes the poverty-stricken Moor with the air of a man who knows that at least in Mogador the tables are turned, and that his are the princely mansion and the good things of this life, while theirs is the pulse and water and the mean homes of the Medinah.

The tinkling of the guitar and the strumming of the piano are nightly sounds too in Mogador, telling that the daughters of Judah have wealth to spend in accomplishments. They delight in dress, as is seen in the cool evenings on the sands or at the watergate, where they turn out resplendent in paint, displaying their full and fat amplitude of charm, clad in freshly-imported gowns from London or Paris, while their daily-renewed complexion and belladonna-brightened eyes are shaded by the daintiest of parasols, from underneath which they know full well how to cast telling glances on the favoured males of their race.

It was our good fortune while at Mogador to make

the interesting discovery that Morocco has not one, but many Salvation Armies, who, in the name of their respective saints, do many strange and horrible things when out with bands and banners on the *holy spree*, in which they indulge on set occasions.

The processions in honour of such spiritual leaders as Sidi Aissa or Sidi Hamadsha are the most stirring events which disturb the even tenor of life in Mogador. Though not unattended with grave dangers, we made up our minds to see as much as possible of the remarkable aspects of religious life in Morocco.

On the 3rd of May there was to be a procession in honour of Sidi Hamadsha. The night before was devoted to the spiritual preparation necessary to develop the intense feeling and religious madness required in those who would take part in the procession, and be fit mediums to show the workings of grace and the wonderful powers of the saint, that thereby all men might recognise that " there was no God but the one God."

Disguised in hooded-*jelabs*, we sallied forth towards the midnight hour to add to our budget of experience and assuage our thirst for adventure.

Nothing could have been more enchanting than the night—nothing more impressive than the unceasing roar of the Atlantic rollers. A full moon overhead flooded the streets and lanes, mottling their every feature with a new charm of light and shade, giving the plain whitewashed houses a ghostly glamour unknown under the fair and more searching light of a Moorish sun.

In the Kasbah few people were astir. One or two Jews passed homewards in billycocks or tiles, mere silhouettes against the white houses, while, spirit-like, no footfall was heard. A Moor now and then mysteriously appeared, a new witchery in his dress and movements in the light of the moon. From the distance a fresh evening breeze brought a subdued barbaric clamour of pipe and drum, which mingled strangely with the notes of "Two Lovely Black Eyes," as lustily hammered forth on the piano by a Jewish maiden in our immediate vicinity.

On entering the Medinah, we had to proceed with more caution, and modify our energetic stride and bearing to the easy-going undulating movement of the Moor. The whole quarter was in an unusual commotion. The streets, usually deserted at this hour, were thronged with men and women alike, who, in their soft white clinging draperies, gave the place the aspect of a city of ghosts. But they were ghosts having a good time of it. Never had I seen a Moorish town more animated. At every corner we were met by bands of men and boys parading the streets, headed by musicians, who skirled out the most plaintive of wild music from clarionet-like pipes, accompanied by the clamour of drums and tambourines and loud singing. Some of these bands moved slowly, bringing in their train groups of women and the more sedate of the Moors, while the music wailed out melancholy ear-piercing notes; others, again, the real followers of Sidi Hamadsha, ran about like madmen, pumping up a spiritual intoxication—their movements the wild antics of devils, their music that of Hades. Here and there they stopped to dance, stamping round with heavy, ungainly movement, jerking their heads up and down,

WOMAN, OUT-DOOR COSTUME.

as if desirous of softening their brains inside. At times, with hands held up in mid-air and faces turned heavenward, the moon disclosed their wild glistening eyes, their foam-circled mouths, and the savage excitement which marked their every lineament as they screamed out invocations to Allah, our Lord Mohammed, and Sidi Hamadsha.

In the vicinity of such fanatics we drew our *jelabs* round our faces and shrank as much out of sight as possible, knowing that we should have but a sorry time of it if it was discovered that Christians were mixing in their pious orgies.

Next day there was an air of excitement and unrest in the town. There was less business being done, and yet more people were moving about. An unusual proportion of country-people had gathered.

As the afternoon wore on, the Jews, who are favourite game for the religious fanatics, either retired into the Mellah, where they massed themselves on the house-tops, or were locked up in their barricaded shops by the Governor's soldiers. The Moors, on the other hand, crowded out into the streets, either to take part in the procession or to act as onlookers. There was a very large proportion of women to be seen, chiefly restricted to the house-tops, where they sat like bundles of clothes laid out for the laundress. Those of the poorer classes freely mingled with the men in the streets, though more commonly they lined the walls.

The route of the procession was from the Medinah, where it formed up, through the southern gate of that quarter, across the sands and into the Kasbah by the Sus Gate, thence traversing the Government square back to the Medinah.

To see the procession properly, we mounted to the top of Ratto's house, which commanded the Sus Gate and a fine view of the sands.

We had barely taken up our position and cast a *coup-d'œil* over the flat beach and the remarkable sand-dunes, when the shrill squeak of pipes and the hammering of drums warned us that the procession was leaving the Medinah. Soon we descried a moving mass of white bundles turning one of the angles of the crenelated city walls. At first we could distinguish nothing but a number of rich-coloured banners, round which crowded a thousand white-robed people. On nearer approach, we discovered that a descendant of the saint mounted on horseback formed the centre of the procession of fanatics. These latter, half naked, could be seen surging round the banners with the mad fury of a whirlpool, or gathering together in front, where they danced to the music with every conceivable uncouth movement. At times, as if animated with a sort of centrifugal force, they broke up and rushed in groups or in ones or twos through the crowd of admiring sympathisers, who formed the major part of the procession, while pulling and tearing each other like hyenas fighting over bones.

On these occasions the banners and horsemen moved forward another hundred yards or so, till again the Hamadshas gathered round their leader, and again indulged in their wild break-down, while the pipers blew their loudest and the tom-toms were hammered with renewed vigour.

As the procession neared the gate, we could distinguish the proper Hamadshas not only by the wildness of their antics, but also by their blood-smeared heads and clothes, their haggard faces and air of madness.

To get a better look at the doings of these remarkable sectaries, we now hurried down, and at great risk joined the crowd. Anything more sickening and disgusting I never saw. The centre of attraction was several men, whose heads were almost featureless masses of clotted blood. They bobbed about in time to the music, and wobbled their heads up and down in the most extraordinary manner, while their eyes, bloodshot and ghastly, remained fixed on the ground. They carried sharp daggers in their hands, with which they made aimless strokes in all directions, to the imminent danger of all around. Now and then these hideous creatures, chosen manifestants of the spirit of Allah and his saint Sidi Hamadsha, seized with an ungovernable excitement, raised their daggers in mid-air, and, with demoniacal gestures, slashed their shaved craniums, making horrible gashes, from which the blood was left to flow over face and neck and fall dripping on their garments or the ground, while they staggered hither and thither in the unconsciousness of semi-madness.

The delighted women screamed shrilly, and around these favoured performers danced the admiring men in wild frenzy. The musicians, rising to the occasion, expanded their cheeks to bursting-point, or made the skin fly from their knuckles as they skirled out their ear-piercing notes and whacked their drums with furious energy. Serene and calm in the centre of this turmoil the horseman sat like a statue of expressionless unconsciousness, his creamy *heddun* or burnous enveloping him from head to feet.

For a time we followed on the outskirts of the fanatical crowd, wrapping ourselves in the magic armour of the British flag, and daring any one to touch us. At length, however, we thought it wise not to test its invulnerability too much. The crowd was evidently being fast carried away by ungovernable excitement. Daggers were being flourished on all sides by religious madmen, under no restraint of prudence or reason. We had not quite lost our heads, and certainly did not desire that our blood should flow in honour of Sidi Hamadsha, or help to secure a good place in Paradise for him who should send us to Gehenna. We thereupon retired to our hotel, to digest as best we might the sickening impressions we had received.

The prevailing feeling among the Europeans who had gathered upon the house-tops to see the procession was one of disappointment. No Jew had been hunted down and done to death, and the Hamadshas had made but sparing use of the knife. No dog had been caught, disembowelled, and devoured on the spot; no bottles broken on the skull; nor, indeed, had there been any of the more curious feats which the followers of Sidi Hamadsha or Sidi Aissa are enabled to do in their name, to the glory of Allah and the confusion of all unbelievers.

CHAPTER VII.

THE BOAR HUNT.

WHENEVER we became tired of the ordinary routine of life in Mogador, we could always pass the time in the favourite British fashion: we could go and kill something.

Under the guidance of "Sarcelle" (Mr. Payton), we had opportunities of deep-sea fishing such as few places can give. For my part, I must confess that these were always occasions of doubtful enjoyment, and it required all the excitement of hauling in sixty-pound *azlimsah*, or the more lively twelve-pound *tasergelt*, to make me forget the natural repulsion of my inner man to anything savouring of a turbulent sea. There is no need, however, for me to describe this particular sport, that having been already done by the skilled pen of the past-master in the gentle craft above alluded to.

It is different with the boar-hunting, for which Mogador is also famous. The wonderful exploits of Mr. Ratto after the "father of tusks" have not had a chronicler, and I may be permitted, though no sportsman, to describe a boar-hunt under his auspices.

On the afternoon previous to the day of the hunt, we

assembled before our leader's house to the number of six Europeans and as many servants, all mounted on mules and horses. All the necessaries for a night out having been safely stowed in the packs, we left the town. Our way lay over the fine sandy beach which lies to the south of Mogador. On our left was the sanctuary of Sidi Mogadul, the patron saint of Mogador, from and to which were passing closely-veiled women and their children. On our right rose conspicuously the remarkable ruins of an old Portuguese battery, and farther south lay a half-buried palace of the Moorish sultans. Along this level sand tract, backed on the one side by drifting sandhills and bounded on the other by the sea, were winding townward long straggling lines of camels driven by wild Sus Arabs. For anything we saw ahead of us, we might have been in the heart of the Sahara.

We speedily reached the village of Diabat, on the Wad Kseb, where the inhabitants have a hard battle with the ceaseless encroachments of the wind-blown sand. Ascending a steep slope, we found ourselves in a few minutes on a low step or terrace which leads to the broken plateau of the interior. To the south the view was bounded by the dark elevations of Haha, while in the distant east the peaks of the Atlas formed a broken skyline.

We now continued our way through a brake of the silky genista, which here flourishes in the sunny sterile sand, and in an hour reached a solitary building known as the Palm-Tree-House, because of its conspicuous

MOGADOR FROM THE SOUTH.

Page 80.

single date tree. This proved to be a country residence of Mr. Ratto's father. Here we laid ourselves out to have a good night of it, with Moorish and Berber music and dances provided by the beaters who had been gathered for the morrow's hunt. One grizzly old hunter specially distinguished himself by his performance on a Shellach reed (*Shellach* is the name given to the Berbers of Southern Morocco). It would seem to be no easy task to play this instrument. The most remarkable twitches of the arms, body, and head, the most extraordinary contortions of the face, were apparently necessary to produce the required harmony. Yet, in spite of all the musician's efforts, some little imp of Eblis would ever and anon burst out with the most startling, ear-piercing squeaks, the unexpectedness of the effect irresistibly reminding one of the itinerant players on tin-whistles who delight country bumpkins at fairs. One of our party next played very sweetly on the Moorish *gimbery*, and then the beaters broke into a wild dance to the deafening music of pipes, reeds, tom-toms, and brass trays. At length, on hearing "Oh, weel may the keel row," dragged out of an accordion, the *perfervidum Scotorum* of three of our party proved too much for them, and was not allayed till it had found expression in a Scotch dance. It was long past midnight ere the varied selection of English, Scotch, Spanish, Shellach, and Arab songs and dances were got through, and we were able to spread our rugs on the floor and seek some needed rest.

We were all astir before daybreak, each one already speaking in subdued tones, as if feeling that the moment had nearly arrived when silence, caution, sharp ears and keen eyes would be all-important in our exciting enterprise.

After tea and a hasty toilet, we sallied forth in the grey dawn, a nasty drizzle overhead and drenching grass and bush under foot not doing much to damp our eager spirits.

Once clear of the buildings, we halted to form up and hold a council of war as to the direction to be taken and the tactics to be pursued to run our game to bay. We looked a formidable party—six Europeans, twenty native beaters, and sixteen boar-hounds, the last the most starved and woe-begone of their kind, and apparently not fit to kill a hare.

Everything arranged, we spread out in line, and commenced our march through the argan forest and painful thorny scrub, which here clad the uninhabited country.

We moved along with the stealthy caution of men who might expect a lion's charge at any moment, and had a reputation as skilled sportsmen to keep up. No sound broke the stillness except an occasional "Hist!" or faint whistle, but all kept a sharp, eager look-out, and searched the ground for boar-signs with the anxiety of men who look for lost diamonds.

Hour after hour passed, however, and nothing added fuel to our bloodthirsty hopes beyond the discovery here and there of a footprint, round which we gathered more eager than geologists round fossil traces of the amphibian. Meanwhile the rain kept falling more and more heavily, and turned us into the most bedraggled of mortals. Our appetites also made insistent demands on our attention. Under these discouraging circumstances, the high-strung enthusiasm with which we started began to cool down. Our movements became more careless, our attitude less watchful. Our guns were carried anyhow,—over our shoulder or resting on our arms. At this moment a hare sprang from a bush and electrified us into new life. The lanky bags of bones called hounds bounded after it with a fierce rush. With one accord we bolted after them, regardless of thorns in our eager excitement.

A sharp squeak as from a Shellach reed sounded through the wood, and gave renewed speed to our flying feet.

A few more seconds, and, panting with our exertions, cheeks flushed and eyes bright with rekindled fires, we were among the pack.

We looked eagerly for our game. Too late!.

The dogs were licking their jaws with unmistakable enjoyment in the consciousness of having dined.

Though none of us had been in at the death, we all felt cheered and reanimated, and each beamed upon his neighbour, as who should say, "Well, boys, the sport begins." The hounds were called "noble dogs" and patted encouragingly on the back.

Heedless of rain and appetite, we pushed on again with redoubled care and caution for another hour.

Just as we began to despair of finding any more sport, a tell-tale squeak made us stand transfixed and breathless.

No hare this time either, but a genuine pig, and, ye gods! a pig that ran too; for now the sound was here, now there. A chorus of half-suppressed exclamations broke forth from one and all, as seizing our guns with a firm grasp and holding them well above the bushes, we tore after the dogs like madmen. There was no picking of steps now, but on we went with a wild headlong rush, slapdash through thorn bushes and over obstructing boulders. Then—sweet music in the huntsman's ear!—then the hounds gave tongue, and their savage growls and yells rang in an inspiring chorus through the otherwise still depths of the forest. "The boar at bay!" was the thought in every mind, but no one spoke, only hurried more earnestly to the arena of savage conflict. A few more minutes and we were close at hand. We slackened our pace, saw that our guns were right, and prepared to meet a possible charge. "Take care of the dogs," Ratto panted out. Nobody replied. With set teeth, which indicated unutterable things, and gleaming eyes watchfully on the alert, we moved forward.

The next moment we emerged from the bush to see the "noble dogs" in one writhing heap, literally hiding the boar from sight. It was a sight which sent the blood into our eyes and made our fingers twitch round the barrels of our guns. But to shoot was out of the question. We waited in momentary expectation of the fierce beast breaking from the worrying pack. Another moment and the dogs fell away. "Take"—— somebody commenced to shout. But his sentence never was completed. He, like all the rest of us, remained with eyes fixed and mouth open.

No boar was to be seen! The battle had been short, bloody, and decisive. Only some drops of blood showed where a baby-porker had met a terrible death.

There was no doubt this time, however, but that the game was of the genus boar, though it had not reached boarhood.

At the moment we all congratulated each other on having got "something like the thing" at last. We had drawn blood of the right sort, and we were now all eagerness to get something to eat before resuming the dangerous sport.

We accordingly made for the appointed breakfasting-place, and speedily dispatched the cold fowls and eggs.

We had not gone far on our way the second time before one of the Shellach shot another pig, and then we had a short time of tremendous excitement, stalking in some dense bush a boar that was *believed* to be there. We never, however, got a glimpse of it, probably owing to some one having made an audible exclamation when a big thorn entered his leg—quite sufficient to make the brute disappear, or rather render itself invisible. We all felt very indignant at the unsportsmanlike disturbance of our friend, and after that he kept in the rear, partly because the thorn made him lame, and partly because he felt that he had disgraced himself.

Meanwhile the Shellach and the dogs had gone off on another scent. We were soon apprised of their whereabouts by one of the former waving to us from a ridge-top, and we hurried towards him. An old sow had been wounded by one of the beaters, and brought to bay by the dogs. It had then been captured and tied, pending the arrival of us Nazarenes, who would have been indignant if we had not been in at the death.

Arrived on the spot, we gathered in an admiring circle round the unhappy sow, delighted with our achievements and proud of our prowess. Mr. Ratto drew his long hunting-knife, and while he felt its edge, we watched him with bated breath, knowing that the climax of the day's excitement had come. The dogs lay or slouched about, all their fierce life gone out of them. Picturesquely the Shellach grouped themselves around the pig, leaning against their long silver-ornamented guns, while in an outer circle we stood or sat on horse or mule eagerly watching Mr. Ratto's movements. Satisfied of the condition of his knife, he set his teeth firmly and braced himself for the last *coup*. Almost before we were aware, the knife had entered the old sow's heart; there was a gush of blood, a death-quiver, and then all was still.

Having thus killed three boars—that is, I mean, our dogs and servants having captured two baby-porkers and a sow—we could now honourably return home.

The sow, after being disembowelled, was placed in the pack-saddle of a donkey; and then, with pipe and song, and men dancing in front, we proceeded back to Mogador, our return from the chase being hailed by admiring crowds.

In all fairness, however, it must be said that boar-hunts at Mogador were not by any means always such as I have described.

On another occasion I had an opportunity of seeing the skill that could be brought to bear in tracking a dangerous boar for hours together, and the final terrific battle when the brute was brought to bay—a truly demoniacal scene of ferocity—the grizzly "father of tusks," firm as a rock in the midst of his worrying enemies, tossing them aside as a dog would toss a rat, gashing them with horrid wounds, now and then breaking through the howling cordon, to be once more brought to bay, and finally to receive a bullet, and so, fighting to the last, fall dead.

BRASS TRAY, MOGADOR.

CHAPTER VIII.

THROUGH SHIEDMA TO SAFFI.

At length everything was ready for our final start. Four mules had all been secured, "real bargains," and were declared to be the best of their hybrid kind at the price.

We were equally congratulated on our good luck in securing such prizes as the great hulking camel and the diminutive donkey, which completed our stud of animals.

All our servants were the most trustworthy, the most intelligent, the most honest, the most superlatively everything, in short, that was virtuous in Mogador servants, and nobody had ever before gone forth to the wilds of the interior so well provided with men and animals. We could not but congratulate ourselves, and set out with a light heart.

Still, travel in Morocco was a new experience to me, and our future success would depend so much on the sort of men we had, that we did not think it wise to start straight for the interior before we had in some manner experimented on the general character of

Moorish travel and the reality of our servants' reputed honesty and fidelity.

After serious consultation, we resolved, therefore, to make a detour through the province of Shiedma to Saffi, where matters might be righted, if by any hap they went wrong.

So far we had been careful to keep our mountaineering plans a secret. To have done otherwise would only have ensured the effectual blocking of the way. We should still have been able to get men, but they would have been such as would have taken very good care that we never left the safe frequented routes of the plains. Under these circumstances, it was thought advisable to engage them simply to travel "in the interior," leaving them to put what interpretation they pleased on the phrase.

In one respect, and that an all-important one, we were placed at a very great disadvantage—we could get no proper and trustworthy interpreter. Three of our servants had a sufficient smattering of French and English for all camp purposes, but utterly inadequate for the more difficult task of collecting reliable information and communicating with the people. Worse than all, this unfortunate circumstance placed us hopelessly at the mercy of our followers the moment they chose to object to any particular route. A very depressing and threatening thunder-cloud this to arise on the bright horizon of our hopes at the very outset of our journey. Turn the matter over as we might, we could not see how we were to arrest or fight against the almost certain storm. As for the outcome, what could we do but shrug our shoulders and exclaim, "Allah will show!"

It was on the 7th of May that we left Mogador. Our little party consisted of five men, five mules, a camel, a donkey, and my horse Toby. My companion had not yet been able to get a charger to his fancy, but trusted in the good providence of Allah and the friendly offices of Mr. Hunot at Saffi to supply him with a suitable mount.

Our small caravan made a picturesque display as, headed as usual by a soldier, we rode through the throng of Moors, Jews, and Europeans collected to see us off, passed under the Sus gate, and on the sandy beach bade our friends good-bye. This melancholy ceremony was short enough, as far as we were concerned, but not so with our followers, who do these sort of things with more decency and order. A hasty prayer had to be muttered, looking eastwards, acknowledging the greatness of Allah and the submission of themselves to his decrees. Pardon also had to be asked for the sin of entering the service of "rebels against God." These pious duties over, they had, with all proper circumlocution and thoroughness, to reply to the good wishes of their friends.

The view outside suggested a hot day. A shimmering haze rose from the sterile sands and hung like a fog over the town, the minarets and towers breaking through with a certain weird and ghostly effect.

Once clear of the beach, we entered the sand-dunes

which clothe the seaward slope of the coast-hills. These dunes had assumed the most remarkable shapes under the steady drifting action of the south-west winds, which in winter blow with great force. At places they curved round in hillocks resembling broken volcanic craters, not infrequently enclosing curious little ponds of water, round which the sand heaped itself in sheltering semicircles.

Over these barren wreaths of triturated sea-shells our way now lay for over an hour, till reaching the top of the hill, we found ourselves on the first of two steps which raise the traveller to the level of the lower plateau of Southern Morocco.

As we took our last glimpse of Mogador, we rejoiced exceedingly at the thought that we were off at last. The worry of preparation was over, and the lazy lotus-eating life of the coast-town cut away from. We were now free. Everything we required for food and shelter was on our mules, and we could see nothing ahead of us but romantic rides through new and ever-varied scenes, or equally romantic camps in shady orange or olive groves, amid all the delightfully picturesque surroundings of Oriental life. How far these enthusiastic day-dreams were realised, and what other and less agreeable elements were added to our experiences, it is the purpose of these pages to show.

Proceeding on our way, we passed over a strip of ground where the winds and sands still struggled to assert themselves among silvery broom-like genista bushes in the hollows and more hardy resin-scented arars on the exposed ridges. Gradually, however, the sands, and with them the arar and the genista, disappeared, giving place to more fertile soils and argan trees. On the gnarled trunks and branches of the latter goats and kids skipped about like monkeys, avidly devouring the leaves and olive-like fruit.

As we continued to travel eastward, the landscape became more and more varied, though retaining the general aspect of a tree-dotted park. There were fields where the natives were reaping their scanty crops of barley by simply cutting off the ears, and there were glades bright with larkspur, marguerite, and marigold. Fortified villages with square and round high towers dominating their vicinity were marked features in the landscapes, the numerous ruins of many more such, affording melancholy evidence of a former prosperity now no longer enjoyed. Everywhere were vestiges of irrigation channels and other signs of a large and industrious population, of which only a remnant now remains, dejected and spiritless waiters on Allah's providence.

At mid-day we reached some very extensive ruins, the chief feature of which was the remains of a fine aqueduct that had supplied the town with water. Though only built of clay and lime, it had resisted the weather wonderfully.

Some distance beyond we struck the Wad Kseb or Diabat, and after a halt for rest and refreshment we resumed our march.

From our halting-place we again diverged from the

stream, and following a small tributary, we marched up a picturesque glen, which conducted us to the top of the second terrace or step, and consequently to the irregular expanse of the lower plateau of Southern Morocco.

From our elevation of nearly 2000 feet we commanded a fine view over the country beneath us seaward, across the argan terrace to the yellow sand-dunes, and Mogador by the gleaming sea; and eastward over a monotonous plain to the snow peaks of the Atlas. The view on the right was restricted by the heights of Mullai Hassan, which form the northern edge of the higher plateau of Southern Morocco, and of the provinces of Haha and Mtuga.

Towards sunset we reached a strongly-built and semi-fortified dwelling, nominally the property of a native, but practically held by one of our Mogador friends, who occupies it occasionally as a summer residence. Here we stayed the night, and were hospitably entertained by the native in charge, who killed his fatted sheep and his best fowls, ransacked the hen-roosts and milked the cows, all on our behalf.

With the morrow came the first cares and worries of travel. The mules were found to be overloaded, and the camel—our camel, of which we had been so proud—turned out to be a fraud, and had already gone lame.

The men had spent the night between gorging and smoking the intoxicating kief, and were roused to their duties with difficulty.

They set about their preparation slowly and sulkily, grumbling audibly against being disturbed so early in the morning. My astonishment was great and disagreeable to see the suave and willing servants of the day before showing very decided tendencies towards mutiny and insolence as I superintended their operations with ever-growing impatience.

Before we got under weigh, El Hadj from Casablanca—who recently had sadly belied the promise of first acquaintanceship—made my temper get the better of me by an insolent rejoinder made to an order of mine.

I seized him fiercely by the *jelab* and shook him till he became livid with fear, though his snaky eyes glittered with murderous thoughts.

It was easy to see that the men took us for two untravelled greenhorns, such as they had hitherto come in contact with, and it was necessary that they should learn without delay that one at least was a past master in the art of travel. If there was to be a fight for the mastery, well the sooner it was over the better.

The day's proceedings were marked by one continued row. The men objected to walk to relieve the mules and camel, but to walk they were compelled. Generally speaking, they all conducted themselves as if under the influence of bang, as at least three of them really were.

The country was grievously uninteresting, presenting not one feature to attract the attention for a single moment. Crust-bound, largely clad with thorns and acacias, it defied the efforts of the husbandman to wrest from its barren bosom the necessaries of life. The bridle-path trended bewilderingly in every direction but straight ahead, while the sun beat down pitilessly, untempered by any cooling sea-breeze. Soon the tip of my nose was raw, and I began to ask myself if, after all, the Ethiopian might not be able to change his skin.

As I looked at this dreary, scantily-inhabited country, noted the sulky, impudent demeanour of our men, and felt myself for the moment little better than an enforced slave-driver, I wondered at the evil chance which had plunged me into such heart-breaking worry and led me to such a cursed country.

At mid-day our worst troubles were over, on our arrival at the featureless clay-built Kasbah of the Kaid of Shiedma. The latter, on learning under what auspices we travelled, dispatched a messenger to entreat us to take up our quarters in the castle; but remembering our experiences at Kaid Aissa's, we politely declined, resolved to stick to our tents.

Once comfortably installed in camp, and with the men in better humour as abundance of cooked and uncooked mona poured in, we began to look on our situation with more genial eyes, and think that after all matters might be worse. Still we found it necessary to keep up a policy of watchfulness and stern repression. We soon discovered that the cunning and villainous men who formed our party, despising and hating as they did all Christians, had been accustomed to do what they pleased with the tourists who fell into their clutches, plundering them right and left, and using them as tools for exploiting the governors and country-people, on whom they saddled themselves.

Their method had been to represent their temporary masters as ambassadors or consuls, or great men travelling with letters from the Sultan, and in their name demand the most outrageous supplies of provisions, which, of course, when obtained, they mostly converted into hard cash for their own particular benefit.

The sale of the provisions was always known to the givers of it, and put to the credit of the Europeans, who were thus supposed to enrich themselves while travelling through Morocco.

This little game we determined to repress at once, and it cannot be said that our consequent proceedings acted like oil on troubled waters. But however bitter the struggle, it was imperative that there should be no doubt as to who were the masters.

In the evening we visited the Kaid, a fat though handsome man, of imposing appearance in his many draperies and massive turban. We found him half-reclining on a Rabat carpet, supported by a cushion of morocco leather. The room was long and narrow, and neither plastered nor whitewashed, and its clay-built humbleness looked anything but becoming the reception-room of a powerful governor. There were no windows, the only light being that which streamed in through the doorway. In the semi-darkness, while our interpreter spoke for us, we could see that one end of the apartment had the appearance of an unarranged general store, there being, among other articles, loaves of sugar, boxes of tea, suspicious-looking bottles, and packets of candles.

From the Kasbah our route turned once more coastwards through a much more varied and interesting country. The Kaid had not only sent two soldiers with us, but supplied a horse for C.-B. to ride, and a camel and a mule to ease our own animals. In consequence there was less friction between our men and ourselves, and we ambled along quite pleasantly over the rocky and but little cultivated country which forms the district of El Kurumut. In two hours we entered a more hilly country, crowned with arar woods, the hollows and slopes enclosed by dykes, and bright with flowery fields and crops of barley.

At mid-day, after traversing a forest of argan, we reached the edge of the plateau, and descended to the lower terrace by a narrow defile cut out of the almost horizontal massive beds of white limestone, and well-wooded with very large argan trees. In less than an hour we emerged from the defile at a charming grove where a Monday market (*Sok thlata*) is held. Thence we rode over beautifully-wooded and cultivated grounds, whose bramble-matted hedges and stone dykes had an unexpectedly homelike aspect, and finally camped at the eastern foot of Jebel Hadid in the district of Takat.

As we sat in a shady nook enjoying the cool evening and our coffee, we could not but think that Moorish travel was not so bad after all. Under shady trees stood one or two small tents, whose open doors displayed their somewhat crowded contents of bed and box, surveying instruments, photographic apparatus, guns, &c. Behind them rose a very primitive erection, constructed of old sacks, the kitchen and head-quarters of Hadj Hamad, whose duties had now become restricted to cooking. Farther off stood a tent of considerable size, which served as a dining-room by day and as a sleeping-room for the men by night, at the same time

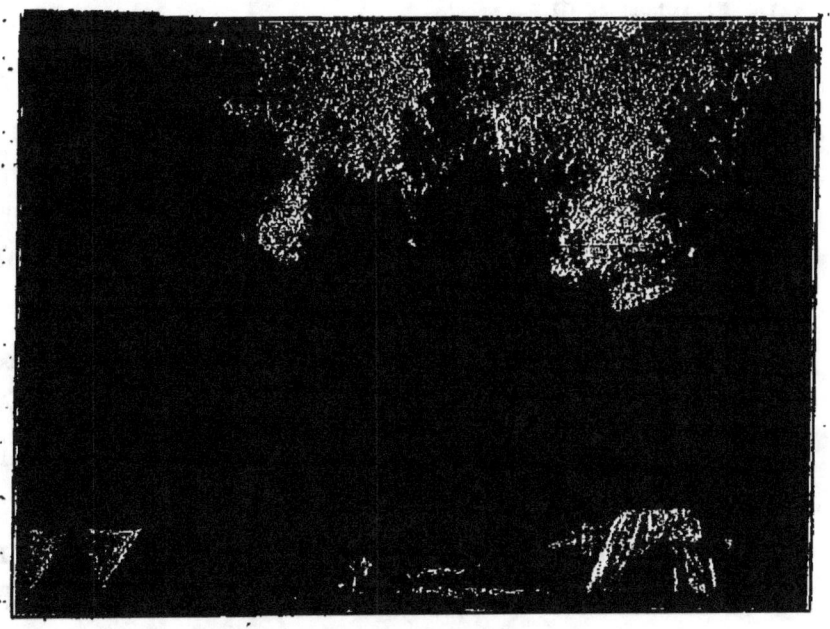

CAMP IN OLIVE GROVE.

giving shelter to the remainder of our baggage. Near the tents stood our horses, hobbled and pinned down to restrain their combative propensities. Some distance from the horses the mules were tethered by the feet to a rope in a single line, and beside them lay the camel and the donkey. The camping-ground was a grove of olives, whose branches threw a chequered shadow over the grassy ground on which our attendants sat or lay in picturesque groups. Farther off little knots of country-men watched us with a kind of passive curiosity, wondering doubtless why Allah permitted such as we to wander over the land of his chosen.

Through the openings in the grove we caught glimpses of the yellow fields of barley, the light-green vineyards, and darker woods of argan which formed the district of Takat.

The men were all in good-humour. We had no occasion to trouble ourselves about the wherewithal to live, food of all kinds having been brought to us in absurd abundance, while the Sheik of the district provided for the safety of our persons and property by posting a line of guards all round the camp.

The day following our arrival at Takat was devoted to an ascent of the celebrated Iron Mountains. We had but to signify our wishes to the Sheik of the district to have a quaint assemblage of natives placed at our disposal as guards and guides. To ensure that no harm should come to us, as well as to keep a watchful eye on our proceedings, the Sheik himself and the Kaid's two soldiers accompanied us.

Leaving camp in the cool of the morning, we followed the base of the mountain till we struck a rugged pathway leading up its side. At first we rode, but the slope soon became too rocky and steep, and we had to take to our feet. We very soon came to a yawning hole, which, on looking in, we could see widened into a large chamber, evidently cut by human hands out of the limestone rocks, here almost vertical in dip. On descending to explore, we found that the excavation cut across the beds of rock and narrowed till the floor and ceiling met some fifty feet into the mountain. What puzzled us was the absence of any marked signs of iron lodes—though for that mineral it was undoubtedly dug—as its position, the nature of the rock, and its shape made the theory of its being a cave-dwelling out of the question.

On leaving this excavation, a stiff climb brought us to the top, at an elevation of over 2000 feet. From the crest of the narrow range we commanded a splendid view, extending from Saffi to far south of Mogador, and from the limitless Atlantic horizon to the haze-veiled peaks of the Atlas. Immediately beneath us, to the west, lay the plain of Akermut, a variegated assemblage of bush, field, and sandhill winding along the coast. On the other side of the mountain we could see the white tents of our camp in its sheltering olive grove, and the whole district of Takat spreading out between us and the plateau edge, with its tracery of olive and argan, vineyard and cornfield, ending in the black masses of arar which clothed the heights from which we had descended on the previous day.

Having satisfied ourselves in addition with a hasty look towards the winding course of the Wad Tensift in the north and the familiar features of Mogador in the opposite direction, we proceeded along the crest of the range in search of the iron-mines.

A sheep-track led us over a bouldery surface covered

with gum-cystus and bright masses of wild thyme, till suddenly we were brought up close to a remarkable pit or quarry-like cavity, quite 100 yards long, 50 to 70 broad, and some 150 feet deep.

"Of volcanic origin," was the explanation which naturally occurred to me, as I looked at its shape and its perpendicular walls and considered its position on the crest of the mountain, not to speak of the extensive nature of the cavity, which seemed to preclude the idea of its being the work of man.

Filled with this idea, I forthwith began to search for further evidence of its igneous origin. With small result, however, beyond determining the fact that the beds were much smashed; there was no marked trace of metamorphism, nor was there any lava debris.

We descended into the pit by a rugged crevice choked with a rank profusion of bush and creeper growing in the interstices of the rocks. Enormous blocks of fallen limestone here and there almost closed the way, but after a severe and somewhat dangerous struggle we got to the bottom. As we peered about, it was gradually forced on our minds that though volcanic agencies had been at work, man also had been no insignificant agent in producing what we saw around us. We were, in fact, in the mines which for unnumbered centuries the Berbers, and later on the Moors, had worked for iron. This metal we could see as a hydrous oxide running in irregular lodes or filling small cavities.

At the bottom of the pit we were shown a small

hole running into the rock, and which we were told penetrated to the heart of the mountain, and opened finally on the mountain-side. We were not provided with lights, and could therefore do nothing, but we resolved to return on the following day and extend our exploration.

To satisfy the religious cravings of our men, we went south to the Kuba of Sidi Yakub, which stands, in its gleaming whiteness, on the topmost peak of Hadid like a spiritual beacon warning reckless navigators on the ocean of life of the dangerous rocks and whirlpools which beset their route, and pointing out the narrow way leading to the peaceful haven of the true believer.

While our men prayed, with heads bowed to the dust, acknowledging the greatness of Allah, and earnestly beseeching the guidance of Sidi Yakub to show them the way to heaven, we fixed our position on this earth by compass-bearings, and by aid of aneroid and thermometer determined the interesting fact that we were 2470 feet above the level of the sea.

On our way down the mountain by an easier path than that by which we had ascended, Crichton-Browne was in momentary danger of reaching the bottom with unexpected and dangerous rapidity. His saddle slipped suddenly forward from the back of his mule, and nearly gave him a very nasty fall. Our men called loudly upon Allah, but secretly sniggered with delight as they saw in this *contretemps* a sign that their prayers had been heard, and that the infidel in all lands would yet be cast down and broken upon the rocks.

On our arrival in camp, a native brought a child which had been bitten by a snake some hours before, in the hope that we could cure it. Useless, however, for it was already in the convulsions of death. As the last spasms of life shook the little body, and its eyes glazed over and became fixed, our men muttered "*Inshallah*" (the will of God), and the distressed father covered the little fellow with his cloak and went sadly away.

In the evening, after the impression of the painful scene had passed away somewhat, finding that the Sheik of Takat was an uncommonly good fellow, we tempted him to sin. Before he was aware of our intention, we spread before him all the allurements in face and figure of some English maidens, as portrayed by the art of the photographer, and expressly forbidden by the Koran. If we had asked his permission first, he would have cried with horror, "Allah forbid!" but now, when his eye rested on the strange dresses and charming outlines of our countrywomen, he ejaculated very heartily, "God is great," and, forgetting everything in the sweet pleasure of sin, looked long and intently at the counterfeit presentments of these the fairest of His creatures.

As he looked from portrait to portrait, we could see his expressive features brighten up as the thought crossed his mind, "*If* Paradise is peopled with such as these!"—or darken as he reasoned, "What a pity that the portion of these fair infidels is Gehenna!"

It was with surly faces, attempted evasions, and vehement protests that such of our men as we required followed us next morning to the top of Hadid, their conduct causing us to ask almost with despair what would happen when the Atlas Mountains had to be scaled.

On reaching the entrance to the underground passage, there was further mutiny, and rather than venture into what might be a dangerous place with unwilling and cowardly attendants, I left them behind, and enlisted the services of two of the natives. One of them led the way with a candle, while the second followed behind with another.

The task of exploration proved more disagreeable, difficult, and dangerous than I had expected. We had simply to wriggle ourselves along like snakes, half-suffocated by the dust we raised as we dragged ourselves through barely passable holes, over and round fallen blocks from the roof, which suggested disagreeable reflections on the possibility of being squashed to death or buried alive. Here and there we had to let ourselves down to deeper levels. The iron veins or lodes had manifestly followed the most irregular course and spread out into the most bewildering ramifications. Not finding any more striking discovery regarding the former miners than here and there a number of wooden props, and becoming alarmed at the nature of the disagreeable labyrinth, with its narrow niches, its turns and twists, and ups and downs, I resolved to turn back. Easier said than done. The different passages were all so much alike, and led in so many different directions among the broken limestone beds, that we speedily became quite bewildered.

We tried more than one passage, only to find that we were evidently on the wrong track. This began to be alarming, and I anxiously calculated how long our candles would last. In little more than half an hour we would be in utter darkness and absolutely helpless. The man who led had declared that he knew the mines thoroughly, but all the comfort we could now get from him, on angrily demanding which was the right passage, was the declaration that "God would show." I must confess that I began to be somewhat demoralised as the consequences of our situation grew up more clearly in my mind. We shouted to those we had left outside. We listened with absorbing attention, but there was no reply. Only mocking echoes came back to us from all sides, as from imps of Eblis laughing at our painful dilemma. Again we despairingly struggled to worm our way out, seeing that "there was no help nor guidance but in God." The candles were getting perilously low. Again we shouted lustily. As we held our breaths, and almost suspended the beating of our hearts, a faint sound which was not an echo reached our ears. But where did it come from? Listen as we might, we could not localise it. Was it from above or was it from below, in front or behind? No matter. We felt that the danger was over now that we were within earshot.

More than once we had to wriggle ourselves back

heels first, there being no room to turn in our burrows. At length a faint ray of light gleamed in upon us, and in a few more minutes we re-emerged into the full brilliancy of mid-day, to be greeted with irrepressible laughter by my companion as he noted my sorry plight and the absurd figure I cut, coated with iron dust from head to foot. I certainly thought he had had the best of it this time shooting "blue rocks," and that Moorish mine-exploration was, to quote one of his favourite phrases, "an over-rated amusement." This reflection, however, did not find audible expression. On the contrary, to show him that I had not been an earthworm for nothing, I held forth to him in these terms, as I seated myself on a rock to recover after my struggle in the mine:—

"We are now in the very centre or focus of eruption by which the almost horizontal limestone beds we have seen all round the mountain have been thrust up, till they stand on end and form the short and narrow range which runs north and south, as you see, like a fish's dorsal fin. This huge pit has in all probability been blown out of the centre of the mountain by an explosion of steam, though largely refilled by the shattered debris. Springs, probably hot, and charged with hydrated oxides of iron, have undoubtedly risen through this nature's safety-valve, and deposited their mineral load among the debris in such irregular veins as I have just been exploring, and in such cavities as you see there in the face of the rock. In process of time these have dried up or found other exits in the moun-

GROUP, TOP OF JEBEL HADID.

tain-side, but something of the residual heat which produced the steam which raised this mountain and deposited that iron is still to be remarked in the hot springs which bubble up in the glen of the Wad Kseb near Mogador."

Satisfied that I had duly impressed my companion with the result of my earth-grubbing, I arose, and, though still aching and skinless about the knuckles, elbows, and knees, hurried back to camp.

After a much-needed wash and some refreshment, we struck camp shortly after mid-day, to the disgust of our men, who did not understand this display of energy, especially when food and water were abundant, shade refreshing, and no danger to be feared.

The day was by no means a pleasant one to travel in, there being not a breath of air, while the sun simply broiled us with its untempered fervour. We travelled north along the base of the mountain to where the upper plateau edge and the range converged to form a narrow picturesque defile, to re-diverge again in a couple of miles, where we entered the small valley of the Wad Ifiri, draining into the Tensift.

We camped some little distance from the *zawia* or sanctuary of Sidi bin Mahida, where the criminal flying from justice may find protection and shelter. These *zawias*, sacred as the burying-places of renowned saints, are, like the *kubas* of the saints in less repute, scattered all over the country, and form inviolable places of refuge, where neither private vengeance nor the hand of public justice can intrude.

The evening was signalised by a terrible fight between the two pilgrims, Hadj Hamad and Hadj M'hamad, which only ended by my appearance on the scene with a horse-whip.

Next morning we resumed our way, crossing the range by a deep depression which almost cuts it in two, the northern part being best known by the name of Sidi Lalkurat, the rival saint on these heights to Sidi Yakub. Passing down a picturesque glen, I was careful to emphasise my geological remarks of the previous day by pointing out the evidences of the volcanic disturbance, and how we were passing away from the main line of disturbance. Numerous salt springs bubbled forth from the red clays which here cropped out. This saliferous water is collected and evaporated in pans specially prepared, and supplies the whole district with salt. Before reaching the Tensift, our men and soldiers made a vigorous attempt to get us to camp, but we obdurately insisted on crossing to the other side to ensure our entry into Saffi next day.

We repassed the sanctuary of Sidi Aissa, and followed the southern and muddy course of the Tensift down its broad valley and along its flat fertile plains, where a recent flood had carried devastation into the rich barley-fields, destroying hundreds of acres.

Early in the afternoon we reached a ford two or three miles above the one we had previously crossed. It looked anything but promising, and for a time it was a question whether we had not better camp where we were in the hope that the flood would subside.

Eventually it was determined to trust to the arbitrament of fate.

I was the first to attempt the crossing. Mounting the tall horse of one of the soldiers in preference to my own little Toby, and stripped to the shirt, I plunged into the swift stream, one naked Moor guiding the horse, and leaving me nothing to do but hold on, while another swam alongside ready in the event of accident. At the first plunge the horse quite disappeared, and the water nearly reached my waist. The crowd on the bank filled the air with cries of "Allah!" or directions to the swimming man. For a moment the situation looked nasty, the rushing water producing in me a momentary giddiness. After a second or two the horse's head reappeared with a snort, and we drifted rapidly down the stream. Soon, however, the horse struck ground, and then wildly plunged forward. After that we got on swimmingly, partly in the literal and entirely in the figurative sense.

Shortly after C.-B., bolder than I was, and desirous of showing the Moors how swimming ought to be done, dashed into the flood by himself. But alas for the pride and the arrogance of youth! He soon found out that he had altogether miscalculated the force of the current, and he drifted down the stream with alarming rapidity, while making almost no headway across. Fifty voices yelled directions in Arabic. The soldiers, who were responsible for our safety, danced about in despair, and having no hair on their heads, tore their beards. A score and more of swarthy natives dashed into the stream, while others ran along the bank gesticulating like madmen.

Happily no harm came of it, the swimmer being drifted on to a sandbank, from which he was helped across to *terra firma* amid a circle of bronze-coloured Arabs. I am not quite sure that it struck me at the time, but I noted in my diary that, with his white skin and smoothly-shaved face, he looked like a water-nymph captured by a band of swarthy fauns or satyrs.

The most exciting incident, however, was the passage of one of the soldiers. In some fashion or other the horse he bestrode was caught by the swift current and rolled over and over, he clinging desperately thereunto. Sometimes a man's head and shoulders would appear above water, sometimes four horse's legs striking madly out, or it might be the horse's head, with wild, terror-stricken eyeballs. He too, however, reached the bank in safety. A mule was nearly drowned, and some of our things were wetted, but no worse damage happened.

Nothing was more applauded than the way our diminutive donkey Ali took to the water, and, assisted by an Arab, swam over. Once on *terra firma*, he cocked his ears, and setting his bellows a-working and his tail a-wagging, he emitted such a bray of exultant triumph or lusty enjoyment of his own vigorous strength as made the welkin ring, and roused a score of answering brays from neighbouring duars and villages.

It took us three hours to complete the fording of the river, and it was sunset before we camped for the night on the high banks some distance from the stream.

THROUGH SHIEDMA TO SAFFI.

Next morning, while quickly demolishing some breakfast before starting for Saffi, I had occasion to remonstrate sharply with our man, Abdul Kader, for allowing Selim, the camel-driver, to wash some dishes in our drinking-water. He as sharply answered, that it was not true. Whereupon, assuming paternal authority, I slapped him in the face, with all due deliberation, as one doing a painful duty for the welfare of the one castigated. His face became perfectly ashy in colour, and his hand sought his dagger. It was not by his side. All the men had seen the blow, and all alike had started as if each himself had received it.

There was a moment of thunderstruck silence. Then Abdul Kader, finding vent to his choking passion, poured out an incoherent torrent of Arabic, English, and Spanish phrases. I did not strike without thought or reason. I had but waited for this opportunity to finally settle the exact conditions on which we were to travel together. My time had come, and I had acted.

To have wavered then would have been to confess myself beaten and afraid of them. No notice was taken of the threats of vengeance and the curses of Abdul. He had his excuse, and our rôle was that of absolute indifference. The other men, however, were sternly bidden pack up, and they saw that in our expression which would not permit of rebellion.

This, then, was the position of affairs when we re-entered Saffi for the second time, to seek the hospitality, the assistance, and the advice of Mr. Hunot.

CHAPTER IX.

SAFFI TO THE CITY OF MOROCCO.

The net result of our first essay at travel in Morocco was far from encouraging.

An altogether unexpected class of difficulties had presented themselves. We had looked forward to the probability of strenuous opposition from officials and a certain amount of danger from the mountaineers, but we had not foreseen that our very greatest peril would be from our own men. To have to fight against outside opposition would only be to experience an added zest to travel, but to know that there was treachery in the camp was to be utterly paralysed. For the first time, as I reviewed the situation, I began to take a somewhat gloomy view. At the very threshold of our enterprise our men had shown themselves not only insolent and disrespectful, but mutinous and intractable in the extreme. They had joined us believing that they could do what they pleased with us, and finding out their mistake, they had "cut up rough."

Never in all my experience of travel had I been subjected to so many petty worries, so many irritating and maddening annoyances. Our servants had acted on the principle that to plunder an infidel traveller was to perform a meritorious act, and to betray him would be secret incense to Allah. With such men we could not hope to be loved; there was nothing left but to make ourselves feared. But how were we to purchase their fidelity—how neutralise hidden treachery? and worse than all, how were we to overcome the dangers attendant on our ignorance of the language? Already we had fallen foul of our best interpreter.

We would willingly have dismissed the entire band if suitable substitutes could have been got; but none such were to be had in Saffi. We resolved to do what we could, however, in that way, and break up the too united gang of Mogador men by introducing antagonistic elements. Selim the camel-driver and Hamad the muleteer were dismissed, and two men recommended by Mr. Hunot engaged in their places. All the others immediately asked for their dismissal also, and were of course refused. They swore by the sacred name of Allah that they would not go with us, and we vowed by the beards of our ancestors that they would either go, or the dungeon would be their portion, where they would lie and rot till we returned. Finding at length that we were not to be trifled with, and that Mr. Hunot backed us up, they submitted to their fate with the resignation of true believers, wondering, however, what terrible sins they had committed that Allah had thus doomed them to be dragged at the heels of cursed Nazarenes, without even the hope of plundering them.

There were other changes required besides those

among the men. The camel had proved a fraud, and had to be sold. With it went our lively little donkey, whose lusty braying, out of all proportion to his size, had given us many a hearty laugh. One of our mules too had broken down, and a substitute had to be bought.

Altogether, the disparity between the promise of Mogador and the realisation at Saffi was strikingly disagreeable.

While this struggle for the mastery and the rearrangement of our little caravan were going on, we occasionally tried to forget our cares and worries by exploratory strolls through the town. There was little to be seen worthy of our attention. To say that Saffi is extremely irregularly built in a compact mass of whitewashed prison-like houses intersected by a complex labyrinth of short narrow lanes; that to the stranger it is remarkable for the filth and garbage which disfigure it, and the flies and pariah dogs which infest its every corner, is only to recount what are more or less the familiar features of most Moorish towns.

The one sight which Saffi possesses worth seeing is the old palace of Mulai bin Abdullah, a Sultan who reigned in the middle of last century, and made himself memorable by marrying an Irishwoman, by whom he had a son called Mulai Ishmael, the bloodthirsty Nero of Morocco.

The palace occupies a commanding site on the hill shoulder, overlooking the town and near the eastern gate. Outside it presents the appearance of an enor-

SULTAN'S PALACE, SAFFI.

Page 114.

mous ugly windowless prison, forming a quadrangle of plain unornamented and unbroken walls. Inside, however, it offers more varied and picturesque features. Here are long vaulted and dimly-lighted corridors, opening into all sorts of unexpected nooks and mysterious rooms; there, grassy courts where fountains have splashed among beds of roses. Here are still to

COURT IN PALACE, SAFFI.

be seen the rooms of the harem, where, unseen themselves, the Sultan's ladies could look down on the town sloping seaward; and there stands still the colonnaded patio of the Sultan, from which open his audience-chamber and his private apartments, all beautified by the hand of the artist in stucco arabesque, in carved woodwork, and brilliant painting, the delicate tracing and lace-like intricacy of the designs being indescribable.

At the back of the palace still stands a Portuguese fort and bastion. From this coign of vantage we can look down upon the massive and picturesque ruins of the palace and the gleaming town fanlike spreading out from it. As we trace the fine sweep of the bay, open to the south-west, we can easily understand why Saffi is the most dangerous port on the coast in the winter-time, when winds from that quarter prevail. As easy is it to understand how Saffi is also one of the hottest towns in summer, and broils under a temperature from 15° to 20° higher than Mogador, only seventy miles distant. The phenomenon is accounted for by the line of heights which surround the bay and town, and shelter them from the cool northern breezes that temper the Moorish summer.

The traveller in his survey will not fail to note with some curiosity and amusement the outer line of defences, behind which the good Moslims of Saffi sleep with an enviable feeling of security. It is formed by the bones of their three favourite saints, which have been laid out with a view to rendering the town safe against the attacks of infidels by sea. On the northern side of the bay gleams the Kuba of Sidi Buzid, and on the opposite side is that of Sidi Wasél, while Sidi bin Muhammed Sal takes the town under his more immediate protection seaward, a host of minor saints keeping watch and ward on the landward side. Thus guarded, the Moorish inhabitants can afford to smile with a sense of security on hearing of "naval demonstrations" or rumours of war. They at least are safe.

On the 19th of May we started finally for the interior. Very different were the feelings with which we now set forth from those with which we left Mogador. Then we hoped everything; now, though we did not despair, we feared everything. Till then we had only seen the bright side of the picture, now we had seen the other also. Turn the matter over as we pleased, we could find no satisfactory answer to the question, how were we to overcome the opposition of our men when they knew where we actually desired to go, dependent as we were on them through our ignorance of the language? All that was in our power was to go and try—go and do our best.

Our first march took us over a series of hummocky elevations and curious hollows, such as we had remarked farther north as being characteristic of Dukalla, and indications of an upraised sea-bed, till at an elevation of about 700 feet we found ourselves on the first step or terrace which raises the traveller to the plateau of Southern Morocco.

Here the step forms a wide plain stretching in low undulations, till, twelve miles eastward, it ends at the base of the second step, which rises abruptly like a low range of hills. This great plain was one almost continuous field of barley in various stages of growth, from the absolutely green to the ripe gold, where already busy groups of reapers were at work cutting off the heads of the grain with sickles.

Some gleaming Kubas, a few wretched hamlets, and the usual shapeless pile of buildings which formed the Kasbah of Kaid bin Tomna of South-Eastern Abda, were the sole other features we were called upon to remark.

The second march led us gradually by a waterless defile to the top of the plateau, at a height of 1500 feet, to find the same monotonous landscape presented to our view, though eastward some irregular hill masses limited the green and yellow undulations. In rising from the lower terrace to the plateau, we had passed from the Province of Abda to that of Bled Hummel, from the raised sea-bed and consolidated shell-sands to the cretaceous red shales and sandstones which have given this district its name of the "Red Country" (Bled Hummel). We camped close to the Kasbah of the Kaid, not far from the small salt lake of Zima, which, lying in a shallow hollow, expands and contracts in size according to the seasons. It is fed by a number of saliferous springs which rise in the red shales. By the evaporation of the water in the dry season large supplies of salt are obtained. Near Lake Zima there is a Kasbah where the Sultan's children are reared and educated, to become little better than paupers on the death of their father.

Everywhere we are called upon to remark the wonderful fertility of these wide plains, and to speculate on the population they might feed, if—if only the rainfall could be depended on; but in that *if* lies the whole question. The rainfall cannot be depended on, and many are the harrowing stories of the periodic famines through drought which the traveller hears on all hands.

Nothing, however, strikes the stranger more forcibly than the evidences of grinding oppression under which the inhabitants groan. The half-starved, weather-beaten, and scantily-clad Arabs, living in squalid, conical thatched huts, are but little better than slaves, while the governors, though living for a time on the fat of the land, with well-stocked harems, and surrounded by numerous slaves and soldiers, their stables filled with fine horses and mules, their pastures rich in flocks and herds, are neither more nor less than human leeches, who for a brief season are allowed to suck the life-blood of the country, till, themselves full to bursting, they are drained by a more powerful blood-sucker.

It is not, however, in a day, or a week, or a month that any adequate notion is obtained of the terrible system of tyranny which holds the country in its blighting and paralysing clutches. It is so all-embracing, digs so deep down, and spreads in so many unexpected ramifications, that the actual condition of things only dawns slowly on the inquirer, and then it seems incredible that such a state of misgovernment can exist for a day.

From the Kasbah of Bled Hummel we ambled on the third day over the same treeless plain, which became, as we proceeded eastward, less fertile and consequently less cultivated. Gradually, too, as we approached the mountains or Rahamna, which for two days we had seen looming up before us, the country began to belie its name of "red." The soil became more sandy and of lighter colour, which we speedily discovered to be due to a change of the geological formation from cretaceous shale to friable metamorphic rocks.

Towards mid-day we found ourselves in the small but lately created district of the Ulad Dlim, a tribe of Arabs brought from near Wad Nun to act as a buffer between the inimical clans of Bled Hummel and Rahamna, as well as to ensure the safety of travellers from the attacks of robbers, who infested the neighbouring mountains. The women of the Ulad Dlim were distinguished by their wearing dark-blue cotton dresses.

From Ulad Dlim we had proposed to strike away from the main road to Morocco, which so far we had followed, and proceed straight through Rahamna and Srarna to Demnat. Our chief reason for avoiding the former city was our fear of being taken too much care of by the authorities there, and saddled with soldiers who would see that we did not diverge from the frequented and safe routes.

With one accord, however, not only our own men, but the people of the place declared that the route was dangerous at present, and that a safer route was to be found some distance farther ahead. With some reluctance and doubts, we submitted to their arguments, and agreed to follow their road.

At dawn on the 22nd, with the usual amount of trouble and worry, I got the men turned out from their tent, after their night of gorging and kief-smoking.

Like so many dogs, they snarled and quarrelled among themselves over the loading of the mules.

As the sun rose we moved out of camp, feeling it deliciously cool in the fresh morning air. We soon reached the end of the great plain we had travelled over for two days, and entered a series of very rocky, rugged hills, which run into peaks and pyramids and a pictu-

H. CRICHTON-BROWNE.

resque variety of other forms, having a general N.N.E. and S.S.W. trend, agreeing with the strike of the almost vertical metamorphic clay slates.

After marching some three hours over rocky passes, and up and down irregular, desolate, uninhabited defiles, we entered a more even country, though here and there, to right and left, rose up sharp ridges of bare jagged rock, which, if they served to add to the scenic effects, also helped to accentuate the air of grey barrenness and desolation which brooded over the landscape. All morning our route had trended suspiciously to the south, and the gravest doubts passed through my mind as to the existence of the second route to Demnat, and more than once we blamed ourselves for not having kept to our original intentions.

All doubts as to our situation were speedily set at rest when, turning the shoulder of a hill, the Atlas range, the plain of Morocco, and the city itself burst upon our view.

For the moment we heeded not the features of the magnificent scene. We were too much possessed with a voiceless rage and an almost overpowering feeling akin to despair as we thought how helpless we were and how thoroughly we had been tricked. Were we also fated to come, like so many travellers who had preceded us, to the foot of that great chain, to be permitted to look and long, and, like them, be sent way baffled?

There was no use, however, anticipating disaster. We had got an unpleasant taste of the quality of the enemy—that was all.

As the first acute feeling of disgust toned down, and we resigned ourselves with the best grace at our command, we began to look around us and forget our disappointments in the engrossing elements of the landscape.

For the first time we saw the Atlas before us in all its kingly elevation.

Hitherto we had only got glimpses of its higher peaks, but now the eye roamed from its dark bush and forest-clad base over its lower ranges to the snowy masses which broke through the grey fleecy clouds that here and there softly swathed its upper zones, and above them gleamed in dazzling whiteness against the blue sky, seemingly not of the gross earth at all.

Thus snow-clad in its higher altitude, the Atlas presented less of the even outline we had been accustomed to picture. There were many prominent peaks which stood out in sharp relief, especially over Misfiwa and Glauwa, but also towards Reraya and the Wad Nyfis.

From where we stood the range seemed to rise with extreme abruptness, dominating the plain with a frowning grandeur not noticeable on nearer approach, where the rise is seen to be more gradual and the central crest far indeed from overlooking the plain, or even its lower ranges.

We could well have spent longer studying the physical features of this goal of our daydreams, but time was precious, and we turned to sweep our eyes over the great plain which lay between us and the mountains. There was but one feature to rivet our attention, and that was a great tower which rose from a dark mass of brown and green, like a lighthouse on a rock at sea. We did not require to be told that this was the tower or minaret of the Kutubia, the one striking monument which Southern Morocco possesses to tell of the former greatness of the empire and its present degeneracy. Around the Kutubia we had no difficulty in distinguishing the walls and houses, the gardens and date-groves, that composed or encircled the city of Morocco. Of the plain itself little need be said. Bounded by the mountains, it seemed but a narrow strip of green and yellow, through which the river Tensift and its many tributaries meandered seaward, conspicuous lines of dark green in their shading of olive and date. Here and there dark patches told of fruit-yielding groves and of inhabitants, and Kubas showed where holy men were buried, though yet living to make intercession for those who believed. Southward the view was lost in hazy distance, and north it was cut off by the broken heights of Rahamna and an isolated hill which lay in front of us.

Having completed our survey, we had still to consider what we would do. Would we go back and pick up the right road, or go forward to the city and stand our chance of the extra obstacles and dangers to our progress there likely to be met?

We elected, though with gloomy forebodings, to do the latter.

By way of putting our men to an actual test, to see how far we could depend upon them, we suddenly left the road and ordered them to follow us. Not a soul moved one step. They stolidly sat on their mules and watched us pushing our way across country. On and on we went, yet there they remained. We lost sight of them at last, and yet we persisted in our experiment. It was well to know the worst. More than one group of harvesters and solitary herdsman were startled by the unwonted apparition of two Europeans unattended by soldiers or natives. It might have gone hard with us, but the very impunity of our movements was our chief safety, and doubtless we were supposed to be the Sultan's European Kaids.

From the crest of a ridge we again got a sight of our rebellious men. To our delight they were on the move and apparently after us. That illusion was soon dissipated. They were on the move indeed, not towards us, however, but towards Morocco. They had determined to take their own way and leave us to take ours, and to experience whatever fate had in store for us. Clearly we were utterly and cruelly defeated.

Thus baffled and disappointed, with almost the last hope of getting into the mountains crushed out of us, there was nothing for it but to return to the road. We soon picked up the men plodding doggedly townwards. It was no use to storm and rage or to threaten vengeance; all would alike have been in vain. So in a sullen line we trudged on under a sweltering heat, the Kutubia growing at each mile more imposing, and the half-hidden walls and buildings of the city showing up more and more from among their shady gardens and groves.

At last we rounded the isolated hill which lies to the north of the Tensift, and speedily reached the banks of the latter. We entered the picturesque date grove which encircles the northern aspect of the town, and crossed the river by a bridge (El Kantra) of some twenty arches, falling rapidly into disrepair. A broad road led us through a succession of rich gardens of dates, olives, oranges, pomegranates, &c., but we had eyes for none of them. We rode along like men who had lost their freedom or prisoners being dragged unwillingly into the town. What mattered to us the beauty of the gardens, the pleasant twitter of the birds in the trees, the animated succession of quaint scenes which greeted our every step, or the life and bustle which told of our approach to a large and busy city.

At length, about three in the afternoon, after having been ten hours in the saddle, the battlemented gateway of Morocco loomed up before us. A few minutes more and we had entered the city. We passively followed our soldiers through narrow crowded lanes, till, reaching a half-ruined house, we were told that this was the governor's residence.

The Sultan's letter was sent in while we waited outside. A messenger soon returned with the windy welcomes of his lord, who, with a boundless hospitality, placed himself and all that he possessed at our disposal.

We mustered up sufficient interest in what was being said to answer with becoming politeness, and then mechanically followed our new guide as he led us back through more winding lanes to the house and garden prepared for us. For the moment, however, we were equally indifferent to what we passed through or where we found shelter. Our thoughts were in the Atlas, where we feared our feet would never be.

CHAPTER X.

MARAKSH, OR CITY OF MOROCCO.

With night and a good sleep came renewed encouragement and revived hopes. We were slightly scotched, but by no means killed. The morning sun and our sanguine dispositions soon added a golden fringe to the dark storm-cloud which had temporarily enveloped us, and we pictured it widening out and out till the darkness was no more, and there remained only the golden glow of success. We had stumbled once, but it did not follow that our next move would be over a precipice. In any case, we were resolved not to succumb to anticipated difficulties till we had tramped right on to meet them, and fairly measured our strength against them.

It was in this cheerful mood that the morning of the 23rd May broke upon us with its summer brightness. We had little to grumble at in the matter of quarters. We were comfortably installed in a vaulted, oblong room, whose whitewashed walls were ornamented with simple upper and lower dados in red and blue. Outside a loggia or verandah, supported on pillars, gave further shade and protection from the burning summer sun and winter rains. Here we could sit and drink our morning coffee, while, otherwise unchecked, the cool morning breezes came to us filtered through the vine-clad arcade that led into the garden. This latter, too, was no mean addition to the amenities of our situation, for after the treeless plains of Abda and Bled Hummel it was refreshing to let the eye rest on fig and pomegranate, olive and apricot, under whose protecting shade grew roses and jasmine, sweet violets, and a profusion of other flowers, adding colour to the scene and pleasing perfume to the air.

In this charming retreat we were thoroughly shut off from the outside world by a high blank wall which surrounded the garden; so thoroughly shut off, in fact, that, for anything we saw or heard, we might have been anywhere but in the heart of a city with thronging thousands.

As we sated our eyes on our surroundings, and noticed with no great relish the care taken of our person by the Kaid, as shown in the numerous soldiers who kept watch and ward over every door and corner of the place, we could not but admit that this was by no means a disagreeable variation in our life.

Under the circumstances we did our best to rise to the situation and receive our visitors with the courtesy and dignity expected of those who travelled under the protection of the Sultan. We first gave audience to the chamberlain of the Kaid, who bubbled over with renewed welcomes on the part of his master, while we tried to keep pace with him in thanks and hopes that Allah would bless and reward him according to his

STREET IN MARAKSH.

Page

deserts. The Kaid, however, did not merely send complimentary phrases. These were substantially backed up by an abundant mona. There were men bearing from him sheep and fowls, loaves of sugar and green tea, great bowls of milk, and baskets of oranges and dates. Eggs, too, there were, and vegetables, with huge dishes of cooked food for the men, and abundance of barley and straw for the horses and mules.

Everything was in proportion to the Kaid's dignity, not to our actual wants, for there was sufficient to have fed fifty men.

We were careful to preserve a stolid demeanour, as if this was only what we had a right to expect, considering our social status.

Our morning's levee over, we were anxious to hurry off to explore the town.

Our hopes were high of seeing something to instruct and delight us; for was not Morocco a city with a history, a city which had been the residence of sultans, and the theatre of civil wars and sieges! Its very name—the City of Morocco—threw a glamour over it, and connected it with all the past glories of the Empire and its achievements in war, in arts, and science.

We would willingly have started off on our exploration attended by only a guide, but our guards would not hear of it. We must go with all the pomp and circumstance of great men. We therefore reluctantly sallied forth on horseback, with one or two of our servants on mules, while several soldiers ran ahead of us, and, with resounding cries of "*Balak! Balak!*"

(beware), followed by a push and a blow if necessary, demanded, in God's name, passage for the "*Anasera*" (Christians). The passage was, of course, given, but often with scowling faces and cursing hearts.

To know, however, that we were being consigned to Gehenna on all sides, and that few there were among those whom we saw who would not have willingly put a dagger in our hearts, if they could have done so with impunity, only gave an added piquancy to our ride.

Our first impressions of the city of Morocco—this southern capital of a once glorious empire—were those of unmixed disappointment. As we wandered through street after street and lane after lane enclosed by clay-built walls and houses of meanest aspect, we saw much indeed of the "havoc," but very little of the "splendour of the East." At every step we found evidence of a nation on a down-grade slide, of a people who had lost all earthly hopes and aspirations, and lived under the most grinding oppression and tyranny. Morocco was a city grown slattern, very much out at the elbows, and utterly careless of its personal appearance. And yet, as we persevered in our exploration, and got rid of our preconceived notions, with all its air of dilapidation the city again began to grow upon us. In the most unexpected places, often midst tumbling ruins and all the signs of rapid decay, we were continually attracted by a group of palms or the sight of some interesting example of Moorish workmanship.

Here it was a fountain on which the artist had

FOUNTAIN IN MOROCCO.

lavished all the wealth of his Oriental imagination, and shown all his manipulative skill in stucco, wood-carving, tile-work, and colour. There it was the horse-shoe-shaped doorway of a mosque overhung with effective mouldings.

We got delightful hasty glimpses of mosque interiors, too, all the more attractive because forbidden and partaking of a spice of danger. These displayed cool aisles and beautiful wall-decoration in stucco, arabesque, and tile-work. There in the subdued light, near the Mihrab, pious Moslems could be seen prostrating themselves before the one God, and shady colonnades surrounded marble-paved courts, where sparkling fountains cooled the air.

It was not, however, in its architectural features that we found the special charm of Morocco. As in all Oriental cities, it was its people and its street-scenes that gave the most picturesque effects. The very beggars carried their rags with such an air—they appealed to the passer-by in such a high-flown and impressive style, that they became not only objects of compassion, but subjects for the artist. The women, swaddled in their absurd blanket-like coverings, carried about with them all the charm and mystery of the forbidden and the unseen. And yet not quite unseen either, for those beautiful eyes of theirs, sparkling with all their liquid brilliancy between black-tipped eyelids and long glossy eyelashes, transfix the gaze of the onlooker and fire his imagination, till he sees not only beautiful eyes, but face and form, and all the other allurements of the sex to match. Not least attractive were the substantial city men of Morocco mounted on quick-pacing mules, or the Government officials on gorgeously caparisoned and prancing barbs, while the

MOORISH GIRL.

weather-beaten Berbers from the Atlas, the gaunt, fierce-eyed Arabs from Sus and the desert, and the shrinking money-grabbing Jew, all formed effective elements in the scene.

It was in the purely business parts of the town, however, that we found most to admire. Motley throngs of buyers and sellers, busy workmen and idle wayfarers, crowded the narrow thoroughfares, and, with the quaint box-like shops on either side, formed an exhaustless vista of picturesque scenes. On these, however, it is not my intention to dwell. Later on we shall once more wander through the streets, and at our leisure see what there is to be seen, and linger over what is worthy of attention and admiration. We can neither see nor linger with satisfaction while the Atlas Mountains loom up largely in the distance, and there is still a doubt whether we shall penetrate their unexplored valleys or climb their snow-clad heights. When these doubts have perished and those feats been accomplished, we shall be able to do the sights and scenes of the city of Morocco some justice.

Our situation at this time was indeed sufficiently puzzling. The danger we ran from the evil machinations of our men was now more than ever apparent, and consequently the necessity of keeping them as ignorant as possible of our movements more important. Happily during the four days we spent in Morocco several things occurred which gave us great assistance and did much to revive our hopes. First we found a Gibraltarian named Bonich, who in the most generous fashion placed his services as interpreter at our disposal while we remained in the city. This rendered us independent of our men for the moment, and enabled us to make very necessary inquiries about routes and passes, without which we would only have floundered in the dark.

Then, in addition, a mountain Jew arrived from Saffi to join us, credited by Mr. Hunot with courage, fidelity, intelligence, and above all, with a most intimate acquaintance with the mountains and their inhabitants. This seemed an almost incredible prize; but we were not long in discovering that Mr. Hunot had not overrated him, and that he at least would not fail us. There was but one terrible drawback—we could not converse with each other, and therefore half his usefulness was destroyed.

One other circumstance there was which gave us unalloyed pleasure and encouragement. We were not, as we had at first believed, the guests of the Kaid of the town, but of a powerful enemy of his, the Kaid of Rahamna. This was a very important fact, as we now felt sure that we should have but little difficulty in slipping away from Morocco without an escort of soldiers, which we dreaded excessively, as likely to put a climax to our difficulties.

Our great object at this time was to obtain, first, the mastery of our men in some way or other, and second, as thorough an acquaintance with the mountain routes and governors as possible, so as to avoid awakening suspicions by having to make inquiries in the neighbourhoods selected for exploration. We must enter these mountain fastnesses, we foresaw, as men knowing exactly where they wanted to go, and as having absolute authority to go whithersoever they pleased.

Everything considered, we still deemed it expedient to keep to our original intentions and proceed to Demnat, where we would make our first essays at mountaineering, and generally feel our way.

The first news that greeted us on the morning of the 27th May was that El Hadj Hamad from Casablanca had deserted, taking with him one or two loaves of sugar and some green tea, to console him while he hid from our vengeance.

We would not have troubled much about him, as he had been an unmitigated nuisance to ourselves and our men, with whom he incessantly waged war, but then we knew that one or two of the others were quite as anxious to quit our service, and it was necessary to show that such things could not be done with impunity. Consequently we set all the machinery of the place at work to capture him, and we vowed that he should lie in prison till we had done with our travels. The men were very much impressed by our energy and our seeming determination to have the last drop of his blood. Some days later we strained our conscience to a considerable extent, and led them to believe that the runaway had been caught and lodged in chains.

The truth was, the rival jealousies of Bin Daoud, the governor of the town, and of Abdul Hamid, Kaid of Rahamna, left Hadj a free field. Bin Daoud's men did not know the runaway, and Abdul Hamid's soldiers would have no dealings with them, not even to the extent of pointing Hadj out. That is a sample of the working of the machinery of Moorish government.

Owing to this unlooked-for occurrence, it was two hours after sunrise before we left Morocco. Our men had been kept in ignorance of our movements till the last moment, to prevent them breeding mischief. Shalum the Jew knew the road to Demnat, therefore we required no guide, while, to show that we travelled under the protection of the Sharifian umbrella, we transformed a Saffi courier into a Government soldier by the simple process of giving him the high-peaked fez which distinguishes the soldier from the civilian.

As we passed through the busy streets, we were in continual apprehension lest we should be stopped by messengers, or find soldiers sent after us to watch our movements while ostensibly looking after our safety. But the gate was reached and no such disaster befell us.

Our course lay almost due east, at first through the zone of well-watered gardens and effective groups of olive and date, which spread themselves over the gentle slope trending to the Wad Tensift. We wonderingly noticed how the whole country was dotted over with mounds of earth, mostly in lines running at all sorts of angles. On examination, these were seen to be formed by the excavation of underground channels for the conveyance of water into the town and to the various gardens. Along these lines at intervals, openings had been made to the surface for the easier excavation of the tunnels, and for clearing them out in the event of their becoming choked up.

In two hours we reached the point of junction of three considerable streams, still swollen by the melting of the mountain snow. These were the Wads Urika and Misfiwa, which took their rise in the central axis of the chain, while the third gathered its waters from the lower ranges which lie between the two rivers. Needless to say these mountain torrents form the chief tributaries of the Tensift.

Having crossed with some difficulty, we travelled over a more sterile tract, undiversified by grove and garden, or even trees. The surface was strewn with large water-borne boulders.

Some time after mid-day we reached the base of the low hills of Misfiwa, but could see nothing of the higher zones for veiling clouds, though more than once a snow-clad peak or crest displayed itself in its supernal whiteness above the grey mists.

We now continued to skirt the base of the mountains, here running almost due east and west, and in the precipitous escarpments we were able to distinguish the flaggy red sandstone and grey and white limestone which composed their lower ranges.

After crossing the Wad Masin we noticed a basaltic dyke breaking through the sedimentary rocks, a fact not altogether unconnected with the sudden improvement in the fertility of the soil which here took place, resulting in the yield of enormous crops of barley.

At sunset we reached the noisy torrent of the Wad Gadat, near where it breaks from its mountain fastnesses, and ascending the opposite ridge, which here hems it in, we entered the dilapidated town of Sidi Rehal.

We did not seek the hospitality of the Kaid in vain. In a few minutes the guest house was prepared, and with laudible promptitude green tea was provided to refresh us after our weary ride. That night, however, in spite of a twelve hours' fast, we nibbled but gingerly at the badly-cooked food sent in to us by Hadj M'hamad, and forgot the vices in remembering the virtues of our late cook, Hadj Hamad.

From Sidi Rehal the traveller commands a magnificent view of the Great Plain of Morocco. In this part are enormous fields of barley, stretching some twenty miles north to the base of the extremely jagged range of peaks which compose the Jebelet or "Little Mountain" of Rahamna and Srarna—the Atlas being *par excellence* the Jebel, though sometimes Jebel Tilj or Snow Mountain. Looking west, the eye finds no boundary except in the haze of distance, though from the neighbouring heights it naturally rests upon the tower of the Kutubia, which, even at a distance of thirty miles, stands forth a conspicuous feature in the landscape, and a perfect godsend to the traveller as a fixed landmark on which to get compass-bearings for the protraction of his route.

It was to the mountains, however, that we naturally turned for something specially noteworthy.

Remembering the dominating and impressive grandeur of the view they present when seen from the Jebelet, we expected that nearer approach would only add to that grandeur and impressiveness—that we would be almost overwhelmed with the sensation of being under the shadow of this stupendous mountain mass. How keen then was our disappointment when, finding ourselves at its base, we sought in vain for the Atlas of the distance with the additional anticipated effects of proximity. Instead, we found ourselves staring up at a series of by no means picturesque low ranges of mountains, gently sweeping up some two or three thousand feet above the plain. A limestone escarpment running in an unbroken line along the face of a ridge, a gully cutting through the same, a whitewashed Kuba on a hill-top, and a Shellach or Berber village clinging to its side, were the sole substitutes for the beetling cliffs, the frowning grandeur of the range, and the snow-clad, cloud-piercing heights which we had been led to expect from the distant north.

There the glittering crest had dwarfed all else; here the minor range at its base bulked chiefly in view, making it difficult for us to realise that we were looking at the lower undulations of a great earth-wave which swept up to elevations of 13,000 and 14,000 feet.

Up the glen of the Gadat and over the shoulder of the heights of Misfiwa we did indeed get glimpses of the highest elevations, but they seemed to be as distant as when we saw them from Jebelet, only infinitely less striking in their effect. They appeared no longer like the snow-capped crest of an enormous precipice frowning over the riant plains, but only the last of a series of great steps.

CHAPTER XI.

SIDI REHAL TO DEMNAT.

On preparing to resume our march next morning, we were nearly deprived in a somewhat violent manner of the services of our new cook, El Hadj M'hamad of Mogador. He was engaged fixing up his pack all unconscious of the fact that his mule and C.-B.'s horse had veered round, till, stern on, they stood in battle-array. Of this fact, however, he was speedily made aware when, passing between the two animals, the horse took the opportunity of violently propelling him against the rear of the mule, from which he was as promptly hurled back and landed on the ground, doubled up and groaning vociferously to Allah and Sidi Abdul Kader. A violent commotion was the result. Horse and mule were driven apart with blows and curses. Every one gathered round the fallen man, but, marvellous to relate, no damage was discovered, though throughout the day he never ceased to groan, and at intervals grunt out the phrase " Ya Allah ! " from which he seemed to derive much comfort.

We would willingly have continued our way with no other escort than our improvised soldier, but the

Kaid would not hear of such a thing. While in his territory he was responsible for us, and he could not possibly let us travel thus poorly protected.

We had no particular arguments to advance against this, and as we had no reason to fear any obstruction as far as Demnat, we submitted without demur to the addition of a horseman to our party.

Our way still lay due east. On our left stretched the great plain, gently sloping northward to the bed of the Tensift. On our right the primary elevations of the Atlas rose in rounded masses, sheltering on their slopes numerous Shellach villages.

There was but little to attract our attention in the wide landscape. A humble wayfarer, a Jew riding towards Morocco on a mule or an ass, long lines of reapers half-hidden in the rich fields of barley, these were the sole points of interest on the lowlands; while the featureless hills only showed, besides the Berber villages, a Kuba here and there, and breaking through the limestone the basalt dyke which we had noticed farther west on the previous day.

Thus thrown back on ourselves, and feeling in a hopeful mood, we did our best to beguile the weary hours with attempts to utilise our Arabic phrases and add others to our list. We tenderly inquired after Hadj's ribs, and cheerfully conversed about the certainty of the runaway cook being in chains. This view of the situation was not taken quite so cheerfully by our men, who among themselves speculated with glum countenances about the fate of their late companion.

In about an hour we reached a place called Tezert, which we learned was the residence of a Sheik of the Kaid of Glauwa, which province here extends as a narrow strip into the plain, cutting that of Zemran nearly in two.

We took careful note of the fact that a route led from the Sheik's house across the mountains to the Dra.

In three hours we reached the Wad Tessaout, one of the chief tributaries of the river we had crossed at Azamor. The Tessaout proved to be a violent torrent running in a deep narrow channel cut out of river debris, the size of the blocks being more suggestive of ice than water transport.

We crossed by a ford some four miles from the hills, the mules having to be unloaded and their burdens carried over on the heads of countrymen, who make this a regular business during the winter and summer.

Shortly after leaving this river we entered the province of Srarna. It was now mid-day, and we began to be sick of the treeless plain and the many reaches of barley crops. The sun beat down with overpowering ardour, and mules and horses required a little more urging to keep them moving at a respectable pace. Even the men ceased talking, and only broke the silence by an encouraging "Arria, arria!" to hurry on their animals.

An agreeable relief was afforded by a series of fine olive-groves and fruit-gardens which we entered some two hours from the river. These gardens we found to be watered by a network of channels leading from the Wad Tedili.

The plain now became more broken and undulating as well as better wooded, and the bordering hills also assumed new and more varied features. Here and there were castellated Sheik's houses crowning prominent eminences and throwing a certain warlike charm over the country. Geologically we were struck by the curious forms into which the limestones were broken and contorted by the intrusion of the basalt dyke, which we could still trace in places on the hillside. These sometimes had the appearance of great V's and W's.

We had left the basin of the Tensitt on reaching the Tessaout, and we could now see to the north-east a number of dark lines winding through the plain, which we knew were other streams flowing towards the north-west, to coalesce and form the Um er Rebia. The Jebelet range had now dwindled down to a few isolated peaks, while ahead of us the mountain masses of the Entifa and Tedla broke from the Atlas and closed up the great plain over which we had been marching east for the last two days.

Towards three in the afternoon we began to diverge from the lowlands and follow a mule-path over more rugged ground.

At length, turning the shoulder of a hill-spur, we found, to our inexpressible relief, the valley of Demnat opening up before us and running into the lower ranges of mountains.

Our path became more and more rugged and difficult

as we proceeded. We crossed deep gullies, so steep of slope that our men had to hang on to the tails of their mules to give them back-weight and to act as a brake in the descent. Even more difficult was the ascent of opposing slopes, up which the animals struggled amid the clamour of all the opprobrious epithets at the command of the muleteers, accentuated by resounding blows.

We here found ourselves among some familiar trees, which we had not seen since we left the coast. Arar and juniper crowned the ridges with their dark resin-scented foliage, or straggling more sparingly down the slopes, mingled with holly-like evergreen oak. Of lighter hue were the oleander bushes which filled the bottoms of the gullies and gave colour to the scene.

Gradually we got past this nasty section, and the sharp ridges gave place to more gentle and less denuded slopes. The olive cast its kindly shade on grassy banks where Shellach boys watched over browsing flocks of sheep and goats, or stood open-mouthed to stare at the strange apparition that burst upon them as we passed. Farther on gardens began to appear terraced in little squares, and near them stood hamlets built of red earth, where the dogs gave us a noisy greeting.

Soon the bridle-path became a veritable arcade, arched over by fruit-trees and walled in by bush and flower and creeper, growing to right and left with all the gipsy grace, wild beauty, and prodigal profusion of the tropics. It had all such a homelike aspect, too, for the pomegranates and the figs were literally smothered under the glorious wreaths of wild-rose and honeysuckle which broke through them and spread themselves over their every branch, till nothing was seen but rich masses of odoriferous flowers. Pleasant to the ear also was the unwonted sound of running and falling water murmuring among stones or rushing over slopes on its fertilising mission.

We no more remembered the weary hours that were past nor felt the burning sun, but lingeringly rode along the lane, no longer dying to reach our destination. We had but little farther to go. A few more windings and turnings, a few more pleasant peeps of terraced slopes, of banks bright with many-hued flowers, and suddenly we found ourselves before the imposing fort-studded walls of Demnat.

We passed under the fortified gateway, and all the sweet charms of nature were shut out. We threaded garbage-strewn streets hemmed in by mean mud-built dwellings. Filthy Jews stared at us in undisguised surprise, and ran after to hear who we were, what we wanted, and whither we were going. The imposing gateway of the Kasbah or quarter of the governor was at length reached, and we halted before the Kaid's house, the centre of an eager group of Jew and Moor and Shellach. The soldiers took the Sharifian letter, and proceeded suitably to announce the arrival of such high and mighty personages as ourselves.

While we waited the return of the messenger, and congratulated ourselves on our safe arrival in such a beautiful district, we were suddenly startled by a clear

K

"Good evening, gentlemen," in unmistakably English tones. Turning in surprise, we looked for the speaker. We could see no one to whom to make reply, till from among the crowd of Jews we were again saluted, and distinguished a somewhat short and fat individual, with features different from those around him. He wore a red fez, which of itself showed he was no ordinary Morocco Jew, none such being allowed to wear anything but a black cap and slippers. We answered him with a very genuine cordiality, as the thought, "An interpreter at last," flashed across our minds.

We soon learned that we were speaking to David Assor, a Cockney Jew, who, by the fortuitous concourse of circumstances, had been landed in these parts, where he had taken to himself a wife and had now been established as a trader for many years.

While we talked our messenger returned to say that the Kaid was asleep and could not be disturbed, whereupon we stormed and demanded who the Kaid of Demnat was that we, the British bearers of Sharifian letters, were to be kept waiting at his gate till he awoke. Let him, we ordered, be apprised forthwith of our presence, else we should show our displeasure by leaving the city and camping outside.

Our fulmination had the desired effect, and soon we received messages of welcome, and were conveyed to an old ruinous building containing but one clean and comfortable apartment. At first we objected, but finding nothing better at the Kaid's disposal, we finally took possession under protest; and after all, if there were nothing else to commend them, our quarters certainly commanded a beautiful view over a finely-wooded glen, on which we looked down from an airy height. At the windows we could enjoy the fresh exhilarating breeze sweeping down the valley from the icy elevations of the Atlas, which in the distance peeped over the green and grey shoulders of the lower ranges of the foreground.

That night we considered ourselves the happiest of mortals, when, over a cup of tea and a biscuit, we were able to shut out our men from our councils, and with Assor lay plans for outwitting not only them but the officials.

As for our new-found friend, we rejoiced his heart and stomach with such delicacies as our scanty stores permitted, and to which he had been long a stranger. We also recounted for his benefit, as far as our limited knowledge went, all about the latest monstrosities that had appeared at the Aquarium and similar resorts, and told him how fatter women and more brute-like men, &c., than had been known in his day. had astonished an admiring world.

Remarkable to relate, too, we discovered that we had some mutual acquaintances. He knew some of my old Swahili friends, from having acted as interpreter to the Sultan of Zanzibar's attendants during his visit to England.

Next morning, feeling in a lively mood of added hopefulness, we thought we would try a new departure, and array ourselves in all the picturesque draperies of the Moor to call upon the Kaid.

First, we drew over our Nazarene legs the *serwal*, the cool, baggy, linen equivalents of the trousers we had doffed, and which, in virtuous Mohammedan eyes, appear as far from decent as does the kilt to Frenchmen. Over these, and hanging nearly to our feet, came the *chamir*, a nightshirt-like garment, drawn round the neck by a string. Over the *chamir* again we drew the *farajia*, an article of clothing somewhat closely resembling the former, but embroidered in white round the neck and down the breast.

The *farajia*, unlike the *chamir*, opens down the front a certain distance, and is provided with numerous soft buttons fastening into loops, the despair of the hasty Christian. Both of these upper garments are of linen, and are drawn in at the waist by a belt of leather embroidered in coloured silks.

We required the assistance and guidance of our men to wind the ten yards of the creamy *haik* around our persons so as to fall about us with becoming grace and style. The fez, turban, and slippers completed our clothing, though we had further to supply ourselves with a dagger and a leather bag, without which no Moor is completely equipped.

We now sallied forth, doing our best to assume the deportment of the faithful, at any rate to appear to be accustomed to this sort of thing. This, however, was not very easy, for somehow or other the *haik* would fall off our shoulders or get entangled among our feet. The loose, heelless slippers on our sockless feet were another source of annoyance to betray the Kaffir masquerading in the garments of the true believer. Mine more than

C.-B. IN MOORISH DRESS.

once by unguarded movements left my feet and preceded me by at least a yard, while C.-B., trying to be more careful, left his behind him. To make matters worse, the firm, gritty sand soon filled them, and rasped and rubbed our bare feet till the skin came off. Happily no native presumed to laugh at us, which would have been the crowning annoyance that might have led to explosions of wrath.

Arrived at the entrance-hall, we were kept waiting a short time while the Kaid made ready to receive us with becoming dignity.

At last our host himself appeared to do us special honour by receiving us in person. Quite black and bullet-headed, Kaid Jelleli had evidently as much of the Negro as the Moor in him. Courteously touching our hands and then his heart, he saluted us with the phrase, "Marhababikum" ("You are welcome"), to which we as courteously replied, "Baraka-lowfik" ("Many thanks"). He then asked various civil questions, whether we were well rested after the fatigues of the journey, whether we had got all that we required, &c., &c.; to all of which we contented ourselves with replying, "Baraka-lowfik." It needed the more pious phrase, "El Hamdu-lillah!" ("Praise God!") fitly to respond to his inquiry if our health were good; which having duly and earnestly ejaculated, we left him to understand by our tone and appearance what we could not find words to express.

The salaam and compliments over, we proceeded to the inner apartments. Having prematurely put off my slippers, I had to return to fetch them, and in my haste to regain my companions I more than once sent my slippers ahead of me or left them behind me, greatly to the delight of some Negro boys who watched me round corners.

Passing along a bare, gloomy corridor, we were at length introduced into a charming garden, enclosed at one side by a colonnaded verandah and overlooked on another by the latticed apartments of the harem. In the centre, and from the midst of encircling rose-

GARDEN IN KAID'S HOUSE.

bushes, a fine marble fountain threw a crystalline jet of water into the air.

Passing round the court by a marble-paved footpath, we passed underneath the verandah and entered the Kaid's reception-room, the door of which was extremely richly painted and carved.

The Kaid now took his seat on a mattress which

did duty as a divan, and we were motioned to follow his example.

In trying to do so in proper Moorish fashion, we ended by flopping down in a most undignified manner and ignominiously drawing our legs under us.

Again the Kaid broke forth into compliments and formal inquiries, but these being beyond our depth, we allowed Assor, who accompanied us, to keep responsive pace with him while we took stock of the room. This, on examination, proved to be most handsomely decorated with a dado of tiles arranged in intricate geometric patterns. Beautiful stucco arabesque surrounded the doorways and windows. The floor, too, was laid in an elaborate mosaic of black and white tiles, partially concealed by couches, rugs, and leopard-skins. At each end of the room was a canopied bedstead resembling an ancient Lord Mayor's coach without wheels.

We were now able to join in the conversation, and do our best to satisfy the curiosity of the Kaid while carefully hiding our actual plans. We simply informed him that we were charged by the wise men of England to collect certain plants for the Government gardens, which were much wanted, and which could only be got in these parts. He was too polite to appear sceptical, and merely exclaimed that God was great—an affirmation which in this case implied that we were Christian liars. He showed himself interested in some of our scientific instruments, but still more in the photographs of our countrywomen which we showed him.

In the midst of our exhibition a small black slave-girl appeared with the tea-tray, and served us with the inevitable three cups of syrupy green tea, of which the Moors drink on every possible occasion—coffee being a rare beverage in these lands. Long before the tea-drinking was over I had discovered that it requires practice to sit tailor-fashion. My legs went to sleep, and I had to stretch them out in the most unwonted fashion before the circulation revived again.

Greatly to our surprise, we were allowed to take some photographs of the court and verandah, and we left the place in the belief that here at least we had no special obstacles to encounter, though the Kaid had warned us that we must on no account venture among the mountains. We might collect plants in the immediate vicinity of the town, but that was to be our limit.

CHAPTER XII.

TOWN AND VALLEY OF DEMNAT.

On leaving the Kaid, I gladly threw off the unaccustomed garments, and in my proper Nazarene character proceeded to inspect the town under the guidance of Assor.

We found little to remark in the matter of architecture, though the Kasbah looked undoubtedly picturesque with its surrounding fosse, its well-preserved and massive fortifications, and its overhanging square towers, from which the Kaid's women, unseen themselves, may look down on the town or scan the varied features of the glen and the distant mountains.

With the exception of the governor's house, there is not a single building rising more than a good English storey in height. All are alike built of *tabia*, or clay, and a little lime, and alike devoid of ornamentation and of whitewash. Still, with all its meanness, Demnat presents a certain air of prosperity, for there are few ruined houses, and still fewer beggars. The inhabitants were all decently dressed, and seemed to want none of the necessaries of life; as indeed why should they in a fertile valley bursting with all the vegetable wealth that nature can give, and when a family can live on fivepence a day with meat at two meals?

We found we were here among a far different class of people from those among whom we had so far travelled. The natives of Demnat had neither the gaunt features and the wild expression, nor yet the tawny complexion of the country Arabs. As little did they resemble the well-fed town Moor, of portly figure, flowing beard, and generally handsome face. In Demnat we were at last among the Berbers of the Atlas, usually known from Demnat westward as Shellach. Neither then nor after months of acquaintance was I able to formulate to myself the particular points in which they agree among themselves as a race, and in which they are distinguished from all other peoples. To me they seemed to occupy in general appearance a sort of intermediate place between the Moor and Arab, a description which applies generally to the Shellach of the lower slopes and the entrances of the various valleys and glens, but which in no respect whatever applies to those living at higher elevations, where they differ more widely in appearance from their brethren of the low grounds than do the latter from either the Moor or the Arab. As a rule, the Shellach may in a very general way be described as being, in the low grounds, a well-built, pleasant-featured individual, with narrow head, well-cut face and good eyes, and but slightly tawny complexion; while in the higher glens and elevations he becomes, chiefly through the hard battle with life and the miserable conditions under which he lives, an under-sized, wizened, and wrinkled person, all bone and sinew, with the brown complexion of leather, and eyes bleared and rheumy, as of men who spend half their lives in semi-darkness and amidst pungent smoke, as is indeed his fate in some districts for two or three months in the year. But we are anticipating. Let us therefore return to Demnat.

One remarks at once, in wandering through the streets and lanes of the Medinah, that the women do not veil their faces. Neglecting in this respect the express injunctions of the Koran, which stringently forbids women to distract the thoughts of the true believers from the contemplation of the sacred attributes of Allah by the display of their charms and ornaments, they move about without the *haik* or any other covering with which to veil the face. What they do show in the way of dress is certainly neither alluring nor becoming. It seems to consist of a single cotton or woollen sheet, which in some mysterious way or other envelops the body over some under-garments; the two ends being fastened together by antique silver clasps, from which hangs across the breast a massive silver chain. On their heads they wear a gaudy-coloured handkerchief to conceal and confine the hair. What pleased us much in mixing with both the men and women was that they seemed delighted to see us, and showed a frank curiosity where the true Moor or Arab would have glared at us with fierce contempt and hatred, and behind our backs muttered, "May God transfix the enemy of the faith."

Under such genial influences we expanded like flowers before the sun, and smilingly saluted all comers with the salaam or invocation that peace might descend upon them, a formula we had latterly been discouraged from using, from being continually, in response to our civilities, by implication consigned to the lowest depths of hell.

Beyond the groups of Shellach we found little to remark in the part more especially occupied by the followers of El Islam, for here there was no properly marked off Mellah, though one was in process of being built. Still the Jew is not happy except when herding among his kind, and speedily by nose and eye we were offensively made aware that we were approaching the homesteads of the chosen race of Israel.

It required all our courage to penetrate into this network of dunghills and indescribable filth; but we considered it our bounden duty as explorers to let no fastidiousness stand in our way.

Stepping along with studied care and watchfulness, keeping down as best we might the unpleasant sensation that would arise, as it had from far different causes at sea, we peeped into various houses and examined with interest the daughters of Judah, who massed themselves round the doors in filthy gowns and repulsive fleshliness.

It was quite irritating to find that some 80 per cent. of the eyes directed toward us were sightless from cataract, disfigured by squinting, or inflamed and swollen by ophthalmia. It seemed almost incredible that such things could be in a small town situated in a well-drained valley, and surrounded by wholesome cooling breezes from the snowy heights in the immediate neighbourhood.

And yet it was no puzzle. No family, however large, occupied more than one small windowless room, though frequently several families are huddled together

MELLAH.

like pigs in a poke. In addition, the rooms are, in almost every case, built round a small court some fifteen feet square, and have a second series of upper apartments similarly occupied, the balcony which leads to the doors affording a partial shade to the court below.

These enclosures are the common family sewers, general reception and work rooms for the women, and happy play-grounds of the children. In addition, they serve as stables for the donkeys and mules of those in the compound who possess such beasts of burden. The sights and smells are sickening beyond description. And yet here, in happy unconsciousness of anything unusual, groups of women spend the day carding or spinning wool, sewing clothes, cooking, &c. Their dress is quite the same as their Shellach neighbours, but necklets of gold coins are more common. Among other things to arouse our astonishment and disgust, was the discovery of the existence of child-wives of eight, nine, and ten years of age, some of whom are mothers at twelve and thirteen.

We had the courage to enter one or two of the rooms which surround these festering, fly-infested courts; but as few will have the temerity to follow me farther, I shall draw a veil over the interiors. In justice to other towns of Morocco, it should be said that, though all the Mellahs are abominably filthy, that of Demnat is in that respect far ahead of any other I have seen.

One naturally supposes that this state of affairs arises from the oppression under which the inhabitants live and have lived. Undoubtedly that supplies a clue to the true explanation, but it has been the oppression of past years which has branded its brutalising mark upon this irrepressible race. The oppression of to-day, such as there is of it specially directed against the Jews—and that is very little in the towns—has nothing to do with the beastly state of filth in which they live. They are, take them all together, much better provided with this world's goods than the Moors, who have their streets clean and their houses and courts wholesome and healthy. In Demnat they are not even confined in a Mellah, and are under no restrictions about the removal of filth. The only explanation is that work the Jews will not except to bring in money. And yet they wonder why God punishes them—His chosen people—with every possible ophthalmic disease, while their hated neighbours, whom surely He has doomed to everlasting perdition, are free from similar troubles.

What a relief it was to escape from this sickening plague-spot, and find ourselves outside the walls, inhaling the untainted mountain breezes, and looking back upon the now picturesque battlements or down into the terraced glen at the edge of which the town is built.

In the afternoon we set forth to visit a remarkable "cave," of which we had heard much from Assor, though he himself had never seen it. As it was only a few miles up the valley, the Kaid made no trouble about letting us go, though carefully providing us with a couple of soldiers, as much to watch what we did as to protect us in case of need.

Mounted on mules, we descended the steep side of the glen on the side of which Demnat stands, till, some three hundred feet below, we found ourselves beside a fine stream, winding in curved and recurved bed, here confined between overhanging precipices draped with masses of ferns, with tree and bush and creeper

DEMNAT.

growing in the crevices and joints of the rocks, there with terraced slopes rising in a bright mosaic of many-tinted greens, of mellow gold, and speckled whites and reds and blues, according as vines and various fruit trees grew in shady groups and groves, or corn lay ready for the reaper, or marguerite and poppy decked the grassy sward.

From the bottom of the glen, where numerous corn-mills driven by the rushing water were actively at work, we scrambled as best we could up the opposite bank, with the delightful murmur of the running water in the network of irrigation channels ever in our ears; and mingling pleasantly with the great plaintive undertones of the parent stream, which from the depths below rose on the wings of the inconstant wind.

As we slowly rose in elevation and wound round the swelling hillsides, we thought we had never seen anything fairer, anything more beautiful, than this exquisitely fertile valley. We could now command a fine view of Demnat. Its walls and towers and the commanding buildings of the Kasbah seemed massive and picturesque in the extreme, and gave altogether a different impression—like so many things Moorish—than when seen close at hand. To add to the natural beauties of the scene were numerous villages romantically perched upon sharp jutting ridges, crowning precipitous hills, or half hid among splendid olive groves, in every case specially disposed with a view to easier defence.

But while we feasted our eyes on those external

beauties, we were not indifferent to the internal significance of things. We had ever an eye for rock sections, which gave us a key to some of the problems of nature around us. Here we came upon the basaltic dyke, which from beyond Sidi Rehal had appeared at intervals, breaking through the limestones, and marking the line where the hills sank into the plain. In this dyke lay the secret of the fertility of the valley; for, decomposed, it forms a rich soil, and when, with rich ingredients, there is a genial warmth, and throughout the year abundance of water, spread by a network of channels over every square inch of ground, what may not be expected?

In this dyke, too, lies the explanation of much of the physical conformation of the valley; and the beetling cliffs and rugged peaks take quite a new interest when we come to understand why they have these forms instead of the swelling slopes and dome-shaped elevations which in places oppose them.

Some two or three miles up the valley we came upon a massive dam thrown across it to raise the level of the stream in the summer and divert its waters into the lower series of irrigating channels. There were two higher series, which derived their supplies from more elevated points of the Wad Demnat, and carried water along the slopes of the valley at a height of 900 feet. This dam was the only modern public work raised for the general good of the community which we saw in Southern Morocco.

Beyond the dam the glen narrowed rapidly on passing

from the more easily decomposed basalt to the compact limestone, and evidently ended abruptly in a precipice. We now left our mules and took to our feet, as the bridle-path had stopped. For a few hundred yards we had no great difficulty, till, nearing a precipice, we were compelled to take to the bed of the stream. As we struggled over enormous boulders, or jumped from block to block over ugly black pools or foam-flaked whirlpools, we had great fun watching the almost despairing attempts of our friend Assor to follow us into these unaccustomed wilds. Never in his life before, even in the pursuit of gold, had he been tempted to leave the bustling street or the well-trodden highway, and now at the heels of two mad Christians he was scrambling, in danger of his life, up a frightful gorge in search of the strange and the picturesque! Even more than ourselves our men took a malicious pleasure in watching his awkward efforts; for to the Moor there is no dearer delight on earth than baiting a Jew. They directed him the worst ways possible, and cheered his heart with jocular remarks. We would have stopped them, but considering that he was likely to associate with us for some time, we concluded that one plunge overhead, after years of abstinence from the bodily use of water, would not be amiss in more ways than one.

This desirable accident, however, did not occur. Losing both his head and his wind, he sat himself down on a rock, and farther he would not budge; and we were fain to leave him to soothe his mind by calculating what he would charge for all these perils and shocks to his system.

Meanwhile, as we scrambled along amid the inspiring roar of water, with precipices closing in and frowning down upon us in ever-growing impressiveness, we were struck by the numbers of very large springs which bubbled up in the bed of the river or gushed forth from the living rock. These we accounted for by the theory that their natural line of drainage had been deranged by the basalt dyke which we had crossed running like a wall through the limestone and sandstone rocks, and even tilting them into vertical positions.

We had but little farther to go, for, turning a corner, we found the way suddenly closed by a precipice 150 to 200 feet high, above which still yawned the upper section of the glen. At one corner of the closing wall a fine cascade leapt from ledge to ledge among the bushes, creepers, and other plants which draped the rugged angles of the rock.

We wondered if this could be the Wad Demnat; it seemed so small beside the torrent which raged around us. Pushing forward more eagerly, we reached a better point of view, and found a great, dark hole yawning in front of us, from which the river came swirling and roaring, as if in mad delight at escaping from the hideous depths of the earth into the fresh air, the bright sunshine, and the bush and flower clad banks. This, then, was "Iminifiri" (the big cave), of which we were in search.

With the greatest difficulty we struggled to the mouth of the cave, determined to solve all the mysteries connected with it. On entering we were struck with awe and admiration at the wonderful sight presented to us.

We found ourselves under a magnificent arch, which swept overhead at a height of 100 to 140 feet. Stalactites of all sizes and shapes hung from the roof in rugged yellow pendants, and the irregular walls were adorned with clustered pillars of stalagmite and other mouldings of Nature's workmanship.

Determined to see as much as possible of the cave, we pushed deeper into the gloom of the interior, ever with the impressive noise of thundering waters in our ears. We had not gone far when, turning a nasty projection of the walls, we were suddenly surprised by a glare of light and a glimpse of the deep blue sky.

After all, then, there was no cave, only a remarkable barrier of limestone rock drilled through by the river. This was rather a damper on our feelings of wonderment, and thinking ourselves somewhat defrauded, and being unable to go further, we returned to the mouth of the arch.

We were now conducted up the face of the precipice near the bordering cascade, which also had all the appearance of springing from the living rock overhead. Right under the roof of the arch, in a curious shelf and pillared recess, we were shown four artificial circular depressions, about three feet in diameter and a foot to fifteen inches deep, each one having also a smaller depression in its centre. Here it is said that holy men from Sus and the Dra, on the other side of the Atlas, come in secret and at night, and by virtue of chanted incantations and written words are able not only to get great store of gold and silver, but to determine where they may be found elsewhere. Undoubtedly this superstition, which is firmly held by the natives, is a survival of some religious rites of the old Nature-worshippers, who in some long-past period of the world's history had looked upon the awe-inspiring Iminifiri as a sacred spot.

We would willingly have continued our exploration and ascended to the top of the precipice, but the day was drawing near a close. Standing on the ledge of rock where heathen rites had been practised, with the deep gorge yawning beneath us, the strange natural tunnel running in fantastic curves far into the blackness of the bowels of the earth, and the rugged precipices and rocky mountains above and around us, we knew something of the feelings which must have filled the hearts of those who had worshipped the terrible forces of the earth. Blended with the awe which our immediate savage surroundings roused were the softer feelings that stole over us as we looked down the romantic glen and saw the smiling fertile valley bathed in all the mellow lights of eventide, cradled in sheltering hills, cooled by fresh breezes, and fertilised by an ever-flowing series of irrigating arteries. One could at such a moment understand that to simple savages, dependent upon what Nature gave them, the sun was no mere source of light and heat, but a very god, that spirits ruled the winds and rain, and regulated the flow of the springs. We at that moment were also Nature-worshippers.

The exigencies of the hour, however, admitted of no lingering, and reluctantly we set our faces townwards.

Next morning I set forth to complete my examination of Iminifiri. But I had other intentions in view as well. I was resolved to make a bold dash into the mountains beyond.

Quite unsuspicious of my intention, the Kaïd allowed me to depart with only one soldier, while I on my part took only my faithful and willing henchman Shalum the Jew with Abdarachman from Mogador, who knew a little English, picked up as a boatman.

This time we passed up the opposite side of the valley, with the object of getting the more easily to the top of the arch. We soon arrived in front of Iminifiri, and proceeded to take some photographs of the creeper-draped natural arch, with its noisy cascade of water dropping ribbon-like at its side.* This accomplished, I set about my more arduous enterprise. To get rid of the obstructive soldier, I gave the camera into his charge, with orders not to leave it for a moment, nor to stir from the spot if he valued his life and liberty. Thus freed, I set forth with a light heart, but still carefully keeping my own counsel.

* These photographs were subsequently ruined by being accidentally re-exposed.

In a few minutes we were on the top of the closing barrier of rock, and then, to my profound surprise, I found that I was not only on the top of a natural arch and bridge utilised by the inhabitants, but also on an aqueduct by which a fine stream was conveyed from one side of the glen to the other, where it fell in the cascade already alluded to.

The explanation of this probably unique phenomenon of a river being conveyed naturally across a gorge 140 feet deep soon became apparent, and proved to be sufficiently simple.

The arch was not composed of the limestone rock of the hills, but of calcareous tufa. The stream that now crossed the glen had primarily fallen as a simple cascade on the eastern side, and being charged with lime in solution, had throughout long centuries continued to deposit its calcareous burden layer after layer. In process of time the tufa or lime thus deposited had gradually grown out till it had reached the opposite side of the gorge and completed the bridge aqueduct, and now, instead of falling on the east side, the stream falls as a cascade on the west side, and there continues its deposition of tufa. Of course, meanwhile, the Wad Demnat was also at work beneath, preventing the choking up of its natural channel while eating away the limestone beds beneath, thus preventing the formation of the massive wall which otherwise would have resulted.

On the bare rocks which overhung Iminifiri I was delighted to discover the rare gum-producing *Euphorbia resinifera*. This was the only place in the Atlas in which I found this cactoid plant, though we subsequently discovered a different species in the neighbourhood of Agadir and on the seaward aspect of the mountains of Haha. The former is distinguished by 3–4 angled branches, the latter by 9–10 angled branches. The Atlas form also grows with shorter and more crowded stems.

Beyond the natural bridge the country opened up into a shallow hillocky valley, backed to the south by a very precipitous range of mountains. Finding a small village of Shellach, we made friends at once with a pleasant-looking native. On asking him if there was any evidences of the Christians having been in this neighbourhood, he told us that on the top of a high conical mountain which he pointed out to us were some ruins of buildings which had belonged to the Rum (early Christians). It struck me at once that this must be the "Christian church" reported by Jackson in his account of the Empire of Morocco.

In any case, this was all I wanted as an excuse for making for some special point in the mountains. Abdarachman smiled in the sickly fashion of a man who thinks another has been joking in very bad taste when I told him to ask our informant if he would guide us thither for half a dollar. At first he tried to put it off, and I had to order him in a very emphatic and angry fashion to do as he was bid.

Pretending to do so, he said that the Shellach would not go on any account. Not believing him, I turned to Shalum, touched myself, pointed to the peak of

Irghalnsor, drew forth a dollar and nodded at the mountaineer. My meaning was caught in an instant, and put in words for the benefit of the Shellach, who brightened up at once, and uttered the magic phrase, "Ya Allah!" (O God!), the starting signal for good Moslems.

It was now nearly mid-day, and no time was to be lost if we hoped to get to the ruins and back to Demnat before dark. We therefore hurried off as fast as we could go.

We crossed numerous low ridges which coincided with anticlines of limestone, the hollows or synclines being characterised by red shales and sandstone. The soil was red, clayey, and poor, and consequently but little cultivated. There were no villages to be seen till we reached the base of the mountain. The steep slope we found to agree with the beds of limestone which here cropped up in one enormous fold. On the lower zones were magnificent groves of olives. Above, however, the soil becomes very meagre, and supports only the hardy arar, juniper, evergreen oak, and various bushes. My eagerness to reach the top of this range of mountains was so great, that I was soon far ahead of both my guide and Shalum; as for Abdarachman, he was left at the bottom.

At length, sadly blown, I reached the highest peak, the top of which I found covered with the ruins of an old building of very great strength and extent, but utterly shapeless, following as it did the irregular outlines of the mountain summit. The walls were of very great thickness and well built, though without lime. Inside, the outlines of chambers could be here and there detected amid the cairn-like mass of fallen stones. In one place there was the remains of an arched and cemented underground chamber, which probably was used for the storage of water for the supply of those who lived in the building.

A glance at the position and surroundings of these ruins soon disposed of the idea that this was ever a Christian church, though not improbably it may have been used for religious rites in a pre-Christian era. This at least seems to be the most reasonable theory to account for such a building occupying the desolate and almost inaccessible position it does, far too from the fields and the villages it would have had to protect had it been merely a fortified place of refuge. Considered solely as an easily defended stronghold, no place could be better adapted. To the east it overhangs a sheer precipice of quite a thousand feet, where a stream has cut through the upturned limestone beds and formed a splendid gorge. To the north, the peak slopes away with such rapidity that few people would care to struggle up in the face of an enemy, however few in numbers. It is only to the west that a neck of the range makes approach fairly easy.

Having satisfied myself of these facts, and ended with the same tendency to believe that the building had been used for religious rites, I turned to take in the wider prospect that spread itself before me.

To my inexpressible delight, I found myself in face of

the central ridge of the Atlas. It was here as we had pictured it from Jebelet, though somewhat shorn of its proportion, and consequently of its grandeur, by the 6000 feet underneath us. In a massive, almost unbroken wall it sprang abruptly from the great undulations of limestone and red shale which massed themselves at its feet, and on one of which I stood. There were few striking features to remark beyond its stern impressiveness, its even outline, and the completeness of the barrier which it presented to all who would cross the chain. The snow still lay in great masses on its summit, and crept here and there down sheltering crevices.

It is proverbially difficult to estimate the height of mountains, but combining what I saw then and afterwards of other parts of the range, I do not think the Atlas at this point far surpasses 10,000 feet in altitude. Geologically, it was abundantly clear that the grey limestone and red sandstone and shales which form the lower ranges also here composed the mass of the central axis—the even level of the top, the long straight lines which run along its face—its whole appearance, indeed, markedly suggesting such a formation. Later we were able to establish farther west by actual observation that this conclusion was correct.

To add somewhat to the impressiveness of the scene before us, a great storm-cloud rested over the mountain, from which continually flashed shafts of lightning, while the thunder rolled and rumbled with awe-inspiring effect.

Fearing not only to be caught in the grasp of the storm but in the darkness of night, we waited but to take one glance at the gorge on our left, widening out into a more open glen, where some small Shellach hamlets appeared in bleak loneliness and amid desolate surroundings. We then hurried as rapidly as we could go down the mountain-side, passed through the yawning gorge, picked up the sullen Abdarachman in the more open valley, and were able to listen smilingly to the passionate reproaches of our exceedingly alarmed soldier, who had not dared to leave his charge, and through the hours of waiting had remained a prey to the fear that he would end his days in prison if anything had happened to us.

We reached Demnat in the evening, and learned that the Kaid was as much perplexed and disturbed by our disappearance as our guard, and that soldiers were preparing to scour the country in search of us.

CHAPTER XIII.

TASIMSET.

FROM Assor we had heard much of a place called Tasimset, situated in the mountains some distance south-west of Demnat.

He himself was personally interested in Tasimset, solely because he had a mother-in-law with a bit of property there, and had occasionally found it cheaper, and also much cooler, to spend a short time within its precincts now and then in the heat of the summer, making use of the opportunity to earn an occasional honest or dishonest penny.

Though not alive to the picturesque, he could not help noticing the fact, however, that there was a fine waterfall at Tasimset, and he had heard the native Jews and Gentiles speak of remarkable caves and other wonders. To these things, as not bringing grist to his mill, he had paid no attention, but he thought they might interest us, and for a consideration he was prepared to act as our guide.

Of course we clutched at the idea. What we chiefly wanted was to know of particular goals to make for, to enable us to assume a more definite attitude with our men and the officials; and now one had been provided for us, and we resolved to use it as a test of the character of the opposition we were likely to have to struggle against in the future. As soon, therefore, as I had refreshed myself after my hurried visit to Irghalnsor, we proceeded to visit the Kaid to announce our intentions. We found him holding a divan in a favourite traditional place of Oriental governors—his stable-yard. In Morocco horses are never bound, but always kept securely hobbled and pinned by their legs to the ground in an open court. It was here that we found Kaid Jelleli, his round half-Negro half-Moorish head peeping cosily from beneath his huge turban and the folds of his *haik*.

After the salaam and compliments expressed in all proper figures of Moorish speech, he upbraided us for having ventured so far into the mountains, to the imminent danger of our lives and against the express instructions of Seedna (our lord). Whereupon we laughed merrily at the idea that anything could happen to British Christians like ourselves—*that* was quite too ludicrous. As for the Sultan's injunctions that we were not to be permitted to enter the "mountains and dangerous parts," that the Kaid must clearly perceive referred only to the Bled Siba (or independent districts), and not to the Bled Maghzan (or country of the Government).

Now here we were in the Bled Maghzan, and what had we to fear while under the potent protection of the great and wise Kaid Jelleli, whom may Allah long sustain and prosper !

Well, the raid into the mountains was an accomplished fact; obviously it had been "written," and who can avoid God's decrees?

It was a very different thing, however, when I announced that on the morrow I was going to Tasimset. I most carefully avoided asking his leave or the protection of his soldiers. My rôle was simply to assume that he had absolutely nothing to do with my movements, and that his soldiers would go with us as a matter of course.

At once he began to make the most emphatic objections. The place was highly dangerous, and he could not permit us to go. We listened to all he had to say with smiling attention, and when he had finished, told him that we were prepared for all the dangers of the way, but that they would in no respect alter our plans. We had business to do there, and go we would, leaving all else in the hands of Allah. Our tone and manner threw him into great perplexity. They were those of great people, of persons having authority behind them. Might he not get himself into trouble if he stopped us? Yes, but was he not more likely to get into trouble if he permitted us to go? In this dilemma he took counsel with his major-domo, with the result that he said we might go if we would return the same day. He would even himself escort us. To this proposition we returned an emphatic negative. We would not be bound by any conditions

He entreated and argued, even threatened, but we remained firm, and at length got up and marched away without waiting to hear more. A few minutes after, a messenger came from the Kaid asking us to give him a letter taking the responsibility of our trip upon ourselves. This we did, not wishing to push matters too far.

Meanwhile our men, getting wind of our intentions, contrived to get at the Kaid, making such representations as caused him to alter his mind, and once more he sent his servant to tell us that we were not to go. Our answer was short, sharp, and indignant. "We had spoken, and we were not Moors or Jews, to eat up our words again."

That evening was marked by a terrific row between Shalum and the Moors. They hated him as a Jew, and they hated him with tenfold intensity because they were afraid of him to some extent, for a bolder or more stalwart fellow did not exist in Morocco. It was a further grievance against him that he would not join with them in their treacherous tactics, and consequently they looked upon him as a spy. They sought every opportunity of telling lies about him, and quarrelling with him. These troubles had now culminated in a terrific outburst, the Moors setting upon Shalum with their knives. No dog's kennel or hyena's den ever presented such a scene of savage clamour and worry as that which we witnessed on rushing to his rescue.

The knives vanished on our appearance, but the clamour redoubled as the infuriated men turned to us and declared with one voice that this dog, this pig of a Jew, had reviled their religion and mocked at their

M

Prophet. We must send him away or they would not go with us. It was bad enough to be the servants of Christians, but to have to herd with a Jew who cursed God's chosen people was unendurable.

That Shalum had been goaded into some such indiscretion was only too probable, for he was the most passionate of men. There could be no doubt either that the others were thoroughly honest in their indignation against him. One of them, Zemrani, utterly unable to articulate words, threw himself in an uncontrollable paroxysm upon the ground and kicked and cried like an enraged baby, and as if he would break his heart.

After we had obtained silence, we learned that El Hadj, the cook, had wantonly broken a caraffe containing native wine belonging to Shalum, who, bursting out in consequence into a passion, had in good set phrase and with astounding volubility cursed the offender from the crown of his head to the sole of his feet, and consigned him and his ancestors to the lowest depths of Gehenna.

Under the circumstances, while sternly reproving Shalum for reviling El Islam and its Prophet, I emphatically fell foul of the others, and warned them that they would have us to reckon with in any further attempts upon Shalum. I also declared that he would not be dismissed for any clamour of theirs. As for deserting —well, let them try, and see whether life in a dungeon would suit them better than travelling with us. They knew what had happened to the Casablanca Hadj; let them take care that such also should not be their fate.

Thus rebuked, I ordered them off, and they went, their hearts full of curses and intense hatred and passion. We were getting too strong for them to dare outwardly to rebel against us, though we could not prevent their covert anathemas and underhand machinations.

On the following morning (31st May) we started for Tasimset, not, however, without a preliminary skirmish with the Kaid, who sought once more to detain us. Finding all his obstructive efforts of no avail, he let us go at last, carefully sending his own right-hand man to keep a strict watch over us and act as a brake on our movements.

Our route lay S.S.W. along a small valley cut out of the easily-weathered basalt dyke. For the first time in Morocco we came upon some clumps of trees worthy of the name; among others, evergreen oak of unusual size and some fine pines (*Pinus halipensis*), a species that occurs only in isolated and restricted areas in the Atlas, but rarely attaining the size of those we now saw. There were also some very large juniper trees.

In about an hour and a half we reached the top of the little valley, and entered the well-cultivated and fertile district of Twaka.

After passing a cluster of villages, we turned more to the west and ascended another elevation. We now descended into a small mountain depression, in the bottom of which welled up a magnificent spring. From this we passed into a second though larger hollow, frowned down upon by a precipitous range on our left, while on easily defended points on our right there appeared several fortified villages.

In about four hours we reached the commencement of a small valley, charmingly diversified by hill and dale, and partially sheltered by mountain masses with rugged limestone escarpments. Fragrant smelling walnut-trees of enormous size lined the hollows, and olives, with their dark-green foliage, spread themselves over the slopes; but more picturesque than all, certainly more familiar adjuncts of mountain scenery, were the fine groups of pines which crowned the hill-tops. On favourable spots were variegated squares of barley ready for the sickle, and vine-clad terraces on the hill-sides. Springs burst in remarkable volume from beneath precipices, and were confined in dams or led in channels to the fields, the groves, and the gardens.

We had not descended this little Eden for more than a mile when we found ourselves confronted by a mountain village, and knew that we had reached Tasimset.

Our escort insisted that we should pitch our tents among the houses, but a look at the crowd which surrounded us and the filthy aspect of the place served to tell us that there was a Mellah here, and we wanted no closer acquaintance with such than the explorer's conscience demanded. We accordingly flatly refused to enter, and, in spite of the protests of both our men and our escort, we insisted in camping on an olive-shaded terrace where we found room to pitch our tents.

No sooner was this accomplished than we set off to visit the falls, of which we had already got a peep through the trees from the village. These we found at the head of a very short though deep notch in the mountain-range which overshadows Tasimset. Here we reached a precipice some hundreds of feet high, from the centre seemingly of which the water burst forth, though in reality it escaped from an irregular cañon too narrow to be at once detected. The fall of the cascade, as nearly as I could guess, was some 300 feet, and it looked very effective in its gleaming whiteness flashing down through a deep drapery of dark-green creepers and bush growing in the interstices of the calcareous tufa which covered the limestone forming the precipice. It was easy to see that here, as at Iminifiri, the origin of the waterfall was due to the junction of the easily-worn basalt dyke and the compact limestone.

In the afternoon we once more returned to the cascade, this time, however, to explore the caves which had been excavated in the tufa deposit which thickly covered the face of the precipice. The only entrance was by an insignificant hole on a ledge of rock and almost hidden by bushes. Through this we had to wriggle like snakes for a distance of several feet, till we reached what looked like a natural niche in the face of the precipice. Several chambers opened from this natural portico, varying in size from six feet by five to thirteen feet by eight or even ten. They were all irregularly excavated, rarely six feet high, and presented no distinctive features from which any conclusion could be drawn. An extremely tortuous and difficult passage led up to a higher series of similar character, lighted here and there by holes to the outside. There was only one room which we found distinguished in any way from the others. This had the style of a nave, supported upon pillars. From it opened two or three chambers. Holes in the rock showed where bars had been employed to mark off or shut in these side apartments. One place had a cutting like a seat. We could discover absolutely nothing to indicate that these caves had ever been used either temporarily or permanently as dwelling-places. The general character of the excavations, the absence of any features such as would have distinguished the abodes of even the most utter savages, the absence also of any blackening of the walls or roofs from the smoke of fires or torches—and many of the caves were utterly dark—all went dead against the theory that these were the caves of troglodytes, while in support of such an idea can only be cited the legend that such cave-dwellers did formerly live in the Atlas. As far as the inhabitants are concerned, they ascribe these excavations to the "Rum," or former Christian inhabitants of the country. In my opinion the caves have either been used as secret storehouses for grain in the ancient fighting days or for purposes of sepulture. I am inclined to favour the latter theory. In such a rocky eyrie, in the midst of the spirit-sounds which echo among the wind-swept cliffs and rise from the falling water, the old pagan inhabitants would almost instinctively seek a last resting-place.

We did not dare, in the presence of the suspicious and watchful natives, to seek confirmation of our opinions by digging in the deep deposit of earth which covered the floor, but we saw numerous fragments of bones which may have been human, and pieces of coarse earthenware which may have held votive offerings to the manes of the deceased.

Upon the whole, we once more reached the light of day in a somewhat nebulous condition as regards the objects for which those excavations have been made.

Anxious as far as possible to elucidate the mystery, we asked to be guided to the other caves which were said to exist near the top of the cliff. Some miserable Jews were ready to show us the way, but as dogs and pigs were sternly cursed by the leader of our escort and driven away. We were not, however, to be turned aside so easily from our projects, and forthwith commenced to ascend the precipice, a proceeding which seemed sufficiently foolhardy to any one not accustomed to such enterprises.

We had got some little way up before our people divined what we were about, but when they did, they began to scream and gesticulate to us to come back. The Kaid's majordomo became specially frantic, fearing a disastrous result to what seemed to him outrageously misdirected energy. The Jews alone sat dumb, while numbers of the natives ran off by the ordinary paths to intercept us at the top of the cliff.

With no small difficulty we at length reached a gorge through which the stream descended before tumbling over into the valley below. A little further on we came upon a natural cave in the tufa, which, by its curious structure, gave one the impression of being under a huge mushroom. The bottom of the gorge, where it opens slightly, was carefully cultivated and wooded, and was overlooked by the picturesque castellated buildings of the Sheik of Tasimset, perched on a high isolated rock approachable only from one side.

In the walls of the cliffs were numerous cave-openings, many of which could only have been reached by ropes or ladders. Those we were able to get at were mostly single-chambered, of no great size, and now used when conveniently situated as granaries and silos for the winter storage of grain and fodder; for, unlike the Arabs of the plains, the mountaineers not only collect all the straw from their grain crops, but also gather hay and grass to feed their sheep and goats when shut in by the snows of winter.

As we peered about in every hole and corner, we gradually became aware that we were being watched on all sides by natives hidden behind rocks, ensconced in olive groves or perched on cliffs. We could see the projecting muzzles of guns and the gleam of their silver mountings. This was of course thoroughly romantic, but scarcely agreeable at the time, and we thought it wise to desist from further explorations. For a time it seemed as if we would have some difficulty in getting back. Happily we struck upon an irrigation channel carried round the face of the precipice with remarkable skill and enterprise, here cut out of the rock, there forming an aqueduct. We rightly argued that by following this canal we would eventually be led to the cultivated slopes of Tasimset, and so find an easy descent. This proved to be the case, and at sunset we reached camp.

Before going farther afield next morning we trolled over to the village, where we were permitted to examine the house of the principal Jew. In an outer verandah were the cooking-places, and a curious dome-shaped erection in which the bread is baked. In this latter a fire is set a-burning till the requisite temperature is attained, a number of small stones being heated at the same time. The fire is then raked out, the stones are stuck in the bread, and thus garnished, the loaves are placed inside the oven, which is carefully covered up till the baking is completed.

The verandah during the summer months is the usual resort and workroom of both men and women. It gave entrance to an apartment which at first appeared quite dark. As we groped our way in with bent back, and so let the light stream in through the low doorway, we gradually saw the main features and contents of the room develop in the gloom.

It proved to be not only the chief living and sleeping room of the family, but also the mule's stable, the cow's stall, the sheep and goat pen, and finally the hen-roost.

There were no windows, and no other means of

light and ventilation than such as was provided by the low doorway, which, of course, in inclement winter weather was kept closed. The house inside was lined with a casing of poles like a palisade, to prevent thieves breaking their way through the walls.

Almost the sole furniture of the room consisted of a few pots. The odour and some other aspects of the place need not be dwelt upon. We were next con-

MOUNTAIN VILLAGE.

ducted to an inner apartment, still darker than the other. With the aid of a lamp we discovered a boy sleeping on what looked like a plain box, but which proved to be a bed intended to raise the sleeper above the cold damp floor. As in the other chamber, there was nothing to remark beyond a number of huge pots for holding oil.

All the Berber houses in this district are built in

exactly the same manner, with the object of keeping out the winter's cold at the expense of light and ventilation, and the preservation of the same happy community of interests between the domestic animals and their masters which makes one family of widely separated members of the animal kingdom. The quadrupeds help to keep the room cosy and comfortable by their vital fires, the cocks warn the careful housewife when day is near, the dogs throughout the long dark hours remain watchfully on guard, while over all the master of the house throws the protective ægis of his presence. The thief may feloniously prowl about, the mountain winds sweep in bitter blasts, the rain fall, or snow hold all things swathed in its icy folds; protected against them all, the happy owner sleeps soundly in the bosom of his family, lulled into sweeter oblivion by the continuous sound of ruminating sheep and goats, the leisurely grinding of many jaws, or the rhythmical heavy breathing of sated cows.

Nearly all the Jews of Tasimset are professedly cobblers and petty traders, who go about to the different markets, which are held on particular days of the week, all over the mountains as in the plains. They chiefly spend their time in utter idleness.

We were shown during our stroll the remains of a substantial building of stone and lime, of which only a part of a wall and a large arch now exist. These are exceedingly well built, and are, of course, ascribed to the Rum. Truly they do not look like any modern Moorish or Shellach workmanship.

Not content with what we had seen in the neighbourhood of Tasimset, we resolved to make the most of our opportunities, and make another dash into the mountains.

After the usual wrangles, to which we were now becoming callous, we contrived to get away minus our escort, ostensibly to revisit the caves at the top of the cliff, but in reality to explore beyond.

Following a picturesque pathway which led round the edge of the precipice, we speedily reached the Sheik's house. Here we refreshed ourselves with some milk, and took a hasty glance down the smiling hollow, and over the broken lower ranges to the plains of Srarna and the broken range of Rahamna.

We now bribed our guide to take us up the upper glen of the Tasimset stream. Leaving this, after a time we pushed our way up an uninhabited and streamless valley, clothed with evergreen oak and adorned with buttercups and other flowers of familiar aspect.

At length we were rewarded for our hard work by reaching the top of one of the mountain ranges at an elevation of over 6000 feet, and finding before us the finest view of the Atlas which we had yet obtained.

We stood on the edge of a great limestone escarpment facing south, and forming a sheer precipice several hundred feet deep, from the bottom of which sloped away an exceedingly steep talus of debris to

CAMP IN OLIVE GROVE.

Page 189.

the bed of the Wad Tessaout, two or three thousand feet below.

A short distance to the west of us lies the little village of Tafrint, its green terraces, small olive groves, and yellow patches of corn only serving to accentuate the oppressive air of desolation which broods over the scene. The river Tessaout, gathering tributary streams from east and west, cuts its way by a deep gorge through the numerous escarped minor ranges which run parallel with the central axis, and southward rise in ever-increasing magnitude till they sweep skyward in one grand culminating crest. The aspect of the limestone escarpments which crown the lower ranges, the bright colours of the red and purple shales and sandstones which occupy the hollows, the deep gorge and radiating streams of the Tessaout, and the snowy table-topped masses which dominate all, make up a scene of the utmost impressiveness.

That evening we spent pleasantly round the lantern, which did duty for the camp-fire, and heard much from Jew and Berber about the mountains and their inhabitants. The story of a grizzly old Shellach who formed one of our guards, describing how he had with his own hand killed his unfaithful wife and her guilty paramour, threw a ghastly light upon the rough-and-ready laws which had prevailed in these parts. Our attendant soldier from Demnat, however, was careful to inform us that under the domination of Seedna (our lord, *i.e.*, the Sultan) such punishment for adultery was not permitted. Instead, the outraged feelings of the husband were soothed by divorce and the payment by the co-respondent of a sum of money, not to him, but to the Sheik or governor, who consequently looked with favouring eyes on such lapses from virtue, till the time came for applying the screw.

Next day we left Tasimset.

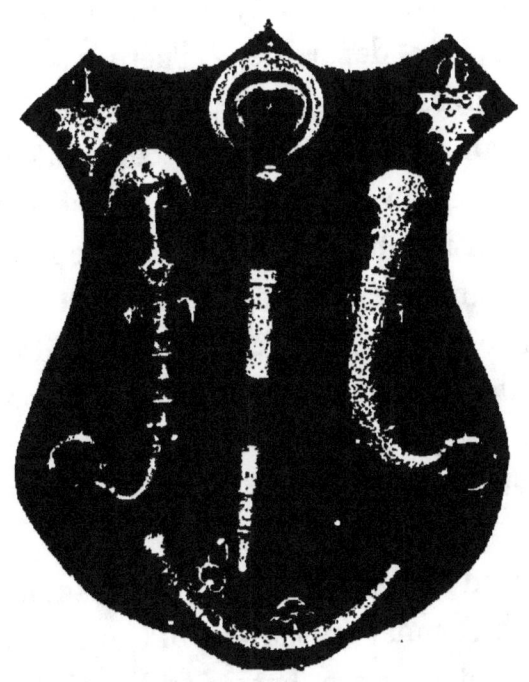

DAGGERS, POWDER HORN, AND ORNAMENTS.

CHAPTER XIV.

THE GLEN OF THE WAD GADAT.

On our return to Demnat after our excursion to Tasimset and the heights of Tazaroch, nothing remained but to prepare for our departure. There was no frequented route across the range from Demnat, nor any accessible Kasbah or town which we could attempt to reach. Farther east we could not go. The mountain regions of the Entifa and Tedla, the "Moyen Atlas" of De Foucauld, being in revolt against the Sultan, were not in a mood to receive strangers, and we could neither afford to be killed nor to be defeated. Our only feasible plan was to try the route through Glauwa to the basin of the Dra, on the opposite side of the mountains.

Having secured the services of David Assor as interpreter, we left Demnat on the 5th of June, ostensibly for Sidi Rehal and Morocco, but in reality for Tezert.

All night long an exceedingly hot, dry wind had blown from the snow-clad mountains, a phenomenon we were at a loss to account for till it flashed upon us that this was a desert wind which had retained its heat in spite of the icy heights it had crossed. In the morning and all day it still continued, reducing us to a dry, feverish state, which only too well agreed with our mental condition.

As we retraced our steps, we had no eyes for either the mountains or the plains. We could think of nothing but the hazards of our position, and how much depended on this our first serious attempt to cross the range. We realised but too clearly that to fail would be disastrous in every sense. The story of that failure would follow us everywhere, supplying not only our own men with an ever-ready weapon against us, but affording to the Sheiks and governors a precedent upon which they would gladly act.

By this time, of course, our men had discovered that we were not going to be confined to the plains and frequented routes, but they had no clear ideas of our plans, and happily were very ignorant of the mountain routes and the geography of the Atlas generally. It was quite evident that our only hope lay in keeping them ignorant, and in every possible way hoodwinking and taking them by surprise. This was a very general proposition, however. Practically, it was all very much a matter of groping in the dark, trusting in the chapter of accidents, and believing with the sanguine faith of a Micawber that "something would turn up."

Shortly after mid-day we neared Tezert, the residence of the Kaid of Glauwa's representative on the lowlands. Pretending to be fatigued and knocked up by the excessive heat, we announced that we would go no farther that day. Our men, ever eager to shorten their journey, fell with delightful unconsciousness and utter absence of suspicion into the trap we had laid for them.

We pitched our tents in one of the courtyards of the building, and gladly kept quiet till the heat of the day subsided. Our reception boded no good, for neither Sheik nor mona arrived—very different this passive toleration from the profuse hospitality of the Arabs and Moors.

Towards evening we bestirred ourselves for action. Taking with us only Assor to interpret, and forbidding any one else to follow, we went to visit the Sheik. He received us in a species of shed, and looked, indeed, like a man who would not be easily dealt with. We commenced at once by taking the bull by the horns. We assumed the insolent and arrogant air of men in authority displeased with their slaves. We demanded the meaning of this niggardly reception. Why had he not sent a mona becoming our importance? Were we Jews, that he thus treated great European Kaids travelling with the Sultan's letters? Did he desire to end his days in a dungeon, or to see his master, the Kaid, brought into trouble?

The poor Sheik, who had met us with contempt on his face, looked at us with startled eyes as the delighted Assor volubly and with added emphasis translated our bullying language. At each new demand, each new terror evoked, we rose in his estimation, till in his fright he could—and would if we had not been Kaffirs—have cringed at our feet and kissed our clothes in abject submission. As it was, he poured forth a torrent of excuses. He had been in the fields and had not known of our arrival. His men had not obeyed his orders. Everything would now be put right, and he begged us in the name of the one God, compassionate and merciful, that we would forgive him.

We softened not our faces, however, nor the angry tones of our voice. Forgiveness would alone depend upon his future behaviour.

Having thus pulverised the unhappy Sheik, and put ourselves on a proper pinnacle in his estimation, we ordered him to have guides prepared to conduct us on the following day on our way to Kaid Madani at Teluet, for whom we bore letters from the Sultan.

This was the last straw that broke the poor man's back. He naturally took it for granted that we were proceeding on special Government business, and he saw nothing before him but ruin and spoliation. He swore that everything would be ready—that he himself would conduct us to the Kaid. This offer, of course, was flatly refused. It would never do to have any one in authority into whose ear our men could pour their story. We told him that two of his men would suffice, but especially we enjoined on him that he should tell no man of our mission; these were matters only for Kaid's ears, not for slaves and servants. This he promised on the beard of his father, and we then left him, hardly deigning to take notice of his humble salutes.

Poor man! how little he thought that the letter which was proving such an open sesame to us was only a general order to his master, in common with other Kaids, not to allow us on any account to enter the mountains. Of course, being only a Sheik, he did not venture to ask for a sight of the missive.

Meanwhile, our men, quite unconscious of the net that was being woven around them, were enjoying themselves thoroughly over the supplies now sent in abundance. We kept a watchful eye on them, however, lest any communication passed between them and the natives.

Shortly after our interview with the Sheik a mountaineer left the compound, who we were sure was a messenger dispatched to the Kaid to announce our coming. Later on, a courier arrived from the coast with letters for us, which gave us an agreeable hour in the midst of the racking uncertainties of our situation.

On the morning of the 6th we were up before dawn, almost fearing to hear that our hopes of the previous evening were quashed. Our men, however, still seemed unconscious of their fate, and already the guides sat waiting to show us the way. We hurried forward our preparations, and at 5.30 were mounted and leaving the compound.

On getting outside, the guide turned towards the hill. Our men, following behind, pulled up with an exclamation of "Allah!" and poured forth a volley of abuse on their conductors, demanding the reason for their choice of a road. These looked to us for instructions. Through Assor they were ordered to proceed.

Our men remained standing, bewildered and obdurate. Hadj made some attempt to argue the matter, and pointed out the right road to Sidi Rehal, our supposed destination. I quickly cut him short, and peremptorily ordered him and the others to move forward in the direction of the guides.

Sullenly and unwillingly I was obeyed. Many were the imprecations, however, "not loud but deep," that were heaped upon our heads; many the exclamations of pious wonder at the inscrutable ways of Allah with His chosen people, and His long-suffering mercy towards the infidels. Elated with the success of our stratagem, we paid no heed to these mutinous mutterings, and bidding the Sheik farewell, we followed in the rear.

Another hopeful circumstance cheered us on our way. The Sheik of Zarktan, the only place of importance on our way to the Kaid, was at the moment on a visit to Tezert, and came after us to excuse himself for not being at his castle to receive us, saying at the same time that he had dispatched a messenger to bid his people prepare for our arrival.

Everything had thus conspired in our favour, and we now saw our way clear as far as Teluet, where the Kaid of Glauwa resided.

The first part of our route lay across limestone ridges, through which a basalt dyke protruded, passing into a district of red shales cut up by deep gorges and glens. Some scanty crops of barley grew on the ridge-tops and more gentle slopes, but elsewhere the sides of the glens lay bare and waste, except where

here and there patches of bush found a precarious foothold, and gave relief to the glaring colours of the red and purple shales. The courses of the rivulets and streams were all shaded and adorned with stripes of oleander bush in flower.

Without being absolutely dangerous, our path was sufficiently difficult to require the constant attention of our men, who grumbled excessively at having to tramp on foot.

Crossing the glen of the Wad Lar, we soon entered that of El Mulha, or the salt river, near its junction with the Wad Gadat. The Wad El Mulha receives its name from the salt with which its waters are impregnated. The course of the stream had all the appearance of being frozen, so great was the quantity of salt crystals which covered the sides and sandbanks.

At the junction of the El Mulha and the Gadat stands the village of Enzel, a place which derives great importance from being a *sok* or market, where the produce of the Dra and the Province of Glauwa is exchanged for that of the northern plains and the city of Morocco.

Up the glen of the Gadat our way now lay into the heart of the mountain and the pass of Teluet. With our entrance to its gloomy and cloud-enveloped jaws our men knew that we were making no mere detour to Sidi Rehal, but were bound for some unknown goal beyond the snowy heights.

They would have rebelled, but that they were too much afraid of us now to do anything openly. The angry passions which possessed them were seen in their faces, however, and found vent in the virulent abuse and curses which they screamed at their animals, but intended for us, as well as in the painful blows that were showered down on the hips of the innocent brutes.

At Enzel the mountains seemed to rise abruptly to a considerable height, but of their upper zones we could see nothing, so completely were they shrouded in clouds and mists. As we advanced up the glen, the sides gradually closed in, leaving no margin along the turbulent torrent by which to thread our way. There was nothing for it but to follow the narrow bridle-path up the steep slopes. Speedily the slopes became dangerous red clay precipices, along the face of which we had to pass, overshadowed by beetling cliffs above, and looking hundreds of feet into the depths below. Here and there lateral streams had cut deep gorges in the cliffs, and round these we had to wind.

With each mile the path became more tortuous, more zigzag, more dangerous, as the glen became narrower and the clay precipices higher. We were kept continually on the rack, ever expecting some disastrous accident. Neither our men nor our mules were accustomed to such tracks, and both were equally frightened. And no wonder! An unlooked-for touch of the pack against the cliff or the slightest slip of the foot was sufficient to have hurled the mule hundreds of feet below. The dangers of the road were immensely enhanced by the fact that scores upon scores of people were hurrying down the glen to Enzel, where a market was to be held on the following day. These carried chiefly dates from the Dra on mules and donkeys. To pass such was dangerous and difficult at all places, and at most it was well-nigh impossible. Deadlocks were of continual occurrence, giving rise to the most terrific wrangles and the continual exchange of showers of abuse and choice epithets, till the whole glen seemed filled with the clamour of shouting men. Thanks to our guides, and no doubt to our own imposing appearance, we usually got the best of the disputes, and, when warned in time of our approach, the mountaineers in almost every case made way for us, whatever might be the risk and trouble to themselves. More than once, however, we unawares got into positions from which it seemed we would never get safely out, it being just as difficult and dangerous to turn back as to go forward.

The sagacity and sure-footedness of the mountain mules on these occasions was amazing, and contrasted strikingly with the paralysing terror and weak-kneedness of our own animals.

At any other time or in more favourable situations, we would have studied the wayfarers with keen interest, but under the circumstances we were more absorbed in the difficulties they added to our march.

We were much struck, however, by the frequency with which we were saluted with "*Bon jour*," showing that the traders on their way to Enzel were also in the habit of frequenting the markets of Southern Algeria.

It was no small relief to us when the clay cliffs with their skirting two-feet pathways came to an end, and we descended once more into the bed of the Gadat, some distance above a once substantial well-built bridge, now half-destroyed.

The clouds now lifted, and displayed in their fullest extent the savage features of the glen. The mountains rose on either side thousands of feet overhead, more imposing in their height and air of solid grandeur than in varied irregularity of outline. The scene gained in savage picturesqueness with each mile we advanced. Here the glen dilated somewhat to form a riant hollow, there contracted to the merest cañon, according as compact sandstone or easily denuded shales predominated. Not a sign of inhabitants was anywhere to be seen.

Towards mid-day the Gadat disappeared into a profound gorge of sandstone, where we could not follow. By a terribly rocky and boulder-strewn path our mules struggled painfully up the mountain-side, ever in danger of breaking their legs or of rolling down to the depths below. At one point, my horse, which I had mounted for a little relaxation, came down very badly, and nearly went over a precipice. Happily I retained my seat, and the horse recovered its legs in time to avert the disaster. After that I did not again intrust my safety to Toby whilst in such places of difficulty and danger.

At length we reached the top of the obstructing mass of sandstone, and obtained a splendid view both up and down the glen. Some distance to the south we could now see the snowy peaks and table-topped mountains of the axis towering over a rugged series of much cut up ridges and ranges, which seemed to run across the course of the glen, defying us to reach the heights beyond.

From this point we descended a couple of thousand feet to cross a lateral ravine, only to ascend to the same height on the opposite side. This achieved, we found ourselves at length facing the central chain of mountains.

The most varied and savagely picturesque prospect we had yet obtained in the Atlas now spread itself before us. Far down at the bottom of the conifer-clad glen lay the romantic district of Zarktan, a little home of human beings sheltered among precipices and gorges and stupendous mountain masses. Berber villages, like swallows' nests, clustered against the steep slopes or under the cliffs, with olive-groves around them, and bright green terraces spreading step-like to the bottom of the glen. Beyond, the Gadat divided and spread itself in radiating tributaries on the northern face of the main chain, out of which it had cut an amphi-theatre-like space, with deep gorges draining into its own basin, and wall-like dividing ridges merging skyward in the snow-clad masses which form the backbone of the chain. There, too, were the table-topped Adrar-n-Iri and the more conical Jebel Glauwi, which formed the two pillars of the mountain portals leading through the axis to Teluet and the basin of the Dra. Both were crowned and streaked with snow.

It was late in the afternoon before we once more reached the bed of the Gadat. Here, on a little knoll backed by pine-clad heights, and with the roaring river in front, stands the fortified residence of the Sheik of Zarktan. Though built of *tabia* (a species of clay concrete), it looked massive, and even imposing, with its tower-like angles and crenelated walls. Here we found shelter and protection for the night,

ZARKTAN.

we ourselves having the guest-chamber outside the main building placed at our disposal, while our men and mules were accommodated in the courtyard and stables.

We spent a very pleasant evening amid our picturesque surroundings, making great friends with the son of the Sheik, a lively boy, who seemed delighted to talk with us and tell whatever we desired. It was evident that his religious education had been sadly neglected, as he had apparently not learned to hate the Christians, nor to curse them in the rich phrases which the Moorish boys know so well how to employ.

We were much annoyed by the impossibility of getting at the names of the various mountain masses in sight; not that there was any lack of names—quite the contrary. But no two informants, when taken separately, agreed, and in most cases we had either to make an arbitrary adoption or give the attempt up in despair.

Our men did not share the now exhilarating feelings of their masters. They grumbled audibly over the barley bannocks with which they were supplied, and sighed after the *kuskussu* and all the choice dishes of the plain. They would have bullied the life out of the Sheik's majordomo, but that they had a wholesome sense of being in the Atlas Mountains, and among people who would stand none of that nonsense from such as they.

CHAPTER XV.

ACROSS THE TIZI-N-TELUET.

NEXT morning we did not start till three hours after sunrise in order to allow of my taking a photograph of the place.

For a short distance we followed the chief branch of the now divided river, till, reaching a point where there was a mellah and the commencement of a magnificent glen, we left the stream.

Ascending an excessively steep ridge of grey shales, which separated like a wall the great glen on the right from that of another smaller tributary of the Gadat on the left, we slowly zigzagged upward, now on one side, now on the other. Beyond the deep gorge on our left rose a still more westerly ridge, behind which again was the defile of the Asif Adrar-n-Iri.

By and bye the gorge on our left with its red shales ended, and our path wound round its head through a forest of evergreen oak, and conducted us to the top of the coalesced ridges. We had now on our right the deep cutting of the Gadat, the stream winding like a thread two or three thousand feet beneath us through repellent grey shales to the foot of Jebel Glauwi

ADRAR-N-IRI AND GLEN LEADING TO TIZI-N-TELUET.

towards the south, and losing itself behind a curve of the ridge to the north. On our left lay the gorge of the Asif Adrar-n-Iri, equally deep, but less mournful of aspect, with its bright ground-colour of red and purple, and mottling of arar and juniper. Here were bright green terraces on the lower slopes, and on points adapted for defence were perched numerous picturesque mountain villages.

Behind us was the short middle gorge which carried us back to Zarktan. Beyond and above towered the dark green table-topped lower range, through which we could trace the course of the Gadat far down to the plains of Zemran. Seen from our commanding height, it was difficult to believe that what lay beneath us was the difficult and dangerous glen we had so laboriously traversed.

To the south the eye followed the sharp irregular ridge between the two minor glens, till it ended like a gigantic buttress or retaining wall against the sides of the fine snow-streaked conical mass of Jebel Glauwi, which rose in a magnificent precipitous sweep of at least 8000 feet from the bottom of the Gadat. Though not without an air of grandeur, the scene presented in this direction was rocky and desolate in the extreme. Hardly a shrub or blade of grass toned down the grey barren slopes of shaly debris; as little did tree or bush relieve the jagged rocks and precipices which protruded from the mountain-sides.

It seemed incredible that mountains rising to elevations of 12,000 and 13,000 feet, as did those before us, should be so scantily clothed with vegetation. It was of course evident that the soil was of the poorest, and that it was being denuded with great rapidity. But that was not sufficient to explain the utter barrenness which prevailed. Later on we learned that hardly a drop of rain falls on these heights during the greater part of the Moorish summer, a fact which goes far to explain their absolute desolation. Having taken some photographs, we resumed our way along the ridge, the vegetation becoming more sparse and insignificant as we advanced. The arar, juniper, and pine were now no longer ornamental factors in the scenery—and arborescent vegetation was alone represented by the gnarled trees of the evergreen oak, which in places struggled to hold their own on the barren ridge. Here and there too we came upon scanty tracts of the hardy gum cystus in its last bloom, but all the flowers of other species we saw could have been counted on our fingers.

On nearing the junction of the ridge with the opposing barrier of mountains, we had to descend into the gorge of the Asif Adrar-n-Iri which divides Jebel Glauwi from the Adrar-n-Iri. This was a task of no small difficulty, and would have been impossible to any Christian and civilised animal, but the mule of Mohammedan upbringing sprang from ledge to ledge and from rock to rock with all the agility and sure-footedness of a goat. The descent was not made any easier by the behaviour of our men, who vented their ill-humour on their animals, and acted as if they would gladly see every one a mass of pulp at the bottom of the abyss. Some such disaster would most assuredly have marked our progress but that we ever kept watchful eyes upon them, and failed not to threaten a horse-whipping if they were not careful as well as helpful.

On reaching safely the bed of the Asif Adrar-n-Iri (stream of the Mountain of Iri), near a small hamlet refreshingly surrounded with hay and barley-clad terraces and fine shady walnut trees, we remarked that the grey shales now became intermingled with black, adding a more sombre and repellent colour to the already bleak and melancholy landscape. These shales were capped by a thick series of quartzite beds, great blocks of which strewed the mountain-sides and partially blocked the course of the stream.

As we scrambled along our rocky bridle-path and penetrated deeper and deeper into the very heart of the Atlas, we could have imagined we were penetrating some gigantic volcanic crater by way of a great rut or fissure through its lava and cinder-built sides. On either side the mountains rose some 8000 or 9000 feet above us in awe-inspiring masses. Hardly a blade of grass or other tuft of vegetation was to be seen on these frowning heights, though that some did exist in favourable situations where springs abounded seemed evident from the occasional bleat of sheep or goats which came wafted to us on the mountain breeze with a melancholy cadence in keeping with the air of death and desolation which brooded over the gloomy gorge. No other sound except the sighing winds along the hillsides and the incessant roar of the turbulent torrent broke upon our ears. And yet the glen was not wholly desolate, for even here the hardy mountaineers, braving all the terrors of winter and the arid heats of summer, had established themselves, and forced from the flinty bosom of mother earth the wherewithal to eke out an existence. With immense labour they had built up terraces along the lower levels, and laid thereon soil fit for cultivation. To these they had led channels of water drawn from lateral rivulets or from the higher levels of the stream, and by such means forced the growth of hay for winter fodder and barley for their own use. These bright patches under cultivation were restricted enough, but in conjunction with a few small clumps of walnut trees they made a refreshing strip of green on either side of the torrent, on which the eye rested with pleasure.

The low clay-built and flat-roofed houses of the mountaineers occupying sheltered situations harmonised well with the scene around them, hardly distinguishable indeed from the slopes and cliffs against which they clustered. Something of the stern sad aspect of the mountains was reflected too in the people themselves. Folded in their black goat's-hair *kanif*, or cloak, with conical cowl drawn over their heads, they sat like inanimate objects on house-top or boulder watching our passing with stern yet somewhat lacklustre eyes, their wrinkled and weather-beaten faces, spare forms, and small stature telling plainly of the hard battle they had to fight with the forces of Nature arrayed against them.

In little over an hour from our entrance into the mountains the gorge began to open out into a pear-shaped expansion, presenting a panorama which strikingly reminded me of the lava and cinder mountains of Aden in its forbidding colouring of black and grey shales and rusty quartzites. The mountains circled round this crater-like depression in unbroken frowning precipices, except where towards the south there was a distinct notch in the general level, which we knew to be the Tizi or pass of Teluet, the last remaining barrier between us and the southern slopes of the Atlas.

In this dreary solitude stood the village of Titula, and here we gladly stopped for the night. The Sheik received us politely enough, though with little of the demonstrativeness of the Moors. A native was turned out of his house on our account, and in one of its dung-plastered windowless rooms we took up our quarters, as it was not deemed safe to remain in our tents, though we would gladly have done so rather than face the evil odours and tormenting vermin which not uncommonly characterise the dwelling-places of true believers.

The natives of Titula showed no effusive desire to cultivate our acquaintance, and what little they did for us was more stimulated by fear of possible consequences than by feelings of hospitality. We knew that, if it could have been managed with safety, our men would gladly have united with the mountaineers to cut our throats; but with the sense of the dignity and charm which hedged us round in our character of British Kaffirs, and made us in a manner invulnerable, we slept none the less soundly that night.

On the morning of the 8th we were up betimes, and by sunrise were on our way in high spirits to cross the pass.

I have spoken of the pear-shaped expansion of Titula as resembling a volcanic crater in respect of its burnt and blasted aspect, but this morning, as we neared the head of the glen, it became evident that ice had had more to do with its formation than fire. Everywhere we scrambled over moraine matter and enormous angular blocks, which had been ploughed up by glaciers in the higher elevations and transported by their agency to where they now lay. This was the first place where I had seen any certain signs of glacial action, and I consequently examined the debris with extra care and interest.

To my geological researches I added botanising, but a more unpromising region for plant-collecting I could not have selected. What was lacking in numbers, variety, and scientific value, was well made up in sentimental interest, however.

Beside sparkling springs with their green circlets of turf, were buttercups and forget-me-nots, veronicas and stellarias. From underneath sheltering cliffs and rocks, white and blue daisies shyly peeped, cosily withdrawn alike from the withering sun and from the bitter blast. The very wayside was made home-like by the occurrence of the gooseberry and the more insignificant plantago. How could we but be touched by the appearance in the midst of these wild African mountains of the familiar flowers of our own fields and hillsides! There were more familiar than strange types, indeed, in the scanty flora of the upper glens, and we gathered such with an added tenderness, souvenirs of home for the moment, to become souvenirs of the Atlas in the time to come.

Meanwhile, as we beguiled the time by botanising, we were still heading towards the pass by an extremely steep path. As we neared the top, all other considerations became secondary to our eager curiosity to see the new regions beyond.

A few minutes more of extra pressure on limb and lung, and we found ourselves where our imagination had long preceded us, and at the point to which we had been laboriously struggling for over three days. To the north and south there was now nothing to obstruct our view into the hazy distance. A single glance sufficed to cast a shadow of disappointment over our sanguine expectations. The scene before us, looking south, though impressive in extent, was far from picturesque. We looked in vain for the Anti-Atlas. As far as the eye could reach, only a slightly broken plateau, 7000 to 8000 feet in altitude, without a single conspicuous feature, met our gaze. At one or two points low table-topped elevations rose like mounds upon the general level, and here and there winding lines trending southward indicated where glens and gorges drained off the winter snows of the Atlas to the river Dra. An even more deadly uniformity characterised the colouring of this mournful landscape. We could not detect a patch of green to brighten up the dull grey and dirty yellow which imperceptibly blended with the hazy horizon, and gave an added air of melancholy sterility to the scene. For anything we saw, it might have been the plateau lands of the Sahara that stretched before us—the Sahara, too, with an oasis in the foreground; for at our feet, 2500 feet beneath us, lay the little valley of Teluet, a bright patch of refreshing green in the lap of the mountains. From where we looked at it, Teluet, with its apparently unbroken circle of mountains, was strikingly suggestive of the dried-up and grass-grown bed of a tarn or lake, as indeed we afterward discovered reason to believe it had been.

To the north the view was infinitely more varied. The eye roamed over the seamed and scaured glen of the Asif Adrar-n-Iri, the better clad heights overlooking the irregular gorge of the Gadat to the yellow plains of Morocco and the partially-seen mountains of Srarna and Rahamna.

Though we thus stood on the watershed of the two opposing river systems of the Dra and the Tensift, we had not by any means reached the top of the Atlas. We had only as yet succeeded in scaling a notch in the range, some 8400 feet above the level of the sea. On either hand grim rocky precipices towered 3000 to

4000 feet above us, and in their apparently impregnable abruptness seemed to laugh at our hopes of ever being able to desecrate their deathlike solitudes or soil the virgin purity of their snows.

When we had taken in the general external characters of the scene around us, we did not fail to note why the Asif Adrar-n-Iri had not succeeded in cutting through the wall-like barrier on which we stood and connecting its gorge with the valley of Teluet.

The hard quartzite which we have already alluded to as overlying the shales and capping the heights suddenly bends down at the pass and forms a compact wall across the glen, effectually defying the eroding action of rains and springs and frosts. But for these quartzite beds, either Teluet might have been drained into the Gadat, or the district of Titula into the Dra, in either case lowering the level of the pass from 2000 to 3000 feet.

After hastily taking one or two photographs, and collecting such plants as grew under the protection of sheltering rocks, we commenced our descent into the valley.

The southern slope was extremely rocky and steep. The men never dared let go the tails of their mules, now to help them round a corner of a projecting rock, now to put on back-weight to steady the poor brutes in their descent, but more especially to arrest an involuntary headlong progress to the bottom in the event of an accidental slip.

The mountain-side resounded with cries encouraging

or vituperative. At times the mule was a sweet one, a gazelle, the very joy of the driver's heart. In tones gentle and soothing it was invited to step along carefully, and warned of the dangers of the mountains. The next moment the unlucky animal had bumped with its pack against a projecting rock, or had stumbled over a boulder and been thrown off the path, to the imminent danger of itself and load. Then it was that the names of Allah, His Prophet, and all the Moorish saints were yelled out with blasphemous significance. Men rushed to grab hold of the pack, the legs, or the tail of the unfortunate animal, to assist in preventing a disastrous catastrophe. Everybody screamed out orders or cursed and swore. Some dusted the mule's hide, or overwhelmed it with such names as pig, dog, Jew, Christian, infidel, or other equally opprobrious epithets, in the midst of which pandemonium of voices the downward progress of the mule was generally arrested. On these occasions, however, it was a constant marvel to me that a single tail was left to adorn the bodies of our animals, so terrible was the unwonted strain put upon them by the combined weight of two or three men. If Tam-o'-Shanter had been mounted on a Moorish mule instead of his auld mare Meg, on the occasion of his memorable ride, he would never, I make bold to say, have crossed the keystone of the Bridge of Ayr.

With our arrival at the bottom of the mountain our path became easier, and as we neared our destination, the misgivings which had pestered us since we left

KASBAH, TELUET.

Tezert came upon us with renewed force. We tried to be hopeful, but it was hard work, and we more often pictured ourselves returning over the pass than venturing further afield.

We rounded a hill of basalt, and crossed several hillocks and mound-like ridges formed of undoubted glacial debris. The country we traversed was stony, and its fertility more forced than natural. Suddenly, on turning the end of a ridge, we found ourselves confronted with a magnificent and imposing castle of the old baronial style.

> "The battled towers, the donjon keep,
> The loophole grates, where captives weep,
> The flanking walls that round it sweep,
> In yellow lustre shone."

We could hardly believe our eyes as we scanned the turreted walls, the crenelated battlements, the fortified gateways and outer lines, which rose before us with such a princely air of military strength and glory, in keeping with the stern grandeur of feudal times, and contrasting strongly with the Brummagem clay-built Kasbahs in which the Moorish lords of these days ensconce themselves.

We had little time, however, to stand and wonder. For some time we had remarked signs of general excitement. Mounted messengers were galloping in hot haste from village to village; armed men were rushing from all quarters towards the castle. The hamlets we passed appeared quite deserted. Something unusual was about to happen. Could it be war? and were we the enemy?. were the questions that naturally rose to our troubled minds. Impossible to say. We had advanced too far to retreat, and there was nothing left but to go forward to meet the good. or ill fortune in store for us.

As we neared the Kasbah, we noticed that the hillocks beyond were crowded with women and children, but no men. More in doubt than ever, we continued our way.

At length we rounded a low ridge which for some time had restricted our view. Imagine our feelings on finding ourselves confronted by a couple of hundred armed mountaineers, drawn up in a double line across our path, supported by over thirty horsemen.

No sooner had we appeared and drawn bridle in painful uncertainty, than a great shout which sounded defiant burst from the crowd of Shellach. Guns were thrown in mid-air or twirled overhead. Next minute half the men were on their knees; their guns were levelled. Before we could make up our minds as to the meaning of this demonstration, a line of pale blue smoke burst from the guns. Almost simultaneously there followed a deafening roar of musketry, which was answered by a score of echoes from the reverberating mountains.

C.-B.'s horse reared and plunged, and one of the mules swerving aside, laid its rider at its feet. The curses that followed showed that nothing serious had happened.

In quick succession the remaining mountaineers fired

their long flint-locks. Suddenly from out the cloud of smoke which half hid the crowd the horsemen appeared. Once free of the footmen, they halted to form in line for a charge. The next moment they started. At first they advanced slowly, though their fiery barbs were evidently straining to break away in a fierce rush. The horsemen were holding their long guns vertically in their hands, the stocks resting on their thighs. Nearer and nearer they came. Fascinated by the sight, we watched them, hardly knowing what they were going to do—not knowing what to do ourselves.

Half the distance between us had been passed, and still they leisurely pranced forward in line, though the pace was increasing into a hand-gallop. Suddenly the leader of the charging party raised his weapon above his head. Thirty others followed his example. The horses, knowing the signal, plunged and curvetted wildly to break away. One moment the guns were whirled in mid-air, the next brought to the shoulder. The reins were now dropped, the horses burst forward like a tornado, their muzzles far advanced, their feet striking up clouds of dust. Shouts from the armed men and shriller screams from the more distant women rent the air. Our horses were rearing in the wildest excitement and the mules scattering in terror. We were confusedly aware of floating *haiks*, of guns in deadly proximity, and the thunder of galloping horses. A deafening volley crashed upon our ears. Almost unseen, amidst the smoke and dust which now enveloped them, the horsemen divided and passed to right and left.

We now knew that we were not the objects of a murderous attack. We were being honoured by a princely reception. Our minds set at rest, we speedily assumed the deportment of men to whom demonstrations of the kind were of daily occurrence. The seneschal or chamberlain of the castle advanced with the welcomes of his liege lord, and these were replied to with suitable dignity and courtesy. Under his guidance we rode forward surrounded by footmen and horsemen, who betrayed in their shouts and gunfiring the lively joy they had in seeing two " rebels against God" the guests of their master.

We were first conducted through a series of courtyards, the walls of which formed outer lines of defence. Traversing these courts through ever-growing crowds of people, we reached at length a strong stone-built barbican. Passing underneath its massive portals, we left the crowd behind and entered the citadel proper, though still outside the castle, into which no stranger may enter. The courts, passages and guardrooms were alive with wild-looking soldiers and black slaves in snow-white dresses. As we passed along, the scenes before us seemed to be those of a dream rather than the sober realities of Moorish travel. We were within a feudal castle, surrounded by everything in harmony, with only an Oriental gilding superadded.

> " By narrow drawbridge, outworks strong,
> Through studded gates and entrance long,
> To the main court they cross.
> It was a wide and stately square:
> Around were lodgings fit and fair,

> And towers of various form,
> Which in the court projected far,
> And broke in lines quadrangular.
> Here was square keep, there turret high,
> Or pinnacle that sought the sky."

As we passed onward we failed not to remark the massiveness of the buttress-strengthened solid stone walls of the main building, pierced only by narrow loopholes and turreted projections, adapted for the use of sharpshooters in times of siege, or in more peaceful periods affording to the ladies of the harem such restricted views of the outside world as were compatible with some scanty measure of light and air.

At the moment we had the pleasurable sensation of knowing that the dark-eyed inmates of the Kaid's earthly paradise were struggling to get a glimpse of the first two specimens of the dreaded Anasera (Christians) they had ever had the opportunity of seeing. We could see no faces, though we surreptitiously got glimpses of *haiks* and heard the sound of eager feminine voices. We would willingly have looked straight up at their peepholes with an unselfish desire to correct their erroneous notions about our personal appearance, but we did not as yet know whether such a proceeding might not be followed in these wild lands by the good old-fashioned Moorish order, "Off with their heads;" so we repressed our laudable inclinations and demurely followed our guide.

We now entered an inner court. Here stood to receive us El Madani, *alias* El Glauwi, *alias* Uld Tabibt, Kaid of the great mountain province of

Glauwa. We saw before us a young man of some thirty summers, of languid manner and pleasant expression, distinguished by high cheek-bones, weak chin, fine brown eyes, and sallow complexion. We hastened at once to dismount and salute him.

Salaams and compliments over, the Kaid himself led us into a pleasant garden, and thence through a colonnaded verandah into a shady room handsomely painted with arabesques, and luxuriously though simply furnished with carpets, cushions, and mattresses.

This apartment we entered with a due show of reluctance, knowing that in walking over the carpets with our big riding-boots we were outraging the most revered customs of Moorish society, as much as if we had entered an artistic drawing-room at home, and proceeded, in presence of the lady of the house, to place our mud-soiled boots on the best ottomans and couches.

At the moment we appeared anything but prepossessing, in contrast to the cool and picturesquely dressed Kaid and his attendants. Not having looked forward to any particular reception, we had taken no thought of the clothes we had on, and had not troubled ourselves about our faces, which presented a villainous appearance in their tawny sunburnt hues and scrubby unshavedness.

These, however, were small matters compared with the terrible consciousness that now took possession of us that our hour of reckoning had come at last, though we fervently hoped that it might be staved off as long as possible.

We at first imagined that the apartment we had entered was the Kaid's reception-room, but we were speedily made aware that it, with the garden and the servants' rooms beyond, now formed the quarters of favoured guests.

We hailed the arrival of green tea with plentiful supplies of cakes and dried fruits as a slight respite before the subject of our business was broached.

Politeness, as well as our capacities, forbade us spending more than a reasonable time over the refreshment, and then an awkward pause ensued. The Kaid was waiting to receive the Sultan's letter and learn the object of our mission.

Further delay was impossible, and the letter was reluctantly drawn forth and handed to our host. On seeing the Sultan's seal, he kissed and touched his forehead with it in token of submission to the Sharifian will. He then passed it on to his *feki*, or secretary, a tall gaunt man of wicked aspect, of whom we feared the worst. This gentleman gravely drew forth his spectacles, and having adjusted them with due deliberation, commenced reading the missive. As sentence after sentence fell from his lips we watched their faces with some anxiety, but not a muscle betrayed their thoughts or feelings. When finished, the *feki* handed the letter back to the Kaid, who received it indifferently. Nothing was said, but his method of returning us the document was significant enough. He did not politely hand, but threw it to us, and then, without a word, the party rose, and left us to our somewhat gloomy cogitations.

Later on, however, we were cheered by the arrival of a princely *mona*. With it came polite messages, and then we knew we were to be treated hospitably, whatever else might be our fate.

CHAPTER XVI.

THE KASBAH OF TELUET.

AT Teluet we were in the very heart of unexplored regions. Northward, toward the yet unscaled summits of the Atlas to the south, lay the but little known basin of the Dra, and to right and left extended the untouched regions of Moharram and Tifnut. To all of these, routes led from Teluet, and over them El Madani claimed to be Kaid, with more or less power of asserting his authority. Of all these geographical attractions, none claimed our attention more than the district leading west-south-west over the mountainous regions of Tifnut to the Sous valley. This seemed to promise most hope of successful exploration, and certainly offered the richest harvest of interesting facts, and the route which lay through it was the one we finally determined to adopt.

It was, however, of the utmost importance to dissemble. To have at once announced our plans would have led to unpleasant wrangles, with no certainty of coming out victorious, and the possibility of being prevented from even doing anything in our immediate neighbourhood. It would be soon enough to speak when the time arrived to start.

There was another reason for keeping quiet. Ramadan (the month of fasting) was drawing towards a close, and till that was over little could be done.

But though we thus assumed the air of men who had reached their land of promise, and had no desire to rove farther into the wilds, our men were not to be deceived. They had no idea of our plans, but they clearly understood that we wanted to go farther, and this they determined to thwart at all costs.

On the second day after our arrival, Abdarachman commenced inciting the only too easily roused mountaineers against us. He laughed at them for giving infidel nobodies like ourselves such a grand reception, and declared we ought to be chased out of the country. This was too much even for his fellow-servants, and Zemrani, one of our Saffi men, in whom we had recently been inclined to place some confidence, promptly informed us of Abdarachman's evil machinations. His unexpected virtue, however, was due less to regard for our safety than to fear of the possible consequences to himself if a popular outbreak took place.

Of more sinister import were the frequent clandestine meetings between Abdul Kader, our personal servant, and the Kaid. We knew that these meetings could have but one object, that is, to learn everything possible about us on the one hand, and to misrepresent our objects and importance with the object of getting us sent back, on the other. At the time, we had no means of knowing what was actually said; but our men were as treacherous to each other as to us, and when too late to be of any use, we learned that Abdul Kader told the most outrageous lies—such, indeed, as could only be believed in a country like Morocco, where there exists alongside the most unparalleled mendacity the most stupendous credulity.

It was represented, for instance, that if we were allowed to go farther, we would intentionally lose or pretend to lose a mule, and then declare that it was loaded with gold and silver, which we would demand from the Kaid.

Of the effect of these stories we saw no outward sign. In the matter of dissimulation we were no match for El Madani. He was content to wait till we showed our hand. But while he waited he proved himself the prince of hosts and entertainers.

Having, like a good Moslim, seen the hand of Providence in our reaching Teluet in defiance of the Sharifian orders, he accepted the situation accordingly. Whether it was written that we were to go on or to go back remained to be seen.

Meanwhile, he, like ourselves, put aside disagreeable questions and became our constant visitor. He was never tired asking questions about Europe and European ways. Much, however, that we told him was of a nature that no Moor could understand. It seemed incredible, for instance, that wealthy and powerful people should be content with only one wife each, to whom they must remain attached all their lives. It was quite beyond his comprehension that people like ourselves should go travelling about the world unat-

P

tended by even one ministering angel, although that again was even less strange than that we should travel about at all, suffering various hardships and dangers —for what? A few flowers, or some such trifles!

He, however, was no more astonished at our extraordinary moral and social codes than were we at the state of things he revealed as existing in Morocco. It was difficult to grasp the fact, which had been gradually boring its way into our minds with growing knowledge of Moorish life, that absolutely the most religious nation on the face of the earth was also the most grossly immoral. In no sect is faith so absolutely paramount, so unweakened by any strain of scepticism, as among the Mohammedans of Morocco. Among no people are prayers so commonly heard or religious duties more rigidly attended. Yet side by side with it all, rapine and murder, mendacity of the most advanced type, and brutish and unnatural vices exist to an extraordinary degree.

These strange anomalies are not confined to any one class. From the Sultan down to the loathsome, half-starved beggar, from the most learned to the most illiterate, from the man who enjoys the reputation of utmost sanctity to his openly infamous opposite, all are alike morally rotten. Punctilious performance of ceremonial duties, acknowledged acceptance of orthodox tenets, these are everything in Moorish religion. Moral conduct counts as next to nothing. Kindred views are not unheard of nearer home, but in Morocco they are carried to their utmost limit.

It was an interesting if revolting experience to witness a Moor reverently bending in prayer before the One God, compassionate and merciful, suddenly stop short in the midst of his orisons to scream a curse or some foul obscenity at a bystander who might have roused his wrath. Still worse to see him pause in the midst of some beastly orgy and hasten to attend the summons of the Mueddin, to return the minute after "like the dog to his vomit, and the sow that has been washed to his wallowing in the mire." The Moor who would lose his character by eating meat not slain in the orthodox way would escape with small censure for foully murdering a man; and envy, malice, and all uncharitableness, with theft and adultery superadded, would be held as venial sins compared with failing to acknowledge the Prophet and the Koran, or neglect of the saying of prayers.

These facts were brought home to us with ever-increasing force in connection with the Kaid and his attendants. They had no hesitation in telling that their ideal of a happy earthly existence consisted in having an unlimited selection of women at their command, abundance of everything that ministered to the brutish and sensual side of their nature, and absolutely nothing to do—no work, no responsibilities, no thoughts even, if these were in any way troublesome.

Nothing, perhaps, revealed more strikingly how thoroughly these principles of life were carried out by those who had the power than what we heard about the Kaid's late brother. It was said of him by the

Jews of Teluet that he had seduced 300 Shellach maidens. This may be an exaggeration; but even if his victims be estimated at only half the number mentioned, the case would still be a frightful one. For this dishonour to their daughters the mountaineers could get no redress, because the Kaid himself was about as deeply implicated as his brother; which means that scarcely a girl in the neighbourhood, on arriving at womanhood, escaped one or other of them. And all this, it must be remembered, among a people where virtue is still something more than a name; where, indeed, prior to the establishment of the Moorish power, seduction or adultery would have been punished by stoning to death.

Such is the blighting influence which Moorish misgovernment is everywhere casting over these brave industrious mountaineers. Up every glen this huge bloodsucking octopus is pushing its horrible feelers, instinct with the lust of power, dragging village after village from its contented and independent isolation to feed with its life-blood the rapacious appetite of the bloated monster. In some places the old independence is still maintained, and there, though almost starved into submission, the Shellach fight desperately for home and freedom.

Elsewhere, though far from being reduced to the semi-serfdom or subjected to the extreme oppression and spoliation of the Arabs of the lowlands, the former independent life is being gradually crushed out of them. Their flocks and herds are rapidly dwindling under the exactions of the Kaids. The heaviness of the taxes on the fruits of their labour is taking effect in the glens as in the plains, with the consequence that groves are less cared for, irrigation channels are becoming choked, and the toilsomely made terraces left to fall to ruin. This, however, by the way.

Among the Kaid's usual attendants were his right-hand man, Abdul Kader, and his secretary, Si Mohammed. The former, as became a great man's parasite and favourite, was always jovial and smiling, ready to make the Kaid's tea, or to enliven the conversation with a story more or less broad. In this respect their conversation mirrored their lives. Nothing could be more frank and free than Abdul Kader's manner, and we thought that from him we would meet with but little opposition in pursuing our plans.

It was different with his companion. Si Mohammed, as became a man with a reputation for learning, preserved a reserved and austere countenance, which did not enhance the beauty of his stern, gaunt features. With him the conversation was always instructive, though on many points about which we should have liked information he seemed to be quite ignorant.

There was one subject which interested us greatly, namely, the question how far Christianity had penetrated into those wilds in pre-Mohammedan days. On this head the traditions extant were as numerous as they were vague. Hardly a glen but had its so-called remains of the "Rum." In every case known, the Rum were spoken of as an alien people, who had previously held sway over the Atlas, and not as if they were the ancestors of the present Berbers. This, of course, may have been largely due to the Mohammedan objection to admit having in any way been connected with the hated Christian. Undoubtedly the mountaineers considered it far less dishonouring to be descended from a race of downright idolaters than from Christians. Hence the difficulty of getting reliable information, and the reason of the possible non-existence now of any traditions throwing light on the subject.

What with our conversation and our display of scientific instruments, we succeeded in impressing our hosts with a deep sense of our learning—a reputation that proved somewhat embarrassing, when, as a *Hakim* or physician, I was besieged by crowds of applicants for cures to their various diseases. Among others, the Kaid's chief wife was a patient by secret proxy, and showed her gratitude for our medicine by sending a present of a pair of embroidered slippers.

Among our various visitors there was none we liked better than the Kaid's brother, a boy of some fifteen years. This youth showed an incredible amount of precocious knowledge. We did not hesitate to draw him out about the secrets of the domestic life of his brother. These had something of the flavour of romance about them, for we heard that jealousy was not unknown in the usually well-disciplined harem. It seemed that the Kaid's life was not altogether a happy one, for on one occasion his chief wife had tried to poison him, and was only prevented from accomplishing her fell design by a lucky accident. It was this wife whom the Kaid afterwards put in bonds unwittingly supplied by us. Having an unused pair of iron horse-hobbles, we made him a present of them, and afterwards discovered that he employed them, not for his horses, but for the inmates of his harem.

We were let into a good many more of the details of the Kaid's *ménage*, but over these it were better to draw a discreet veil.

Of course, while we thus quietly awaited the fit time for action, we were not confined to our room. The courts and passages of the castle afforded us endless matters of interest. It was not only in respect of its architectural features that the Kasbah realised all our ideas of what a feudal castle must have been in the olden days. In everything around us we saw reflected something of the life likewise. Soldiers grouped themselves about the fortified gateway and the guardrooms. Slaves and servants in great numbers dawdled about the passages, or hastened on special business. Mounted messengers left the castle for Morocco, the Sultan's court, or a distant district; others came bringing news of petty tribal revolts, of crimes committed, and wrongs to be avenged.

Sheiks and headmen of tribes arrived daily to render an account of their affairs or to arrange for some raid. Hunting-parties were arranged, and, accompanied by magnificent packs of huge boarhounds, left for the bush to track their game, or for the mountain-tops in the more arduous pursuit of the "*aoudad*" or *mou-*

tion. Hawking, too, was indulged in, and the sportsmen made a gay show as they pranced out of the castle on gorgeously bedecked horses—only no lady fair accompanied them.

In two courts stood fifty splendid barbs always ready for action, fitly to receive a friend or charge an enemy. Fifty cooks, in relays of ten daily, worked in the kitchen to supply the wants of the military and domestic household.

No wanderer was turned from the gates. Lavish hospitality and prodigal profusion reigned everywhere. Once a week a market was held in the neighbourhood, and then the outer courts gave shelter to those who came from far and near, and the travelled hundreds were fed at the Kaid's expense.

It was, in truth, no mere resemblance to a scene of the feudal times that we saw before us, but the feudal system itself in full force. The Kaid was but a lord appointed by the Sultan to rule over certain lands, on condition of supplying him with a certain number of men and a certain amount of money, and bound to hold himself in readiness to join his liege's standard in time of war. He again was regarded as the leader by the different clans who came under his jurisdiction. To him they looked for justice and protection, while ready to rise in arms at his call, and to supply him with supplies in kind and money. The whole machinery of government was sufficiently simple. The Sultan looked to the Kaid solely as a channel through which to collect men and money. If that was done to the satisfaction of the central authorities, no questions were asked about his administration, for the Kaid existed for the uses of the Sultan, not for the benefit of the people. As for the governor, as became a Mussulman, he ruled according to the legal code of the Koran, that is to say, as far as that code did not interfere with his own personal interests and passions. Nominally the people could appeal to the Sultan if his rule was oppressive or tyrannical; practically that was impossible, except the Sultan wanted an excuse for squeezing him of his plunder.

Apart from these varied and interesting sights and studies, we could have had no more charming place than Teluet in which to spend a few days in the lotus-eating, easy-going style of the Moors.

The early summer climate of the little mountain valley is simply perfect. The temperature usually rises from 68° in the early morning to 72° in the shade after noon. The heat of the sun is at all times tempered by the cool winds from the encircling mountains. The air is of the most marvellous purity. Peaks twenty or thirty miles distant seem close at hand, and the highest elevations of the mountains only suggestive of a pleasant morning's constitutional. The slopes of the Atlas when in shade had the appearance of being covered with a pall, so black was their aspect and utterly hidden their rugged irregularities. The sky, when suddenly looked up to, had all the aspect of a black canopy, so blue was the expanse overhead.

In all other respects, however, Teluet was by no

means attractive. Hardly a tree or bush gave variety to its semi-sterile and stony fields. Such vegetation as there was, grew along the banks of the streams, or where irrigation channels carried water over the ground, and in a manner forced a scanty yield of grass and corn. The extensive garden of the Kaid was the sole redeeming feature to the monotonous outlook, and in it were a number of fruit trees and flowers, among which the Kaid delighted to spend the afternoon hours, drinking tea and talking.

The valley lies at an elevation of 6000 feet above the level of the sea, and runs parallel with the Atlas. In length it does not exceed eight miles, and in breadth three. On the north, it is dominated by the abruptly rising main ridge of the range, which towers over it to a height of from 12,000 to 13,000 feet. On the south, it is enclosed by the escarpment of the Dra plateau, or Anti-Atlas, to retain the term applied to the heights fronting the main axis, and generally believed to be a secondary range. This plateau, where it overlooks Teluet, attains an elevation of 7300 feet. To the east, the encircling walls of the valley present a break, through which is seen the conspicuous, comparatively isolated, dome-shaped mass of Jebel Unila, which, I should say, rises to a height of at least 12,000, but may be a thousand feet more. Unila is described as having a deep lake at its top, which, taken in connection with its isolated position and shape, suggests a volcanic origin. To the west, the mountains form a less well-marked and abrupt wall, though rising from

7000 to 8000 feet in elevation. Numerous gorges and glens may be seen cutting their way through the plateau, drawing the rains and melting snows of the higher mountains away to the Dra, and farther west o the Sus. The route through Tifnut to Gindafy and Ras el Wad is described as one interminable series of ascents and descents in the crossing of the numerous sharp mountain ridges and deep narrow glens. Over this region the Kaid of Glauwa holds little more than a nominal sway. Only a month before our arrival, a tribe called the Ait Umast had even gone so far as to make a descent on Teluet; where, however, close to the castle, they were defeated with a loss of sixty men.

In the valley itself there are a surprising number of villages, to most of which Mellahs are attached. Altogether there cannot, I think, be less than 500 families, and probably as many as 700, or some 3000 souls in all. Of these, 600 to 800 are Jews.

One of our first excursions after our arrival at Teluet was to the plateau to the south. Crossing the Asif Marren, we immediately commenced the ascent. We remarked the sharp foldings of the purple, grey, and whitish shales, and fine-grained sandstones which composed the plateau, and gave some rich colouring to the scene. We saw little vegetation of any kind, till, nearing the top, we found ourselves among some isolated arar trees of considerable size.

The view from the summit was extensive, and towards the north imposing in the extreme, but need not be dwelt on again, as the characteristic features of the surroundings of Teluet have already been described. We did not fail to notice, however, how sharply the central range rises from its plateau pediment, and, without spurs or terraces, sweeps up to a height of from 6000 to 7000 feet. In this respect it differs widely from the opposite side of the range, except over Demnat, where the central ridge rises with a similar abruptness.

This sharp crest we could trace unbroken in one grand mountain wall as far west as the part overlooking Gindafy and Reraya. The view to the south is what I have already described from the Tizi-n-Teluet—a monotonous melancholy expanse. One feature, however, specially attracted our gaze on turning to the south-west. This was what appeared to be a fine range of mountains, fronting, though not running parallel to, the Atlas. In its centre the range rose to a conspicuous elevation, snow-streaked, and probably attaining a height of 10,000 or 11,000 feet. At the moment, we thought that here at last was the Anti-Atlas range, but subsequent observation, together with the observations of De Foucauld, led me to conclude that though this was what had been called the Anti-Atlas, it, at least in this part, was not a range, but the southern side of a great broad valley, cut out of the Atlas pediment or plateau by the numerous rivers flowing to the Dra and the Sus from the main range.

One of the most interesting sights in the valley of Teluet is its caves, which, like everything strange and inexplicable, are ascribed to the Rum. These lie at the eastern end of the valley, near the village of Tabugumt. Proceeding thither, we were conducted some little way up the Asif Marren, to where a high clay cliff overhangs the bed of the stream. Here we could descry a doorway of very modern aspect surrounded by a stone wall, and led up to by a species of natural staircase.

On clambering to the entrance, we found a passage to the right of the door, which led some fifty or sixty feet straight into the heart of the hill. From this passage there opened sixteen cells, eight on either side. These were all excavated after the same pattern, and measured some ten feet long by six broad and seven high. The walls and roof are undoubtedly blackened by smoke, though whether from ordinary fires or a conflagration of possible corn and hay stores it is impossible to say. In front of each cell or chamber there is a hole or trap-door giving entrance into a species of cellar.

The caves are at present utilised by the Jews of Tabugumt as granaries, and this may have been their original use, though on this point no information could be gleaned from the natives. We could discover nothing conclusive on the subject in the caves themselves, but what we did see gave some colour to the idea that they might have been used either as cave-dwellings or as granaries rather than as places of sepulture.

On the way back to Tabugumt we noticed the prevalence of particles of antimony in every direction, and made a collection of flowers and beetles from the meadow which borders the stream.

At the village we had a piteous reception. The Jews crowded round me with their halt and blind and diseased, in hope of cures. They grasped my clothes with nervous fingers, and attempted to kiss my boots as they besought me to give them medicines. An old woman—a Moor, if I rightly recollect—carried her supplicating abasement to the extent of drawing her hand across the sole of my boot and then kissing it. Her son had been thrown into prison, and she desired me to intercede for him with the Kaid.

The Jews of Tabugumt, as in the mountains generally, proved to be a more cleanly people, though far from being ideally so, than their brethren of the plains. We found here an extremely neat and clean whitewashed synagogue, quite the best we had yet seen.

On the evening of our return from visiting the caves, the ill-feeling exhibited to Shalum by his Moorish companions came to a climax. By accident we discovered that M'hamad, the cook, though a *Hadj* (pilgrim), had been surreptitiously mitigating the hardships of Ramadan by appropriating to his own uses milk sent to us. Taking it into his head that Shalum had been the informant, he proceeded, still smarting from the rebuke we had administered, to look for him. Finding him at last sitting in a corner, El Hadj went up and kicked him in the mouth, cutting Shalum's lip. Shalum, however much of a Jew, could not stand that, and gave his assailant a blow that sent him spinning. A terrific row was the result. El Hadj, like the cowardly bully that he was, raised a howl that Shalum had been cursing their holy religion. This was quite sufficient to bring all the others to his assistance, and, yelling and screaming like a pack of fighting-dogs, they came running to me, Shalum not the least noisy among them.

It was with difficulty that the story could be heard, but I was not long in determining on whose side lay the blame, and at once made tracks for my hunting-crop.

A minute later Shalum rushed in with a bleeding hand, part of a finger cut off. Hadj had attacked him in the dark and tried to stab him. I at once sent to the Kaid to have the offender put in prison. Hadj, however, had been before me with his story, that he had only been upholding the sanctity of their holy religion against the defiling tongue of a dog of a Jew. The Kaid was loth under these circumstances to do as I desired, as indeed it was disgraceful to throw a true believer into prison for any crime whatever against a miserable Jew. Getting up in a towering rage, I seized Hadj by the throat and shook him till he quaked again, and then, still holding him, I turned to Abdul Kader, the Kaid's messenger, and swore that if he was not put in prison forthwith, I should myself administer the thrashing he so richly deserved. This would have been a crowning dishonour for any good Moslem to put up with, and the Kaid, to save him from such a disgraceful punishment, threw Hadj at once into the dungeon.

That dungeon must have been a horrible place, for the vicious brute was rendered so humble by a single night of it, that he kissed my hand and vowed to be a good boy ever afterwards, on being let out on the request of the Kaid.

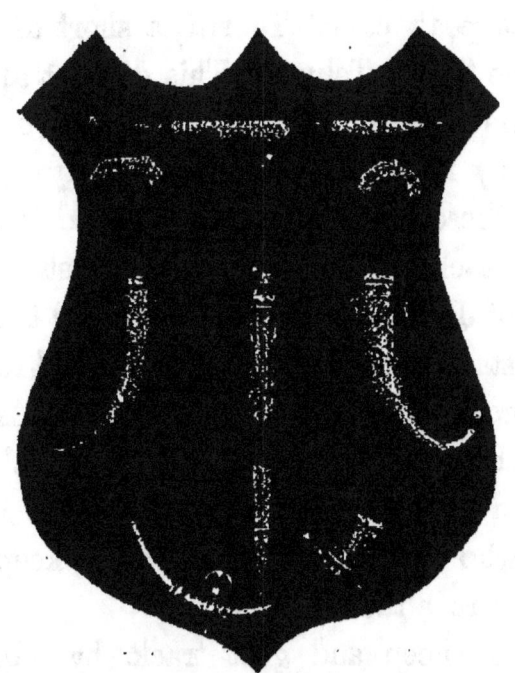

DAGGERS AND POWDER HORN.

CHAPTER XVII.

ASCENT OF TAURIRT.

FROM the day of our arrival at Teluet we had remarked a conspicuous peak called Taurirt, a short distance to the east of the Tizi-n-Teluet. This did not appear by any means the highest point in the range, but it was an elevation by itself, and seemingly fairly approachable, and for these two reasons we resolved to select it for our first attack on the actual Atlas crest.

The 13th of June was the day chosen for this enterprise. We started at sunrise, and went three miles north-east across the valley to the village of Ait Humwali, where the Kaid has a second castle, almost as well built and imposing as that at Glauwa. Here we got a guide, who carried out his duties by keeping out of sight in the rear the whole way.

Following a sheep and goat track, by which the herds go up and down the mountain, we crossed an outcrop of basalt, whose angle of dip coincided with that of the sandstone beds between which it lay. A thin division of shale cut the basalt into two beds. Rounding a small ravine cut out of the dividing shales, we speedily reached the top of the igneous rocks, where

Q

we found that a second ravine marked the junction of the latter and the red sandstones, which formed the mass of the mountain. Here was neither grass nor bush, only a few tufts of spring plants, and in sheltered nooks one or two flowers. Rocky desolation reigned everywhere.

The outcropping ends of the highly tilted sandstone beds presented a curious step-like arrangement, due to the peeling off, as it were, of the upper beds, which in a manner showed how the mountain had acquired its conical form.

In little over an hour we had attained an elevation of 2000 feet above the valley.

Rounding the corner of a precipice, we found ourselves confronted with a fine spectacle. At our feet, and running westward to near the path which leads over the Tizi, was a deep gorge cut out of the sandstones. On our left looking east rose a great precipice facing Taurirt. On our right towered the peak itself, like a cyclopean pyramid streaked with snow, but showing little else than grey or reddish rocks. Between the two spread a brilliant patch of meadow, all aglow with buttercups and watered by numerous springs. No garden ever seemed more lovely than did at the moment that acre of flowering green sward; no waste more bare and blasted than its walls of enclosing rock.

From the meadow a sharp climb over rocks and boulders brought us among the snow-wreaths, and speedily we were on the summit of Taurirt, at an elevation of 11,180 feet.

It was somewhat annoying to find our view blocked to the north by the Adrar-n-Iri, which rose in a flat-topped mass from 500 to 1000 feet above us. We could, however, look down on the glen of Titula.

From the point we had attained we were enabled to guess with greater approach to accuracy the height of the Atlas in our vicinity.

To the west, on the opposite side of the Tizi-n-Teluet, there was no mistaking the fact that the central ridge rose far above us. The large amount of snow which still lay on its top and extended far down its sides was in itself sufficient proof. In that region, and including Jebel Glauwi, part of which we could just see, I calculate that the Atlas attains a height of at least 13,000 feet. Farther west the general elevation does not exceed 12,000 feet, and here and there may be even a little less, till it rises once more over Reraya. Eastward probably no point rises above 12,000, if so much, with the possible exception of Jebel Aiachi east of Demnat, and near the head of the Tessaout the height sinks to 10,000 feet or less.

Of the extensive view which spread out before us it would be tedious to speak again. It was exactly what we had seen from the Tizi-n-Teluet, but with a wider horizon, the isolated mass of Jebel Unila and the range-like elevation of the Anti-Atlas—a name which I retain for convenience—thrown in. More interesting, certainly more pleasing, was it at the moment to discover some lovely tufts of veronica growing in the shelter of the rocks, and several gooseberry bushes among the crevices.

Having completed our observations, we commenced our descent. On our way down we employed ourselves collecting such plants and beetles as we could lay hands on. It was very disappointing, however, to find not more than fifteen species above a height of 8000 feet. Here, more markedly even than on the northern side of the range, the scarcity of vegetation was due to the aridity of the summer climate, hot desert winds, and the sterility of the soil.

When some few hundred feet from the top, an incident happened which distracted our attention from our botanising, and afforded fresh proof, if that were needed, of the sort of men with whom we had to travel.

Among our little party of four who accompanied us in our ascent was one Sioma from Saffi, who so far was the most trusted among the Moors of our caravan, though that did not mean much. On reaching Ait Humwali, he had been much disgusted at having intrusted to his care a small bag containing some provisions. Though weighing only a very few pounds, he tried to get it foisted on a Shellach on the promise of payment by me. The Shellach finding that I would not recognise the transaction, gave the bag back to Sioma. The lazy fellow then fell into a towering passion, and volubly protested against having to carry anything up the mountain. To all the clamour he raised we paid no heed. On reaching the summit, Sioma broke once more into a storm, although for the life of me I could not understand why he should make so much trouble over such a trifle. Finding me imperturbable, he suddenly sank into silence, and went off by himself to sulk in a small hollow which conveniently presented itself. When we left, he with the guide and two of our men remained behind. As already said, we had descended some few hundred feet, and were absorbed in our plant and beetle collecting, when we were arrested by a shout from the mountain-top. With difficulty we were able to make out that Sioma had taken ill, and that I was wanted to go back to see him. There was a suspicious suddenness about this illness which did not tend to awaken my sympathies, and as I did not see what good I could do even if I were beside him, and knowing also that he had to come down in any case, I merely ordered the others to help him, if necessary, to come to me.

A few minutes later the party at the top could be seen commencing their descent, Sioma carefully supported by his companions. Resuming my botanising, I thought no more about him as I peered here and there for plants, and turned over stones for beetles.

Suddenly a startling shout rang from the heights above. Another and another followed. Electrified by the tone of the cries, I hastily looked upward. To my astonishment, there was the erewhile sick man, Sioma, tearing down the dangerous mountain-side as if possessed by ten thousand devils driving him to destruction. His ample garments floated behind him, and high overhead he brandished a stick. From boulder to boulder and rock to rock he leaped with all the agility of a goat, and ever as he ran he made the welkin ring with mad outcries. After him, but more carefully, came the other three men, shouting to him to stop his headlong career.

C.-B. and I stood aghast, riveted by the extraordinary spectacle, wondering what delirium had seized the man, and expecting each moment to see a terrible fall. Our attendants, equally astonished, ejaculated, "God is great!" "God the Merciful!" "The Eternal!" and a dozen other exclamatory phrases, as at each leap they expected to see a collapse and hear of a broken head or limb.

For a moment I thought that, seized by a fit of madness, he was making for us with murderous intent. But while we watched his miraculous progress, he suddenly stopped short, raised his arms overhead, and then sank out of sight among the stones.

In a few minutes his pursuers were beside him, and we could see them bending over and finally assisting him to his legs. We drew a breath of relief when we saw that at least he was not dead—no bones broken even, to judge from the way in which, with some assistance, he came down the mountain. We now hurriedly cut across the slope to meet him in his descent and see what was wrong. The group had arrived at the buttercup meadow before I reached them, and there lay Sioma squealing like a pig and shaking all over as if with ague.

Hurriedly I felt his pulse; it was normal. I

placed my hand on his brow; it was quite cool—wondrously cool considering the run he had just had. I stood for a moment perplexed. Then the truth began to dawn upon me. All this was nothing more nor less than an exhibition of temper, let off in the hope of being exempted from all further mountain-climbing, to which all my followers had a very decided aversion.

When I curtly said that he was only shamming, and bade the men leave him alone, they looked indignant at my infidel brutality.

Not desirous of pushing matters too far, in case there really was some little thing wrong, before resuming my botanising I ordered them to assist Sioma on to a mule which the Sheik of Ait Humwali had brought with him half way up the mountain. On their trying to do so, he screamed as if in the greatest agony, and had to be laid down again. It was new to my experience to learn that a strong healthy man could become a prey to delirium in the course of twenty minutes, and be free from it again in five; for by this time the patient showed no traces of any mental wandering. The more I thought of it, the more certain I was that the whole thing was a pretence. I therefore ordered the men to leave him alone and let him come round by himself. With great reluctance they obeyed and followed me. For a time Sioma lay still, then hearing no sounds about him, he looked up. His cure began to work rapidly when he saw us fast retreating down the mountain-side. He was next seen to struggle to his feet as if in great pain, and begin to hobble after us. His groans came at intervals to our ears, making my men doubtful, but leaving me obdurate.

Finding that he was not making sufficient progress, the groans began to abate and his pace to increase, and by the time we reached the village where we had left our mules, he was almost up with us. By way of preserving some show of illness, he entered Ait Humwali still leaning heavily on his stick, and with many heartrending sighs and moans. The mules were brought forward. Sioma looked to the men to help him to mount. This they were about to do when they were sternly commanded to desist, and a savage glance shot from the sick man's eye as he saw himself baffled on every hand.

We were just about to start when with one agile bound this *malade imaginaire* vaulted to his place beside Abdarachman, and amid roars of laughter we left Ait Humwali, the most obtuse of our men seeing how thorough the sham had been.

In the good spirits produced by the successful ascent of the mountain and the ludicrous exposure of Sioma's pretended illness, C.-B. and I had a mule-race. We were only provided with pack-saddles, and had men seated behind us. The result was somewhat ignominious for me. Zemrani, who was my fellow-rider, suddenly swayed, and as he was holding on to me, I was overbalanced. The mule at the same time swerved, and the next moment Zemrani and I both came headlong to the ground, and the race accordingly ended.

Not the least interesting among our exploratory strolls in the neighbourhood of Glauwa were our visits to the Mellah close to the castle.

Nowhere, perhaps, is the astounding persistency of type and the tenacity of race more remarkably shown than among these mountain Jews. For unknown cen-

ATLAS JEWS.

turies they have lived an alien, hated, and despised race among the mountain-fastnesses of the Atlas, without losing in one particular their distinguishing physical characteristics. Their manners and customs have alike remained untainted by contact with the followers of Islam who surround them, and the general wave of progress which has affected their brethren in more civilised lands. Persecution and hatred have only had the effect of binding them more closely together, of making them stick all the more tenaciously to every tenet and ordinance of their creed, and strengthening their conviction that they are the chosen people of God. No matter where the traveller comes in contact with the Jews of Morocco, whether it be in Mogador, or the city of Morocco, or in Tabugumt in Teluet, he feels the moment he enters a Mellah that he is among a people as sharply marked off in appearance, manners, customs, and religion from the people outside the gate as is the Englishman from the Chinaman on the other side of the globe. The Mellah may consist of only six families, as in an Atlas village, or of hundreds, as in the city of Morocco, yet the distinction is equally marked and absolute. Your ways are not my ways, nor your God my God. We have no point in common. Yours may be the power in this world, and ours the shame and servitude; but in the world to come our portion will be Paradise and yours hell and all its terrors. These are the ideas in which the Jews envelop themselves—ideas that have gathered round them as the stony petrifying crust from calcareous springs gathers around the twigs and moss on their brink. They are, in fact, animated fossils, phenomenal survivals of a former great nation and religion.

Spite of the bad impression of the Moorish Jew we had carried with us from the cities—and on this point we shall have something to say in another chapter—

we could not but mete out a measure of admiration and compassion to his brother of the mountains. Here he did not present himself in the revoltingly dirty guise we had become familiar with in Mogador and Demnat; nor was he the repulsive parasite, feeding upon the cancerous sores of the diseased country, which we had in most places found him to be. On the contrary, he revealed himself as a hardy, useful, and hardworking member of the dual community. In the mountains he showed himself as a small but enterprising trader, who faced extreme dangers and hardships in passing from tribe to tribe and market to market, to collect on the one hand wool, hides, oil, walnuts, and almonds, and sell or barter these on the other for a little tea and sugar, cotton, and the various articles required to supply the simple wants of the mountaineers. In other cases he attended the *soks* or markets simply in his capacity as blacksmith, cobbler, or tailor.

It must not be supposed, however, that the Jew can travel about with impunity merely in his character as a Jew bent on a useful errand. He travels safely as being one under the protection of a Shellach. Each Jew of the Atlas—except where under the immediate protection of a Kaid, as at Teluet, is compelled to secure for himself a *sid*—i.e., lord or master—to whom he becomes practically a serf or slave, on the principle that it is better to be plundered by one man than by everybody. The *sid* undertakes to see that no one maltreats him more than may be permitted to a good Mussulman bent on asserting that there is no

God but the one (Moslem) God. A reasonable latitude is allowed in this respect. In the matter of plundering, however, the *sid* is more particular, for then the affair begins to touch his own pocket. The Jew's gains are his gains, and therefore for any one to rob his Jew is to rob himself, which is what no *sid* could stand.

Of course there is no limit to the *sid's* exactions but his own prudence and foresight. He therefore spares his Jew much as the Abyssinian spares the live bullock from whose quivering haunch he cuts his daily steak, stopping just short of the point where his usefulness and power of gain might be impaired. He works him judiciously, and assists him as much as possible to make money, knowing that in the long-run it will all come into his own coffers. And strive to make money the Jew necessarily must, first because it is in the blood, and not to do so would mean atrophy and death; and secondly, because if he fails in this, his first duty to his superiors, his disgusted *sid* will suddenly cut up rough some day and seize everything that belongs to him. Nor from this state of things can the Jew escape. True, he might himself escape, but only by deserting his family and goods, and laying open his relations to severe exactions. To prevent desertion no Jew is ever allowed to travel anywhere with his wife and family. If he goes on a journey, these are always held as hostages for his return. Even the marriage of a Jew's daughter is a source of income to the *sid*, for the intended bridegroom must ransom her for a sum proportionate to his reputed wealth.

Under these circumstances the life of the Atlas Jew becomes a burden to him, or rather would be a burden, but that, brought up to it, and never seeing any reflection of a freer life, he adapts himself to the situation—all the more uncomplainingly that he sees in his miserable condition only God's punishment for the inherited sins of his forefathers, and at the same time nourishes the belief that for his tormentors a day of reckoning is coming. Then it will be the Jew's turn. His oppressor will be thrown into hell-fire, where, from his heavenly throne, his whilom victim will joyfully watch him as he stews and frizzles side by side with the arch-fiend Mohammed and all the devil-saints of Morocco.

The dress of the mountain Jew is the same as that of the Shellach, with the exception of the black slippers and the greasy black fez, which is almost always doubled in at the crown. They are without exception slenderly built, thin-faced, and spare of form, but evidently wiry. The nose is distinctly aquiline as a rule, and the eyes are keen black or brown. The Atlas Jew is rarely seen without his love-locks hanging from the temples. The persistency of the Jewish type is, of course, due to the fact that they never marry outsiders. The exceptions to this rule are so rare, that the case of a Jewess having married a Moor at Tikirt, on the Wad Dra, convulsed the whole Jewish community in the mountains. In the coast-towns cases of Jewesses marrying Moors are less rare.

The nationality of the Jewish women of the mountains is much less easily recognised than that of the men. They dress exactly the same as the Shellach women. They wear a single sheet of woollen or cotton cloth wound round the body, the ends meeting over the breast, where they are attached by two silver clasps of quaint design. Underneath they wear other garments according to the time of the year. The upper sheet is further fastened and adorned by thick cords in gay colours coiled round the waist. Strings of gaudy beads and silver coins adorn the neck. On the head are worn two brightly-coloured handkerchiefs—one spread over the head and hanging down the neck to conceal the hair, the other tied round the head to form a band.

The hair is generally dripping with henna, the common cosmetic among the Shellach, who use it to such an extent that it trickles over the face and neck and down upon the shoulders, with results that may be better imagined than described. On Sundays and gala-days they paint the brow, nose, cheek, and chin in various designs. The eyebrows are frequently shaved to the merest line and painted black. The Jewesses have all magnificent eyelashes.

In the Mellah at Teluet we saw several child-wives. Some of these very young girls were rather piquant and attractive in their appearance, but we saw no Jewess above twenty that we desired to look upon a second time.

Neither at Teluet nor anywhere else did we ever hear anything about a tribe of warrior Jews of which we had seen mention in books.

CHAPTER XVIII.

INCIDENTS OF LIFE AT TELUET.

On the evening of the 11th June every one was on the alert for the appearance of the new moon, which would announce the end of Ramadan, the month of fasting. The walls and house-tops were crowded by eager gazers, and everywhere were groups of mountaineers gazing intently towards the west to see the silvery crescent emerge from the afterglow of the summer sun.

The blessed sign at length rejoiced the hearts of the pious Moslems, and universal joy was displayed. Women trilled out their shrill screams from the house-tops, and men shouted loud congratulations to each other, and danced about, firing off their guns in the most reckless manner. Thereafter they betook themselves to their devotions, men on all sides prostrating themselves in the dust, and muttering prayers the while.

The following day was kept as a grand holiday and time of rejoicing. Those who could afford it donned new clothes, and men and women alike arrayed themselves in their best.

From early morning all the poor people of Teluet

kept flocking into the castle, where barley was distributed with no stinted measure. Sheiks mounted on horses or mules arrived from far and near, bringing with them presents in money or kind for the Kaid, who sat in state all morning to receive the same, as well as the congratulations and compliments of his friends.

After breakfast we went ourselves to call upon our host. We found him occupying a small suite of rooms over the inner gateway. These apartments, which formed the reception-rooms of the Kaid, were ornamented very effectively, though somewhat gaudily with painted arabesque.

El Madani seemed exceedingly happy. He welcomed us effusively and conducted us to his place at the end of the room. All his kinsmen and Sheiks sat round the wall in dignified silence. After the proper congratulations and compliments we took our leave.

In the afternoon we were called back to witness a grand native entertainment expressly got up by the Kaid for our benefit. All the male musicians as well as the women of the neighbourhood had been requisitioned to dance and sing before us, and in response to the summons scores of women had flocked into the castle to act either as performers or onlookers.

From an embrasure in the defending wall of a roof we were enabled to see the performance to advantage. We looked down upon a large irregularly shaped court, surrounded by the outer castle buildings, of which the lower rooms were used as stables and the upper as stores and granaries.

In one corner lay twenty or thirty huge Tidla boarhounds, utterly indifferent to the unwonted scene of animation. Grouped in every direction were large numbers of Shellach women and children in snow-white dresses, set off by the brilliantly coloured silk handkerchiefs on their heads, and the thick cords of red and gold around their waists. Their necks gleamed with gaudy beads. Their hands and feet were henna-dyed, and their faces painted with lines and dots.

The men, also, were in great numbers, and moved about more restlessly. They mostly wore the black *kanif*, in which the deep orange elliptically-shaped patch behind showed with curious effect. Others, however, were in grey or white, and nearly all had some sort of apology for a turban, the fez being rarely seen in the Atlas.

Easy to recognise in this interesting gathering were the Jews. These, of course, sat somewhat apart from the faithful, though not so far as to indicate that their presence was actively obnoxious.

More handsomely dressed than the country people were the Kaid's slaves and retainers, mostly black of countenance, but picturesque in well-draped *haiks*. These moved about from group to group with an air of authority, ordering people about, and generally putting matters to rights.

Our appearance was the signal for the dance to commence. Some forty men, of whom half carried large tambourines, the only musical instrument used, arranged themselves in a semicircle. About as many women took up their position in a straight line, forming, as it were, the chord of the arc.

At a given signal, the men, slowly and with solemn faces, chanted a sentence in the tone of worshippers who invoke a hidden power. To this the women replied in their shrill treble. Holding their tambourines before them, the men next struck them three times, chanting sonorously and slowly the while. Bending down till their instruments touched the ground, they again struck them three times with due deliberation, the women joining in the accompanying chant with plaintive cadence. Once more the men stood erect. The tambourines were now raised high overhead, and once again three notes were struck.

A weird, wild air was next lustily sung out, though still slowly, and with a strain of impressive solemnity, the tambourines marking time. The women stood upright with grave faces, holding their closed hands against their breasts in an attitude of prayer. By and bye their heads began to nod in time to the music, the closed hands, moved vertically from the wrist, wagged in company. This new part of the performance continued some little time. At length the leader of the orchestra held up his tambourine and struck it vigorously three times. This marked the commencement of a livelier measure. Bob, bob went the women, as if practising the old-fashioned curtsey in time to music. The heads nodded quicker; the hands, still moving vertically, were softly clapped. Every moment the music grew faster, with a corresponding acceleration in the nodding, the bobbing, and the clapping of hands; and every moment we looked for the feet to join in the general movement and break into a Berber hornpipe. Nothing of the sort happened, however. The strange performance had reached its climax.

The leader raised his tambourine overhead and struck three discordant notes. The entire orchestra raised their instruments in a similar fashion. Knees ceased to bend and heads to move. The hands gradually became still and the shrill voices died away. The song and dance were over.

Before another measure commenced, two women went round the semicircle of men and threw upon each one's right breast a scented powder called *B'hor*, about which we were unable to learn any reliable or precise particulars.

Meanwhile I had become aware that I was not only an observer, but one of the observed.

Above and behind me rose one of the high towers of the castle. Happening to cast my eyes upward, I discovered that a number of white-robed and veiled women occupied the openings of the crenelated walls which surmounted the roof for the use of riflemen. This knowledge caused me to divert my attention every now and then from the scene below to turn with guilty conscience but imaginative eye towards the forbidden quarter. So much of the glamour and charm of Morocco had been ruthlessly demolished by the rude realities of experience, that we clung with pertinacity to the pleasing idea—illusory or not—that there were still Moorish beauties in the harem, if they could but be seen. Hence the eagerness with which we scanned the forms of the veiled women, ever hoping to get a glimpse of some ravishing beauty, whose image we might carry away on the ever-ready photographic dry-plate of our heart, and print on the tablet of our memories as a bright souvenir of El Mograb. I felt none the less eager to steal a glimpse of the jewels of the Kaid's harem that I knew the owner himself, or his slaves, might detect me in this outrage on Moorish good manners.

It was not long before I discovered that C.-B. was equally aware of the proximity of the women, quite as fidgety as myself, and even less restrained in the exhibition of his curiosity. In some excitement he came to tell me of their presence, though it was news to learn that a tower beyond held by far the best of them. Dissembling my own feelings, I severely reproved him, and warned him of the consequences of showing any indiscreet curiosity. But all the same I wanted to see the women as much as he; so by and bye I strolled round to where my friend sat, and went in for a little strategic small-talk.

First we discussed the dance for a few seconds. I then turned the conversation on the imposing character of the castle. "Where could a more ideal baronial residence be found than this?" I asked with an oratorical flourish of the hand in the required direction. "How picturesque its outline, how effective the towers!" As I spoke I swept my eyes over the building. There, true enough, were some bundles of clothes at openings of the wall, one or two faces and brilliant eyes peeping from the folds of the dress; but my glance was too hasty and too guilty to allow me to distinguish any special allurements; and not daring to look again, I speedily returned to my own place.

For several hours the dances continued with but slight variation in the music and movements. In one, the women with bent knees moved slowly backwards a few feet and then forward. In another they moved sideways round the men, who seated themselves on the ground.

The whole performance was of a remarkable character, and suggested to me a survival of some old heathen rites. Its tone and character had all the air of a religious invocation. I could not, however, elicit any very satisfactory information regarding it, and had to be content with guesses. Getting tired of it at last, we sent a present of five dollars for the performers, and then retired to our quarters.

With the close of Ramadan it became necessary to prepare for our departure. We had done everything in our power to ensure the good-will of the Kaid and his people. A valuable rifle, a binocular, a hunting-knife—everything, indeed, that could possibly be spared, and which our host showed a fancy for, was sent to him. Nor were Abdul Kader and Si Mohammed forgotten; they also were propitiated with presents.

On the 14th of June, taking the opportunity of a visit from Si Mohammed, we told him that in a day or two we were going to leave Teluet for Tifnut and a place called Gindafy, which we understood was near the head of the Wad Sus. Si Mohammed betrayed no surprise, but said that the project was an impossible one. The road was as a road in Gehenna, and the people *en route* were the very agents of the Evil One himself, and in revolt against the Kaid.

We smiled at his description of the toils and dangers of the way, as if these were our special delight, believing that the Kaid, after the friendly relations we had established, would not throw obstacles in our way, though he might not assist us.

In the afternoon Abdul Kader paid us a visit while I was out, and I learned that he had spoken quite as emphatically against our intentions as had Si Mohammed. This was more discouraging, for we had never seen Abdul Kader except wreathed in smiles, like a true-born courtier, and we had always calculated upon his being our friend.

Our next step to precipitate matters was to dispatch Assor officially to the Kaid to notify our intended departure for Gindafy on the 16th. He returned with a peremptory prohibition. Letters taking all the responsibility of the affair on ourselves were of no value to him whatever. Our death, which he declared was certain, would mean his utter ruin, and he considered it his duty to prevent us going, even should he have to imprison us, and send us back in chains to the plains, from which we had come in violation of the Sultan's commands.

Our hopes now went down to zero. We still cherished the idea that if we could but get an audience of the Kaid himself we would be able to get round him. That, however, was exactly what the Kaid took care we should not have, being, I believe, genuinely put out at the situation that had arisen.

In our profound disappointment and chagrin the wildest projects entered our head. C.-B. was ready for everything and anything; but though I dallied for a time with some reckless ideas, I knew full well that without the Kaid's concurrence and assistance we could never leave Teluet.

With the exception of Shalum, not one of our men would budge one step, and, with the Kaid to back them up, we could not force them. As utterly out of the question was it to bolt away in disguise. That the people of Tifnut were dangerous and in revolt was undoubtedly true, and we could not but grant that the Kaid was taking up a position such as any one in authority would have assumed in similar circumstances. Still, the pill was too bitter to be swallowed easily, and we could not help breathing defiance and threats.

Next morning matters became worse, our men, who had helped to bring the situation about, could not refrain from showing their exultation over our discomfiture, and with my own hand I had to chastise El Hadj for insolence. The castle attendants displayed an altogether altered demeanour, reflecting the temper of their superiors. The lavish *mona* was no longer forthcoming, and we were confined to our apartments. Everything was evidently to be done to show that we were troublesome guests, and that we might expect no favour till we submitted to the will of the Kaid.

We spent the day in a bitter and melancholy fashion, chewing the cud of our reflections. No Kaid arrived, no ray of hope appeared in our gloomy horizon.

On the 16th matters had not improved. The Kaid positively refused to see us till we had renounced our intention, nor would he be induced to receive Assor. There was nothing for it but to submit to our fate, and that with the best grace possible, for it was better to part friends than enemies.

In the afternoon we sent to tell our host that we proposed to return to the plains on the morrow. About sunset the Kaid arrived, and being desirous to smooth over matters as much as possible, in case we might do him damage at the court, he brought with him a handsome gun with powder-horn and bullet-pouch as a present, in addition to what he had already given us. He also brought with him a large supply of biscuits, dates, almonds, and raisins, as provisions for the road. We received these tokens of friendship as graciously as possible, but none the less the Kaid seemed ill at ease. Before leaving he asked us as a special favour to remain another day, in order that he might prepare a feast for us to speed us on our way and celebrate our renewed friendship. To this arrangement we reluctantly consented.

Next day, knowing that the feast would be an affair

of some magnitude, and wishful to show, by partaking heartily, that we harboured no malice, we deemed it advisable to fast all morning, so as to give our appetites a keener edge and blunt the fastidiousness of our palates. For the same reason I thought it well to take a constitutional. To do this I had to slip outside, as if merely taking a stroll about the castle. Some distance beyond the outer wall Shalum met me, bringing with him a couple of mules, one for me and one for himself. My goal was a low range or ridge closing in the valley to the west, beyond which was the glen of the chief tributary of the Asif Marren, a spot I had long been desirous of visiting. As I was afraid of being pursued and captured before attaining my object, we hurried forward as fast as possible.

The morning was exquisite in its fresh purity and cool bracing temperature, its brilliant sunlight, and marvellously deep blue sky. The spice of possible danger in front and of pursuit behind gave the necessary zest to make our ride thoroughly enjoyable.

We had passed more than one village without being molested or questioned. At length we neared the bottom of the hill which we had to ascend in order to look down into the valley. We had still, however, to pass a large village and cross a stream. The former we did without trouble, and had almost reached the stream, when we were suddenly startled by excited cries behind us. Turning sharply round, conceive my astonishment on finding an infuriated mountaineer rushing towards us and making violent efforts to escape from two men, with the very evident object of shooting me.

The peril of my situation was only too evident. I was unarmed, though that mattered little, for if I had shot my assailant, there would have been no escape from his fellow-villagers. Shalum was equally defenceless. To make matters worse, we had no common language, and in the excitement of the moment I could only ejaculate in English. Shalum, being a Jew, dared not interfere; but to his honour be it said, he did not attempt to save himself by flight. With look and gesture I mutely demanded why the mad fanatic—for such I deemed him to be—wanted to take my blood. I deprecated any such violent proceeding with upraised hands, and made animated marks of exclamation with my shoulders and eyebrows.

Nothing more was left to me but to sit on my mule and watch with painful personal interest the progress of the struggle. Every now and again it seemed as if my would-be assailant would succeed in breaking loose, and his gun would come dangerously near the horizontal. At such moments it was no joke to have no other alternative open to me than that of helplessly sitting still.

Nothing had any effect on the foaming maniac. Neither the severity of my looks, nor the dignity that doth hedge the British subject, were of any avail. As little use was it to try to fix him with my eye; for, to my added discomfiture, among the armed crowd that was rapidly gathering, another fanatic, excited by the behaviour of his friend, commenced a similar disagreeable demonstration in my rear, and it became an interesting speculation with me, as I turned first to the one and then to the other, which was likely to be the first in shedding my Christian blood.

Matters were becoming worse at each moment. War-cries were echoing all round, bringing out scores of armed villagers. The crowd around me surged and clamoured. Some wanted to give the fanatics a free hand, others objected on the ground that I was the Kaid's guest. A few there were who seemed to turn over in their mind the propriety of killing me, and more than once I caught sight of guns raised and then lowered.

I began to think my last hour had come. There was but one course open to me, namely, to attempt retreat. To my agreeable surprise, the crowd, as such, made no attempt to stop us, though the two madmen, now weak with their violent exertions, still struggled to free themselves.

Restraining my desire to put my mule to the gallop, and disdaining to appear afraid, though I never got such a fright in my life, I gathered together such remnants of my dignity as still were left, and calmly ambled away, not deigning to look back, but wishing with my whole soul that I had one eye at least in the back of my head. For over a hundred yards I momentarily expected to hear the report of a gun, and feel one sharp moment of agony. Happily no such catastrophe happened, and after a time I felt that without loss of dignity I might look round. I drew a deep sigh of relief from an intolerable mental tension on finding that we were not followed, though we were still watched from the heights by groups of people.

My first care on finding myself out of danger was to warn Shalum to be absolutely silent as to what had happened, knowing that if it came to the ears of our men, they would make splendid obstructive capital out of it. For the same reason I resolved to say nothing of it to the Kaid, though I longed to demand soldiers and return to the village with vengeful intents.

On reaching our quarters without further adventure, C.-B.—who, meanwhile, had been peacefully working up his diaries—C.-B. and I proceeded to array ourselves in Moorish dresses, as being cooler, and more in keeping with the function in prospect, as well as—if I may be permitted to say so—allowing of more comfortable expansion as the banquet proceeded. For the rest of the afternoon there was nothing for us to do but loll about on our mattresses and cushions—a Moorish fashion which did not suit our temperament. It was satisfactory, however, to feel that our appetites were getting ravenous.

At length, as the Mueddin ended his call to afternoon prayers, the sound of slippered feet came welcomely to our ears. As we half-raised ourselves in eager expectancy, a dozen slaves in snow-white dresses defiled before us in an appetising train that made our mouths water with anticipatory joys. Each stalwart negro perspired under a circular legless table, behind

"DINNER READY."

Page 268.

whose huge conical cover he was almost hidden. Their steaming burdens were deposited in a row, like so many beehives, stretching from our door half-way down the garden. The slaves looked at us with beaming faces, mutely congratulating us on the coming feast, as they stood over their respective tables flicking away the clouds of flies with long cloths. Our men

WAITING FOR DINNER.

gathered around like jackals, and licked their lips, awaiting the moment when their turn to eat would come.

We had not long to wait for the Kaid and his two henchmen. We rose to receive them at the door with salaams and compliments, and then, without loss of time, arranged ourselves for action, the governor, however, not joining us.

First a slave appeared with basin and ewer in which to wash our right hand—the left never, if possible, being used to convey food to the mouth. Every one having washed, we seated ourselves tailor-fashion in a circle.

Abdul Kader was again all smiles and jokes. Even Si Mohammed relaxed the dark severity of his countenance, while we did our best to assume an air of subdued hilarity, such as might become our dignity.

The nearest table was now placed in our midst, and the beehive-shaped cover taken off. Before us appeared a large glazed earthen dish, like a wash-hand basin, half filled with melted butter, in which swam four roast-fowls. As many loaves garnished the edge of the table. With one accord we ejaculated "*Bismillah!*" (in the name of God), with which phrase the good Mussulman puts a divine stamp on whatever he does.

In my hurry to show how much at home I was, I made the vulgar mistake of breaking bread before Abdul Kader, who acted for the Kaid, did it for me.

There were, of course, no knives or forks, and we had to make the most we could of our fingers. Our attempts were miserable failures. As we could only use the right hand, it was difficult to separate the meat without drawing away the fowl or making a terrible splash. In our impatience we restrained ourselves with difficulty from using both hands, than which nothing would have been more low-bred.

Abdul Kader, seeing our embarrassment, hastened

to separate the choicest pieces with his own fingers, and either placed them beside us, or as a special compliment popped them into our mouths. This, however, only made us more anxious to succeed in our own attempts.

Having made some impression on the dish, the remainder was passed on to our men to finish off, giving us time to suck our fingers clean in the manner of little boys who have been at the jam-pot.

In quick succession three other courses of fowls, all cooked differently, were placed before us. Next followed, one by one, three *tajen*, or stews of beef and mutton, like the chickens, all swimming in butter or oil.

Of each and all we were expected to partake, and as our appreciation was understood to be in proportion to the amount we consumed, we began to see the wisdom of our choice of clothes.

After the six courses of stews and chickens, we felt ready for anything, and in capital form for whatever might turn up. Our eyes became moist with mingled emotions on seeing half a baked sheep hoisted into our midst, oozing forth fat from every pore and steaming with appetising odours. In my desire to show how much I was enjoying myself, and what a good time I was having, I dug my fingers too eagerly into the juicy meat and burnt them. Naturally the pain made me raise them involuntarily to my lips; but recollecting myself, I dissembled, and made believe that I had only been trying the flavour of the mutton, and that nothing could be more delicious.

A pillau of rice and fowls was an agreeable variation to the more substantial solids that had hitherto been presented. We made, however, but a poor show when the Moorish national dish *kuskussu* was placed before us. This consists of wheaten flour granulated and steamed over a stewpan in which meat is being cooked.

In eating *kuskussu*, little balls are formed by a peculiar motion of the half-closed hand. These are then raised to the edge of the fist and dexterously propelled into the mouth by the thumb. To do this properly requires a great deal of practice; and not having had it, we failed so ignominiously, that it would have been well had we provided ourselves with bibs.

Our failure, however, was again Abdul Kader's opportunity. With his own greasy fingers he made balls for us, and then on the signal "*Kul !*" cleverly shot them into our open mouths. Of course we stammered out "*Baraka-lowfik !*" (many thanks), and made faces expressive of our delight and appreciation of the high honour done us; but none the less the balls went down our throats with difficulty, though by this time there were perhaps more reasons than one why that was so.

The *kuskussu* marked the end of the feast proper. We piously acknowledged the true Giver of all the good things that we had eaten by ejaculating "*Hamdulillah !*" (praise the Lord), and then thoroughly washed our hands.

Tea, cake and fruit in lavish abundance followed as

dessert and top-dressing. But we had not yet quite done with all the accompaniments of the banquet, during which we had literally put through our hands twelve fowls, some fifteen pounds of stewed mutton and beef, eighteen loaves of bread, half a baked sheep, and other less substantial viands.

First, an array of bottles and other utensils more or less mysterious were brought in, and I had to place myself in the hands of Abdul Kader, who proceeded to drench my clothes and person with rose-water till I looked as if half-drowned. Next I had to be perfumed with the smoke of odoriferous aloes wood, benzoin, and ambergris placed with charcoal in a burner.

Abdul Kader first wafted the smoke over my face, then I had to stand over the incense-burner, so that the perfume should penetrate everywhere, with the result that I speedily emitted smoke from neck and sleeves like an active volcano.

After this crowning ceremony the governor rose to leave. We conducted him to the door of our apartments, where, after exchanging salaams and compliments again, and commending him to the keeping of Allah, we returned to dry ourselves and resume the ordinary dress and ways of civilised life.

CHAPTER XIX.

TELUET TO AMSMIZ.

On the 18th of June we bade farewell to the Kaid, and in anything but an amiable mood commenced our return to the Plain of Morocco. In little more than two hours we were again on the Tizi-n-Teluet, lingeringly taking our last look of the riant valley, as before we had taken our first. Regrets were useless, however, and there was nothing for it but to turn our faces to the north, and hope for a more lucky turn of the wheel of fortune in other parts of the Atlas.

On our way to Zarktan, El Hadj chiefly claimed our attention. Since our arrival at Teluet, he had been unable to obtain any kief, and being an inveterate smoker of that deleterious drug, he had been reduced to the verge of lunacy. The deprivation made him a danger to himself and those around him. He now chose to let out his spleen on his mule, and swore he would send it to the bottom of the glen. So reckless was his behaviour, that I dared not leave him one moment; but even my presence was no great restraining influence, and our march was one continuous wrangle, varied by threats of my hunting-crop, and other violent demonstrations, indispensable unfortunately, and loathesome to my soul. On the ridge over Zarktan his brutal treatment of the mule nearly ended in the animal's death; for getting bewildered and terrified by the way in which it was being pulled about, it missed its footing and fell from the pathway, only escaping destruction by a miracle. After that the poor brute became utterly paralysed, and could only be got along with the utmost difficulty. The near realisation of his expressed hopes for the moment slightly sobered Hadj, but none the less I kept my hunting-crop ready for immediate application to his shoulders on the next lapse from proper conduct.

In the evening we reached Zarktan, where we were once more hospitably received.

Next day we were much disgusted at being compelled to farther retrace our steps down the valley of the Gadat, instead of being able to cut westward over the mountains, as we had been led to expect.

El Hadj was more than ever contumacious and brutal in the treatment of his mule, which, on its part, was more than ever frightened. Again I had to resume the revolting task of going behind him like a slave-driver with ever-threatening whip. At last, not daring to show the mad rage which possessed him, he bolted off and left his charge. Happily a native of Morocco returning from Teluet volunteered to bring the mule along, else we should have been in a quandary. As for Hadj, I resolved to let him alone till I reached Misfiwa, where, I made up my mind, he should once more meditate in a dungeon.

In four hours we reached the bridge above Enzel, and here we cut away from our old route. The Kaid's brother had so far accompanied us, but here he left us. His last request was that Hadj might be forgiven, and though greatly enraged against the scoundrel, I could not refuse this parting grace to our youthful friend.

Ascending the hills by a steep path, we kept west by north, over red shales backed up by intrusions of basalt. At the top we were on the undulating surface of the first mountain terrace, with escarped hills to the west, formed by a capping of limestones over softer shales and sandstones. Irregular anticlines and synclines brought these beds to the surface in different directions. What chiefly attracted our attention, however, as we entered the drainage basin of the Wad Masin, was a clearly defined mound-like moraine, extending from the back of the high mountains overlooking Zarktan well across the lower slopes. Though of no great breadth or thickness, and only some five or six miles in length, this was by far the most important evidence of glacial action we ever saw in the Atlas. This fact makes me extremely sceptical of the glacial origin ascribed by Maw to an enormous series of "boulder beds" a few miles farther west of the Wad Masin. It seems incredible that glacial drift could have been deposited, as he describes, to a thickness of one or two thousand feet in a restricted area of a few miles, while elsewhere, from Demnat to the Atlantic, and in the very heart of the Atlas itself, only the most insignificant evidence of glacial action exists. In Misfiwa and Urika, where these so-called glacial deposits are found, there is nothing in the height or conformation of the mountains to indicate more favourable conditions than elsewhere for the formation of glaciers or the deposit of ice-transported matter.

The geological features of the mountain terrace we were now crossing were interesting in other respects. Evidently the intrusion of bosses and walls of basalt had been the principal factor in the formation of the folds and curves which distinguished the rocks. At one place we passed along the axis of an anticline, where the tension on the sharply curved beds had been too much for the limestones and shales, which had consequently been fractured, and formed a sharp V.-like valley. This valley farther north opened into a great circular hollow, occupied in the centre by a hillock of basalt, from which the opposing escarped circle of limestone beds dipped away in all directions. Through this curious depression runs the Wad Misfiwa.

Our route now followed this fine mountain stream, up whose picturesque and frowning glen we got tempting glimpses of the snow-clad heights beyond. The bold physical features of the inner ranges needed not the confirmation of river debris to tell us that there the geological formation differed from what we had found in the Gadat. Still the drifted blocks of greywacke, porphyry, and diorite which strewed the bed of the Wad Misfiwa gave us more definite data regarding the nature of the geological change.

It was three in the afternoon when we once more

emerged from the mountains and found ourselves among the olive groves of Iminzet, with the yellow monotony of the Plain of Morocco stretching away northward.

To our delight, the Kaid of Misfiwa was absent in Morocco—a circumstance which enabled us to dispense with the presentation to him of the introductory letters supplied to us by El Madani. We well knew that they were more than introductory, and contained hints and warnings regarding us which would have been acted upon had we tried to penetrate the mountains of Misfiwa, and passed on also to the next governor we desired to visit. By the happy accident of the Kaid's absence we would now be able to obliterate our traces in a manner, and start afresh with a Kaid unbiassed by previous knowledge and unsuspicious of our movements.

Taking everything into consideration, we deemed it well to make no attempt in the meantime to ascend the Misfiwa glen, but rather to throw our men off the scent by pushing on to Amsmiz, and there, if possible, cross the mountain.

Meanwhile, to impress the Sheik in charge with a proper sense of our importance—which otherwise he would have held to be of no account—Assor bullied the life out of him to bring *mona* in fitting quantities. In this our men—backward in all else—joined heartily, till at length we were elevated to a proper pinnacle in the Sheik's estimation, and he hastened to kill the fatted sheep and lay before us his choicest chickens—a proceeding in this case recognised by us with a suitable gift of money.

Next morning we started for Amsmiz by way of Gurguri. Our course lay south-west, over the stony, treeless plain, and skirting the base of a low flat escarped hill, at the base of which rose a dyke of basalt. The one agreeable feature in the landscape was the numerous villages along the edge of the hill. The greater part of the crops—here somewhat scanty—had now been cut and gathered into heaps awaiting the thrashing. In about two hours we reached the Wad El Mulha, where the basalt dyke ends, and the low hills sharply curve south, and form a great bay, having Urika in its centre. As we travelled on, the plain became more fertile and more varied by winding strips of olives and fruitful gardens, to which a perfect network of artificial channels led the needful water. Some three hours from Iminzet, at a place called Tamarakt, we remarked an undoubted line of ice-borne boulders, many of great size, and from this part we could see the collection of rounded hillocks at the foot of the Atlas composed of the "glacial drift" of Maw.

About mid-day we crossed the Wad Reraya, where we all nearly came to grief in a quicksand in the middle of the stream. Two hours later we entered a magnificent series of olive groves, and found ourselves close to the Wad Reraya at Taghnowt (Tachnowt).

At this point we left the plain to cross the mountain spur of Mulai-Ibrahim and Gurguri. At a height of 4000 feet we found ourselves at the top, with the holy *zawia* or sanctuary of Mulai-Ibrahim on our left. There is no more highly revered saint in Southern Morocco than Mulai-Ibrahim; and our men hastened to jump from their mules and mutter a prayer for his blessing. This done, they threw stones upon some huge cairns that lined the wayside, built up by the additions of successive generations of travellers, who, unable to visit the holy man's tomb, yet desired to add something to the rude monuments thus raised to his honour.

After crossing an outcrop of metamorphic rocks we entered the curved and folded series of cretaceous date.

It was near sunset when we found ourselves at the western edge of the Gurguri mountains and looking over the plain. Half way down the exceedingly precipitous slope we passed the Kasbah of Gurguri, perched like an eagle's nest on a projecting shelf of rock. The Kaid here being from home, we had to descend to the castle of his Kalifa or lieutenant, which we reached long after sunset, having been over fourteen hours in the saddle.

Our reception was far from hospitable, and we gladly moved on next morning to Amsmiz, which we reached in four hours, our animals dead beat with the forced marches of the previous three days.

From what we had been told of the Kaid of Amsmiz by Shalum, who belonged to that place, we expected not indeed such a reception as at Glauwa, but entertainment quite as lavishly hospitable. He was known to be a man of catholic tastes, who delighted to number some European vices amongst others more strictly Moorish. A man who enjoyed his bottle like any good Christian, was not, we imagined, likely to look upon us too suspiciously, though we were not sure how far the couple of bottles of whisky we carried among our stores would be an open sesame to the portals of the Atlas heights and fastnesses. We did not, however, get an opportunity of trying the experiment. The Kaid was absent in Morocco. When we arrived, the Kalifa or deputy-governor was in the fields, and the servant in charge showed us into the court and guest-chamber of the common herd of travellers. We resented this very much, but had to submit on finding the Kalifa on his arrival powerless to open the other rooms. Still it was necessary to impress him with a due sense of our importance, and we failed not to express ourselves in the most indignant terms, with the required result.

At Amsmiz we were once more at the entrance of a mountain glen leading to a pass across the main chain to Gindafy and Ras el Wad in Sus. Here, as elsewhere, we kept our plans to ourselves till the moment for action had arrived. At present, it was absolutely necessary to give our mules a rest to recover from their late journey.

There were certain things in our favour which gave us ground for hope. In the first place, the Kalifa was not likely to act so energetically, or feel so sure of his ground with us, as the Kaid. Then we had the precedent in our favour of having been to Teluet, and there regally entertained. Our men, too, were not so suspicious of our intentions, as the familiar road to Sus lay farther east, up the Wad Nyfis.

Amsmiz lies at the foot of the outer mountain terrace of the Atlas, and close to the entrance of a narrow glen, through which may be caught a glimpse of the backbone of the range, only some eight miles distant. The town stands at an elevation of 3020 feet above the level of the sea, according to our boiling-point thermometer, though Hooker's aneroid registered a height of 3382 feet. My experience with the two different instruments leads me to accept my own observation as probably the more correct. Bearing on this point I may mention that among the mountains my aneroid differed from the B.P.T. to the extent of several hundred feet, each ascent producing a new error in the reading. Yet on starting, and on returning to the coast, the aneroid read correctly, and agreed with the B.P.T. Consequently, if I had relied entirely on the former, and had not had the latter to compare it with, I should have left Morocco with the impression that I had been in possession of an admirably correct instrument, whereas in reality the readings among the mountains would have been enormously wrong. It must, therefore, be understood that the elevations given in these pages and the accompanying map are either deduced from the temperature of the boiling-point—as is the case with all the important points—or from aneroid readings corrected by the B.P.T. This fact will explain the re-

AMSMIZ.

markable discrepancies which geographers will not fail to note between my elevations and those given by such trained and accurate observers as Hooker and Ball.

The population of the town of Amsmiz we guessed to be somewhere about 2000, of which a very considerable proportion are Jews. Here, as elsewhere, these children of Israel are terribly overcrowded. Greatly to our surprise, however, we found among them a certain measure of cleanliness, not only in their persons, but in their houses and streets. Of course the cleanliness was purely comparative. With this better sanitation there was a corresponding improvement in the health of the Mellah. Physical deformities were more rare, and without exception the Jews of Amsmiz were by far the finest developed men and women we met anywhere in Morocco. In other respects too they attracted our favourable notice; for they had a manly and independent air about them sufficiently rare in these lands, and seemed to be on very good terms with themselves and with the Government.

Among the various problems presented by the Jews in Morocco, none appears more curious than this, that in every town and district they develop a characteristic physical appearance without losing the distinctive features of the race, so that the observer can at once say that this one comes from Amsmiz, and that from Demnat—from the city of Morocco, or from the Atlas Mountains. This differentiation is of course to some extent due to the different pursuits, conditions of life, and climate which mark their various spheres; that, for instance, of the Jew of Morocco as compared with his brother of the mountains. But a far more important factor in effecting this specialisation was the old state of things—now only existent in remote corners of the Atlas—which prevented Jews from leaving the places where they were brought up as semi-serfs. A third was their prevailing habit of marrying among relations in order to keep their hard-won money from going outside the family.

Child-marriages we found to be the rule in Amsmiz—not, be it remembered, between a boy and a girl, but between a man of mature years, frequently old even, and a child of from seven to ten. These child-wives live with their husbands, though, as may be understood, only for protection till they attain a certain development. Mothers at ten are not, however, unheard of, and are not rare at thirteen or fifteen.

The surprising thing about these early marriages is that they do not appear to react upon the physique of the population. As far as Amsmiz was concerned, the custom seemed to result in the production of fine healthy men and women.

JEWISH CHILD-WIVES, AMSMIZ.

CHAPTER XX.

GLEN OF THE WAD AMSMIZ.

ON the 23rd June, the mules being sufficiently recovered, we resolved to broach our plans to the Kalifa. So far not a breath of our intentions, as far as we knew, had got out. In addition to keeping everything secret, we had called the worst of our men before us, and given them a frightful " blowing up." We told them that we knew all about their evil machinations at Glauwa, and said that if such practices were continued we would take a terrible revenge. We left them to imagine for themselves what that revenge would be, giving them a wide margin of speculation between death by shooting or flogging, or by torture or starvation in a dungeon. In any case, we gave them to understand it would be something unusually severe, and failed not to emphasise our threats with demoniac faces, tones, and gestures, till, in shaky undertones, they could be heard muttering, " God help me! God help me!"

Nothing occurred to disturb our hopes during the two days we remained quiet; but then that did not mean much. In Morocco, the man with a mission launches his bark without apparent opposition. Sanguine of success, he glides peacefully down a smooth broad stream. In time he sees his goal looming up ahead, and already feels success assured. Then is his moment of greatest peril. Almost without fail a barrier of rocks will rise up before him, or, still worse, he will find himself being swiftly carried over a waterfall, or a hidden snag will swamp his frail craft, sinking all his fair hopes and sanguine expectations to the bottom, and him with them. It had been so with us at Teluet; was it to be so again at Amsmiz?

On being ushered into the presence of the Kalifa—who, like the Kaid of Demnat, was more of a negro than a Moor—and the usual compliments over, we simply told him, with the air of men who had no doubts about their position and rights, that on the morrow we were going to continue our way to Gindafy, for whom we had a letter from the Sultan. We desired that he should have a guide provided for us. As Assor translated our authoritative language, we watched the face of the Kalifa with no small anxiety and doubt. Would he put a pin in the grandiloquent bubbles we had inflated to overawe him? No! "*Wakke!*" (very well) was the word which fell sweetly on our ears. "Inshallah! (please God), the guide will be ready." After some ordinary talk, we walked away as if we had not any material body to support.

Next day, there in very truth was the guide, and no countermanding orders from the Kalifa. Still, as long as we were in the neighbourhood of the town, we feared the worst. The men would have rebelled if they had dared, for they saw once more the hard work, scanty fare, and dangers of the mountains before them, and behind them the easy life, princely feeding, and safety of the plains. They had, however, acquired a

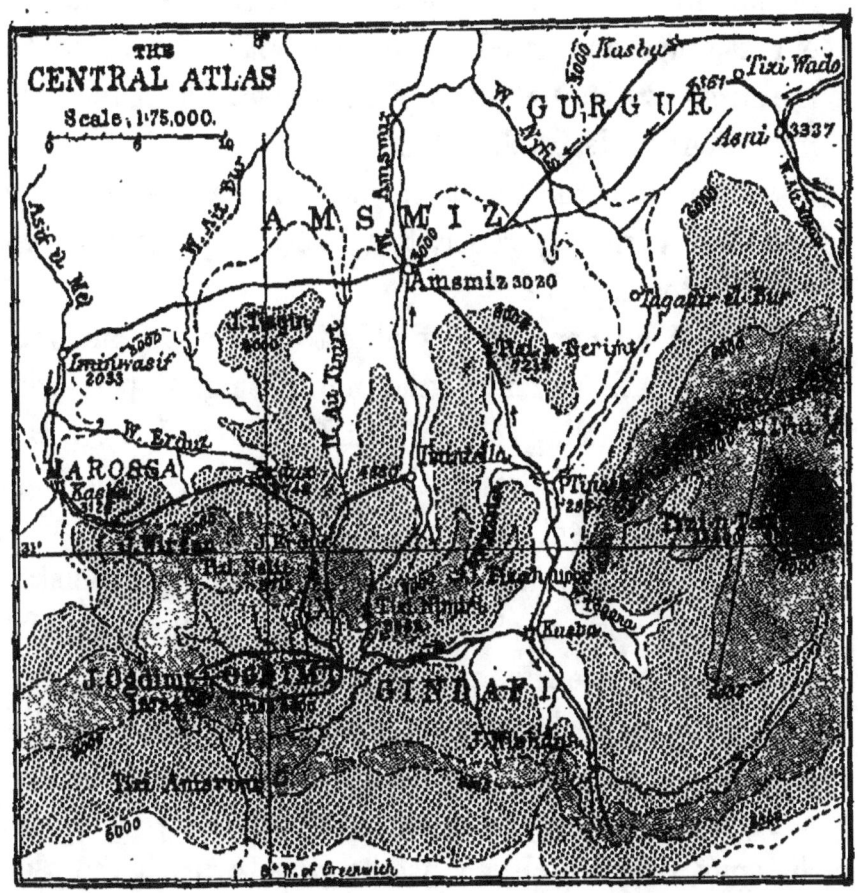

salutary fear of us, and only showed their feelings in their faces, and by the tardy manner in which they loaded their mules.

As we passed through the ill-built yet picturesque town, we were greeted by numerous inquiries as to our destination. "God will show," we replied evasively, wrapping ourselves in our cloaks of Moorish reserve.

"A path of peace to you," greeted us more commonly as we passed through the Jews' quarter, and many of its inhabitants hurried forward to kiss our hands effusively, while the lame and the halt clung to our stirrups and tried to embrace our very boots, till the necessary "*flus*" or coppers caused them to desist from their undesirable attentions.

"Beware of the Shellach," was the last warning we got from a friendly Moor, to which our pious cook replied, "God help us!"

In half an hour, hardly able to believe in our good luck, we had traversed the undulating slopes, with their rich mottling of vine and olive and corn, and had reached the base of the outer range. We commenced the ascent of the mountain by a rocky gully. The lower slopes were here bright with gum cistus, and aglow with a rich bloom of wild thyme, which gave an unwonted look of brightness to the sad, grey air of sterility which is the usual summer garb of the Atlas.

In about an hour we had reached the shoulder of the spur, over which we had to pass to reach the glen leading to the main range. From our coign of vantage we could now take in the wide sweep of the lowlands we had left, the grove-circled town of Amsmiz, and the tree-shaded streams from the Atlas winding like green snakes through the yellow burnt-up plain of Morocco. Faintly, too, through this weird summer sheen could be descried the garden-mottled city of Morocco, from which the great tower of the Kutubia rose conspicuous. Of more immediate interest was the glen of the Wad Amsmiz, cutting deep into the lower ranges, and opening up a varied scene. Massive precipices of slightly dipping yellow limestone contrasted with the irregular surface features of grey friable metamorphic rocks which cropped up from beneath; while away towards the head of the rugged glen the backbone of the Atlas rose abruptly, the peak of Tezah, with the snow still gleaming in its sheltering nooks, giving variety to its otherwise monotonous features. The cool breeze from these lofty heights came refreshingly to us after the burning heats of the plains, and the brawling torrent a thousand feet below sent to our ears the soothing sound of its rushing and tumbling waters.

Along this glen our way now lay. A bridle-path wound along the precipitous and rocky slope, appearing and disappearing in its many irregularities of surface, a mere thread in the wild waste.

Once more we were preoccupied with the difficulties of the pathway. Once more our mules engrossed the larger share of our attention, and the air became musical (or otherwise) with the sound of Moorish curses and words of encouragement.

In spite of everything, one mule did go over—the mule, too, which carried our kitchen utensils. We rushed with dismay after the unhappy brute, expecting to find a mass of broken bones and flattened stew-pans. With difficulty we raised it to its feet, and proceeded hastily to examine it and the contents of the pack. We piously said "Amen!" to Hadj the cook's exclamation, "There is no conqueror but God!" when we discovered that the mule's bones were whole, and that the damage to the cooking utensils was of the slightest.

For a good part of the way we kept some hundreds of feet above the bottom of the glen, passing through a bush and tree scrub of resin-scented *Calitris* and juniper, of holly-like evergreen oak and the omnipresent arbutus, almost the sole woody competitors for elbow-room on these uncultivated slopes. It was only on descending to the bottom, where water throughout the year is abundant, that our eyes were gladdened with the nobler presence of walnut, carob, ash, poplar, almond, and pomegranate, which here rose into the dignity of trees, and shaded the cultivated terraces of the mountaineers.

Our first march was a short one. Owing to the absence of supplies farther up, we had perforce to camp while the day was still young.

It had never before been our good luck to find such a charming camping-ground. In the Atlas flat pieces of ground covered with green sward and sheltering trees are extreme rarities; but here, in the glen of the Wad Amsmiz, we had a delightful bit of turf on which to pitch our tents, splendid walnut trees to shade them, a noisy torrent to babble at our feet, and majestic mountains to fold us in their giant arms and cool the tropic heats. Berber villages also were at hand, to send us store of corn for mules and horses, milk, eggs, and fowls for ourselves, and *kuskussu*, *tajen*, and barley-bannocks for our attendants.

We learned that there were some so-called Christian remains in the neighbourhood. Taught by former experience, we were somewhat sceptical as to their reputed origin, but we nevertheless started off to visit them and determine, if possible, what they really were.

Our course lay up a most charming ravine cut out of beds of yellow and white limestone and sandstone, whose rugged angularities were veiled and beautified by a rich draping of ivy, dogrose, honeysuckle, and bramble. Among their bright green foliage numerous springs splashed and trickled, giving the leaves a fairy covering of glistening water-drops wherever the rays of the summer sun happened to fall. Above everything we were delighted to find among the fallen blocks, and in the shady nooks of the ravines, a profusion of daisies, perfect counterparts, except for a dash of blue on the petals, of our own dear familiar field-flower.

While delightedly peering about and struggling from rock to rock in search of new plants, quite forgetful of the primary object of our stroll, we were suddenly astonished to find ourselves standing upon a beautifully quarried and dressed block of stone weighing from a ton and a half to two tons. "Something of the Rum" (Christians) "at last," we mentally ejaculated, as we remarked the well-squared and moulded shape of the block. A little farther off was another, and speedily we had discovered quite a number, of varied size and shape, but all equally well quarried and prepared for the chisel of the mason. "But what were they intended for?" we asked ourselves. Nobody would dream of building a house such as needed stones of these dimensions in a desolate glen like that of the Wad Amsmiz. They must, therefore, have been quarried for some building out in the plains. That conclusion only opened up another difficulty; for how were stones, weighing in some cases quite two tons, to be conveyed down a rocky gorge which half-loaded pack-mules traversed with difficulty? No planking could be laid down, and rollers were out of the question. No solution of the question occurring to us, we gave the puzzle up, while we canvassed a second problem. Could the Romans have quarried these stones with their customary building enterprise; or had it been the Moors in the good old days when they led the van of civilisation, and were shining lights even to the peoples of Europe?

It had never been made out that the Romans were established so firmly at the base of the Atlas as the quarrying of such building materials would naturally imply, while it had been shown that the Moors had been capable of great building enterprise. We could not, therefore, but conclude that the balance of argument was decidedly in favour of the Moors. Still there was the question, How were such blocks to be conveyed down the glen?

Our puzzled speculations took a new turn when, in the search for enlightenment, we wandered farther up the ravine, and found a new source of interest in the discovery of a magnificent spring bubbling up in crystalline clearness from a hole at the bottom of a precipice, and in such volume as to form a very fine stream.

The natives declare unanimously that there is a huge iron grating across the mouth of the spring, firmly fixed in the solid rock. This statement was corroborated by Shalum, whose information we had always found phenomenally trustworthy for Morocco, and he declared that on a previous occasion he had seen the grating, and described the bars as being as thick as a man's wrist. We ourselves could not see the grating, owing to the turbulent boiling of the water, which was then dammed back to raise it to a higher level for conveyance by an artificial channel to the terraces of the mountaineers. Of course a halo of romance gathered round this wonderful spring with its sealed mouth. Treasures were unhesitatingly spoken of, and magic seals. Marvellous virtues were ascribed to its waters, and dire punishment predicted to any one who would have the hardihood to violate its charm-protected sanctity.

We began to ask ourselves if there could be any connection between the dressed blocks and this magical spring, but laughingly concluding that there could be no end—certainly no satisfactory end—to the questions which might be asked, we hurried on to inspect some ruins close to the village of Imintella, also ascribed to the Christians or Rum. The situation and character of these remains were certainly very remarkable. They were undoubtedly ancient, but a glance at the style of architecture, and at the lime and mud-formed concrete of the walls, was sufficient to tell that, if of Christian origin at all, they must have been the work of the native Christians, who seem to have largely occupied Morocco before the Mohammedan conquest, but of whom almost nothing is known but a name.

On our return to camp in the cool of the afternoon, and while refreshing ourselves with a cup of tea, our attention was attracted by the sight of a humble wayfarer descending the glen. He was driving a lowly ass before him, with many resounding whacks on its scantily covered bones, and lusty invocations of Allah to witness its obstinacy. Heedless, however, alike of voice and arm, the ass's ears and tail wagged with the same pendulum regularity, and its little hoofs pattered at the same even pace over the rocky pathway.

There was something in the dress and appearance of the wanderer, as well as in the basket which was securely strapped to the donkey, that suggested an Aissawa—that is, a follower of Sidi Aissa, in whose name the true believer is enabled to resist the poison of snakes, to eat glass, and to do a number of horrible things with perfect security and enjoyment.

Eager to see some of these feats under such favourable circumstances, I hurried forward to secure him ere he passed.

"Welcome, oh stranger, to our tents," I cried, anxious to practise my Arabic. A scowl alone showed that the inheritor of the promises had heard my greeting and scorned the hospitality of a Nazarene and rebel against God. "Peace be with you," I once more ventured hesitatingly.

"Peace be unto the *true believer*," he replied briefly and with marked emphasis.

My Arabic and my good spirits here failed me; but Hadj M'hamad came to the rescue. The eye of the Aissawa glistened on seeing the pipe of *kief* (bang) which Hadj carried in his hand.

"Listen, oh happy believer in our Lord Mohammed (on whom be peace), to the words of the Anasera (Christian). Show him your miracles. He will enrich you with silver, and perchance he may yet acknowledge, through the grace of Sidi Aissa, the One God and His Prophet."

The frailties of the flesh were, happily for us, stronger than his spiritual repulsions, and decoyed by Hadj's kief pipe, the snake-charmer was brought into camp. Further mollified by the soothing fumes and the sight of a dollar, he consented to exhibit the miraculous powers given to those who follow the banner of Sidi Aissa.

Laying the basket of snakes on the ground, he commenced to circle round it with a curious step, chanting meanwhile an invocation to his patron saint. He accompanied his wild chant with a large tambourine, which he vigorously thumped with his hand. Commencing at first slowly, with a plaintive wail in his voice, and a depressed worn-out look in his spare and haggard features, he gradually warmed up to a more exalted condition of religious excitement. His eyes became brighter, his expression more animated, as he struck the tambourine with ever-increasing vigour, and whirled round and round the basket with floating garments, and long black hair falling down his back in matted locks. Suddenly, in the midst of his wild gyrations he stooped down, fearlessly inserted his hand into the basket and dragged forth two snakes.

The music was now over. Only the brawling stream broke the silence. For a moment the Aissawa stood still in wild elation, the venomous reptiles coiling round his uplifted arm, while we sat breathless watching the strange scene. Time after time, the snakes bit his naked arms viciously, he calmly and unflinchingly looking at them. The performer now took an onion leaf, and with it scratched his leg till he drew blood. After that he returned one of the snakes to its basket. For a moment he held the other aloft by the neck, man and reptile glaring fixedly at each other, as if trying which had the superior power of fascination. While we still wondered what was to be the next move, he suddenly raised the snake to his mouth. A vicious snap and the snake was headless, though it still wriggled in unceasing convulsions. With incredible rapidity the snake's head was chewed and swallowed. Our disgusted protest was unheeded, as, rigid, with eyes fixed and air of intense absorption, the charmer next bit off several inches from the body of the snake. His eye now assumed a stonier glare, and he appeared to be utterly oblivious of his surroundings. The poison of the snake was coursing through his veins, and he was in the fell clutches of delirium. Once or twice more he tore with wolfish appetite at his now passive victim. Then his madness took a new form. He threw himself prone on the earth, and on all fours jumped about with brutish gestures and wild animal howls, gnashing the ground with his teeth or chewing mouthfuls of grass. A more strange or sickening scene it would be difficult to imagine—the snake-charmer, in the paroxysm of mad delirium, grovelling on the earth with the howls and action of a wild beast, his hand still clutching the half-eaten snake; around him the awestruck circle of spectators—the two Europeans fascinated yet disgusted, their Jewish followers shrinking behind them in terror, lest, as sometimes happens on these occasions, the fanatic in his maniacal fury turn upon them; and the believing Moors calling upon Allah and His Prophet, upon Sidi Aissa and all the saints of the Moorish calendar, to save and protect their servant. The deeply-foliaged walnuts threw a sombre shadow over all; the Wad Amsmiz swept past at our side with mournful roar, and far above the grey mountains frowning down upon us in majestic silence.

At times the madman sprang to his feet, tossed his arms with wild entreating gesture towards the heavens, his eyes glaring like an enraged beast or fixed in ecstatic contemplation of space. Then again and again he would snap ravenously at what remained of the limp snake, or once more throw himself down on the ground, clutch it with his claw-like fingers, and roll about in all the abandonment of excruciating agony.

In one of these latter paroxysms Hadj M'hamad slipped to the side of the unconscious and writhing Aissawa, and waiting his opportunity, snatched the remainder of the snake from him, substituting for it a tough piece of raw mutton. Seemingly unconscious of the change, he tore at the mutton with undiminished relish and ferocity. By and bye the height of the frenzy passed away. The man lay still or restlessly rocked himself from side to side. Again Hadj was equal to the occasion. Picking up the tambourine, he commenced slowly dancing and drumming round the other's prostrate form. Soon, but without taking any apparent notice of these attentions, the snake-charmer commenced moving about in a weird, wild dancing step, in which Hadj joined. All at once he sank to the ground paralysed, moaning and quivering as if in his death-throes. Hadj, bending over, vigorously fanned him. The crisis soon passed; the moaning ceased, and his limbs were still. The Moors continually muttered their prayers with bent heads and hands held in an attitude of supplication. The Jews said not a word, and we ourselves were also silent, struck by the impressiveness of the scene in the fast gathering shadows of evening. Finally the Aissawa looked up. His eye wore a softer expression, though the foam still rested about his mouth. His face was haggard and of death-like hue. The deadliness of the poison had been overcome and the delirium driven away. With one voice the Moors acknowledged the greatness and omnipotence of Allah, and hastened to assist the exhausted servant of Sidi Aissa to rise and proceed to the camp-fire, where kief, the earthly consoler, soon soothed his unstrung nerves.

An hour later, while I sat in my tent chronicling these doings as I now place them before you, I was disturbed by my companion calling upon me to come out at once. There was something in his tone which made me lay aside the pen forthwith and hurry out into the darkness. Round the glowing camp-fire our men were gathered, their swarthy lineaments and white robes contrasting picturesquely in the ruddy glare with the fair face and European dress of Mr. Crichton-Browne. While I stood for a moment enjoying the romantic aspect of the scene, my eyes were suddenly attracted to the Aissawa. From the centre of the glowing embers he drew forth a piece of charcoal, held it—I will not say coolly—between the tips of his fingers, while he blew it to a white heat; then with a preliminary "Bismillah!" he calmly put it into his mouth, and leisurely munched, then swallowed it, with evident signs of enjoyment, while the Moors broke into cries of "Allah Akbar!" ("God is great").

Apparently, the Aissawa had eaten his dinner first and was cooking it afterwards. He helped himself to the charcoal, not once or twice, but several times, till evidently he was sure that his snake was thoroughly done. At any rate he had demonstrated to the satisfaction of all the assembled believers that there was none but the one God, that Mohammed was His Prophet, and Sidi Aissa not the least among the saints.

CHAPTER XXI.

GINDAFY.

WE left our charming camp of Imintella as usual at sunrise for our second crossing of the main range. Our route still lay along the Amsmiz stream, crossing its rocky bed every few hundred yards, according as the exigencies of the gorge demanded, and winding through a narrow strip of magnificent walnut trees.

As we pushed our way deeper into the mountains, we remarked the appearance of a new factor in the geology of the Atlas. On the east side of the glen the formation was metamorphic, consisting of clay-slates and schistose rocks pierced by porphyry veins. On the west the rocks were yellow and reddish sandstones and limestones, unconformably overlying the older series, the straight lines of bedding shown along the hillside, and the even terrace-like surface, being in marked contrast with the jagged outlines of the debris-strewn slope of the opposing metamorphic areas.

A mile above camp the cretaceous (?) rocks ended suddenly against the friable clay-slates and greywackes, which abruptly rose from beneath, and towered high up in the central mass of mountains.

In an hour we reached a point where the Wad Amsmiz divides and embraces the massive front of Jebel Tezah, a conspicuous peak in the main axis, ascended by Hooker, and rather erroneously named so by him; "*tezah*" or "*tizi*" simply meaning in the Shellach language a pass or a mountain over which one crosses. The name, however, may be retained for convenience.

Following the chief branch, we found ourselves penetrating in a south-westerly direction deep into the central mass, the gorge narrowing as we proceeded, the slopes rising more abruptly and ruggedly to a height of 9000 feet on our right, and from 10,000 to 11,000 feet on our left. But for the prevalence of walnut trees of great size and an occasional hamlet, we might have imagined we were penetrating a mountain glen in the Southern Scottish Highlands, so similar were the general characteristics of the scene. The surface features and geology were the same; the wild thyme gave the glow and colour of the heather, while spleenworts and scale ferns decked the rocks, and daisies bloomed in every sheltered spot.

Near the division of the stream there were numerous ruins of hamlets, the sight of which at first gave rise to moralisings on the sad results of Moorish misgovernment. We speedily found, however, that the desolation was due to an even more terrible curse, and that some ten years previous a drought and consequent famine had swept off the inhabitants.

Two hours from camp we reached the end of the stream, or rather the point where it breaks up into numerous rivulets, spreading themselves over the face of the peaked mountain that ends the gorge, as Tezah fronts the main glen of the Wad Amsmiz. At this point we had to commence the ascent of the range. In the marvellously clear atmosphere this did not seem a great undertaking, but in reality we had a climb of some 5000 feet before us. A zigzag pathway, apparently fit only for a goat, could be faintly traced running up the mountain-side, marking out the route rather than assisting us in the ascent. The rock formation being an exceedingly friable clay-slate, the slope presented a desolate appearance of barren monotonous uniformity, sparsely dotted over with a few stunted prickly shrubs, and rarely brightened with a flower. The higher we climbed, the steeper and more dangerous became the slope, till we feared we should have to unload what little the mules carried to enable them to struggle to the top. Of all the animals, however, Toby most deserved sympathy. Assor, our interpreter, besides being lame and fat, was totally unaccustomed to mountain-climbing, yet somehow or other we must contrive to get him to the top. His mule not being equal to the task of carrying both him and its small pack, there was nothing for it but to let him ride my horse. The plucky little beast did not belie its reputation for hardiness and sure-footedness, but more than once I held my breath in expectation of some frightful accident, or clung with might and main to Toby's tail in order to avert the impending catastrophe. All along the grey barren slope we saw no sign of bird or other living creature, and the only sounds which fell upon the ear were the mournful sigh of the winds sweeping along the mountain-side, and the melancholy sough of the stream two or three thousand feet below. Our men, however, failed not to waken the echoes of the glen with their cries of threat or of encouragement.

By dint of patience and many persevering struggles we at length reached the top, at an elevation of little short of 10,000 feet. On halting to regain breath and look around, the first thing I became aware of was the disagreeable fact that Gindafy, for which I was bound, did not, like Teluet, lie on the south side of the Atlas, but in the very heart of it. This was a most disappointing discovery; for when I expected to see the southern lower ranges, and even the valley of Sus, at my feet, there lay scattered an opposing though somewhat lower barrier of mountains called Wishdan, and between, the great yawning glen of the Wad Nyfis, running parallel with the main axis. This cleft in the range was Gindafy.

The scene around, however, gradually made us forget for a time our grievous disappointment, for, without exception, it was the grandest and most strikingly varied mountain landscape we had yet seen in the Atlas. A bewildering assemblage of range and peak and glen surrounded us; on all sides serrated outlines and fantastic forms. Five thousand feet beneath were the green fields and terraces of Gindafy. Dark masses of arar and evergreen oak mottled its cradling slopes, and the crests of the circling mountains were chequered with wreaths of dazzling snow. On the east the glen was closed by the great amorphous snow-clad masses over Reraya, which rise to a height of 14,000 feet. To the south the southern tip of the cleft range, having Wishdan as its conspicuous feature, was remarkable for the gleaming aspect of the crystalline limestones which cropped out along its axis. To the west the glen could be seen to divide into two great gorges, separated by a narrow mountain ridge, and quickly closed by the curving round of the Wishdan range to join the one on which we stood. Near the head of the Nyfis, in bold isolation, rose a conspicuous snow-clad peak called Ogdint.

The whole aspect of the scene differed widely from any we had hitherto looked upon farther east. There the Atlas had exhibited table-topped heights, escarped ridges, and straight lines of bedding running like walls of masonry along the ridge of the slopes, while the surface colours had been bright with a rich mottling of red and purple. Here instead was a much more denuded region, distinguished by sharp peaks and ridges, jagged and rugged outlines and slopes, for the most part covered with grey slatey debris of mournfullest aspect. The explanation lay in the geological formation. We were now in a metamorphic area of exceedingly friable clay-slates and stiffening masses of less easily weathered greywackes, while to the east were grey and white limestones and red and purple shales and sandstones of the cretaceous age. Though wanting in some of the effects, and especially in the rich colouring, the mountain scenery around us was more effective and picturesque. What it wanted in massiveness it made up by the sharpness of its fantastic peaks, the serrated outlines of its ridges, the depth of its glens, and the generally more varied character of its outline. But we had still far to go to reach our destination, and we could not afford to spend much time over the landscape around us.

If the ascent of the Tizi Nemiri from the north side had been bad, the descent on the south side seemed from where we stood to be utterly out of the question. Never in the course of all my mountaineering have I seen a mountain path of such exceeding steepness. There was nothing for it, however, but to shrug our shoulders and re-echo our men's pious expressions of trust in Allah that the descent would be accomplished somehow. At the same time, mindful of the saying that "Heaven helps those who help themselves," we failed not to exhort our men to keep firm hold of the mules' tails, as they hoped for a place in Paradise, and to escape punishment at our hands.

In an hour we had descended quite 4000 feet to a lateral feeder of the Nyfis. Our course, though less dangerous, then became more rough and toilsome down the rocky bed of the stream. No Christian mule or horse could ever have descended that rocky defile, but ours, reared in a different religious atmosphere, went along with all the agility and sure-footedness of a goat.

By and bye the narrow rugged glen became an

impassable gorge, and we were compelled to leave it and cut across the mountain buttress or spur which separated us from the main glen of the Nyfis. This was by far the nastiest bit we had yet met with, and more than once with breathless expectancy we watched our mules as they passed dangerous places where the slightest touch of the pack on the opposing cliffs or rocks would have sufficed to precipitate the unlucky animal to the bottom of an abyss. The hair-breadth escapes, seeming or otherwise, were many, keeping us continually on the rack, all the more as mules and men alike were unaccustomed to these mountain paths and dangers, and were alike afraid. Moreover, the drivers were indifferent to our affairs, and were being forced into these wilds against their will. Consequently they cared little what happened to our animals so long as they themselves were safe. Constant threats and remonstrances and never-tiring vigilance were required to keep them to their duty, our enjoyment of the scenes and of the pleasant excitements of the route being thus continually spoiled. In spite of all our precautions, one man all but came to a sad end. A pack suddenly slipped from a mule which was trying to climb up a steep rock, and coming down on the driver before he was aware, nearly hurled him into the depths below.

Without further accident the shoulder of the spur was reached, and there before us, now only a thousand feet below, lay the valley of Gindafy. After the bleak desolateness of the upper heights, the groves and fields which clad the bottom of this mountain cleft looked quite luxuriant, and certainly very pleasing. I was much surprised by the discovery that here, in the very heart of the Atlas, in what was little more than a deep longitudinal hole or pocket in the central axis, was a sharp syncline of red sandstone, like a crust or lining to the sides of the glen, and overlying the metamorphic rocks which form the mass of the chain.

This unexpected sight set my brains aworking, and opened up an interesting vista of geological speculation. Had this little—for little comparatively it could be seen to be—had this little syncline of sandstone, with its angular stones disseminated through it, been simply caught up in the primary folding or crumpling of the rocks which had produced the Atlas range; or had the sandstone been deposited in some mountain tarn, the forerunner of the valley of the present day, and subsequently squeezed into its present form and position by a second series of foldings? The latter theory then and afterwards most commended itself to my mind.

From the point we had now reached we could see numerous villages, but we were specially attracted by the sight of a massive castellated building in the very centre of the valley, past which winded the fine stream of the Nyfis. This building we had no difficulty in identifying as the Kasbah of the Kaid of the province.

We speedily reached the bottom of the glen, and then by an easy pathway pushed on rapidly along the banks of the stream.

It was with no small misgiving that we approached the Kasbah. The glen had only some two or three years before succumbed to the power of the Sultan. The Kaid and his people were known to be still smarting under the ruin brought on them in the long period during which they had strenuously fought for their independence. That independence had only been half lost, and the Sultan's supremacy was more nominal

KASBAH, GINDAFY.

than real. Under these circumstances, we were coming not only in the character of hated infidels, but as *Kaffirs* under the partial protection of their cordially detested master—anything but a recommendation. Our death or spoliation could be followed by no bad consequences to them. We hoped the most, however, from the kindlier feelings and less virulent antipathy to Christians which prevail among the Shellach.

It was nearly sunset when we approached the castle. A couple of hundred yards from it an awkward pause ensued. Assor's mule had lain down and thrown him over its head. A relief party had to return to raise the mule and hoist him on its back. Meanwhile a great flutter was observable about the castle on the sudden appearance of our strange party. People crowded on the roof and the terraces. They filled every door and window, awaiting the development of events. Intense evidently was the speculation as to the meaning of this mysterious inroad into these dangerous and unfrequented parts.

At length two messengers left the castle to accost us, and at the same time Assor came up with us.

Our credentials having been shown, and our rank and dignities announced, we were properly welcomed in the name of the Kaid. The wordy welcome was better than the practical fulfilment. We were led round the castle and shown into a miserable windowless room in an outhouse, reeking with dirt, and evidently swarming with bugs and fleas.

We expressed our indignation in no measured terms, but we were told that that was all the Kaid had to give us. Our *mona* was as scanty as at other places it had been abundant.

Next day matters were no more encouraging. The Kaid would not see us or receive our messengers, and no food was sent, a fact which on the plains would have made our gluttonous men rage like demons, but here only threw them into a state of sullen resignation, born of the fear of worse to follow. Defiantly we tried to penetrate within the precincts of the castle, but had the door slammed ignominiously in our faces; and, fearful of a bullet from one of the flint-locks carried by the mountaineers on the castle-walls, we retired crestfallen. We were watched on all sides as dangerous animals, whose habits must be carefully studied before they could be approached with safety or even tolerated in the vicinity.

It was late in the afternoon before a satisfactory conclusion was come to, but Assor did at length get an audience of the Kaid, and again we were made welcome.

We were now permitted to leave our vermin-infested room and camp in an olive grove a couple of hundred yards down the stream. Our hopes brightened further when, later on, the Kaid—El Taiby by name—came to visit us, and showed a physiognomy by no means repellent, and suggesting some force of character. Nothing could have been more promising than his assurances, and on his leaving we at once set about drawing up our programme of excursions, with a due regard to the claims of geography, geology, botany, and mouflon-hunting. The Kaid had said we might go wherever we liked, but in Morocco bridges rarely lead from promise to realisation. For my friend at least there was to be no realisation this time. About midnight, while writing my diary, I was suddenly disturbed by C.-B. coming to me in some excitement and evident pain, borne, however, with the utmost stoicism, to tell me that he had just been stung by a scorpion while putting on his pyjamahs. He was still grabbing hold of the latter with the venomous insect inside. We soon disposed of the scorpion, and proceeded at once to apply undiluted *eau de luce* to the spot on C.-B.'s thigh which marked the sting. So copious was the application that several inches of skin peeled off. To further counteract the poison, from which fatal effects were not unknown, I thoroughly dosed the sufferer with brandy, of which we happened to have a single bottle, with the happy result that he soon became quite talkative and jocular over his really painful wound. Although no dangerous results followed, C.-B. was *hors de combat* for the next fortnight, than which nothing could have been more annoying to his ardent temperament and his eagerness to make the most of the opportunities afforded to us.

Next day, on my trying to take advantage of the leave given us to go wherever we liked, the old troubles began. A score of obstacles were at once thrown in my way. No guide or escort was ready, and the Kaid was declared to be asleep and could not be disturbed. I went off a short walk by myself, and this led to a display of the utmost excitement and the most energetic protests. Hour after hour went past, and then it became too late to do what we proposed.

Matters seemed to improve in the afternoon, for the Kaid, nettled at hearing so much of the magnificence of El Glauwi, sought to throw him into the shade with the vulgar display of the parvenu he in truth was. He sent for our inspection some of the most beautifully worked daggers with gold and silver sheaths that we ever saw in Morocco. Afterwards he came himself with quite a bundle of huge coarsely made women's jewellery in gold and silver. The gold and the silver were the proceeds of the spoliation of the valley by the late Kaid when by power of arms he reduced all the petty Sheiks and transformed himself into their paramount lord. He had just succeeded in establishing his position, after several years' struggle against the combined forces of all the neighbouring governors, when he had to succumb to the authority of the Sultan.

To ensure that his daggers and jewellery should not cost anything, the Kaid's father had employed a Jew of Amsmiz to work on them for over two years, then paid him the stipulated amount and sent him away rejoicing, immediately after, by order of his employer, to be murdered and robbed as he passed through the gorge of the Nyfis. For our inspection Taiby also sent his horse trappings, which undoubtedly were extremely valuable and gorgeous. There were three sets of bridles and saddles one mass of gold and silk. We calculated that each would cost from £150 to £200—that is to say, if they had been paid for, but the gold was the hard-won money of the poor mountaineers. As for the workmanship, which was of the best, it had not cost much either; for an Algerian Moor famed for his skill in this class of work was beguiled into the mountains, and there forcibly kept for twenty years, with no better remuneration than his food and clothes. That at least was the man's own story.

The Kaid having, as he thought, outdone El Glauwi by the magnificence of his vulgar display, and also duly raised himself in our estimation, became somewhat mollified. He promised to let us visit some reported caves up the Wad Agandice, one of the principal tributaries of the Nyfis, and uniting with the main river a couple of miles below our camp.

True enough, in the morning no obstacle was thrown in my way. A couple of guides were provided and off I started; C.-B. very much disgusted at being compelled to remain behind. The reported wonderful caves proved to be an utter fraud, or, if they did exist, they were not shown to us. All that we saw were some petty excavations in the face of a cliff, formed by the natives in search of the iron ore which here and there occurs in small veins and pockets.

We had no reason, however, to regret being led to the Wad Agandice by false reports. Following the course of the stream to where it seemed to disappear in the precipitous front of Wishdan, we turned a spur of the mountain, and found ourselves at the entrance of the most magnificent gorge or cañon it has ever been my lot to see—such an one, indeed, as may be found in America, but seldom seen elsewhere. Imagine a great yawning crack running right across a range of mountains. Picture yourselves at the bottom. On either side you look skyward over 5000 feet of beetling cliffs and precipices, broken into by areas of extremely steep slopes and deep-cut crevices, and capped by fantastic rocky peaks and turret-like masses. Pine-like arar trees give a dark shaggy covering to the ravines, and add picturesqueness to the cliffs and frowning projections. Intermingled are patches of the brighter green prickly oak. For almost the first time the Atlas presents some of the savage grandeur and awe-inspiring effects one connects with a mountain range reaching heights of 12,000 and 13,000 feet. Everywhere before there had been something to disappoint us. Here it was not so. There was neither the frightful feeling of desolation and death, nor the grievous monotony of outline which had so frequently oppressed us at other places. The arar and the juniper were in unusual luxuriance, and in keeping with the rugged rocks. The roar of the turbulent boiling torrent accorded well with the feelings of awe and wild exhilaration which the scene evoked, and the unusually fine strip of walnut and almond, carob, poplar, and ash, which bordered its banks served to throw into relief the wilder aspects of the frowning mountain-sides.

Up this yawning cañon we struggled and splashed, compelled to wade up the bed of the river, stumbling unexpectedly as we went into deep pools or over obstructing unseen blocks. Of almost as much interest as the scenic effects was the insight into the geological structure given by this magnificent rock section.

For the first mile we crossed the vertical much-smashed crystalline limestones which form the northern half of Wishdan, then with great abruptness right across the axis of the mountain the metamorphic area became replaced by more massive beds of yellow sandstones and purple and blue shales and grey masses of limestone. Between these we detected an intruded layer of diorite, and farther on a conformable bed of basalt tuff or breccia, evidently contemporaneous with the igneous rocks.

About four miles from the entrance to the gorge the stream divides, one branch flowing from the east and the snow-clad heights of the Tizi-n-Tamjurt overlooking Tifnut, and the other from the south-west behind Wishdan. Here the scenery attained its most strikingly varied aspect and grandest effects; for from a projecting mountain-shoulder we could command a view into three great gorges, each of surpassing interest in its wild savagery.

On reaching this point, my thoughts became divided between the scene before me and another sight which presented itself farther ahead. The mountains which closed in the view in that direction seemed to have a low elevation as compared with the main mountain mass through which we had passed by the Agandice gorge. What if I could reach the top? Tifnut would then be at my feet on the left, and Ras el Wad and the valley of the Sus on my right.

Our soldiers, however, had received orders to go no farther than the division of the stream where the Kaid's authority ended and the territory of inimical mountain tribes began. Moors, however, I argued to myself, would do anything for money, so I took the leading soldier aside and tipped him the wink very broadly, not to speak of giving him a sight of a massive coin. He looked intelligent, and the minute after, accompanied only by himself and Shalum, I was puffing up the mountain-side. We had not, however, got more than a thousand feet above the stream when our guide, as if all unconscious of what we intended to do when we started, commenced energetically protesting against any attempt to go farther. "It was against the Kaid's orders. We would all be killed." Another dollar acted like oil on the troubled waters, and again I pushed on with feverish energy, hopeful, yet fearful, of success. It was no use, however. Our guide became more and more excited and noisy. He placed himself time after time in our way, and with the gesture and looks of a madman demanded that we should turn back. He did not hesitate to draw his sword, nor to make a show of lifting his gun at us, and otherwise conducted himself with such terrible earnestness, that I could not believe he was acting merely to extort more money from us.

By dint, however, of maintaining a determined front, and the timely doling out of sundry further francs, we were allowed to proceed stage by stage. At each new effort we thought our end would be gained, and always we were disappointed. The extraordinary purity of the atmosphere made heights extremely deceptive, while each ridge was attained only to find another and higher beyond.

At length, after a terrific scene of yelling, gesticulation, and wild threats, I was reluctantly compelled to give in. We could easily have forced our way in spite of the guide, but we knew that such action would utterly spoil any chance of exploring farther about Gindafy. Then the day was on the wane, the heat was terrific, and I was exceedingly ill from indigestion, from which I had been suffering for two or three weeks.

Having unfortunately left my aneroid in camp, I could only roughly estimate our height at 8000 feet, and that probably another 300 or 400 feet remained to be scaled.

Crestfallen and disappointed, we now turned campwards, and safely reached our tents at nightfall.

That was the first and last bit of exploration we accomplished from Gindafy. The old work of treachery had commenced. The friendly relations which were springing up between the Kaid and us were soon blighted by the evil machinations of our men, who, ever fearful of that dreaded journey into Sus or worse places, stopped at nothing to secure its defeat.

We were confined as prisoners to our tents, and on no account allowed to go outside. Bluster and threats were as useless as expostulations and promises. It was terribly hard, however, to find ourselves in such a centre of exploration and be compelled to leave it with so little done. But we were enveloped in the unseen, intangible meshes of a net, from which we could do nothing to free ourselves. We were avoided by the inhabitants, and had almost no food sent to us. In spite of everything, we held out for a couple of days, in the desperate expectation that something might turn up; but at last, seeing how hopeless the case was, and how increasingly dangerous our position was becoming, we reluctantly made up our minds to return to Amsmiz.

On the 3rd of July we left camp. A mile to the east the narrow valley suddenly contracts into a narrow gorge or glen, where the red sandstones end and the metamorphic rocks begin. The glen of the Wad Nyfis, unlike most of those we had hitherto followed in the mountains, wound in great curves, here expanding somewhat, there contracting to the merest gorge, due to the presence of intercalated stiffening masses of greywacke among the friable clay-slates. Many of the curves of the Nyfis were very picturesque, with their outer grand sweep of steep rocky mountains, the glistening semicircle of rushing water at their base, and the projecting spur or cone running into the concavity, crowned as usual by some quaint village, surrounded by its olive and walnut groves, its cultivated terraces, and tree-shaded irrigation channels. Every now and then ravine openings gave us peeps into the higher ranges beyond.

An hour from camp the Wad Teguna joins the Wad Nyfis, its sharp defile affording a route leading down the shoulders of the Tizi-n-Tamjurt to Tifnut. The Nyfis itself, it should be remarked, affords not only an

entrance into the valley of Gindafy, but is the chief route by way of Wishdan to Ras el Wad.

We were greatly delighted during our descent of the glen to find some undoubted remnants of lateral moraines at various heights on the mountain-sides, with boulders in several instances unmistakably striated. At one or two places also we were so fortunate as to discover some smoothed and polished rock surfaces, which had been preserved unaltered by a covering of moraine debris.

About half way down the glen we camped at the village of Tinesk, on the Wad Ait Hosein, which flows from the north side of Jebel Tezah.

Next day we left the glen of the Wad Nyfis and struck across the Tizi-n-Gerimt at Amsmiz. Our wonder was continually evoked, in crossing these frightfully desolate heights, as to where the inhabitants of the numerous small hamlets, which clung like clay-mounds to the mountain-sides, found subsistence. Yet the people seemed well off, and contrasted favourably with the miserable and poverty-stricken looking Arabs of such fertile plains as Bled Hummel.

At mid-day we re-entered Amsmiz, and resumed our former flea and bug infested quarters.

CHAPTER XXII.

MAROSSA AND THE ASIF EL MEL.

From the Tizi Nemiri and the valley of Gindafy my attention had been attracted by a snow-streaked peak at the head of the Wad Nyfis, which rose conspicuously far above the neighbouring heights.

A great desire to visit and ascend this mountain had taken possession of me, and on my return to Amsmiz, I determined to attempt the adventure.

By dint of inquiry, I discovered that there were two routes—one a roundabout, by way of the Asif el Mel and Marossa, the other a direct one across the mountains. I resolved to take the former, to enable me to throw the Kalifa off the scent by pretending that I only wanted to visit the petty province of Marossa.

In order not to be thwarted in my enterprise by my men, I resolved only to take three. One, of course, was the ever-willing and faithful Shalum, the second Zemrani, on whom I could depend fairly well, and the third Abdarachman—the beau ideal of the insinuating and treacherous Moor, a perfect Moorish Iago. This last we took with us as interpreter. He had picked up a strange medley of frightful oaths and cant phrases from English and Spanish sailors while working as a Mogador dock-labourer. These fragments of speech he employed in such an unusual fashion that frequently we could not help laughing, even when his language was of the lowest, it being clear that he had rarely any idea what it meant. He knew, however, a few common sentences fairly well, and with these and what I myself knew of Arabic, we contrived to get along somehow. That he would do his best to have us stopped before getting far into the mountains I felt quite certain; but he would be unsupported, except by the soldier, and by dint of careful watching we hoped to neutralise his evil influence. Assor and the rest of the men were left behind with C.-B., who still was unfit for much travelling—a state of things as much due to the very drastic character of the cure as to the sting of the scorpion.

It was my policy to take both my men and the natives by surprise. I therefore struck while it was hot, and before any one had time for reflection.

The Kalifa made no objection to supply us with a guide to the comparatively safe district of Marossa, though he ordered the soldier who was to act in that capacity not on any account to allow us to go farther, or to cross the mountains.

On the 6th July, the second day after our arrival from Gindafy, we left Amsmiz. For some twelve miles we travelled rapidly west, skirting the base of the abruptly rising outer heights, most prominent and unusually picturesque among which was the scaured and rugged limestone peak of Jebel Tisgin, rising to an estimated height of nearly 8000 feet.

On our right spread northwards the Plain of Morocco in its yellow garb. Shortly after our start we crossed the Wad Tinirt, and some miles farther ahead the Wad Ait Bur, both refreshingly bordered with olive groves and green fields, thanks to their irrigating waters.

In somewhat more than three hours we reached the Asif el Mel, a mountain stream of no great dimensions in the summer, but which later on becomes a raging impassable torrent, as the depth and character of the channel sufficiently showed.

At this point we turned sharply south into the mountains by way of the glen of the Asif el Mel. The scenery along our route calls for no detailed description. The glen winds in many sharp short curves, with slopes comparatively smooth and even, rising to a height of two to three thousand feet overhead. The formations are clay-slates with a capping of cretaceous rocks, the escarped faces of which help to break the monotony of the view.

Midway up the glen we passed the village of Albedur, and shortly after mid-day a second, called Tiginsdel, at the commencement of the tiny Kaidship of Marossa.

At 1.30 we reached the head of the glen of the Asif el Mel, and the residence of the Kaid. We found the Kaid and his people up in arms. All the inhabitants of the glens beyond were at war with him, and only a short time before had burned his house to the ground and carried off nearly everything he possessed. Naturally he was by no means pleased to see us, as only adding to his responsibilities. He would not hear of our pitching my tent outside, as he was in daily expectation of further attacks. With some difficulty a room was found for me—alive with vermin, as usual—and there I took up my quarters.

At Marossa the Atlas springs up very abruptly from the 5000 feet of its lower ranges to more than double that height, or from 10,000 to 11,000 feet. At the same place the glen of the Asif el Mel divides into three profound gorges—those of the Wad Ait Gair running south-west, and of the Wad Amsmetirt, to the south, cutting deep into the heart of the range. The third, or defile of the Wad Erght, is of less imposing depth, and runs east along the line of junction of the upper and lower heights. Between the Wads Erght and Amsmetirt lies the extremely precipitous and conspicuous mountain of Wirzan. The cretaceous rocks attain a development of some 2000 to 3000 feet at Marossa, where they end abruptly against the main axis, a great fault marking their junction with the metamorphic strata. Though almost horizontal to within a hundred yards of this fault, the sandstones and limestones are there tilted and crumpled in the most remarkable manner. This interesting fault runs in an almost straight line along the base of the main chain to the division of the Wad Amsmiz.

That night at Marossa was one of the most uncomfortable I had experienced in Morocco. Foreseeing that it would be one of wrestling, I took such precautions as I could to improve my situation. I had happily provided myself with some insect-powder, and this I liberally distributed over the cork mattress and rug which formed my bed. Then I thoroughly dusted my sleeping suit inside and out, besides carefully tucking my pyjamahs into my socks. Thereafter I drew forth a huge cotton bag, specially carried for such occasions, and put myself inside, tying it well round my neck. Thus enveloped, I smiled as I thought how thoroughly I had outwitted the enemy, and in hopeful mood lay down. Soon I closed my eyes and—and did not fall asleep. The heat in my unventilated bag was excessive, and I speedily streamed with perspiration. Mosquitoes began buzzing outrageously about my ears, and what with their sharp itching stings and my inability to slaughter one, or in any way to let off my wrath, I was by and by reduced to a state of madness. I am certain, too, that one or two rats, discovering my helpless condition, enjoyed the exciting amusement of scuttling across me. How I tossed, and groaned, and sighed, and cursed (as far as my principles would permit)! At length, drenched and dripping, itching all over my face and neck, and "frenetic to be free," I burst my bonds, and tearing that delusive bag open, struck out wildly in the darkness of night. It was undoubtedly an immense temporary relief to let off my passion in action, no matter how inane, but the rubbing of afflicted parts only served to add to the irritation. Of course, a perfect battalion of fleas took advantage of the break in my defences to precipitate themselves inside the bag, and then it was all up with me. The morning found me limp, bedraggled and dishevelled, feverish and irritable. It required all the soothing virtues of deep potations of tea to bring me back to my normal condition.

The 7th being Saturday, or the Jews' Sunday, Shalum would on no account ruin his character by travelling, though addicted to breaking nearly all the other commandments. We could not, of course, travel without him, and were perforce compelled to stay at Marossa.

Lured by the report that caves of the Rum were on the other side of the glen, we went thither; but as at Agandice, found them to be a fraud. More interesting, however, were the ruins of some singular massive walls, thirty yards in diameter, which we discovered encircling an isolated hill. These walls were three feet thick, and well built with stone and lime. They may possibly have been merely fortifications, but that I think doubtful.

With the exception of a walk to the mouth of the Wad Amsmetirt gorge, the Kaid would on no account allow us to explore in his neighbourhood.

Next morning we ostensibly commenced our return to Amsmiz by way of the mountains. It was understood we were to stop at a place called Erduz, which I had contrived to discover lay on the way to Ogdimt, as well as to Amsmiz. Our guide, quite unsuspicious of my intentions, made no trouble about varying our return route. Travelling east, we ascended the glen of the Wad Erght, which runs along the line of fault, and junction of the cretaceous and metamorphic series. The road was rather nasty at places. Abdarachman's mule coming against a projecting rock with its pack, was precipitated over a low cliff, but, strange to relate, landed on its feet.

Half way up the glen we crossed a terminal moraine formed by a glacier descending from the heights of Wirzan. The moraine was full of great polished sub-angular blocks in a matrix of finer material. Some of these blocks had been weathered out, and now crowned short pillars of the matrix, presenting the appearance of gigantic mushrooms.

In about two hours we reached the top of the glen, and found immediately beyond us another glen running at right angles to our route.

Still following the base of the upper range and the line of fault, we reached about 10 A.M. the wonderfully fertile valley of the Wad Erduz, and bivouacked in a grove of the finest walnuts we had seen in the Atlas. The rest of the day was devoted to botanising, with excessively poor results.

We here noticed some women watering plots of ground, to which water could not be conveyed by channels.

My fears that Abdarachman might yet succeed in thwarting my plans were considerably intensified on finding him in earnest talk with the soldier-guide and the Sheik of the village. That more villainy was in the wind was soon made certain by Shalum coming to me and by words and signs letting me know that Abdarachman was up to some mischief or other. All day long he had acted as if he could not translate into English anything said to me, and otherwise made himself as artificially dull and stupid as possible. None the less he understood very well the blowing-up I gave him and my angry tones and gestures.

That evening I sat solitarily, wondering whether I should succeed on the morrow in my attempt. I bitterly contrasted in my mind the hopefulness and trust with which I had faced infinitely greater trials and dangers in the wildest depths of Central Africa with the feelings I now experienced at finding myself so helpless before the underhand treachery of one or two Moorish servants.

My thoughts kept me long awake as I lay wrapped in my rug on the hard ground, canopied by a gigantic overarching walnut-tree, my eyes sometimes attracted to the stars seen twinkling through the branches, more often to the fire-lit face of Abdarachman, for whom I wished many unutterable things. It is impossible, however, to travel all day and remain awake all night, especially in a bracing mountain atmosphere. In time the not unpleasant rush of the stream at our feet, the low tones of my men's voices, and the soothing sound of rustling leaves sent me into oblivion. Thither Abdarachman could not come to disturb me, nor did the hard ground make my sleep less sound or enjoyable.

CHAPTER XXIII.

THE ASCENT OF JEBEL OGDIMT.

At daybreak I awoke with dew-washed face, refreshed and braced up to encounter, with renewed courage, the difficulties and troubles before me.

A cup of tea and a couple of eggs disposed of, I asked Shalum the way to Ogdimt. This was my first intimation of the goal I had in view, and every one stood speechless, though Shalum instinctively pointed out the road. The attractive expression disappeared from Abdarachman's face, and rage and fright expressed themselves in his chameleon eyes. Our soldier-guide in time found voice, and protested with voluble energy against any attempt to proceed farther. He quoted the governor's orders. In my calmest but most determined manner I told him that the governor's orders were matters of the utmost indifference to me, that he himself could go back if he pleased, but that to Ogdimt I would go. The soldier, however, dared not leave me. He wept, implored, cursed, and generally comported himself like a madman, but for sole answer I mounted my mule and moved Ogdimt-wards.

That the enterprise was a dangerous one was evident

from the blank faces of Shalum and Zemrani, who showed no great alacrity in following me. For a time the guide kept pace with me, laying hold of my clothes, entreating, even threatening me, but I was immovable. Finding all his arts in vain, he was fain to mount his donkey, never ceasing for over an hour to curse his fate, and calling upon Allah, the Prophet, and the saints to stop me. Abdarachman with more malice was overheard trying to comfort him by the expression of a hope that this time I would be killed, and release them from further service with such a cursed infidel. That, however, was poor comfort to the soldier, however innocent he might be, for my death would mean his incarceration for life in a horrible dungeon.

That there was some little danger in penetrating to Ogdimt, however, was made apparent when even Shalum and Zemrani, on our arrival at the foot of the main axis, refused to budge another step till I loaded my rifle, guns, and revolver, and held them ready for action. Thus prepared for whatever might happen, we set ourselves to scale the excessively steep crest of the central mass of the range, which so far we had only skirted.

We had not ascended more than a thousand feet above the mountain step or terrace of Erduz, when we found ourselves enveloped in a dense mist. Our men ceased their talk, and even the soldier sank into silence, as we slowly zigzagged upward and penetrated deeper and deeper into the all-enveloping mist, which might also prove to them their shroud and winding-sheet. For over an hour and a half more we continued the ascent, seeing almost nothing but one another appearing and disappearing in the mist. At the end of that time, however, we were delighted to note a gradual lighting up of our surroundings, and in half an hour we emerged rom the cloud zone and found an intensely clear blue sky overhead, and underneath one of the most weirdly beautiful and striking spectacles it is possible to imagine.

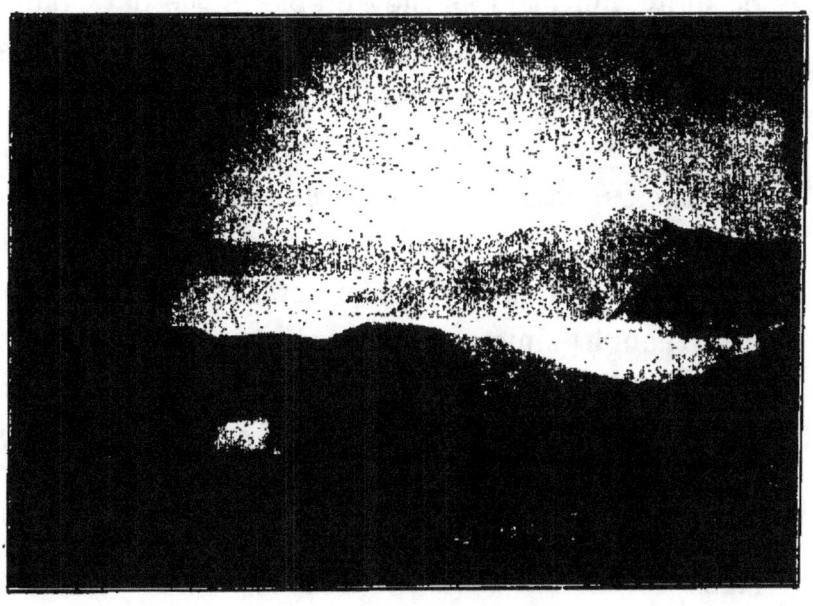

THE CLOUD SCENE, TIZI NSLIT.

The monotonous grey mist through which we had passed stretched out before us in an illimitable ghostly sea ot tumbling billows, breaking in snow-white foam. From this fleecy expanse of dazzling white the main axis of the Atlas rose sharply defined, its frowning mass in marked contrast to the sea of clouds, though patches and streaks of snow still defied the summer sun. From the central ridge a number of spurs projected towards the north, forming jutting headlands and promontories, between which the snowy clouds penetrated like so many arms of the sea. That nothing should be wanting to complete the illusion, the cloud billows driven before a morning breeze dashed themselves against the apparent precipitous rocky coast-line, and were transformed into the most perfect resemblance of spray and foam as they crept up the dark mountain sides. The whole scene was made more impressive, more spectral, by the preternatural silence which prevailed. Such a combination of the weird, the beautiful, and the grand I have never elsewhere seen.

Gradually, as I stood giving myself up to the influence of the marvellous spectacle, the fog began to lift, though almost imperceptibly, dissipated by the morning breeze and the ever-increasing heat of the sun. One or two of the more prominent elevations of the lower mountain terraces peeped out from the encircling cloud wreaths, and showed themselves like black rocks and islands, round which the ghostly billows dashed and foamed, though to the ear came neither roar nor murmur.

I could have dearly wished to sit and watch the slowly changing scene, and the disrobing of all the features of the hidden landscape below; but we had still far to go, and dangers and difficulties lay in our way, so, after hurriedly photographing the scene in the hope of fixing on paper some of its fascinating aspects, I resumed my tramp.

Soon we reached the Tizi Nslit, the pass which leads over the Atlas range to the district of Ogdimt. The landscape panorama which now held us enthralled was of a very different character from the one we had just turned from. To the south and south-west no clouds threw the glamour of another world over a magnificent assemblage of sharp, barren mountain ridges, profound gorges, and glens, all grouped round one grand central mass, which, snow-streaked and commanding, reared its massive head far above the surrounding mountains. That central mass was the mountain of Ogdimt, my immediate goal.

My men made one more attempt to turn me back at this point with highly coloured representations of the wildness of the independent Berbers who occupied Ogdimt. Here they declared the long cuttlefish arms of the Government could not reach, and nothing would give the mountaineers more pleasure than cutting the throat of one who to them would appear not only as an infidel but as a spy.

Arguments and warnings like these had often been dunned in my ears, but, as before, I remained deaf, and set my face towards the mountain. From the pass of Nslit a gradually deepening glen led downward to the inhabited zone and the head-waters of the Wad Nyfis. Besides its cañon-like depth and narrowness, and its grim and enclosing mountain walls, the glen presented no feature specially worthy of note, though there were places where we had some uncomfortable half minutes in skirting precipices and

JEBEL OGDIMT FROM THE TIZI NSLIT.

ascending or descending places verging on the impassable.

After a time we crossed a wall-like ridge, and entered a glen running parallel to that of the Tizi Nslit. It was with no small difficulty that we reached the bed of this glen, but thereafter our way was comparatively easy as we rode down among cultivated terraces and through groves of walnuts and almonds, getting peeps here and there of oddly perched Berber villages, stuck on the steep mountain-sides like swallows' nests against a weathered and ruined wall.

My men wanted me to stop at the first village we came to, but that did not suit my purpose, and I doggedly held on my way, though not without fear that the villagers might turn us back or end our farther progress in an even more unpleasant fashion. No such disagreeable incident occurred, however, though it was evident from the demeanour of the natives that they were extremely suspicious of our intentions, and were not quite sure how to receive the first Christian who had ever ventured into their mountain fastnesses. Some time after mid-day we reached the noisy stream of the Wad Nyfis, and on its banks I camped under shady walnut-trees and hemmed in by enormous precipices. Matters looked far from promising. Nobody came to speak to us except one old man, who was sent to inquire our objects in venturing into those parts, and generally to take note of us and our doings. From among the rocks and trees, however, armed men could be seen peering out, keeping a close watch upon us, and making us feel distinctly uncomfortable as we thought of possible "pot shots." My men thought it more than uncomfortable—dangerous, in fact—as people from the plain were looked upon in the light of enemies by the mountaineers. It was therefore more than the cold breeze from the snow-streaked mountains which caused them to sit doubled up, the picture of wretchedness, awaiting what Allah might send, and no doubt wondering what heinous sins they had committed that He had doomed them to be dragged at the heels of a hated Christian into these wild and dangerous parts. Shalum was the least concerned of the party, accustomed as he was, in his character of Jewish trader, to venture with impunity into the worst parts of the Atlas.

If we had had something to eat we might have taken a more cheerful view of the situation, but nothing was forthcoming, and an empty stomach does not dispose one to take a sanguine view of things. Happily towards evening matters somewhat improved. One or two villagers came into our camp, and these were cajoled and bribed into bringing us some eggs, rancid butter, barley-meal scones, and walnuts, on which we made a sparing meal.

For the first time since we left Mogador, we were able to indulge in the luxury of a splendid camp-fire. So far charcoal fires, which required the aid of bellows, had not realised our ideal of that important adjunct of camp life.

As the night passed on I withdrew from the cheerful

blaze, and in the privacy of my tiny tent sought to solve the problem how I was to reach the top of that mountain mass which lay so tantalisingly near and yet seemed so unattainable.

My cogitations brought me no consolation, and I could only make myself cheerful by reiterating to myself that "it had to be ascended somehow."

That "somehow" was still undefined on turning out of my rug—I cannot say my bed—next morning. To give up the attempt was out of the question, however. I could not consult with my men, that would have ensured failure, and with Shalum, the only one on whom I could at all depend, I unfortunately could not hold converse. But there was no time to lose, as the entire day would require to be devoted to the task.

I therefore called the old man who had visited us the day previous. I explained to him that I wanted to collect some medicinal herbs which I had been told grew on the slopes of these mountains. To this he objected at once. No stranger was ever allowed to go there, and all the people in the different glens were at constant feud and looking out for whomsoever they could shoot. The sight of some dollars made him take a more hopeful view of the situation, however, and, to my delighted surprise, he offered to take me to a shoulder of the mountain which he pointed out to me. That was all I wanted. Once away from the village, and Abdarachman and the soldier left behind, I felt sure of attaining my object.

The bargain was clinched at once, and taking with

me only Shalum and the soldier, I started off accompanied by our old Berber friend and a companion, an addition I did not so much like. Crossing the stream, we at once commenced the steep ascent of the sharp ridge which runs east from the central mass and divides the upper course of the Wad Nyfis. I pushed on with a certain feverish energy, trying my powers to the utmost. To my delight, I soon discovered that the soldier was lagging wearily behind, the result largely of his bang-smoking. With well-simulated commiseration for his weakness, I stopped, and taking my rifle from him, told him he might go back to the camp. Suspecting no trick, he gladly turned down the mountain. I was now free of my chief danger, and for the first time assured of success. The guides were ahead, and with a look at Shalum and a nod at the peak overhead, I apprised him of my intention. Shalum smiled grimly, and for answer buckled up his voluminous clothes a little more, and took the rifle from me.

Half-way up the steep shoulder of the ridge, the view of the end of the Wad Nyfis glen looked very striking. From our camp the stream divided and spread itself out in a semicircle of radiating torrents, cut off from each other by narrow ridges which broadened and heightened till merged in the semicircle of snow-streaked mountains which circumscribed the view and formed the watershed. So complete was the semicircle, so regular the radiation of the stream and ridges from a small central hill, that I was irresistibly set thinking of a cyclopean wheel, of which the hill was the hub, and the ridges the giant spokes running into the great rim. All the streams were sharply marked out by fringing walnut trees and green terraces, above or among which stood picturesquely situated villages, the whole in refreshing contrast to the barren grey ridges on which hardly any vegetation found a footing or hid the jagged metamorphic rocks and their weathered debris.

In two hours we ascended 4000 feet, and had attained an elevation of about 9000. We were here on the crest of the sharp ridge, and from it I was delighted to get a good view of the Sus Valley and the glen of the Wad Nyfis, from which I had been driven a week before by the Kaid or governor of the district. I could afford to laugh at him now. At this point our guides sat down with the air of men who had got to their farthest limit and meant it to be mine also. To this I made no remonstrance. Happily Shalum was one of those men to whom a wink and a nod are sufficient to convey no end of things, and by that simple means I told him, "You wait here for a time with these two men, while I, on pretence of collecting plants and beetles, make for the peak;" and he, with his cunning Jewish eye, told me to "leave it to him and he would pick me up."

I would not, perhaps, have started off with such a light heart if I had known how the pass over into Sus was infested by robbers on the outlook for chance travellers, as well as by the armed sentinels who continually kept watch on the passes and glens. As long as I was in sight of my guides, I was assiduous in my naturalising, but soon I got an elevation between me and them, and then I literally took to my heels and ran along the ridge of the grassy slope for quite half a mile. No one was yet in sight, but I soon descried Shalum hurriedly following up and alone.

I could not learn from him how he had got away from the guides, but he made it clear to me that there was still risk of being stopped besides danger to our lives, and he hurried me on till it seemed as if we were running a race. Without breaking into a run, we tramped along at our utmost walking rate, determined that we would keep a good distance between the mountaineers and ourselves.

As we reached the pass which leads from Ogdimt to Sus, Shalum, who was fully conversant with the dangers of the country, placed himself ostentatiously at my side, holding my express rifle ready for instant use, while by voice and gesture he hounded me to greater exertion. I laughed at the time at his precautions, though touched by his solicitude on my behalf. And yet his presence and the ready rifle probably saved my life, for at that very moment, all unconscious to myself, I was under the cover of the gun of a mountaineer, who, hidden behind a rock, watched my passing. In spite of Shalum's precaution, one of us would probably have dropped before the robber's fire, but our guides had meanwhile discovered our flight, and at that moment had raised a tremendous hue and cry behind us. We turned but to see where they were, and then gave renewed speed to our movements—not so much that we were afraid of them alone, but in case they got assistance to stop us. That this fear was not without grounds we soon discovered on looking round and seeing our pursuers joined by two other men, who seemed to have sprung from the earth. These were two Ogdimt robbers, who had been on the point of shooting us from behind a rock near which we had passed.

For a time our way was comparatively easy, along the crest of the ridge leading towards the peak, and we made splendid progress. This, however, ended abruptly, and to our dismay we found ourselves confronted by a jagged piece of crystalline limestone, projecting like a gigantic saw from the back of the ridge. For a moment we despaired of being able to pass, but at length, with some difficulty, we succeeded in getting over the nasty obstacle.

We now began to feel comparatively safe, our guides and their friends having rather lost on us, though they never ceased to gesticulate wildly and scream vociferously to us to stop or come back. Still Shalum, who had fallen behind some distance, kept urging me to peg away; and peg away I did as if for dear life, though the exertion was frightful at the elevation of over 10,000 feet we had now attained. After crossing the jagged crystalline limestone barrier, a terribly steep part lay before us. My legs were trembling with the unusual exertion, while the rarefied condition of the atmosphere made breathing painful. This steep part over, we need fear no opposition, however, and therefore I went for it with all the will and energy I possessed.

By slow degrees, and with many short stops, this step was accomplished, and I fell rather than sat down beside a patch of snow, of which I eagerly ate to assuage my thirst. Shortly after Shalum rejoined me, and later still the guides, foaming and full of wrath, but, thanks to their age, more exhausted than I was.

What made me feel rather uneasy was the disappearance of the two men who had joined them at the pass. Could they have gone to get reinforcements? and was I going to run into a trap?

Meanwhile my escort by turns entreated and threatened to get us to turn back, but seeing me determined and implacable, and feeling their inability to stop us, they yielded to the necessities of the situation and the seducing influence of a couple of dollars, and gave up all opposition. Still I was suspicious, and lost no time in recommencing the ascent of the remaining and most difficult part, though it seemed but the work of an hour. We had not well set out, however, before we were confronted with the very nastiest piece of rock-climbing I had ever encountered. This was another jagged outcrop of weathered crystalline limestone, projecting in dangerous teeth, where a fall of a few feet would have produced the most terrible wounds. To evade this barrier meant a considerable descent, and I therefore tried to cross it, as in the other case; but after a painful and perilous attempt I was forced to give it up on reaching an impassable overhanging abyss. To return was now nearly as difficult as to go on, but happily, after much loss of time and a dangerous descent, I found a middle path, by which I managed to scramble to the foot of the ridge. I had now to struggle over a nasty talus of loose debris, lying at such a high angle that at each step I slipped down the hill, and more than once I thought I would have gone to the bottom of the mountain in the midst of an avalanche of stones.

The limestone precipices thus rounded, I had to recommence the ascent, a task of no small difficulty in the loose, slippery rubbish. Moreover, I now felt the result of the race I had run to escape from my keepers. I had overstrained both limbs and lungs. This, combined with the ever-increasing height, made each step a painful toil, so that every few moments I had to sit down to recover myself.

All this time I was alone, as Shalum and the natives had taken their own roads and been lost sight of. After a series of determined spurts, I thought my task was nearly accomplished, when to my dismay I found myself at the foot of a new precipice 150 feet in height, which not only seemed impregnable, but shut off the view in the direction I was chiefly anxious to survey. As I sat down in disgust and disappointment to recover breath, my almost despairing gaze fell upon a narrow rift in the rock which I determined to try, relying upon the sharp projections and the undiminished strength of my arms to bring me safely to the top.

The climb was safely accomplished, only, however,

to find a new disappointment awaiting me. I had struck the wrong peak. Beyond me lay another and a higher. Nearly exhausted as I was, I would fain have given in. As it was, I sat down to consider whether or not the attainment of the other peak was worth the trouble, and whether it would not be enough in the interests of science simply to estimate the remaining height. While I carefully cogitated these important matters, Shalum came up with me, shortly after followed by the guides and three wicked-looking tribesmen. Shalum appeared very uneasy, and warned me by his looks to be on my guard. As if to pass the time, I looked at my revolver and opened and shut the breech of my rifle. At the same time I gave the chief a franc, knowing it was best to make matters go smoothly if possible, since the sound of a rifle-shot would make every man in the radiating glens rush to arms. The sight of our weapons, our air of confidence, and the small *douceur* of money did all that was required, and the banditti, for such they were, left us, though we kept them under watch till well away.

Somewhat recovered by the rest, we now struggled up the crowning peak, and exactly at mid-day reached the top. My first care was to throw myself down for a quarter of an hour to recover from the terrible climb, or rather from the earlier exertions of the ascent. Then I gathered myself together and began leisurely to examine my surroundings.

The most varied and magnificent view presented along the entire range of the Atlas lay spread out before me. Immediately around the metamorphic rocks which run from the central mass of the range were cut into a wild series of gorges and glens, divided by sharp mountain spurs and ridges, here and there rising into snow-streaked peaks. Everywhere was desolation, barrenness, and preternatural stillness. Hardly a patch of green gave variety to the monotonous drifts of shaly debris and the jagged ribs of rock which protruded above the surface. It was only in the middle zone that dark masses of *Callitris* and stunted trees of the evergreen oak found a footing, while along the bottoms of the glens the terraces of the mountaineers added refreshing bits of colour. Numerous villages clustered against the steep mountain-sides, and under the blaze of the African sun, and with the proximity of walnut and almond groves, seemed almost desirable residences.

From my immediate rugged surroundings my gaze naturally turned southward and roamed with delight over the almost unknown Sus Valley, which, seen from my commanding elevation, spread all its physical features in one striking sheet 10,000 feet below me. From among the massive ranges to the south-east the Sus River could be seen emerging and winding in a quivering silver thread through the plain seawards. From either side numerous streams showed themselves meandering to augment its volume, here lost in dark green patches which spoke of date and olive groves, or gleaming in silvery reaches where they glided along the yellow burned-up grass plains. Curling smoke indicated the site of towns and villages, and Shalum, proud of his knowledge of the country, pointed out such places as Iminebha, Talkjunkt, and Ras-el-Wad. It was much to have the unique pleasure of looking down as on a map on all these places; but it was still more to trace the wall-like grandeur of the "Anti-Atlas," which ran seaward, a southern bounding barrier to the great Sus plain. Hardly a prominence broke the almost even level of its summit, hardly a spur jutted from its stern, precipitous sides. So it seemed at least, but a haze hung round its lower zones, and possibly hid some such features.

Turning to the east, the glen of the Wad Nyfis led my examination towards the narrow mountain valley of Gindafy, from which a week before I had been driven back. It now looked cosy and smiling, cradled among its circling mountains. Northward lay only rugged mountain peaks and ranges, with no specially striking feature, and bounded by a dense haze.

After allowing myself to revel in the varied aspects of this magnificent panorama for some time, I had to recall myself to the more prosaic duties demanded of me. Having ascertained to my satisfaction that I had reached nearly 2000 feet higher in the Atlas than any previous explorer—the height being 12,734 feet—having also taken a round of angles for mapping purposes, it was necessary to recommence my descent without loss of time.

Keeping round the head of the glen (not daring to return by the road we had come), we descended some 4000 feet with great rapidity, till we reached the bottom of a deep gorge, in which the snow still lay to a great depth, forming a beautiful but treacherous tunnel, through which ran the head-stream of the Wad Nyfis. At Irg, the first village we reached, we were received with profound astonishment; but happily Shalum discovered a trading acquaintance, and thanks to his good offices, we got a little milk and some walnuts, which greatly refreshed us.

Finally, after sunset we safely reached our camp, and relieved the fears of our men, though we did not lessen the excitement and suspicion of the natives, who were now convinced that we were spies. The villagers kept clear of us and brought us no food, and I was fain to content myself with some more walnuts, and then turn in, more weary than I had ever been by a seventy-mile walk in Central Africa, though more from the forced exertions than from the actual work achieved.

On the following morning we left Ogdimt with pardonable alacrity, for it had become too hot for us, and a diet of walnuts, though doubtless nourishing, was more than my gluttonous men could stand or than I exactly relished. We recrossed the mountains by a more easterly pass, and descended the Wad Ait Tinirt, till midway we crossed to Imintella, and arrived on the same day safe and sound at Amsmiz, to find all well.

The governor fumed and stormed on hearing where we had gone in defiance of his orders. He threw the innocent soldier into prison, from which I rescued him with the utmost difficulty. He also threatened Shalum with all sort of penalties, but that worthy Jew figuratively wrapped himself in the British flag and dared him to touch a hair of his head.

CHAPTER XXIV.

MARAKSH.

ON the 13th of July we re-entered the city of Morocco. Our reception by Ben Daoud, the governor of the town, was of the most inhospitable character, though we succeeded in getting a commodious house in the heart of the Medinah. In some respects this was a desirable state of matters, as we were left quite free to move about as we pleased, unwatched and unhampered by troublesome soldiers.

There were various reasons for taking up our quarters in the city at this time. C.-B. was still unfit for travelling, the heat had gradually become unbearable, and finally, we wanted some stores from Mogador. We calculated that we would be able to see all that we wanted of Morocco, and be off again in ten days or a fortnight. Our calculation would, no doubt, have come right in any other country in the world, but then we were in Morocco, where the expected rarely happens; and, in spite of ourselves, the fortnight ran into five weeks before we were able to resume our mountaineering. We had thus ample time to look about us and form a very fair idea of the town and its ways of life.

VIEW OF MOROCCO FROM THE HOUSETOP.

Page 347.

We did not recommence our exploration of the city with quite the same hopeful enthusiasm which characterised our first look round. Much of the glamour and charm which our imagination had woven round the thought of Morocco and the Moor had long since disappeared. There was indeed a veneer of fascination still left, but underneath we had discovered little but what was disgusting and revolting. Of the latter the ordinary tourist sees almost nothing, while ever confronted with the former; and therefore those who are only anxious to view strange and unusual sights may still wend Morocco-wards, and find much to delight them; only, if they want their pleasure unspoiled, they must not scratch beneath the surface.

Before saying more about the Moor, however, let us try to form some more comprehensive idea of "Maraksh" than we have hitherto obtained. Let us commence by taking a *coup d'œil* over the city.

From one corner of the verandah which surrounds the inner court of our house a short flight of steps leads up to the flat roof. Our house towers, as you see, quite a storey above the neighbouring dwellings, and in its central position enables us to see not only all over the town, but actually to violate with our infidel gaze the sacred privacy of various courts in our immediate vicinity. To these we shall, for the moment, virtuously shut our eyes. The view which Maraksh presents from the house-tops, as from the streets, is miserable and disappointing. On all sides stretches a comparatively even expanse of flat-topped houses, the level only here and there broken by a slight variation in the average height, as in the case of our own house, for instance. As far as colour and general appearance go, we might be looking over a newly-ploughed red-clay field. With the exception of a bit of whitewashed wall, or the green-glazed tile roof of a mosque, there is absolutely nothing in the buildings themselves to relieve the prevalent reddish colour of the city. Apart from the houses, however, it is refreshing to see in various directions groups of date-palms raising their bright green graceful leaves above the mean, half-ruined houses and wider areas of gardens which are extensively scattered through the town.

The special features which distinguish the city, as seen from the house-tops, are the square minarets of some ten mosques, which rise above the general level to heights varying from 60 to 100 feet. These, with their small, moulded, open windows, and their walls ornamented with variously-coloured tiles in arabesque patterns, are the sole features of architectural interest which greet our eyes. Among these minarets one deserves special mention—that of the Kutubia. This fine minaret within a radius of thirty miles had been seen by us as the one conspicuous feature in the Plain of Morocco. From the mountains of Rahamna, as from Sidi Rehal and Amsmiz, it had attracted our attention in its kingly isolation; and close to it as we now were, we could form a better idea what a contrast it presents to the insignificant erections around, rising as it does to a height of 270 feet. The one was a type of the Moor who conquered Spain, and excelled the Christian alike in war and all the arts of civilisation; the others were fit expressions of the degenerate Moor of the present day, who, lost to all enterprise, and void of any trace of the good qualities of his ancestor, seeks but to prevent annihilation by the most absolute isolation from contact with the outside world,

THE WALLS OF MOROCCO.

waiting for that day when Allah will arise and destroy the infidels and replace His chosen on the pinnacle from which they have fallen.

The city as a whole forms a slightly irregular quadrangle eight miles square, to which is tacked on the palace garden of Agdel like a pendant or tail. It is surrounded throughout by a high wall with square forts at intervals, both alike falling rapidly to decay. With the exception of the gateways, of which there are eight, the building material of the fortifications is *tabia*, a species of concrete composed of clay and lime, which, when well made, forms a wonderfully durable compound. As a protection against an organised assault, neither walls nor forts would be of the slightest value. The smallest piece of artillery in any European army could smash it to pieces with the greatest ease.

It would be difficult to estimate the population of the city, but my own conclusion is that normally it does not exceed 30,000, of which a third are Jews. When the Sultan takes up his residence, the number will rise to something like 60,000, which then includes the army and all the camp and court followers.

Like other Moorish towns, Maraksh is divided into the Kasbah, which has a governor of its own, and contains the Sultan's palace and its adjuncts, the Medinah or Moorish civilian quarters, and the Mellah. The Medinah, besides having its own proper walls, is also intersected by others which divide it into secondary quarters, capable of being shut off when necessary—an arrangement no doubt intended for the easier isolation of any outbreak among the inhabitants.

Having thus formed some general idea of the city as seen from the house-tops, we may now descend and commence a more detailed exploration of its sights and scenes.

In the more business part of the town there is absolutely nothing to remark but the passing people.

Narrow lanes run everywhere without plan or reason, hemmed in by blank walls of *tabia*. These walls, like the Moors, are for the most part in a sadly degenerate

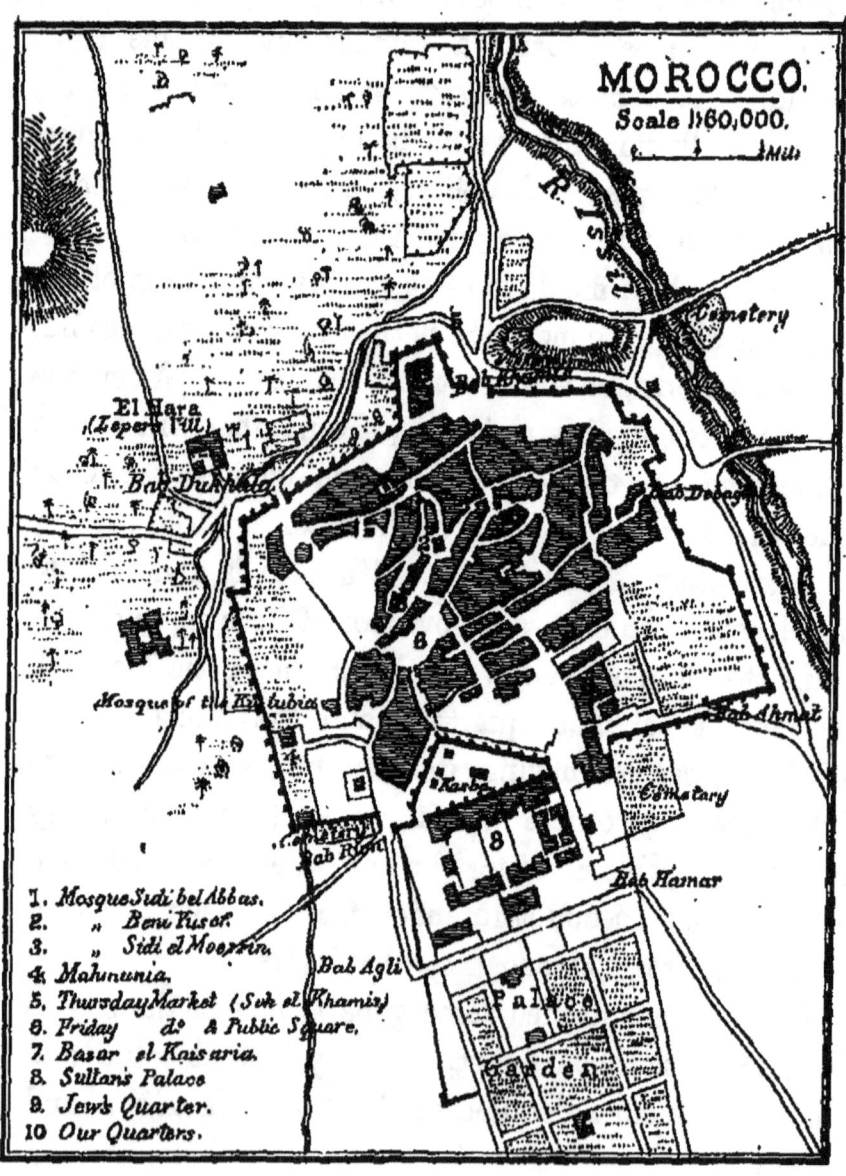

condition, waiting, indeed, like their owners, for the fate which Allah has decreed for them. The Moorish idea seems to be that it would be a sinful flying in the face of Providence to bolster up the tottering wall or patch up its dilapidations, and hence one meets at every step buildings in the most dangerous condition overhanging the street. Beneath these, however, the inhabitants, strong in their faith that their day and hour is fixed, pass with the same leisurely step which characterises their daily walk. Not less soundly do the owners sleep inside. Yet there are few days without a disastrous catastrophe, and every squall or strong breeze which crosses the city leaves behind it ruined houses and people buried beneath them. During our stay several such accidents occurred, but excited no remark. It is in the commencement of winter, with its rains and stormy weather, that most of these casualties occur, not a day passing without its tale of disaster. Probably few towns in any country present such a death-list from the falling in of houses.

Outside the business quarter there is almost nothing to attract the traveller. There are a few mosques, but most of these are so buried up that nothing but a bit of the minaret and the open door can be seen. The little one does get glimpses of is tempting enough, and suggests a rare treat if one were but permitted to stroll inside and enjoy the subdued lights and cool temperature of the sacred building while revelling in the examination of its artistic features.

One or two of these mosques are of considerable antiquity, and doubtless preserve specimens of the earlier and better genius of the Moors.

MOSQUE OF THE KUTUBIA.

That of the Kutubia shows nothing in its great barrack-like buildings to call for description. The tower is the only one of its kind built of stone in Maraksh. It is square in form, with some handsomely carved and moulded windows, while its sides are cut in relief in effective fretwork, and further adorned with bands of geometrically arranged tiles in green and black. A small lantern surmounts the tower, bearing three gilt globes, which threaten to topple over. The lantern is reached by a winding plane, there being no steps.

From whatever point of view the Kutubia is observed, it dominates the town in a most striking and impressive fashion, and neither in town or plain can one escape from it. Unlike all the others, too, it stands alone, surrounded by open squares and fine gardens, which throw its architectural features into full relief, and add to its impressive beauty by an effective framing of trees.

The modern rival to the Kutubia is the huge Brummagem mosque of Abdul Aziz, the patron saint of the city. This mosque is the special pride and glory of Morocco, but no more approaches the architectural impressions of the Kutubia than does the degenerate Moor of the present day resemble his high-souled and enlightened ancestor of five hundred years ago.

We did not venture to make a near examination of the mosque in question, and what we saw of it from a little distance calls for no remark.

Abdul Aziz, besides being the patron saint of

Morocco, holds that position also in relation to the blind, the crippled, and persons otherwise deformed. It is reported of him that on one occasion, on meeting a rival saint called Si Hamad u-Musa, and being in an irritable mood, he cursed him, and swore that all his descendants should be beggars. Si Hamad u-Musa was at once put on his mettle, and swore in retaliation that the children and children's children of Abdul Aziz should all be deformed. Hence the fact that all beggars claim the one as their ancestor or saint, and the presence of the crowds of the diseased who gather around the shrine of the other.

No one ever goes to the mosque of Abdul Aziz empty-handed. He must take something with him in money or kind to deposit in the treasury. The Sultan himself, when in Morocco, sets the example by going in great state and contributing several hundred dollars to this charitable fund. By this means many hundreds of deformed and diseased poor are supported.

There is a story current in the city that Morocco is doomed by Allah to be overrun by a French army as a scourge to the faithful, but that on its arrival at Maraksh the general will proceed to the mosque of Abdul Aziz, and on his entering he and his whole army of infidels will at once recognise that "there is no God but the one God, and that Mohammed is His prophet."

There are several other important mosques in Morocco, such as Sidi Yusuf, Sidi Wasan, &c., but their exteriors present no features worthy of description.

Outside the purely business and manufacturing quarters the only other structures deserving of notice are one or two gateways, the *fundaks* or business places of the wealthy merchants, and several fountains.

Of the gateways, the finest is one leading into the Kasbah, no great distance from the Kutubia. This is really a very handsome massive structure of stone,

ENTRANCE TO PALACE COURT.

beautifully carved in arabesque scroll work. Like the Kutubia, and all things artistic in Morocco which command our admiration, this Kasbah gate belongs to the old order of things. The date of its erection is, as far as I am aware, unknown, but it is probably not less than four hundred years old.

Among the later buildings of the same character, the most effective are those to be seen inside the precincts of the palace. One of these, communicating between two courts, is perhaps in the best style of modern Moorish art. Its chief characteristics are the fine arch surmounted by effective projecting mouldings, a sloping top or roof covered with green tiles, and a small pinnacle on either side. The colour is white with a bordering of lake to represent layers of bricks. Even this palace gateway is constructed of *tabia* and sun-dried bricks plastered over and whitewashed.

In the palace grounds nothing but crenelated walls and open squares are open to the inspection of the European, so that what there may be of the beautiful and interesting remains hidden out of sight.

In one corner we saw a private doorway with its surrounding decoration of tiles. Our attempts to photograph some of these gateways and doors gave rise to various amusing and exciting incidents. It was of no use to ask permission. That would only have resulted in a blank refusal and steps being taken to stop us. Our only plan was to make up our mind beforehand what we should photograph, and then take the palace servants and guards by surprise. The courts being open to the public and used as thoroughfares, we trotted quickly up to the place chosen, dismounted, and proceeded with all possible dispatch to focus the camera and take the negative. It seemed always to take some time before the guards and others clearly understood what was about to happen. The moment they did so, they rushed to stop us, shouting and waving their hands in the fashion of people who try to frighten back animals venturing into tabooed enclosures. Of course we paid no heed to such demonstrations, and usually completed our work before the excited people reached us, when, our object achieved, we were able to receive them smilingly as we leisurely put up our apparatus.

It was different in the streets and market-places. There we got photos with the utmost difficulty. No matter how empty either might be, a minute after our arrival at a selected spot crowds were swarming round us, more or less troublesome and obstructive. On more than one occasion these crowds became threatening, and we had to fly precipitately to escape being mobbed, or at least having our instruments ruined. At these times we missed the services of the Kaid's soldiers, for without them we dared not drive back the reviling crowds, who would have promptly resented any attempt of ours to lay infidel hands upon their sacred persons.

The city of Morocco is unusually well supplied with water. Deep underground channels convey it in abundance from the Wads Urika and Reraya to all parts of the town. There are many open channels also, for the watering of the outer and inner gardens.

The fountains where the inhabitants supply themselves for household purposes are usually neat, handsomely decorated with wood-carving, stucco arabesque, and beautiful tile dados of the most intricate patterns. The best, of course, are the oldest, the modern fountains being usually of the plainest description. The former frequently appear among ruined walls, melancholy relics of better times and better deeds, and well merit such a title as "Serb-u-Shuz" ("Drink and gaze!"), applied to one of them. One usually stumbles on them by accident in the most unexpected places. Some are attached to mosques, such as that of Sidi Wasan. It would be useless to attempt to convey any idea of the wealth and character of the decoration of these charming structures by any amount of word-painting, and I leave the camera to speak for me.

We may now venture to enter the business part of the town. Here we need look for no architectural characteristics. The streets are dirtier and more full of garbage, the houses are even more mean and more dilapidated than elsewhere, rarely rising above one storey, and as seldom showing a relieving bit of ornament; but the traveller is hardly aware of the fact till afterwards. He is caught up by the busy life that throbs around him, and stands enthralled with the sights and scenes which pass before him in endless succession. The narrow streets are thronged with hurrying currents of human beings; the market-places are packed with ghostly crowds, and from a dozen quarters comes the inspiring din of a hundred industries. After all, it does seem that some work is done in Morocco, and that, whatever be the aim and ideal of the Moor's life, the many have still to do something to keep soul and body together. The most of the streets in the business quarters are shaded in some way from the fierce summer sun. In one it is a vine that gives the needed protection, in another mats or branches, in any case producing a much-needed shade, and enhancing the quaint, picturesque effects of the streets.

The principal thoroughfares are mostly occupied by butchers, greengrocers, &c., and petty shops to supply

A POTTER'S SHOP.

the daily domestic wants of the city. From these on either side lead the special quarters of particular classes of workmen. Here it is the silversmiths', where each workman sits cross-legged, close to his little furnace, with all his apparatus within arm's reach, so that he requires not to rise. There it is the carpenters', who also, as far as circumstances will permit, sit cross-legged at work. Farther on we may explore the gunsmiths', and watch the interesting processes of turning out the old-fashioned flint-locks, which the Moor still clings to. Processes and tools alike are of the simplest, though the results are remarkably good in many instances.

Another quarter is devoted to the manipulation of Morocco leather, for which Maraksh still retains its ancient reputation, though European nations are now competing with it in its production. Here we may see the artisan at work turning out the handsomely embroidered bags which are the indispensable hold-alls of the pocketless Moor. Others are at work on the plain yellow slippers which cover the feet of the men, or the richly embroidered red ones worn by the ladies. Most interesting is it, however, to watch the method of ornamenting the leather for cushions, tray-mats, kief-pouches, &c. By the simple process of cutting out the intricate patterns in which the Moor delights on red, green, or lavender coloured leather, and picking off the epidermis or outer skin, the desired result is produced, as is shown in the illustration of the leather tray-mat. This class of artistic work is done with great rapidity. Only a few guiding lines and circles are drawn, and then, without further sketching in, the workman commences with a chisel like a graver's tool, and with skilled hand cuts out his arabesques. Then there are the saddlemakers' quarters, the tanners', the dyers', the cobblers', where the seemingly irrepar-

ENTRANCE TO ONE OF THE BUSINESS QUARTERS, MARAKSH.

Page 361.

able is repaired; the blacksmiths', where horses and mules are being shod, with their owners standing by. At places we pass long lines of Jewish women mending shirts and sewing on buttons for bachelors and travellers "while they wait." Everywhere is subdued animation, and a deprecating air of haste, as of men apologising for being in a hurry.

Among the mean houses and booths shaded by vine or mat the *fundaks* and quarters of the well-to-do merchants, who deal in the more valuable cloths and goods, rise with a certain prosperous and comfortable air. Many of them have no small pretension to style and magnificence, their entrance doorways opening into well-built and well-roofed arcades, on either side of which are the cells of the various merchants, who sit doubled up among their merchandise like animated Burmese gods. Some of these *fundaks* are built in the fashion of a house surrounding an open court, the lower rooms being the shops for the transaction of business, and the upper the stores.

Of all the places in the business part of the town, none proved more interesting than the Kaseria. This was an arcade devoted to the sale of certain kinds of linens, cottons, and so forth. Its attraction, however, for us lay in the auction-sales of new and second-hand dresses, jewellery, &c., held in it every evening. We attended these auctions assiduously, and became quite learned in all matters connected with male and female apparel. There were some half-dozen *delals* or auctioneers, who ran about among the crowd with the articles for sale, showing them off, and announcing the last bid they had received. We were thus enabled to secure several things at very moderate prices, though at first the auctioneers tried hard to cheat us by calling fictitious bids. As bearers of the Sultan's letters, we were not required to pay the Government tax of five per cent. on everything bought. Men's *haiks*, and women's *kaftans*, *hazams* or waist-bands, huge coarse gold ear-rings with red coral pendants, and silver wristlets, were the chief articles sold.

The Kaseria was a great place for the *demi-monde* and the "mashers" of Morocco. Considerable numbers of the former were always sitting about, trying the effect of their fine black eyes on the bystanders. Many of them also were there to watch the sale of their dresses and jewellery, to which necessity the incessant vicissitudes of fortune and the exactions of the Kaid were continually reducing them. It is a common mistake to suppose that this class of women is comparatively unknown in Mohammedan countries. So it would be if the laws were carried out, but in Morocco, the most strictly religious of them all, this is far from being the case. There is no town in the empire where they do not exist in considerable numbers, and in this respect Maraksh has quite a notoriety. There are laws of course, against them, but they are applied with a judicious eye to the Kaid's advantage, not to the discouragement of vice. Either a regular tax is levied upon these unfortunates by the extraction from them of continual bribes, or they are judiciously nursed till they have acquired a little money or some handsome clothes and jewellery, when they are swooped down upon, stripped of everything, and put in prison until such time as their friends are prepared to secure their release by the payment of an additional fine. After that they are allowed to resume their old life. Many of these women are very pious and strict in attending to their religious duties, and I myself have encountered a number of them on a painful pilgrimage to the sanctuary of Mulai Ibrahim in the mountains of Gurguri. So little are the denunciations of the Prophet regarded, that we have it on the very best authority that descendants of Mohammed himself are among the ranks of these fallen ones. This, however, by the way.

Next to the various quarters where articles are made and sold, the various daily marts scattered about throughout the city are of the greatest interest. Not far from the Kaseria is the grain-market. The crowd which usually collects here, of which a large proportion are women, has an appearance remarkably suggestive of a ghostly host swathed in grave-like cerements. Almost without exception the buyers and sellers are in white or creamy-coloured *haiks*. There is less movement and bustle than in the streets, the crowd being usually too dense to allow of much movement, but a thunderous din rises from its midst, and tends to dissipate the effect of the weird appearance of the shrouded multitude. Close to the grain-market is the slave-market. To the Nazarene this is forbidden ground, but none the less we contrived to penetrate within the gate, and get a glimpse of a small square, or rather large court, surrounded by a pillared verandah, with cells or rooms beneath. Here were groups of handsomely-dressed Moors gathered critically around various women, well dressed, and evidently born and brought up in Morocco, their only rivals being one or two raw slave-girls fresh from the Sudan, with hardly a rag to cover their well-knit figures, and no veil to partially hide the hideousness of their faces. Before we had time to see more, our intrusion was discovered, and we had to fly before a volley of curses and threats.

In another place was an oil-market. In many ways this was the most interesting of all, for here we could contrast with each other the weather-beaten features of the mountaineer, the fierce-eyed and gaunt forms of the wild Arab of Sus and Ras-el-Wad, the debased Arab of the surrounding country, and the sleek Moor and cringing Jew of the town.

Besides the daily markets for such produce as grain and oil, there are two great weekly *soks*. At the Sok-el-Khamis or Thursday market, horses, mules, camels, donkeys, cattle, &c., are sold. It is held outside the Bab-el-Khamis, which we entered on coming from Saffi. Thousands throng to it for miles around, and make a wonderful show. Here, as at the Kaseria, the animals are sold by *delals*, who mount them when mules and horses, and show off their paces very much in the fashion of people at horse-shows at home. Inside the walls, and not far from the Bab-el-Khamis, is a secondary *sok*, where second-hand articles of all sorts, with pottery, spices, native medicines, &c., are sold. Itinerant jugglers and other public entertainers, including the omnipresent snake-charmers, take advantage of the crowd to show off their skill for the expected *flus*. The scene at this market is always very effective, the crowd being broken up and shown off by large mounds of rubbish, and surrounded on one side by fine date-groves and gardens, while spreading away on the other is the great city.

The second or Friday market is held in a large square in the very heart of the town.

Of all the public sights and scenes which Morocco presents, none attract and delight the traveller more than the exhibitions and entertainments held in the evening in the square of the Friday market. The fierce heat of the day is past, and the cool breezes which spring up make it delightful to turn out of the now heated courts and rooms to enjoy the invigorating freshness. The Moor naturally wends his way to the market-square, for it is his public recreation-ground, his music-hall, his reading-room, his everything, indeed, that ministers to his enjoyment.

There is a small group of venerable be-turbaned men listening attentively while some one reads a chapter of the Koran. A little way off is a blind man singing a sacred song in praise of Mohammed. There is something touching in the sight of the picturesque old singer standing in the midst of his sympathetic audience and emitting his sonorous guttural notes, while his face is turned upward and his sightless eyeballs twitch involuntarily. We pass on to another group gathered about a Shellach musician, who plays a reed, and draws from it quaint and not unpleasing music. Men with tambourines accompany him, and a boy dances to his piping with many strange wrigglings of the body. Farther on is a juggler, one too who has shown his skill in European circuses, and by virtue of his master, Si Hamad u-Musa, has astonished the Nazarenes. His dress and manners tell that he is a travelled man, and the English or French phrases which he shouts at us make the matter certain. His tricks do not attract us much, but it is different when we find ourselves before another circle of eager listeners. Here a genuine story of the "Arabian Nights" is being recounted to the believing crowd, exactly as it has been recounted for hundreds of years, and delighting an Arab audience with its never-waning interest. How we long to understand the rich gutturals which fall so volubly from the narrator's lips, and feel that if we could but get a clue to the story he tells, we could follow his animated movements and supply meaning to the sounds. There is another who while he talks keeps up a running accompaniment on a gimbery, his narratives apparently mostly humorous, to judge from his pantomime and the laughter he evokes, and probably turning upon some dubious adventure among the fairer sex.

The entertainments provided are endless—music, dancing, fencing, and shooting at such marks as an orange held on a stick ten yards off. Most popular of all, however, is the snake-charming. This seems to be a never-failing source of amusement to the Moor. It is awanting at no *sok* or market; it is on nightly exhibition in every town. As the national and characteristic amusement of Morocco, it has no rival. We ourselves never tired watching the performers. Their acting had a strange wild charm about it which attracted us far more than the actual feats they performed. Their very appearance—gaunt face, eyes with a restless gleam of madness, and long matted locks hanging from the crown of the head down the neck—was in itself sufficient to rivet our attention.

The stamp of religion was put on all their doings. They commenced with invocations to Allah and Sidi Aissa, raising their hands imploringly. At times they would address a prayer to Mohammed, and then all hands were held in a supplicating attitude. Three or four men sat with tambourines, and thumped them with greater or less vigour as circumstances seemed to demand. In his performances the snake-charmer goes through a regular series of evolutions. For a time he dances round with the uncanny movements of a witch who brews a potion or works a charm. He seems to be imbibing the spirit and faith of the apostle of his order, becomes more and more excited, more and more oblivious of his audience. The proper ecstatic mood attained, he bends down to the skin-covered cylindrical basket, and draws out one or two snakes—a deadly looking cobra and the even more repulsive *lefa* or puff-adder. The former rears a foot of its body from the ground, and holds its head at right angles, ever ready to strike. The *lefa*, on the other hand, lies flat, watching the performer with its cold glittering eyes. We are just getting absorbed in the sight, and think the special feats about to begin, when a stoppage takes place. Allah and Sidi Aissa are again invoked. The crowd, with hands held before them, join in prayer, and a small contribution to defray expenses is collected. Then

A MOORISH AUDIENCE.

the snake-charming commences. The charmer tempts the *lefa* to spring at him, while he moves round with swaying body and a dancing step, chanting continuously. As he thus turns and twists, the cobra ever keeps itself partially erect, watchfully following the movements of its owner, its head turning round on its body as on a pivot. At times it strikes at him. Louder grows the din of the tambourines and more excited the behaviour of the performer. Suddenly he draws out a small snake and holds it up before him. He pushes out his tongue, and the snake bites it. He applies it to his leg, with a similar result. The onlookers now stand in hushed expectancy, while the noise from the tambourines is redoubled. We also stand for a moment expectant, looking for some strange *dénouement*. The *dénouement* comes, but hardly as we imagined. For the performance stops at the most interesting moment, when the smallest contributions are thankfully received. We throw in ours, and having seen enough for one night, move slowly back to our quarters.

LEATHER TEA TRAY MAT.

CHAPTER XXV.

LIFE IN MARAKSH.

During our stay in Maraksh we tried in some measure to live the life of the Moor. In certain respects there was but little difficulty. The terrific heat of midsummer made inaction during the most of the day almost a necessity.

On our arrival, the thermometer, in the best shade we could obtain in our house, registered a temperature of 65° in the morning, and 85° in the afternoon; but thereafter it rose daily, till on the 25th the heat was 95°. On the 29th it rose to 98°. These readings were obtained in the doorway leading from our principal room to a shady verandah, where the heat was 5° higher. The minimum temperature was more variable, and ranged from 68° to 80° degrees. On the 28th a south wind blew during the afternoon, and seemed like a blast from a furnace. Yellow clouds of fine dust obscured the sky and everything beyond our immediate neighbourhood.

During the following week the temperature fell till it reached as low as 89° on the 1st of August, and then commenced to augment till it reached 100° on the 5th, at which point it remained till 6.30 P.M., when it fell to 99°. This high temperature was again due to a desert wind from the south, bringing with it suffocating clouds of fine dust. The night following was hot and feverish, making sleep impossible. In the morning the thermometer still registered 86°. At 9 A.M. it had risen to 90°. At 2 P.M. the hot wind again set in from the south-west, with even more violence than on the previous day, accompanied by thunder and lightning and the same suffocating clouds of fine dust. Under its influence the temperature in the verandah rose to 112°, though by keeping the door closed it registered only 96° in the inner room.

The heat of the succeeding days continued to be excessive. The respective maximum temperature of the verandah and the inner room with closed doors were: the 7th, 108° and 97°; 8th, 108° and 97°; 9th, 104° and 95°; 10th, 102° and 96°. On those dates there were hot south-west winds and clouds of dust. On the 10th I removed the thermometer to the head of the staircase, where there was a draught and the best shaded corner in the verandah. On the 12th, 103° was registered; 13th, 101°; 14th, 98°. On the 18th the heat had gone down to 90°, but rose again on the 23rd to 101°. There were indications, however, that the worst was past, and the cooler months setting in.

Needless to say, with a heat of from 96° to 112° F. little could be done. Our usual course was to quit the inner room early in the morning, leaving the door open till about 8 A.M. After that time the door was shut to keep out the rapidly increasing heat of the day atmosphere, while retaining the cooler night-air inside. Such business as we had to do was then transacted, the mules and horses seen to, and perhaps a market visited.

Our household expenses were by no means excessive, though everything that Morocco could supply was lavishly procured. The daily cost of the keep of ourselves and Assor, seven servants, two horses, and eight mules, amounted only to the small sum of ten shillings at most. Mutton and beef, milk, eggs, fowls, with melons, cucumbers, tomatoes, onions, potatoes, grapes, figs, &c., were supplied in abundance at ridiculous prices, as well as straw and barley for our animals. A dozen pounds of the most delicious large grapes, resembling our best hot-house grapes, could be obtained for less than a penny a pound.

Towards mid-day, when the heat was approaching its worst, there was nothing for it but to retire to our inner room, shut the door and lie quite still in semi-darkness, divested of every article of dress we could spare. Of course there was absolutely not a breath of air, our chief object being to prevent any circulation when the outer temperature was several degrees higher than that of the room. Our experience of life in Morocco under these circumstances enabled us to see the reason for the windowless rooms of the Moors. The arrangement prevailing in most Moorish houses is calculated to keep the temperature lower during the day and higher at night.

OUR QUARTERS, MARAKSH.

It may not be out of place to describe our quarters. They may be accepted as typical of the houses of the well-to-do townsmen. The entrance-door led into a long somewhat narrow passage, which ran right across the side of the house to a small open court beyond, which could be used as a stable for mules and horses. Half way along the passage a door opened into another passage running at right angles, and leading into a handsome court, at least fifty feet square. One side of this square was arched to form a verandah, which shaded an inner room, undecorated, and without windows or other means of ventilation than the doorway.

On the right side from the passage was a second large windowless room, the door being simply shaded by projecting eaves. The side facing the lower verandah had also a room of similar dimensions and style, but better ornamented. All these rooms were long and narrow with high ceilings.

At one corner of the court a steep, awkward flight of steps led to the upper storey. Here a finely-arched broad verandah ran round three sides of the house, from which, however, opened only one very large, well-plastered room, thirty feet long by ten in breadth. At one corner was a small room with a window, while at the opposite was an even smaller apartment which served as a bathroom. The court and the apartments described are the master's special rooms, where he might without impropriety receive male guests, who would neither see nor be seen by the inmates of the harem, to whom due notice is always given of the approach of a visitor, so as to enable them to clear out of the way. In our house the harem was divided into two parts. The principal one was situated over the entrance passage, from which a door gave admittance to a flight of steps. It consisted of a suite of three small rooms. The middle one was lighted from the ceiling, and served to transmit light to the other two. These three rooms, though small and cramped, were exceedingly handsomely decorated, especially the middle one, with its polygonal dome and skylight. Brilliant colours and graceful stucco arabesques, brightened up and adorned every nook and corner, and even the doors were handsomely panelled, carved, and painted. Every precaution was taken that the wayward ladies should not be tempted to stray by anything they could see, and still less to let wandering feet follow wandering eyes, for the sole opening in the wall was firmly barred with iron.

These rooms were probably devoted to the use of the principal wife, or it may have been a favourite slave. The other division of the harem or private apartments lay on the opposite side of the square from the entrance-passage. Here a door led into a small secondary court, round which were the kitchen and one quadrangular room, and an upper suite of small rooms.

It need hardly be said that the furniture of a Moorish house is of the simplest. Such things as objects of art are unknown. Everything that is agreeable to the eye is a fixture. Such are tessellated

WOMEN AT DOOR OF THE HAREM.

pavements and floors; cool glazed tile dados round the rooms, mostly in black and white; handsomely carved and painted doors; stucco arabesques round niches and doors, and gorgeously coloured ceilings. Where ventilation other than by the doorway is desired, it is provided for by an open stucco fretwork like delicate lace arranged in three charming little arches over the door.

The house we occupied was not permanently occupied, but under other circumstances it would have had a garden in the centre, with a bubbling fountain probably, and tile-paved walks.

A gorgeously coloured carpet, one or two mattresses, and several cushions form almost the sole appointments of a Moorish house. There may be a rude box for small articles and letters, one or two candlesticks or more elaborate candelabra for use at night placed on the floor, and among the very well-to-do a European clock, more ornamental than useful; but these are usually the sum of the requirements of the Moor. Throughout Morocco there is nothing more disappointing to the traveller than this absence of things beautiful, whether for the adornment of the person or the house. One naturally expects to find all sorts of beautiful and quaint objects, to see picturesque houses, and even get peeps into the most delightfully fanciful interiors. That some such things existed in earlier days is made every now and then apparent as we wander through the town and assiduously attend auction-sales. But to know that an object is beautiful, that it shows careful and loving workmanship, and reflects the graceful fancy we associate with things Moorish, is also to know that it is old. In everything we see there is evidenced a frightful degeneracy in genuine workmanship and artistic taste. To the painter, the enduring colours of other times are as much unknown as is his ancestor's skill in blending them in effective scroll-work. The stucco arabesque is equally becoming a thing of the past, simply because there is no demand for it, and consequently the workmen are dying out, with no others educated to replace them. The rugs and carpets reflect the same degeneracy. Aniline dyes of gorgeous hue have almost entirely replaced the enduring vegetable colours formerly employed, and with the colours the skill in effective and harmonious arrangement is also disappearing. The beautiful glazed tiles are now not made, except to a small extent at Tetuan; Fez still keeps up a certain reputation for coarse though bold and effective pottery and beautifully worked cloth waistbands for women; Rabat for carpets and embroideries; Mogador for brass trays and silver ornaments, and Maraksh for various kinds of leather-work. At each of these places the tourist may pick up a few objects worth taking away, but even then he will find that the best things are old, whether carpets, daggers, or guns.

There is no difficulty in detecting the cause of this degeneracy. It is the notorious misgovernment which is at the root of this, as of all the other evils which are ruining the Empire. What temptation is there for any one to set up for himself a handsome well-built house, when the chances are that he will not be allowed to die in it, and that sooner or later it will pass into the hands of the Sultan or of strangers? As little is he tempted to amass around him things beautiful—which in his heart he loves—in a country where justice is unknown and security to property non-existent. To show any sign of luxurious tastes, and of wealth to gratify them, would only serve to apprise the Government of the fact, with the inevitable result of entailing on the owner a ruinous contribution, or imprisonment till such time as the authorities were satisfied that there was nothing more to be squeezed out of him.

Then, against the preservation of anything beautiful or artistic, militates the fact that there are no hereditary governors or Sheiks, no powerful families who might pass on their treasures from generation to generation. Wealth of any kind will never remain two generations together in the same family before the Sultan has swallowed everything in his omnivorous maw. Few Moors, without having placed themselves under "the protection" of a European Government, are ever allowed to die wealthy. To avoid spoliation, the first idea of any one—except the Jews—who has amassed some money is to bury it. The amount in Morocco of such buried treasure, of which the secret has been lost, must be enormous.

An even worse influence than this system of wholesale plunder tends to the rapid deterioration of Moorish art and the disappearance of skilled workmen. These latter are now becoming so rare, that the moment one is discovered to have greater capabilities than his companions, he is immediately impressed into the service of the Sultan or the governor. Not, however, to be petted and honoured and made much of, as was the good old fashion, but to be compelled to work for little more than his bare livelihood. I have mentioned two instances of this in connection with the Kaid of Gindafy. Hundreds similar could easily be adduced. It is the ruin of a workman to get a reputation for genius or cleverness in any branch. His only way of escape—and it is one not unfrequently adopted—is to botch his work and subject himself to a flogging, and eventually to dismissal if he persists in his deliberate error. That is how the descendants of the people who built the Alhambra and made their reign in Spain glorious by their marvellous buildings encourage and foster art in these days.

After this digression let us resume the records of our life in Morocco.

The one great obstacle to our realising the everyday life of the Moor, was the sad fact that we were bachelors. The Moor can in no way imagine life on earth, still less in heaven, without the solacing presence of women. They are his sole companions and friends at home, his dolls or toys, his entertainers, servants, everything that any one can well be to him. Without them he can undertake no journey, and he cherishes them as the apple of his eye. Not that it follows that he cares much for them in our sense of the term. On the contrary, he may even go so far as to hate individuals among them; but he nevertheless cannot bear

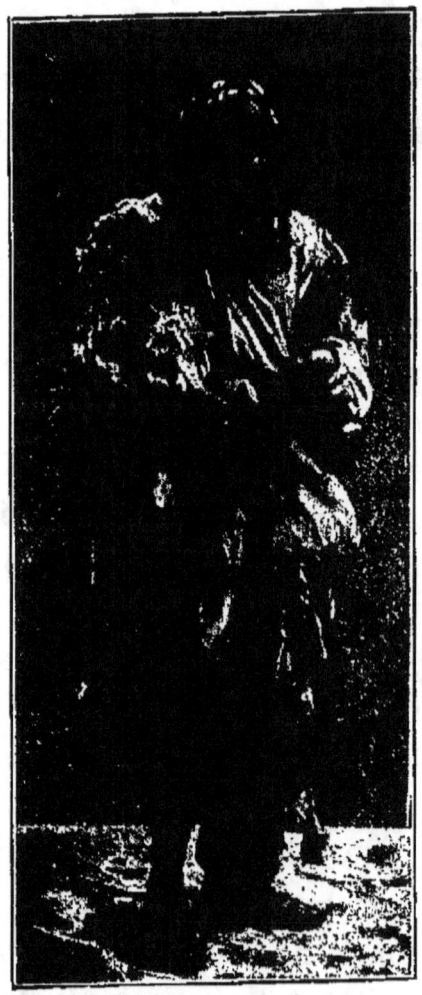

ITINERANT MUSICIAN.

the thought of others getting a glimpse of the living treasure which has become distasteful to himself.

Failing this prime essential of a Moorish existence, we had to fall back for a little variety in our monotonous existence on such public entertainers as could be hired. Of these, none amused us more than the itinerant half-Negro half-Arab musicians from Sus and the desert. These generally go about in pairs, got up in the most fantastic fashion, with rags, skins, bands of cowries, and iron bells about their legs and ankles. One performs with a drum, the other with a curious species of iron double cymbals. Their antics are of the most absurd description, and sometimes irresistibly comic. Their appearance and performance, however, had an added interest to me in bringing vividly to my memory entertainments of a similar character in the Sudan, where I had first formed the idea of visiting Morocco. At other times we brought in a troupe of Jewish singers and dancers, who had the reputation of being the best of their kind in Southern Morocco. That may have been so; but if it were, it said very little for the singer's and dancer's art in these parts. The women in frightfully shrill voices screamed out Arab and Jewish songs, accompanied by violin-grinding and tambourines. One man danced in the Moorish fashion, and that was all.

By dint of such arts as one may employ in Morocco, we obtained a coveted invitation to the house of a Moor. Needless to say he was one of lax morals, though otherwise of firm religious principle; that is to say, he would, for a consideration, hand over the key of the house in which was his wife and daughter to another, though he would have thought twice about eating forbidden meats. In our case, we wanted to see the interior of an inhabited Moorish house, and if possible get a photo of some Moorish women, one of the most difficult things to obtain in these parts.

Of course we had to go in disguise, as the idea of allowing a Christian into a Mohammedan household would have been too horrifying a scandal, even for the gentleman in question, and, if discovered, would have been followed by very serious consequences to both parties.

Under the guidance of our Gibraltarian friend Bonich, we started on our adventure some time after mid-day, when the excessive heat had driven every one within doors. We did what we could to adopt the Moorish stride of a man of substance, and with apparent success, for no one took any notice of us. I soon, however, had something else to think of than what people were thinking of us, for the slippers I had on began to chafe my sockless feet, and take, with the assistance of the fine gritty sand which got plentifully inside, the skin from my toes and instep. If my feet had been rubbed continuously with sandpaper, as they were indeed with sanded leather, I could not have been more painfully flayed. Under these circumstances, dignified easy motion was out of the question, while the skinning of the toes made the necessary pressure to retain possession of the slippers extremely difficult. My walk became an awkward shuffle, and more than once my slippers came off. But for the fact that there was hardly a soul in the broiling streets, we would have been detected and probably followed. At last we turned to the right and entered a blind alley, at the end of which was a door where Bonich knocked. A woman's voice replied; the next moment the door was opened, and with guilty haste we slipped inside, turning round as we did so to see that we were not observed.

We now found ourselves in a dark passage, with an unveiled woman beside us. Of course, in a well-regulated household no woman would have opened the door, and the announced approach of a male visitor would have been followed by the flight of the women to their own sanctums. We were first conducted into a small garden enclosed by walls and shaded by an overarching vine and a large fig-tree. In this deliciously cool retreat mattresses and cushions were laid for our comfort, and with no small delight I divested myself of the most cumbersome of my Moorish garments, and especially of my slippers. The woman who had let us in, seeing the pitiful condition of my feet, hastened to bring water to wash them. The master of the house now arrived, a villainous-looking fellow of fluent speech, plentifully garnished with the name of Allah and phrases from the Koran. While we exchanged the courtesies of life with this detestable fellow, his two wives, one of about thirty and the other about thirty-five, waited on us. They brought us first fruit and melons, then bread and honey, followed by a *tajen* of stewed beef in rancid butter. A little of each course went a long way in satisfying our appetite; no more, in fact, than politeness demanded.

The mid-day meal over, the master of the house retired to say his prayers, and his daughter arrived resplendent in her best clothes. She wore a *kaftan* of rich yellow brocade, partially veiled by an upper garment of fine muslin. Her dress was drawn in at the waist by an embroidered belt. Her black hair, covered with a brilliant crimson silk handkerchief, was gathered into two plaits tied together at the ends and hanging down the back. Heavy silver wristlets encircled her arms, and strings of beads her neck. The adornment of her person was completed with henna tints on her hands and feet, black-painted eyelashes and eyebrows, and tattooed dots and squares on the middle line of her brow and chin and on her arms. Her face was broad across the cheekbones, which were prominent, and her mouth was somewhat large, displaying a magnificent set of white teeth. Her great attraction, however, were her almond-shaped eyes of the most brilliant black. These were wide apart, and had glossy, luxuriant eyelashes. Upon the whole, however, she could not be termed handsome or pretty, though her figure, as far as we could judge, seemed well-made, and certainly the feet and hands of this Moorish damsel of fifteen or sixteen were all that could be desired in size and shape.

When on this subject of women, I may take occasion to remark that, as far as we got opportunities for judging—and these were strictly limited—the Moorish ladies were not remarkable for their beauty. We were apt to acquire erroneous notions on this point from only seeing their eyes, and these were frequently quite fascinating; but more than once, on seeing our unconcealed admiration, and no Moor being nigh, our expectations of seeing a beautiful face to match were belied on the *haik* being coquettishly drawn aside, and withered features and general ugliness displayed. Of course we only got glimpses of the faces of the older women, and those of the very poor and the loose. Beauty naturally gravitated into the harems of the wealthy, from which it never came out except by night, so that we had no means of acquiring correct notions on the subject. My observations, however, such as they are, make me believe that young women from fourteen to twenty-five years of age are exceedingly well-proportioned, and sometimes very beautiful. After that age, figure and beauty alike disappear with great rapidity.

The dress of the women is almost identical in make with that of the men, even to the trousers. They employ, however, much more expensive materials—gorgeous brocades, silks, &c., generally covered by a gauzy stuff. The wealthy have exceedingly heavy *hazams*, or waistbands, worked in silk in the most beautiful manner, and varying in price from eight to two hundred dollars. The *haik*, in which they are shrouded when they go out of doors, is nothing more nor less than a very large woollen blanket, heavier than any used in England. At Saffi and Mogador no face-cloth is used, and absolutely nothing but one eye is shown. In Morocco generally, a face-cloth of light open material is worn, and the *haik* is drawn round by the chin and held there by the hand. At Amsmiz the *haik* is held by both hands in such a way as to form a narrow slit quite a foot long. This must be the most troublesome of all the ways of wearing the cumbersome garment. The shoes of the women are distinguished from those of the men by being red in colour, and frequently daintily embroidered.

This habit of always having to think of hiding the face has aroused the curious feeling among them that it is more indecent to show it to a stranger than any other part of the body. In the hot weather it was no uncommon thing to see women going along the streets with their faces jealously veiled, and their breasts more or less exposed.

Though the women we now saw before us were by no means shy, and could make use of their charms with all the consummate skill of a Frenchwoman, we soon got tired of trying to keep up conversation. We hastened thereupon to take some photos of them, no easy task, for they thought it a terrible sin to have their portraits taken.

This done, we would willingly have bolted; but that was impossible, for we had to await the arrival of a servant to smuggle away the apparatus, and— I blush to mention it—to bring me a pair of socks, without which I could not venture to trust my feet in Moorish slippers again. While we waited, we explored one or two of the rooms of the house, only to find it absolutely devoid of all furniture other than rugs, mattresses, and cushions. The walls were plainly whitewashed. Everything was clean and neat.

Needless to say, my socks drew the attention of passers-by and revealed our identity; but we did not now care, as we were on our way to our own quarters.

In pursuance of our design to "do" Morocco as thoroughly as possible, we resolved to have " a wash and brush up" in the native fashion. The hammum in Morocco, as in all Mohammedan countries, is an institution. Every quarter of Maraksh has one or more of them.

There was one great obstacle to our carrying out our wishes. The hammum was sacred to the faithful, and no Christian had ever been known to desecrate the hallowed precincts. That of course was the more reason for going; for what else did we travel but to do and see things that other people had not done and seen. Our hope lay in this, that after the *Acha*, or supper-prayers at 9 P.M., the baths are reserved for families, and those who can afford to take them for the night and bring with them their own servants, &c.

We accordingly dispatched our most intelligent and fluent liar of a servant with *carte-blanche* to exercise his special talents to secure the hammum for our use, of course strictly hiding our identity with anything infidel. To our delight he succeeded in arranging the matter. Needless to say, it was as necessary to go in disguise to the hammum as when visiting our Moorish friend.

LIFE IN MARAKSH.

After the call to prayers had resounded over the city, we started off, accompanied by most of our men, all in a great funk, and very reluctant to go,—no one more so than Assor, who, to the fear of detection,

IN DISGUISE.

added all the imaginary horrors of a thorough washing, an operation of which he had had no practical experience in his whole lifetime.

We had barely left our quarters before we had nearly spoiled all. Each, in his absurd eagerness to see that the other looked the Moor, broke more than once into audible English speech, till energetic tugs from the men brought him once more to his senses. These latter did their best to surround us and ward off inspection, but the narrowness of the streets and the numbers of people still moving about made that next to impossible. At one place an unmistakable reference to Christians was made. All that we could do was to take no notice and hurry on, quite unaware whether we were being followed or not. It seemed not, however, as we reached the door of the hammum without obstruction or disturbance. Here we were again nearly caught; for thinking that the baths were deserted, we were about to bolt inside the moment the door was opened, when we found ourselves face to face with several bathers carrying lanterns. Instinctively we turned our backs, and our men crowded round us and kept up a continuous gabble till the enemy passed out. There had clearly been mismanagement somewhere, for we soon discovered that some people were still left in the hammum. To escape these, we were huddled into a small cellar, used apparently as a refuse bin, and there, in complete darkness, and hardly daring to breathe, we were kept for several minutes, till it was quite certain every one had left.

We were now ushered through a badly-formed passage and into a filthy vaulted chamber with square pillars. We had only a couple of candles to light up the place. What we did contrive to see hardly realised our idea of an Oriental bath, with its couches and luxurious fittings. Few European cellars would compete with the black and repulsive chamber which served as an undressing and cooling room. It was not even whitewashed, and a damp, mouldy, flea-populated straw mat was all there was to represent the soft cushions and comfortable divans we had looked forward to. A singularly horrible smell assailed our nostrils too, instead of sweet perfume and incense, so that everything was in harmony. Though disappointed, we were in too high spirits to be very much put out. As we tried to pierce the gloom, and remarked the dimly-seen flitting naked figures of our tawny or copper-coloured attendants, and heard their half-suppressed whispers, we concluded that this was something to be seen *once* in one's life.

While we compared our own appearance with that of our men, and noted our general surroundings, we began to picture ourselves as white captives in a Moorish dungeon, and about to be put to the torture, which might consist in being boiled, to judge from the steam which filled the room. Assor looked very much as if he felt the awfulness of his position, and indeed it was a terrible ordeal he had to face, a whole lifetime's washing at once. How terrible too for the operator, we thought! Encouraging each other with jokes, as of men who knew how to die, we half pushed, half dragged the interpreter to his fate, the Moors grinning with delight at the prospect of scrubbing him. From the black hole we had undressed in. we groped our way, with the aid of a single candle, into a second warmer chamber full of steam, our men following with wooden pails. This was more gloomy, more dungeon-like than the other even, and poor Assor groaned aloud. After encouraging him with an account of what was still in store for him, we penetrated to another and the warmest chamber, full of steam like the others. This inner sanctum was an oblong vaulted room which had never been plastered. At one side was a tap for drawing the necessary hot water from the boilers on the other side of the wall. There was no operating table, and there was nothing for it but to lie down on the smoothly cemented floor. The temperature, as far I could judge, would be about 150°. Our cook turned out to be a skilled shampooer, and he kneaded and rubbed, pushed and pulled, sat upon us, and rolled and tumbled us about with all the style of an old hammum hand. He failed not to give us a professional slap to mark the end of any particular operation.

The great affair of the evening, however, was the shampooing of Assor. Everybody was anxious to lend a hand, we, because for the moment he represented all Moorish Jews and their Mellahs, and our men because they saw he was frightened, and that here was an opportunity of paying off old scores long accumulating against the race of Israel. Seeing his protests to be in vain, he submitted to his fate on our promising to give him the treatment of a baby. Needless to say, our delighted followers pounced upon him right gleefully, with the most satisfactory results. If ever a man knew what it was to put off the "old man" in the physical sense, that individual was David Assor, who at the age of forty-five got his first and probably his last Turkish bath.

On our return to the dressing and cooling room, the odour which had assailed our nostrils on entrance came upon us more overpoweringly than ever. A hasty examination revealed to us a most horrible open sewer. Sickened by both sight and smell, and heedless of possible colds, we hurried on the most necessary of our clothes and fled from the place.

The night was finished off by an exhibition of Moorish dancing. The dancers being women, they had to be smuggled in disguised in men's *jellabias*, otherwise they would have been watched and captured by the Kaid's soldiers. For the same reason it was necessary to bring them at night.

The dancing-women were introduced with a great air of caution and mystery, and showed much bashfulness in taking off their *haiks* and exhibiting their mature charms to infidel eyes. Finding, however, that we were not exactly ogres, and warming under plentiful libations of tea, they were soon quite at their ease. By and bye a wicked-looking wall-eyed individual who accompanied them strung up his native guitar or *gimbery*; one of our own men tapped on a brass tray, while the others kept time by clapping their hands. Thus invited to foot it on the carpet, one of the dancers stood up and circled round once or twice, accentuating the measure with her heel as she glided round. All at once she stopped and gave a sharp stamp with one foot. Next moment both feet were at work, much as if she had found herself on a hot plate from which she could not escape. This vertical rhythmical motion next developed into a sort of shake up of the whole body, every muscle being brought into play. The movement became faster and faster, till suddenly a climax was reached. The all-round and up-and-down motion ceased, and she essayed with a wriggle to tie her legs in a knot before finally plumping down on one knee before us to receive the expected largesse.

The other girls next showed their skill, growing more lively and animated as they became accustomed to our unwonted presence, and the one-eyed Cyclops broke into a song on the pleasures of love, our men assisting in the chorus. The feat of the evening, however, was to load a brass tray with all the accessories of tea-drinking, including the filled-up cups, poise it on the head, and then dance as before without spilling a drop of tea.

Upon the whole, the performance was neither particularly interesting nor graceful. The girls were by no means good-looking, and we were glad to get rid of them after suitably rewarding them.

CHAPTER XXVI.

THE AID-EL-KEBIR.

During our stay we had the good fortune to see the celebration of the "Aid-el-Kebir," or Great Feast, which marks the close of the ceremonies connected with the pilgrimage to Mecca. Following the practice of the whole Mohammedan world, as well as of the actual pilgrims in the valley of Mina, every Moor who can afford it sacrifices a sheep, a goat, or a cow, dresses himself in his best, and holds high holiday.

In Maraksh the celebration of the day is made the occasion of a great state function, and the gathering of all the Kaids of Southern Morocco to do homage to their liege lord the Sultan, and fill his treasures and the coffers of his ministers with so-called presents of blood and tear-stained dollars. The Sultan being absent at Mequinez, his place was taken by the Viceroy, Mulai Othman.

The state function was to take place outside the town, and we resolved to attend it, though we knew that there would be no small danger of a fanatical outbreak at our intrusion upon the religious ceremonies.

We found the streets presenting an unusually animated aspect, with their thronging thousands all clean-shaved and in refurbished or new dresses. The shops were shut, and only sweetmeat and cake sellers plied their trade, though everywhere the tinkle of the distinctive bell of the water-seller could be heard, and now and then he could be seen bending under his large goat-skin bag, from which he dispensed the re-

WATER CARRIER.

quired refresher. The great mass of the crowd were mounted on donkeys, mules, or horses, the last mostly ridden by soldiers hurrying to collect under the banner of their respective Kaids.

Among others, we were interested in seeing the soldier who had prevented my finishing the ascent of the southern range of the valley of Gindafy. He, on his part, on discovering us, drove his huge spurs into his horse's ribs and charged us at full gallop. In the course of his wild career through the stampeding crowd, he screamed out something about Allah, threw his gun up in the air, caught it again, and turning round in his saddle, fired at an imaginary enemy, and then, amidst a cloud of dust, pulled up his horse under our noses.

Our way to the meeting-ground lay through the palace square, and our hopes of seeing something noteworthy rose as we saw squadron after squadron of wildly picturesque horsemen gallop up to the chief gate of the palace to salute the Viceroy before proceeding to their posts.

We were soon outside the walls of the town. Two miles beyond the gate, and close to the Agdel garden, were massed a great concourse of horsemen and people on foot. The horsemen mostly stood in line, but we could also see parties galloping along furiously, firing volleys while at full speed.

In a few minutes we neared the crowd close to the gate of the garden, from which the Viceroy was to appear. From this point far out into the plain were ranged two lines of horsemen a hundred yards apart. At the farther end could be seen some kind of erection, round which the pedestrians and townspeople were gathered in their thousands.

Pending the arrival of the Viceroy, the various parties showed their skill in horsemanship and the use of arms by engaging in *lab-el-barud* or powder-play, the one sight in Morocco of which the traveller never tires.

For a time we stood and watched this strikingly picturesque spectacle. By and bye the gate of the garden opened and a party of cavalry galloped out. Behind these came two magnificent horses, all fully caparisoned and led by grooms. The next to appear was a fine-looking venerable old Moor, with a beautiful white beard, a huge turban, and voluminous *haik*, and enveloped besides in a creamy-coloured burnous, the hood of which covered his turban, while the skirts hung down over his feet. This was the Viceroy, riding on horseback, surrounded by grooms on foot and men who flicked long cloths in the air to keep the flies at a distance from his regal person.

It now became necessary that we should proceed to the other end of the lines if we wanted to see the ceremony. With the cool, calculated impudence which does marvels in such a country as Morocco, we started off just ahead of the Viceroy, and pranced along the route kept open and guarded for him. We heard no sound, but we were none the less aware that from both sides, before and behind, a terrific volley of maledictions were hurled at us. No man, however, presumed to stop our course or turn us aside, and, otherwise unmolested, we reached the end of the lines and mingled in the deep circle of townspeople.

The erection we had remarked from the other end we could now see to have a striking resemblance to the gaudy hoardings of a shooting-gallery at a country fair. Its object was of a more sacred nature, however. On this occasion it had to do duty for a mosque, and there we could see the painted imitation of the Mihrab or prayer-niche, indicating the "Point of Adoration," the direction of the sacred city of Mecca. There also was a pulpit for the reader and expounder of the Koran. In front of the gaudily-coloured hoarding was spread a considerable area of matting for the comfort and cleanliness of those about to engage in the religious exercises of the occasion. In dignified procession the Viceroy now moved towards the extemporised mosque. Arrived at the edge of the mat, he dismounted, took off his slippers, and marched across to the Mihrab. Those of the faithful who were not soldiers hurriedly ran to take places. Barely had the Viceroy reached the prayer-niche when the call to prayer rang out sharp and clear on the fresh morning air, every guttural and syllable clearly enunciated and dwelt on lingeringly, musically, and lovingly. For the moment the galloping of horses and the thundering volleys ceased, the din of the talking thousands was hushed, and hardly a sound broke in upon the impressiveness of the half-chanted call to all true believers to come to prayer.

Never before had I looked upon a more interesting spectacle, to south and east for over thirty miles spread the monotonous expanse of the Morocco plain, with something of the grandeur of the boundless sea. Beyond rose the dark towering range of the Atlas, half veiled by the summer's haze, which cast a weird glamour over the mountain heights. Behind were the fort-studded city walls, encircling date groves and gardens, the domes and towers of mosques, and flat-roofed red houses. Around us pressed the thronging thousands of the city and surrounding plain—Arab and Moor, Shellach and Negro, all were there. Almost every one was enveloped in a white robe and a turban, only the boys and children adding bits of colour in their crimson or yellow *kaftans*, and helping to make the crowd less ghost-like. The scene was completed by the long lines of horsemen, sitting statuesque, their guns resting on their saddles, and inclining forward at a slight angle, and by the crowd of courtiers and well-to-do officials and townsmen who squatted on the mat, all in snow-white raiment, save for the high-peaked fez which distinguished the military men. We had hardly well noted the elements of the spectacle when the call to prayer ended with a long-drawn dying cadence.

Next moment the Viceroy rose from his squatting posture, and, like machines moved by a common impulse, the devout crowd who surrounded him followed his example. He it was who led the prayer. As every one muttered in unison, there were bendings of back and knee; foreheads were pressed to the ground, bodies were swayed backwards and forwards, and faces turned slightly upwards with an air of absorption. Submission to God's will, humiliation before His greatness, deprecation of His wrath, supplication for His continued long-suffering and mercy—praise—thanksgiving—all were alike expressed in word and action;

and still in the silent intervals of devotion one could hear the reverberating volleys of troops of soldiers, and on turning round, could see clouds of dust and pale blue smoke, from the midst of which broke a wild array of galloping horses and *haiks* floating like white standards in the breeze.

What most surprised us while we stood looking on the faithful at their devotions was the equanimity with which our desecrating presence was received. We had come quite prepared to be driven away, and yet no one molested us, beyond dinning in our ears the customary curses, which familiarity had led us to treat with contempt.

At the end of the prayers the congregation once more sat down "all of a heap," looking very much like bundles of clothes capped by conical hoods. A *tolb*, or learned man, now entered the pulpit and commenced reading from the Koran a lesson for the day.

Meanwhile the Kaids with their followers had broken up the lines, and were massing themselves one behind the other in order of precedence, forming quite a small army of cavalry. This rearrangement had hardly been completed when the reading finished, and every one hurriedly got up, sought his slippers, and hurried to his horse or mule.

We now pushed forward to see the next development of events. This was the cutting of the throats of several sheep, under the superintendence of the Viceroy. For the lower classes of the city this is the great event of the day, it being made the occasion of a remarkable competition. A prize in money is offered to the man who, on the sheep's throat being cut, picks up the animal in his arms, and, mounted on a mule, first reaches the palace door with the sheep still alive. To do this, of course, he has to grasp the sheep's throat in such a way as to stop the effusion of blood while still allowing it to breathe. The throat-cutting itself we did not witness, but from out the centre of the excited crowd we saw some twenty men on mules riding away as if for dear life, screaming and whacking their animals the while. Among these, only some two or three carried sheep, the rest were friends anxious to assist and encourage those who competed. After this party went helter-skelter the whole donkey-riding costermongerdom of Maraksh. In a twinkling we were left standing almost alone. The Viceroy had mounted and moved some distance on the way towards the Kaids, and there stopped. Next moment the first double line of horsemen trotted towards him, the Kaid and his standard-bearer in the centre. Arrived within five yards of where he stood, a chamberlain or master of ceremonies demanded the name of their tribe or province and of their Kaid, and proclaimed the same to the Viceroy, who throughout what followed spoke not one word, but sat with his hands in the Mussulman attitude of prayer. The chamberlain, speaking for his master, now said, "The Lord help you," to which, with one voice and bending low, the right hand on the breast, the Kaid and his men shouted, "May

Allah preserve our master's life." With almost no interval the chamberlain next cried, "You are welcome to town," to which, with the same pantomime, they answered as before, "May Allah preserve our Master's life." "May you enjoy the holiday," was the next observation, which was followed by the same reply. Finally the Kaid was dismissed with, "Allah leave you in peace," to which for the fourth time he and his people answered, "May Allah preserve our master's life," as they faced to the left and rode off the saluting-ground. Exactly the same thing was repeated as the Kaid of each province or his representative rode forward. They were, of course, variously attended, according to their position, from the Kaid of Gindafy, who was represented by a single soldier, to the Kaid of Rahamna with his two hundred splendidly caparisoned horsemen. A soldier mounted on a mule represented one of the divisions of Haha. With the last presentation ended the state function. The Viceroy returned as before, and each tribe and Kaid wended their way citywards.

We of course followed their example. An ugly incident marked our return. As we were entering the gate an attempt was made to rush us. Happily, it was frustrated by some horsemen of our friend the Kaid of Rahamna, who helped to keep off the crowd.

Though the religious proceedings and state ceremony were over, the festivities connected with the Aid-el-Kebir had still to commence. The afternoon was to be devoted to a grand display of powder-play, and never having seen this national game to advantage, we resolved to be spectators, whatever might be the risk. As a matter of fact, we thought that there could be little danger in mixing in a crowd gathered for secular enjoyment when we had been allowed to go unmolested at a religious function, where there might have been some excuse for attacking us. To be on the safe side, however, we sent to the Kaid and asked for an escort. We were not surprised, considering our strained relations, when he informed us that we had no business to be out. This, however, did not agree with our ideas of our rights and privileges as Britons and bearers of a Sharifian letter, and, escort or no escort, we determined to go.

In the cool of the afternoon we accordingly set forth with some of our men for the square of the Friday market. Here we found a crowd of many thousands of people gathered to see the game.

The powder-play had not commenced, and to pass the time we entered a café, where we drank some coffee. Returning outside, we found the mob crowding in an unusually uncomfortable manner round the door, there being many country-people, who had never seen a European before. As we stood and watched the gathering horsemen and the strange scene around us, it became very evident that mischief was brewing, and that our presence was obnoxious. We had long been accustomed to scowls and revilings, but there was now a tendency to hustle us. We could only form a very hazy idea of the import of the curses, and we replied to them by good-humoured smiles and jokes. It was different, however, with a young man, the nephew of our friend Bonich, who accompanied us as interpreter, Assor not daring to venture out. Arabic he knew better than his own tongue, and his fiery Spanish blood could not brook hearing the revered bones of his ancestors consigned to the lowest depths

FACES IN THE CROWD.

of hell; he chafed accordingly. One great hulking Negro showed himself specially obnoxious in his language, and he speedily brought matters to a climax. I had turned to watch the arrival of a party of horsemen, when a savage clamour broke out behind me. Wheeling round, I discovered to my dismay that the rash boy, utterly forgetful of his situation, had rushed at his black reviler and struck him in the face. The next moment he was stunned by a heavy blow from the Negro's club. A howl of execration burst from those around, and Bonich was being hustled into their midst, from which he would never have escaped alive. However great might be our own danger, it was impossible to stand by and see our companion murdered before our eyes without doing what we could to save him. It was not a time for thought or calculation, only for action. Involuntarily I rushed to his rescue. Those in front of us fell back. The Negro was about to deal another blow at Bonich when I struck him with my fist full in the face. The next moment I was over him, pinning him to the ground by the neck, and, like Bonich, forgetting my surroundings, soundly belabouring him with my hunting crop. It was too much, however, for a Moorish crowd of fanatics to see one of their number thrashed by an infidel. With fierce yells they rushed at me. I turned to look up. A club was descending on my head. I dodged, and received the blow on my left shoulder, paralysing the arm but saving my life. I let go the Negro and stood erect. Letting out the huge lash attached to my hunting-crop, and throwing all the fury and strength at my command into one fell stroke, I swept it round the faces of the closing crowd. Taken by surprise, those in front fell back with skinned faces, howls of pain mingling with their curses. With ampler sweep, I once more struck out with all the concentrated force of one who fights for dear life. So vicious was the blow, that the lash, though thicker than my finger, broke off at the fastening.

I was now standing clear of the crowd, exposed to a new and more terrible danger. In the midst of the wild pandemonium I was able to detect phrases of sinister import—"Stone the dog of a Christian." "Kill him!" "Send the Kaffir to Gehenna."

From all sides hundreds of stones came hurtling through the air. I was aware of blow upon blow, but I felt no pain, not even any sensation of fear. My excitement was too great, the danger of the moment too supreme. Time after time a levelling blow on the head seemed inevitable; but no! Marvellous to relate, my skull escaped absolutely untouched, though I was knocked black and blue over leg and body. My situation in those few seconds was intensely critical. Our servants had shamefully fled, and at any moment I might be knocked senseless. So far I had been too much absorbed in my own position to know what my companion Crichton-Browne and young Bonich were about. I now, however, became aware that they were bravely making a diversion in my favour. Slowly I retreated in that direction, still facing the yelling fanatics, still brandishing my hunting-crop, and happily forgetful of my revolver. A few seconds more and I had rejoined my friends near the café. To our relief the door was open. Had it been otherwise, our position would have been hopeless, for on either side stretched a blank wall with no point of escape. Amid the angry cries of the baffled multitude we bolted inside and shut the door.

Though we had thus obtained a temporary respite, we were far from out of danger. The clamour for our death rose more angrily than ever, and hundreds of stones hammered with a terrific din against the door. We felt sure that they would attempt to force an entrance and dispatch us like rabbits in a warren. We had little time to think, however. A new and sharper note was sounded by the crowd. The rattle of stones became less insistent and continuous. We looked at each other, and only our eyes spoke the thoughts within us. Almost unconsciously we loosened our revolvers in their belts, and kept our fingers on them. We could only await the last critical moment.

The medley of excited cries now retreated some distance from the door. In a slight lull a muffled sound reached our ears. With bated breath and closest attention we listened, trying to fathom the significance of the sound. Quickly it gathered in volume. It approached our refuge. Yells, howls, and execrations followed in its wake in a demoniac roar. A moment more, and we expected to see the door flying into splinters. But no! The thundering sound swept past, and then we knew we were saved. The sound was that of a fierce rush of galloping horsemen driving back the infuriated Moors. Assured of this fact, we threw open the door and walked straight out again in face of the crowd. A roar of execration greeted our appearance, and stones whizzed past us to the imminent danger of our persons. But our blood was up, and we were determined not to be driven away. This lasted for a short time, till some soldiers were posted round us, and then the fanatics contented themselves, as at first, with cursing and reviling us. Though sadly bruised and sore, and still far from being in a safe position, our British pride would not permit us to leave the ground, and we remained to see the powder-play, which now went continuously on. We speedily became absorbed in the picturesque display before us.

At the far end of the square, with the Kutubia some distance beyond overlooking all, the various tribes are massed, line behind line, all in most unsoldierlike costumes, but a perfect artist's dream of artistic effects. In front of them stretches the space in the square kept open for them, having the Moorish crowds on either side, and the walls of the adjoining houses covered with eager onlookers. The first line now begins to move forward. The horses are restrained to a trot, and display their fine action as they dance forward instinct with fiery life. Their long tails sweep the ground, and the tangled bushy manes and luxuriant forelocks add to their wild appearance. Their trappings are of the most gorgeous description, bridle and saddle alike being ablaze with yellow, green, or crimson housings. Their riders, swathed in voluminous creamy dresses, sit like born riders, their swords at their sides, the crimson cords of their daggers and powder-horns, helping to retain their *haiks* on their shoulders. They hold their long flint-locks in their hands, the stocks resting on their thighs and the muzzles pointing skyward. The Kaid or leader rides in the centre, and is distinguished by the fineness of his

POWDER-PLAY.

haik, but more by the magnificent horse he rides and the splendour of its trappings. He sits among his men as becomes a Kaid, ever turning an eager commanding eye to right and left to see that all are in line and acquitting themselves properly. Meanwhile, the pace increases. The horses try to break away, impatient of the bit and the delay. The party near the middle of the square, and are almost opposite us, and still they proceed at a hand-gallop. At this moment the Kaid raises his gun, still holding it vertically, high in the air. As if moved by a common impulse, twenty others do the same. The horses, feeling that the moment of action is coming, are restrained with difficulty. The guns, still held overhead, are now brought to the horizontal, every movement being led by the Kaid. The next moment the flintlocks are lowered, and the stocks pressed against the shoulders. The reins are dropped and the horses bound forward in a magnificent rush. For a moment nothing is heard but the dull thunder of galloping feet, nothing seen but a line of levelled guns and an indefinite mass of white dresses and horses half-hidden in a cloud of dust. Horses and men are darting straight for a dead wall, as if to their own destruction.

As we watch with breathless interest the living whirlwind, a crashing volley sounds in our ears, and then we are confusedly aware of guns again twirled overhead, of floating *haiks* and red-peaked caps partially seen amid clouds of yellow dust and curling wreathes of blue smoke. In a twinkling the reins are regained, and, almost touching the dead wall, the horses are thrown on their haunches and arrested in their wild charge. Then from out the dust and smoke the party returns in single file to the starting-point.

Kaid after Kaid shows the disciplined skill of his men in horsemanship and the use of arms with varying success and applause. At times the lines get broken, or a soldier fires his gun prematurely; when the charge has to be made over again.

Most interesting of all, however, were the feats and antics of those who rode singly or in twos. These displayed the greatest skill, and added something of realism and dramatic interest to their exhibition. They searched for the enemy. Shading their eyes with their hands, they pranced forward looking eagerly in all directions. The enemy was seen, and charged with fierce shouts of "None but the one God!" Mocking cries or bloodthirsty threats were hurled at the imaginary foe. Then came the firing, the sudden halt, and the gallop back. Some there were who displayed special feats, such as firing their guns while held in all sorts of unusual positions, or throwing their weapon up in the air while at full gallop, catching it again and then firing at an imaginary enemy in front or rear. In these and other feats one man from Sidi Rehal carried off the honours of the day. Going in a straight line at full gallop, he stood erect on his saddle, tossed his turban in the air, slipped into his seat again, and, still at full gallop, turned and stood on his head. At another time he stood on his saddle while going at full speed brandishing his gun overhead, dropped as before into his seat, and, quick as lightning, turned round and fired at an imaginary enemy chasing him. A third feat was to simulate being wounded while pursued by the enemy, and by way of carrying out the fraud, to sway about in his saddle as if disabled. The pursuer, thus thrown off his guard, was allowed to come near, when at once the seemingly wounded man was erect, and the enemy done to death before he had time to recover from the surprise.

This interesting exhibition went on till after sunset, and then it became a question how we were to get away. At first we thought of remaining in the café till after dark, but that idea was given up on considering the additional dangers of a possible mobbing in the dark and with no cavalry at hand. We resolved, therefore, to leave on the moment. With difficulty we got our horses brought to us, our men having recovered from their first panic. We at first rode away quite leisurely, amid renewed howling and curses of all sorts; several stones were thrown, but without doing us any harm. Matters, however, became so bad in spite of the presence of several of the Kaid's soldiers, that we had to put our horses to the gallop and run amuck through the crowd. We speedily got outside, and without further misadventure reached our quarters, where our first care was to attend to our bruises, which were numerous from neck to foot.

Next day, our blood being still up, we determined to revisit the square, just by way of asserting our right to be there. We started off in the morning, with the double purpose of giving the Kaid a bit of our mind, and of making a reconnaissance to find out the disposition of the enemy. With difficulty we got two of our men to follow us. The streets were considerably crowded. By the way we were looked at it could be seen that the disturbance of the previous evening was in every man's mind, and that every one wondered at our temerity in venturing out again after what had happened. No one molested us, however, and we rode on to the Kaid's. That official was all excuses, vowing that the disturbance was all the work of the country-people. He asked us what would have been done in England if a Moor had been assaulted as we were. Of course we said that the guilty person or persons would have been put in prison. To which he triumphantly answered, "Allah! what have you to complain of then? For I have thrown thirty people into dungeons, whether guilty or not." He did not further explain that the captures were made less with an idea of punishing guilt than of filling his own pockets with the fines extracted.

We would have had more compassion for his victims, but that we knew that, whether they took part in the attack or not, they were all morally guilty, and thoroughly rejoiced in and sympathised with it. We were weak enough, however, to ask their freedom, which, the fines having been extracted, was willingly accorded.

In the afternoon we once more rode back through the crowd to the café door. Our appearance was greeted with hooting, and one or two stones were thrown. We thought we were in for another attack, but happily the imprisonment of the thirty men had become known,

THE AID-EL-KEBIR. 413

and no further molestation was offered us At the café we found several soldiers awaiting our arrival. Nothing worth mentioning happened to mar our enjoyment of the powder-play, and we retired as before, with a sense of coming out of the conflict the victors.

THE KUTUBIA.

CHAPTER XXVII.

THE JEWS.

AMONG the many attractive studies which Morocco presents to the mind of the inquirer, none is of more surpassing interest than the position of the Jews.

We started from England on our quest of the new and the wonderful with the current ideas regarding the shameful oppression under which, in the Sultan's "happy dominions," the Jews are supposed to eke out a miserable existence. We understood that they were in a position of semi-serfdom, compelled to huddle together in filthy stys, known as Mellahs, subjected to the most degrading restrictions, liable to be murdered and tortured with impunity, their wives and daughters the legitimate prey of the lustful passions of their oppressors—that theirs, in short, was the life of the pariah dog, glad to escape with no worse than curses, kicks, and blows, and thankful if allowed unmolested to pick up such scraps and offal as might be gleaned from the garbage of the Moorish dunghills.

For a time we retained these impressions in all their fulness. The first superficial glance at the outward aspect of things around us seemed only to corroborate the tale of horror and degradation we had heard in England. With our own eyes we saw the overcrowded Mellahs and the resulting physical and moral evils. No account of the terrible filth conveyed half the truth as to their actual condition. The stamp of degradation and the ravages of disease seemed marked on the face of every inhabitant. Hated like poison, and looked upon by the Moors with profound contempt, our first feeling on beholding these suffering children of Israel was one of unmitigated commiseration and pity. Our indignation continually welled over to think that in this nineteenth century such a state of things was permitted to exist. More than anything we wondered to find that among the Europeans of the coast towns there was a marked reflection of the attitude of the Moors. Not one of them but would sooner consort with a Moor than with a Jew. We ourselves, fresh out from home, and burning with ideas about equality of race and religion, full likewise of sympathy with the downtrodden and the oppressed, were anxious to prove our sentiments in action, to hold out to the victim of tyranny the right hand of fellowship, and do what in us lay to help him.

Had we made no more than the usual personally-conducted tourist trip, and obtained only the cursory glances of native life which are the common lot of such travellers, we should have returned home ready to draw a harrowing picture of Jewish wrongs and grievances, and to preach a new crusade to Christian Europe, calling on it to rise in its might and free this unhappy people from its worse than Babylonish captivity.

The true position of the Jews, like the character of Moorish misgovernment, was only borne in upon us gradually. With more frequent and intimate contact came a fuller knowledge and the dawning of new lights.

As we penetrated beneath the surface, it began to appear that the Jews herded together in their Mellahs as much from internal instinct as from external compulsion, and that, if not confined to one, they would only form several—so many more reeking dunghills to stink in the nostrils of the cleanly, sweet incense and perfume loving Moor—so many more plague-spots to infest the air he breathes and poison his blood; for where the Jews are, there also are filth, vermin, and disease. In this respect there is no race on earth so absolutely repulsive as the Barbary Jew. He hugs his dirt as he hugs his gold.

By degrees we discovered that the Jew is not liable to conscription, that he is not taxed for the support of the Kaids and the Sultan, and that, as compared with the Moor, his life and property are safe. Though an alien and despised people, they are the only section of the community to whom some measure of justice is meted out. They are largely governed by their own laws, administered by their own Sheiks, and with their own code of punishment. The Moor, for a trivial or no crime at all, is continually liable to be chained and thrown into the most horrible dungeon; and no matter how monstrous the injustice, not even his nearest relative dares raise his voice in protest. The Jew knows

DAVID ASSOR, SHALUM,
AND JEWS OF MARAKSH.

only prisons, comparatively sweet and clean, and where chains are unheard of. During a period of confinement for any offence, he is allowed the occasional companionship of his wife or friends, and is even permitted to go into the town to transact business. The slightest injustice done to a Jew is sufficient to convulse the whole of Morocco, and set every European Minister at work, by the united outcry of the Jewish community, who make every molehill a mountain, and every assault a brutal murder. The Moor, on the other hand, might be flayed alive or done to death with every conceivable torture, and not a soul in all the land would venture to make a remonstrance. We never once heard of a Jewish maiden suffering at the hands of a Kaid or other official, whereas no young woman of the dominant race was safe. Examine matters as we might, we ever saw the advantage on the Jewish side —better laws, better treatment, greater security of life and property; spoliation, murder, and rapine were reserved for the true believer. True, the Jew is subjected to a variety of restrictions. He must wear a black fez and slippers. In the Medinah he must walk barefoot, and not ride a horse or mule. But what are such things to him so long as he is allowed to make money unmolested? To be prevented from doing that would be the only restriction he would feel acutely. He is not allowed to hold land—as neither are the Europeans—but practically he may hold as much as he pleases, simply by having a Moor as partner and nominal owner.

As time went on and our studies grew wider and deeper, we further came to the conclusion that between the Government and the Jews the Moors are between the devil and the deep sea. Into the respective hands of these two bodies the whole wealth of the country gravitates.

As money-lenders the Jews are as maggots and parasites, aggravating and feeding on the diseases of the land. I do not know, for my part, which exercises the greatest tyranny and oppression, the Sultan or the Jew—the one the embodiment of the foulest misgovernment, the other the essence of a dozen Shylocks, demanding, ay, and getting, not only his pound of flesh, but also the blood and nerves. By his outrageous exactions the Sultan drives the Moor into the hands of the Jew, who affords him a temporary relief by lending him the necessary money on incredibly exorbitant terms. Once in the money-lender's clutches, he rarely escapes till he is squeezed dry, when he is either thrown aside, crushed and ruined, or cast into a dungeon, where, fettered and starved, he is probably left to die a slow and horrible death.

To the position of the Jews in Morocco it would be difficult to find a parallel. Here we have a people alien, despised, and hated, actually living in the country under immeasurably better conditions than the dominant race, while they suck, and are assisted to suck, the very life-blood of their hosts. The aim of every Jew is to toil not, neither to spin, save the coils which as money-lender he may weave for the entanglement of his necessitous victims. Let me mention one or two cases in illustration of these remarks.

Here is an incident, told us by our interpreter David Assor, in which he himself was the lender. He lent $25 to a native of Demnat at an interest of half a dollar per day, and received as security three donkeys, two cows, two guns, and one sword, with the use of the donkeys and cows meanwhile. When he left our service, the interest had been running on for twelve weeks, and therefore amounted to $42, or nearly double the principal. The result would be in the end that he would receive $40 or $50 in money, and retain the animals and weapons.

This, it must be remembered, was repeated not to prove what a sharp fellow he was, but to show his moderation and good-heartedness; for he told us he could have got a dollar a day instead of half a dollar, so great was the necessity of the borrower, a Moor who had been swooped down upon by the Kaid, and had to pay the $25 or be deprived of all he possessed, and he himself thrown into prison. By borrowing from Assor, he had been enabled to stave off the final ruin for two or three months.

The following is another case which came under our own notice:—To enable him to get his brother out of prison, a Jew lent a native of Dukalla $300, to be repaid at the end of three months with $200 of interest. At the end of the three months the $200 of interest was paid, and the principal left at the same rate for another three months. At the end of that time $400 were paid, leaving still a debt of $100, on which the Jew was to receive the same rate of interest. At the proper time $100 were paid, $75 being still left. In nine months the Moor had thus paid $700 for $300, and naturally enough perhaps thought he might be freed of the remaining obligation. But the Jew would not hear of it. He must have the uttermost farthing of what was due to him under the bond, or the man must go to prison. To avoid such a fate, the latter sold his mule for $45, and gave it to the Jew. He now asked to be allowed to go back to Dukalla to borrow the remainder from his friends. Afraid, however, to lose sight of his prey, the Jew demanded to be paid on the spot. With difficulty his victim contrived to raise $25, leaving still $5 unpaid. But even yet he was not permitted to escape. The Kaid was hand and glove with the money-lender, and to prison the Moor must have gone, but that at the last moment the remaining dollars were scraped together, and the unfortunate was free. The Jew had thus received $475 in a year for the use of $300.

In the towns, on the very best security, the lowest rate of interest taken is 30 per cent., but more commonly it rises to 120 per cent., or higher. To people who have to raise money at once to satisfy the ravenous maw of a Kaid, the common way is to lend $100 at an interest of $50 for three months. Of course, at the end of that time it is rarely paid, and the Jew gladly adds the $50 to the $100, and lets the accumulated amount go on at the same rate of interest.

JEWESSES, MARAKSH.

It must be admitted, however, that whatever may be our disgust at discoveries such as these, the Jews are not altogether an unmitigated evil to the country of their adoption, or rather, to put it more correctly, they are of no small value to the merchants of other countries. Their keen mercantile spirit makes them a capital medium of commercial intercourse, and does much to keep the country open in some measure to the trade of Europe.

Before saying more about the general position of the Jew, it may not be out of place to pay a visit to him in his own quarters. Thither, however, I would not advise any of my readers who are easily upset by sights and smells to follow me.

In going to the Mellah, we have to pass through a considerable part of the Medinah, in which we ourselves are located. We shall not, however, waste time over the scenes which meet us *en route*, beyond remarking, for the purposes of comparison, the snow-white dresses and well-washed persons of the Moors, and the calm dignified grace with which they move along, as of men to whom the affairs of this life are but matters of trivial import, and to be attended to at any time. There, too, are the women gliding past, shrouded in their white *haiks*, ever attracting us by their beautiful eyes and the outlines of the well-shaped nose pressed against the muslin face-cloth. The streets are clean though ruinous, and picturesque though mean. We get peeps into market-places, and linger at the doors of quaint workshops.

Here and there a thoroughly Eastern odour of perfumes and spices permeates the air, and harmonises with everything we see and hear around us. We cross the square of the Friday market, pass the house of Ben Daoud, the governor, and finally find ourselves within the gate of the Mellah.

At once we notice a striking change. We are in a new town, inhabited by a totally distinct race of people, who seem to have almost nothing in common with those we have just left. There is more animation, quicker movement, more earnest work, and but little evidence of drifting easily through life, trusting implicitly in what Allah will send. An eager purpose shines in each man's eye—a purpose which absorbs his whole soul, and keeps him restlessly, intensely on the alert. We do not need to be told that greed of gold is the moving principle in the Mellah.

With a different type of features you remark a change in dress. An ugly blue handkerchief with white spots, or still uglier, greasy, black cap, replace the ample folds of the turban or the bright red fez of the Medinah. By the well-to-do dark-coloured or black *kaftans* are worn instead of gauzy *haiks*. Everywhere more pronounced colours meet the eye, everywhere dirtier faces and hands. No shrouded beauties attract our attention. In their place, brazen-faced, disgustingly fat, and repulsively dirty women meet us at every step. No veil hides their deformed eyes or disease-marked faces, a white sheet hung over the head and drawn in at the waist being the only equivalent. Their tawdry gold-embroidered open bodices seem specially designed to show off their gross charms, and the skirts of their dress and the greasy handkerchief which covers their hair are in keeping with their general air of uncleanness.

The gate of the Mellah leads straight into the principal business street, which in parts is shaded from the sun by boards and mats thrown across from the housetops. As we pass along, the street begins to narrow and the shops to become fewer. The air, which so far has smelt of the odorous ingredients of Jewish shops, now becomes more and more redolent of the effluvia of Jewish sewage, of which the sole channels, the sole resting-places, are the streets, no matter what its nature. Each side-lane opens up vistas of dunghills, the gradual accumulation of which has raised the original level of every street several feet, so that to enter the houses a corresponding descent is necessary. Clouds of flies rise in buzzing myriads at every step. In these we see the chief disseminator of the ophthalmic diseases which afflict "God's chosen people." Everywhere are wranglings and quarrellings. No uncommon sight is to see two old men clutching at each other by the beard, and, with faces thus drawn close to each other, pouring forth an uninterrupted torrent of yells and screams. They weep, too, in their rage, like ill-tempered children, and snarl and snap and tug at each other like worrying dogs. Everywhere the public sights and scenes are unseemly. We look in vain for one redeeming feature, one object on which our eyes may rest with some sense of pleasure. We had often longed to see Moorish women unveiled; here we should be glad of any covering to conceal the faces of the Jewesses who crowd the doorways to watch our passing. The consciousness that they are trying to bring their squinting or sightless eyes to bear upon us haunts one like a nightmare, their large, sensual mouths, with lips wide apart, displaying ugly sets of teeth in harmony with themselves and their surroundings. There, too, are the children wallowing in the filth, many already marked with ophthalmic disease, and not a few just recovering from small-pox; some in their mothers' arms fearful to look upon.

Matters are little better inside the houses. We cross the family dunghill, conveniently placed at the doorstep. The interior arrangements are much the same as in the Moorish quarter—the familiar *patio* or court surrounded by two storeys of apartments. Here, however, the resemblance ends. Instead of being occupied by one family, there are from eight to sixteen, according to the poverty of the inmates. A beastly sink, full of liquid sewage, and peopled by wobbling ducks and hens, replaces the clean tesselated pavement or the rose-perfumed garden. Dishevelled women, with strident voices, scream at each other in acrid tones,— very different from their more musical-voiced Mohammedan sisters. Seldom has a family more than one room; and too frequently that room becomes the dwelling-place of two families. These apartments are, as in the Medinah, long and narrow; but, unlike the Moorish rooms, they are marked by dirt and untidiness. They are absolutely destitute of ornament, though the roughly painted outline of a hand to ward off the evil-eye might be mistaken for an attempt at such. Another favourite charm is the rude sketch of a scorpion executed on paper. This is supposed to render its possessor proof against the venomous pests which infest the city. At first we are led to believe that the numerous red spots which mottle the once whitewashed walls are rudimentary attempts at decoration, especially as in some places they are more numerous than in others, and form a species of arch. We are soon disillusionised. These rude red splatches mark the spot where bloated bugs have met a bloody death under the ruthless hands of vindictive Jews. The arches mark the favourite sitting-places of the owners; the radius of the arch is the length of the human arm. Needless to say, other vermin lead a cheery existence in the mattresses and straw mats which cover the floor, ever attracting attention to their presence by their merry leaps and bounds, or more markedly by repeated incursions on our legs and ankles.

Few people are more hospitable than the Jews, and the mistress of the house lays down her child—painfully hideous from an attack of the small-pox, now raging in the city—while she washes the cups preparatory to giving us some green tea. Politeness demands that we should pay for our curiosity by acceptance. To wash down the nauseous mixture we ask for some water. A tin pannikin is picked up from the filthy floor, and without more ado dipped into a large earthenware jar in the corner, leaving us to imagine that the same process has been going on since morning and to calculate the probable condition of the water in consequence. That water was never swallowed.

But enough of the amenities of Jewish life. Only the pen of a Zola could fitly portray its various repulsive aspects.

Like the Moor, the Jew sticks to the doctrines and ceremonial observances of his religion with the most unchangeable pertinacity. Elsewhere he has become influenced by his environment, has dropped much and altered much, and in some measure has brought himself into harmony with his surroundings. Not so with the Jew of Morocco. Persecution has had its usual result. It has cut him off from outside influences, and has compelled him to use his religion as a force to preserve the race from destruction as well as show it the way to heaven. The Jew's creed has become the formula of a national union, subscription to which ensures the protection of the entire community. In it lies his safety. To permit the slightest variation in the received views is to undermine the bulwarks behind which he has entrenched himself. But while Judaism in Morocco has petrified into an unchangeable crust, it has, like Mohammedanism, lost all its moral force. The Jew will break almost any of the ten commandments without exception, rather than violate a ceremonial observance. To omit saying his morning prayers would lie heavier on his conscience than stealing. To touch fire of any kind on Saturday, to eat meat not killed by the proper Rabbi, to ride on a mule or donkey on the Sabbath, would be more heinous offences, and would be viewed with greater reprobation, than vicious practices, lying, or even murder. He rejoices in over eighty feasts, fasts, and holidays per annum, when it is not lawful to do work of any kind; and so great is the tyranny of the Jewish priesthood, that not a soul dares violate the custom. He may have more than one wife. Divorce is easily obtained; but is rarely taken advantage of, as, except in the case of the blackest offences, the wife's dowry must be given back. This is an effectual veto. Rather than relinquish wealth once acquired, a Jew would remain tied to a perfect devil.

In justice to this remarkable race, it must be admitted that the frightful and loathsome state of things which exists among them is the result of past persecution. Till well on in this century, their position could not have been worse. To be treated like human pariahs and moral lepers, to be buffeted, spat upon, degraded, and kept apart, could not but have the effect of making them in some measure what they were assumed to be. It will take generations of better government to alter the filthy habits and smooth out the moral warps which have thus been produced.

Among the mountains and south of the Atlas, the Jews are as much deserving of commiseration as ever they were, but it is different in the towns and in Morocco proper. The Lord has delivered the Philistines into the hands of His chosen people. As their ancestors lived in bondage to the Egyptians, and were at last enabled to despoil their oppressors, so now, in a slower but more effectual fashion, they are revenging themselves for past wrongs. To the former tyrants now belong the stripes and the dungeons. It is their turn to be robbed, tortured, and ground down. Justice this, perhaps. Yes, but with the merciful the sympathy and pity are ever for the sufferer. In Morocco, which is the sufferer—Jew or Moor—it is not difficult to decide.

CHAPTER XXVIII.

THE HOUSE-TOPS.

OUR pleasantest hours in Morocco were those spent on the house-tops. When our evening meal was over, and the fierce splendour of the summer sun veiled in the west, we invariably hastened from the stifling oven-like atmosphere of our rooms to seek fresh air and cool breezes overhead. Our appearance in this forbidden region was always the signal for a commotion among such of the women as had already ascended to the neighbouring house-tops. Most of them immediately scuttled below, like rabbits suddenly disturbed in their warren; but, like rabbits too, they not infrequently found courage to turn round on reaching the staircases and trap-doors to examine, with true feminine curiosity, the rude violators of their privacy. Some there were who ensconced themselves behind walls and other bulwarks, and there took notes of our persons. A few occasionally stood fire, but these were mostly such as we could well have dispensed with the sight of. Those we longed most to see—the young and beautiful—were treasured up too securely ever to be permitted to accompany their riper sisters to their favourite rendezvous, where there could be no security from the prying gaze of unauthorised male eyes.

It required a certain amount of temerity on our part to venture outside as we did. The house-tops are absolutely restricted to the use of women, and any man trespassing on the forbidden region is liable to fine and imprisonment. We, however, as British infidels, considered ourselves outside the pale of Moorish laws, and made exceptions for ourselves, on the plea that we were religious lepers, of whom no good Mussulman need be afraid as likely to disturb his domestic peace or attract the wandering eyes of his ladies. But there are unreasonable people everywhere, and we had every reason to believe that twice we were shot at with murderous intent, one of the bullets whistling uncomfortably near us. Not to be too offensive, we rarely ventured up till darkness was setting in, by which time hardly a woman was to be seen, the jealous-minded Moor being careful that his womankind keep their own apartments after dark.

Pleasant it was in these cool, balmy evenings to watch the changing after-glow or the swift gathering shades of evening over the Atlas Mountains. How different they looked now, divested of their snowy mantle, only the highest elevations showing here and there a spot or streak of white. That mountain region was no longer a *terra incognita* to us. We could now identify its peaks and glens. Eastward we could trace the course of the Gadat through the flanking lower ranges to the conical mass of Jebel Glauwi, bringing back to our recollection the toils and worries of our first attempt to cross the mountains. . From Jebel Glauwi to Jebel Tezah the range presented a comparatively even and unbroken summit, gradually rising westward, till over Reraya, where the slopes were still streaked with snow, it undoubtedly reached its highest elevation. Cutting deep into the flanks of the mountain we could see the gorges of the Wad Urika and the Wad Reraya. At the head of the former a prominent peak broke the general level of the crest. This was the Jebel of the Asif Sig—none other, as was easily demonstrable, than the "Mlitsin" of Washington, over which geographers have disputed so much. Our eyes ever turned with special longing towards this peak, for we had marked it in our minds for an exploring assault.

West of Reraya a sudden drop marked where the Wad Nyfis cuts right into the heart of the range and forms the valley of Gindafy. Through the great notch thus hewn out might be seen the heights of Jebel Wishdan. From the Nyfis westward the massive comparatively even level of the Atlas ridge becomes more broken into conspicuous peaks, chief among which were Jebel Tezah and Jebel Erduz; the latter jutting out somewhat, and hiding Jebel Ogdimt and the westward continuation of the main range.

When darkness set in, there was little to tell that a populous city lay around us; no glimmering street-lights, no glow in the sky, no lighted window even to brighten the gloom and tell of cheery homes and the happy domestic circle. There was no hum of busy life, yet the city was not altogether without some characteristic sounds. The firing of guns, the squeak of pipes, and the noise of drums which accompany a marriage procession were of nightly occurrence. More frequent even than these were the lamentations and shrieks, painful to listen to, which announced a death. During our stay small-pox was raging in the city, especially among the children, and was carrying off the little ones by scores. Sometimes in our immediate vicinity three or four families with their friends might be heard simultaneously announcing their bereavement.

The house-tops afforded us some otherwise unobtainable glimpses of Moorish domestic life. Placed as we were, we not unfrequently became involuntary listeners to matrimonial disputes. One night we were made aware that, however lowly may be the place of women in the Moorish social scale, they still retain the right to give their lords and masters " a piece of their mind." The wife of our neighbour, who was no less than a Sharifia, or descendant of the Prophet, had discovered that her husband had been spending his substance on strange women. She opened fire upon him accordingly. Such a torrent of virulent abuse I never heard in all my life. It was no hysterical outburst quickly subsiding into silence, but one continuous scream, kept up at the pitch of her voice for hour after hour, and indeed far into the morning. The husband's voice was never once heard, but whether his silence arose from a guilty conscience or from sheer inability to edge in a word, I cannot say. Next night, however, told another tale. We heard the lady's voice again, this time not in abuse and invective, but in terror and pain. It was now the husband's turn, and he wasted no time in idle words, but gave the rebellious fair one a most thorough castigation.

At times we ventured to take a peep into the court of an adjoining house, where we could see the inmates moving about. The centre was occupied by a charming little garden, overlooked by a cool, airy verandah. Everything was supremely neat and clean.

Not infrequent on these summer evenings were the sounds of unholy revelry. A little way off some unattached women had taken up their residence, and syren-wise sang nightly the praise of love and the joys of meeting black-eyed girls in the light of the moon. It was not a pleasant sort of music, and came to our ears in jarring contrast with the impressiveness and neverending charm of the call to prayers at *Asha* or suppertime. At 8.30 lights might be seen ascending the mosque towers, till, the top being reached, they shone like stars in the darkness. Suddenly from one of the towers would burst upon the night-air the summons to prayer, chanted by a full magnificent voice, another and another taking up the cry, till the whole city rang with the phrase—"Allah Akhbar! Allah Akhbar!"—which called the faithful to their evening devotions. In the stillness of the starlit night those sonorous guttural sounds came to us with added effect, and it is doubtful if there were a dozen of the true believers around us who listened half so attentively or were so genuinely touched by the beautiful solemnity of the Mueddin's cry as we hated Christians, who sat on the house-top listening to what was not intended for us.

That all Mohammedans are not alike uninterested in the performance of any save the imperative ceremonial duties of their creed, we had an opportunity of learning also from our post of observation on the house-tops. A number of the faithful nightly gathered on a neighbouring roof for prayer and the reading of the Koran, the devotions being led by a venerable old man, seated near a lantern, which half lighted up his fine face and the picturesque group of listeners.

Sights and sounds like these could not fail to draw us into reflections about Mohammedanism and its influence as a religion for good and evil. The result of our investigations had been far from encouraging. How different its effects in Morocco from what I had known them in the Sudan! There I had seen it burning with the old fire of its early days in Arabia, when it transformed a scattered congeries of nomad tribes into religious propagandists and the conquerors of half the semicivilised world. Similarly, in the Central and Western Sudan, it had commenced a new era of hope and progress to the Negro, and with the watchword of Islam a race of shepherd-serfs, called Fillani, had burst their heathen bonds, and established Mohammedanism as their religion, and themselves as the rulers of a region extending from Lake Chad to the Atlantic. But it was not alone a mere conquering force, leading men to battle and victory. It had proved itself a great civilising agent, raising the social status of the Negro, instilling the germs of morality into his darkened mind, substituting Allah, the one God, compassionate and merciful, for his old idols and fetishes, and sweeping away the gross mass of superstition and horrible practices which marked his state of barbarism.

Not least valuable had been its influence in stemming back the advancing flood of gin, which, with a few Bibles, largely represented Europe's civilising agents. Wherever Islam penetrated in these barbarous regions, there was a concomitant enormous advancement in civilisation, morality, habits, and customs, as well as in arts and industries. Compared with it, no religion was doing such magnificent work or producing such splendid results. There was an adaptability and a simplicity about it totally awanting in the other proselytising creeds—or rather, to put it more correctly, in the methods of those who undertook the propaganda; for the failure of Christian missionaries is more due to their insane methods of going to work than to any inherent unsuitableness in their religion to the minds of the peoples approached.

But if in the Sudan we found Mohammedanism instilling a new life and vigour into barbarous races, and setting them on the road to spiritual, moral, and material advancement, in Morocco we found it doing quite the reverse. Here it was preventing all advancement, suppressing all higher and nobler impulses which happened to be alien to its spirit, cutting off the believer from all outside genial influences, and acting as a blight upon his whole nature. Like Judaism in the case of the Jews, Mohammedanism had become to its Western adherents a petrifying crust, as incapable of expansion from the inside as of being penetrated from without. Superficially it presented a fair and seemly spectacle, unquenchable faith, scrupulous attention to ceremonial duties, and most absolute submission to the will of Allah, but underneath all was maggots and rottenness.

Mohammedanism had here proved itself to have that amount of good in it which could raise a degraded people to a considerable level of civilisation, and give the main impetus which made their arms all-conquering. Further than that it could not go. With the dying-out of the first intense missionary enthusiasm came the dissociation of religion and morality—the petrifaction of the one and the rapid decadence of the other. The results of these two processes are seen in Morocco in their most advanced stage. Here we are confronted with the astounding fact that the most religious people on the face of the earth is at the same time almost the most immoral, and find that the force which made the empire great in the world has become the agent which will prove its destruction.

The government of Morocco was another fertile topic of discussion and reflection. The existing state of things seemed almost incredible to European eyes. I had never seen anything to compare with it, even among the most barbarous races of Central Africa. The Moorish principles of ruling may be summed up in two words—poverty and disunion. Keep the people ground down to the dust and foster tribal animosities, and there will be no rising against the constituted authority. In the poverty of his subjects and the disunion of the tribes lies the strength of the Sultan. For the people to become wealthy, or the tribes to unite among themselves, would be manifest dangers to the state. Consequently, every penny of money is squeezed out of them by regular, and especially by irregular, taxation. The most absolute restrictions are put upon the exportation and importation of important articles. Such a port as Agadir, the natural outlet of the trade of Sus, is kept closed to commerce, solely with the same end in view. A scarcity of food existed last year in the south, while in the north there was abundance. Nevertheless the Sultan refused to allow of a trade in grain, because, on the one hand, those who were starving would get their food too cheap, and, on the other, those who sold would get too much money, and might make themselves troublesome. Rather than that, let the people starve and the food rot.

Too much starvation, however, it is seen, may engender discontent with the Sultan's and God's decrees. Therefore, to prevent co-operation among the tribes, everything is done to keep up an inimical feeling. No two neighbouring governors are ever friendly with each other. To be so would be to lay themselves open to suspicion. A little war between two such neighbours is not discountenanced by the Sultan as long as it helps to ruin their respective districts. Sometimes it is purposely encouraged, till the Sultan, seeing his opportunity, turns round in virtuous indignation, and throws into prison the governor who has been most enriched by spoliation and plunder, the ill-gotten wealth thus finding its way into the Sultan's treasury. Everything exists for the ruler; land and people are alike his. The whole system of government is arranged with a view to impoverishing exactions. The Sheiks drain the people, the Kaids the Sheiks, and the Sultan the Kaids, the result being as complete as the drainage of a given area into the ocean by a river and its tributaries. The people have no rights, save such as the Sultan more or less temporarily accords them. Justice, or the reverse, is dispensed to the highest bidder, and crime winked at under the influence of bribes. A man's sole safety in Morocco lies in absolute poverty. To have money, or the reputation of having it, is to live in constant fear of chains and the dungeon, of torture and starvation. The tenure of office of a Kaid or Sheik entirely depends on the amount of money he manages to divert into the coffers of the Sultan and his ministers. Few there are who do not know the inside of a dungeon; fewer still who are allowed to end their days in peace. Formerly the Kaids had a certain measure of power, and could at times even set the Sultan himself at defiance. Now that power is much broken. In order to break it still further, to promote further disunion and more thoroughly drain the country of its wealth, all the larger provinces, such as Abda and Haha, have now several governors, besides *Amins* or Government tax-collectors.

The result of these measures is seen in every corner of the country. Ruin and desolation are marked on every square mile, deserted homesteads and rich plains lying uncultivated telling their own tale of spoliation and rapine.

As we wander from province to province and from city to city, and see the poverty and degradation of the inhabitants, it seems difficult to believe that these are the descendants of the people who conquered Spain, who, when all the nations of Europe were little better than semi-barbarians, encouraged the arts and sciences, and built noble palaces, mosques, and public buildings, which have remained the wonder of succeeding generations; a people, too, who were renowned for their love of music, poetry, and literature in general, and who set an example of rare liberality of thought, of polished manners, and of ruling genius never surpassed by any nation in later times. The Moors of to-day are, as a race, the identical Moors of Spain, but how much deteriorated! Not a trace remains of the old enlightened traits. Everything that made their ancestors the admiration of the world has been completely blotted out, and has been replaced by its opposite. All this has been brought about by the system of government. Since the expulsion of the Moors from Spain, it has gone from bad to worse, till now art and learning are unknown, the material prosperity and happiness of the people unthought of, and religion has become a barren formula. Hatred and suspicion of the foreigner replace the open-hearted hospitality of other days. From being in the full tide of the current of life, Morocco has now become a stagnant backwater, full of noxious germs and rotting weeds, utterly irreclaimable, and bound before long to sink in the foul mud of its own making. There is absolutely no hope of its becoming better through ordinary outside pressure and contact with healthier influences.

Morocco knows that its very existence now depends upon its isolation and its firm determination not to allow entrance to European reforms. Every innovation is looked upon as another door opened to the invasion of the hated infidel and the assertion of his power. It might be thought that people living under such grinding tyranny would naturally hail with pleasure the interference of European powers in their behalf. No greater mistake could be made. In the first place, they rarely complain of their condition. All things happen according to the decrees of God, and He it is who has ordained that they should be thus afflicted. To rebel against His minister on earth would be to rebel against Himself. This the Moor has not yet learned to do, and accordingly he accepts his fate with the most admirable resignation. Again, no Moor believes for a moment that his condition would be improved under a European Government. It seems to him that he would only be exchanging oppression under a ruler of his own faith for oppression under a Christian—a disgrace and dishonour he could not bear.

Nor is he altogether without reason for this belief; for in Morocco the honour of more than one European country is continually being dragged in the mud by its representatives, who in many cases *buy* their places, not as a means of watching over their national interests, but in order to traffic in the sale of "protections," which put the Moor or the Jew outside the pale of Moorish law, permitting him to indulge in legalised plunder, and so adding another to the numerous diseases under which the country groans.

France is no small offender in this respect, but America is the most shameless sinner. With no trade, no genuine subjects, no real or imaginary interest to look after, there is yet not only an American Minister at Tangier, but Vice-Consuls, mostly Jews, in the chief coast towns, some of whom are no honour to their country. Nay, more; America does not hesitate to make a naval demonstration to compel the payment of bills run up in the Jewish fashion—a few paltry hundreds of dollars becoming in a year or two thousands upon thousands.

One thing we may congratulate ourselves upon. Our hands are clean. With such a man as Sir Kirby Green at the helm, we shall know how to make ourselves respected in just causes, but will have no participation in anything disgraceful or underhand. With Consuls like Mr. White at Tangier and Mr. Payton at Mogador, and Vice-Consuls like Mr. Hunot at Saffi and Mr. Hunter at Casablanca, we need have no fear of our national honour. They belong to the class of men who have made our name and our influence for good great in the world.

What will eventually become of Morocco I do not venture to predict. It would indeed have ceased to exist as an empire long ago had not national jealousies prevented its absorption into Algeria or its division between France and Spain. Both of these powers watch and wait for the hour when it shall become a part of either or both of their possessions. No other nation puts in a claim to a share of the spoil, yet none will allow either France or Spain to enter, to their real or fancied detriment. Spain alone could not conquer Morocco, or, if conquered, could not keep possession of it. Even France would think twice before venturing on the work of conquest. A very considerable army would be required, and, with a troublesome population in Algeria and the war-cloud hanging over Europe, that could not well be spared. The defeat of Germany, in the event of war breaking out, would determine the fate of Morocco. Then, without a doubt, France would take possession of the region she has so long looked to as her natural right, whatever Spain might say to the contrary.

This is not a pleasant development to be looked forward to by us, but, all things considered, it must be admitted it would be the best solution of the question for Morocco. The French, though no colonists, have shown themselves capable of great and unselfish sacrifices in opening up the regions in Africa of which they have taken possession. Of course it will be asked, what about our retention of Gibraltar and our power in the Mediterranean? On that subject I do not pretend to speak as an authority. Doubtless we should know at the proper time how to take such steps as might be necessary for the safeguarding of our own interests. In any case, the state of affairs in Morocco is a disgrace to the century, and we cannot be justified in countenancing it because, forsooth, some real or imaginary danger to our position at Gibraltar is foreseen by the substitution of an improved European government. Shaky and rotten must be the foundations of our position in these parts if it is dependent on the continued existence of the Moorish empire as it is at present.

AMONG THE GARDENS, MARAKSH.

CHAPTER XXIX.

URIKA.

TOWARDS the end of August we began to see our way to leave Maraksh. The heat had considerably abated; the stores we expected from the coast had arrived after an excessive delay; but best of all, some sores on my feet, from which I had been suffering for over a fortnight, had taken a favourable turn.

The one alloy to our delight at leaving the city was the fact that we would once more be thrown upon the tender mercies of our men. David Assor had made up his mind to return to Demnat, leaving us dependent on Abdul Kader as an interpreter. This arrangement would have disturbed us more, had it not been that Abdul Kader was now three months in arrears of wages; and although we still had to revisit the mountains, yet we were in a manner on our way to Mogador.

As the time for our departure arrived, however, it seemed as if we were likely to be deprived even of Abdul Kader's services, for he fell sick. For several days he made our quarters dismal with his groans, and brought our spirits down to zero by the sight of his pain-stricken and woebegone face. He reduced Assor to tears by the recital of his agonies, as he besought the latter to lay his case before us, and ask us not to seek to drag him away to die on the road. It seemed indeed as if it would be necessary to leave him behind. And yet, without Assor and Abdul Kader, how were we to get along? where find a substitute? Our perplexity and annoyance was great. Happily, one day I came upon the sick man by surprise, and, to my astonishment, found him in a joyous mood, solacing himself with the companionship of a dark-eyed countrywoman. On seeing me, his smiles vanished and a look of pain settled upon his face. A pang of agony doubled him up and forced a groan from the depths of his inner man. Grieved at the sight, I retired to reflect. I recalled how, on a previous expedition, I had quelled a rebellion and cured no fewer than a dozen sick men with a single bottle of castor-oil. My course seemed clear. Armed with a dozen pills—dose one to two—I hastened back to my suffering attendant. The damsel—no ministering angel in time of sickness—had disappeared, and Abdul Kader was writhing on the floor. Ordering him to sit up, I administered the pills in one dose, and then laid down my ultimatum with no uncertain voice. He must either be completely cured by the morrow, or he would be turned out of the house without letter or wages. Under the circumstances, I allowed him the day and night to recover. Next morning he came up smiling.

It was on the 28th of August that we once more took the field. As on the occasion of our previous departure from the city, we did not think it necessary to acquaint the authorities with the fact, and we were allowed to leave untroubled by obstructive soldiers.

Our primary destination was Urika, with the object of penetrating the glen of that name, and ascending the Jebel Asif Sig—one of the most prominent of the few elevations which break the even outline of the main ridge.

In six hours' rapid riding we crossed the burned-up plains, from which all the crops had now been gathered, leaving nothing but yellow stubble and withered grass, and reached the base of the mountains once more. How we rejoiced to be away from the dusty town and our oven-like quarters, and find ourselves once more near a brawling torrent, under shady olive trees, and with the mountains towering over us. We camped at Achliz, near the entrance to the glen. We were invited, for safety, to take up our quarters in the Kasbah, but we preferred our tents and a spice of danger to the Kaid's guest-house, with its inevitable fleas and sense of confinement. The Kaid was at a second residence in the mountains, so that the Kalifa had to act for him.

The day of our arrival being a market-day and Achliz a *sok*, we saw a picturesque assemblage of mountaineers and country-people. Their presence simplified the gathering of our *mona*, with which we were always lavishly provided. On our appearance,

MOUTH OF THE WAD, URIKA GLEN.

the Kalifa sent down at once and collected together the Sheiks of villages. To these he gave the necessary orders, and they again sent instructions to those under them. As the afternoon wore on, one messenger after another arrived laden with provisions. From one village came a contribution of a donkey-load of charcoal, from another eleven fowls, and from a third a sheep. From various other quarters came two or three dozen eggs, a dozen pounds of butter, onions, and a mule-load of barley. The Kalifa, on the part of the Kaid, added a loaf of sugar, a packet of candles, and a quarter of a pound of green tea, besides half a dozen loaves of bread, fruit, and several dishes of cooked food.

Rather to our surprise, almost everything collected was handed over to us—a most unusual occurrence, our appearance being usually a splendid opportunity for the most outrageous exactions in the way of food, nominally, of course, for us, but in reality for the Kaid and his Kalifa, while the Sheiks also took the opportunity to help themselves. On these occasions it was useless for us to protest that we would rather buy the food, for the exactions would have been made all the same. As little use was it to offer money to recoup the poor people from whom the supplies were levied; it never would have got past the Kaid or his underlings.

In our communication with the Kalifa we missed Assor very much, and had always a most unpleasant feeling of suspicion regarding the integrity of Abdul Kader.

Next day, though the Kalifa was anxious that we

should stay till the Kaid arrived from the mountains, we insisted on going up to where he was. We started accordingly with only half our men, also leaving our horses behind, as less suited to dangerous mountain-paths.

Our way lay up the bottom of the glen, sometimes in the bouldery bed of the river, sometimes winding along its olive-clad banks. Near the entrance we crossed a series of vertical beds of white limestone and red shales passing into red sandstones, which formed irregular arar and cystus clad hills. On the slopes and crests were several picturesquely disposed villages, with their red clay-built walls and curious open verandahs in the upper storeys of the houses. At this place also there was an outcrop of the basalt, which occurs so frequently among the cretaceous rocks of the lower range.

An hour from Achliz we were quite put out on descrying on the dark bush-clad mountain-side the white dresses of a party of horsemen. We knew it could be no other than the Kaid and his attendants.

When within a quarter of a mile of each other we halted and dismounted, as if each was a suspicious party and required to be carefully approached. At length we met, and we were pleased to find the Kaid a lubberly-looking and apparently simple-minded fellow, with whom we could probably do as we pleased. He at first wanted us to return with him to Achliz, but on our insisting that we could not think of doing so, he gave in and turned back with us. We had not

VILLAGE IN URIKA GLEN.

Page 448.

far to go before we were shown a charming camping-ground in a grove on an excessively high bank of river, or more probably glacial debris, as the absence of stratification and the huge size of the enclosed boulders seemed to suggest.

Here we were supplied in absurd abundance with all the luxuries that Urika and the Kaid's stores had to offer. The Kaid's care of our valuable persons was not so gratifying. It took the form of his camping out beside us, to keep strict watch and ward over us and our movements.

The conversation we had with him was apparently of the most encouraging nature. We were told that everything he possessed was ours to command, and that we might go wherever we liked in his province. He then proceeded to let us down gradually. First, the upper part of the glen was shown to be a part of the province of Misfiwa, with the Kaid of which he was on bad terms. Next, we were told that the rest of the glen, with its bordering mountains, were in revolt against him, and that he himself could not go a mile farther up. We had a strong suspicion that we were being duped between the seemingly simple Kaid and the wily Abdul Kader; but what could we do? How ascertain the truth? In the evening we attempted to take a walk, and were speedily stopped by a dozen soldiers, who would not allow us to proceed farther, on the plea that we should be killed. At night a triple line of guards surrounded us, presumably for our protection, but in reality to make sure that we did not leave camp.

Next day, in spite of the protestations of our host, we insisted on being allowed to ascend the glen, though we were by no means sanguine that we would get far. The Kaid at length gave way, and commended us to the keeping of Allah and half a dozen soldiers.

Our suspicions that we were being hoaxed grew ever stronger as we were led up the rough bed of the river in the most rambling fashion, our guides apparently desirous of gaining time. Shalum unfortunately knew absolutely nothing about this district, so that, whatever might be our suspicions, we were utterly dependent on the soldiers.

We had barely got half a mile from camp, and were nearing a point where the glen suddenly narrows to a gorge, the mountains springing abruptly to a height of from 7000 to 8000 feet, when we noticed signs of commotion in the numerous villages here dotted about. Great numbers of men were hurrying along, apparently with the view of reaching a point ahead of us. At first we thought that the Kaid, seeing our determination to proceed into the dangerous parts, had ordered the mountaineers to join us. Our escort seemed as much interested as ourselves, and watched the gathering natives, freely commenting among themselves on the situation.

It soon became evident that the Shellach had no intention of acting as a reinforcement or of assisting us in any way whatever. They could be seen collecting in olive groves and behind rocks and other favourable positions for defence and concealment. Every one was armed, and the glint of silver-mounted guns could be seen from every grove ahead of us. An unusual interest in what was going on was displayed by the women, who were crowding out in front of the villages and on the house-tops. Our hearts sank within us as a large party suddenly burst from behind a projecting ridge, and took up a position right in the centre of the glen, a cordon of armed men being thus drawn across our path some two hundred yards ahead of us, with the evident intention of stopping all farther progress. At the same time our escort, with every sign of determination, threw off their cumbersome cloaks, and began to buckle themselves up for action. They loaded their guns, and then, in the manner of sharpshooters, scattered and advanced to meet the enemy, taking advantage of tree and rock to cover their movements. We ourselves remained where we were in unpleasant perplexity, doubting whether the whole affair was a ruse of the Kaid's to stop us without implicating himself, or a genuine case of obstruction on the part of the mountaineers. In either case, our prospects of advancing further were nil. We thought it well, however, to test the real character of the opposition. Accordingly we advanced in a body towards our scattered escort in front. The enemy immediately displayed great excitement. They brandished their guns at us, and screamed out that we must go back, else they would shoot us. The soldiers of our party, who had advanced alone with such apparent bravery to oppose a force ten times their number, seemed annoyed at our coming to their support, and at the sight of our ready rifles. At each step the mountaineers became more frantic. Scores of guns were levelled at us, and we knew that their owners were all good marksmen. To add to our difficulties, at this moment we had no interpreter, Abdul Kader having been left in charge of the camp. At length, seeing how hopeless and even dangerous it was to push our way through the excited cordon, and anxious to avoid intentional or accidental bloodshed, I called a halt. C.-B., with his military instincts, wanted to charge and force our way through, but I would not listen to any such proposal, and gave the word to return to camp.

On regaining our tents, we angrily taxed the Kaid with getting up the opposition. He earnestly swore on the sacred name of Allah that it was not so—that he himself was in constant danger from the wild tribesmen, and at the moment was compelled to camp out on the watch for possible attacks. Only a few days before our arrival he declared that he had treacherously captured thirty of the rebels and thrust them into prison, and that in consequence they were in greater ferment than ever.

How far he spoke the truth we had no means of determining, for we could not believe a word Abdul Kader told us. On the subject of an interpreter, however, our minds had now happily been set at ease, a courier having arrived the night before from Bonich, offering his services as such to Mogador. Needless to say we had clutched at the proposal at once.

Whatever reason there might be to suspect the Kaid of treachery, he at least gave us no cause of complaint on the score of *mona*. Here was our bill of fare for the day, our party being six in number:—

    6.30.—A huge wash-hand basin of soup, with eggs, milk, and charcoal.
    8.—A second enormous supply of soup and a melon.
    8.30.—Green tea from the Kaid's own tea-service, four loaves of bread, and several pounds of fresh butter.
    9.—Four large dishes of cooked food.
    12.—A large basket of grapes.
    12.30.—A decanter of rose-water.
    3.30.—Two dishes of kuskussu and half a baked sheep, followed by tea.
    5.—Two dishes of cooked food with four loaves of bread.
    8.—One live sheep, a loaf of sugar, and a quarter of a pound of tea.
    9.30.—Ten live fowls and more cooked food.

Finding ourselves no match for the combined craftiness of our henchman and the Kaid, we gave up all hopes of reaching the Jebel Asif Sig, and accordingly returned to Achliz, deeply enraged and disappointed. This was unfortunate for Abdarachman, who, against my express orders, had sent a miserable little mule with a frightful sore on its back into Morocco for Bonich. I at once, in presence of the crowd, administered a sound castigation to the fellow, and ordered him off with another mule.

During our absence a man had been murdered in our camp, the murderer flying for safety to the neighbouring province.

Mr. Bonich arrived in camp the same afternoon, having missed Abdarachman, who evidently had gone on to Morocco. Next day the latter turned up at 9 A.M.; and after resting the mule and my pony Toby for a couple of hours, we set off for the Wad Reraya.

Shortly after mid-day we reached that river at Tachnowt, where it leaves the low range of heights, which here projects north from the Atlas.

At Tachnowt or Taghnowt the glen is comparatively open, displaying outcrops of white limestone and red shales, forming an anticline whose axis is parallel with the mountains. A mile up the winding river the glen suddenly narrows to the merest gorge, where some metamorphic shales and crystalline limestones run at right angles to its course, and have been less acted upon by denuding agents.

In passing through the gorge, there was no other path than the bed of the river, till once more the cretaceous rocks reappeared, with a coincident widening out of the gorge into an open glen. At the point of junction of the two classes of rocks, our attention was drawn to the ruins of a house built on the top of a desolate rocky peak, and said as usual to be the work of the "Rum."

Shortly after entering the rewidened section of the river's course we turned due west, still following the river. At each half-mile the country became better cultivated and better wooded. This alteration in the character and direction of the glen proved to be due to the occurrence of a dyke of very decomposable basalt, a probable continuation of the one we had seen at Urika, and possibly more or less connected with those we had seen at Sidi Rehal and elsewhere, as far east as Demnat.

Towards evening we reached Asni or Hasni, where the glen once more turns south and penetrates into the heart of the Atlas. Here, close to the house of the Sheik, we camped in a fine olive grove.

We render ourselves liable to be misunderstood when we say that it was with no small delight we heard that the Sheik himself some time previously had been thrown into a dungeon for the heinous offence of not being able to satisfy the rapacity of the governor. His absence we knew would facilitate the accomplishment of our plans, more especially as his son, who represented him, was but young, and had no experience or authority.

POWDER HORN AND BULLET POUCHES.

CHAPTER XXX.

THE ASCENT OF THE TIZI LIKUMPT.

In 1872 Sir Joseph Hooker and Mr. Ball had visited Asni, and following a branch of the Wad Reraya called the Ait Mesan, had succeeded in reaching the central ridge of the Atlas. To the left of the Ait Mesan was a second stream called the Wad Iminnen, leading, like the former, to a pass over the mountains called the Tizi Likumpt. Naturally we elected to attempt the ascent of the latter.

It would be tiresome to tell in detail how we laid our plans, how we dissembled, and bullied, and bribed, and puffed ourselves out into demoniac shapes and dimensions, till our unhappy young victim was reduced to acquiesence and a proper degree of malleability.

On the 3rd of September we found ourselves, despite of all the painted terrors in store for us, leaving Asni with light hearts, though with unwilling attendants, who had done their best to set the Sheik against us, to avoid going with us. Our guide was the same man who, sixteen years before, had led Hooker up the Ait Mesan valley.

It was beautiful and bright after the clouds and

showers of the previous day, which had shown that the unsettled weather of winter was commencing. In about an hour from camp we reached the entrance to the main mass of mountains. It is at this point that the Wad Reraya divides, forming the but slightly divergent glens of the Ait Mesan and the Wad Iminnen. At the head of the former we could see the notch in the mountain crest which marks the Tizi-n-Tagharot, with the flanking prominent peak of the Tizi Nzaowt.

The first part of the course of the Wad Iminnen is a narrow gorge cut through a series of variegated sandstones, shales, and limestone, which form precipices and steep slopes more or less clothed with evergreen oak, arbutus, and arar, and towering some three thousand feet overhead. Not far up this gorge we passed the remains of a very solid concrete dam, formerly used for purposes of irrigation, and of course ascribed in these days to the Rum.

Above the dam the gorge widens out somewhat, and affords some small space for cultivation, and here are several hamlets and a few olive groves and cultivated terraces. An intrusion of porphyry at this point alters the dip of the sandstone from a slight one south to a sharp one north, the latter farther up becoming vertical where they abut against a series of metamorphic rocks. With every hundred yards the scenery becomes grander and more picturesque. The mountains tower some five thousand feet overhead, displaying every feature of rugged scenery, everything awe-inspiring, desolate, and terrible. In this part there is no room for cultivation; for there is not a flat piece of ground to be seen, nor, if there were, is there any means of carrying water to it. There is not even room for a mule-path at the bottom, and the bed of the river is too rocky to permit of its being used as such. The track ascends the mountain-side and winds round the face of a great precipice five hundred feet deep and in broken jagged sections rising a thousand or more feet overhead.

Less than an hour takes us through this wild and dangerous part, and once more we find ourselves on a less difficult slope, though nearly as grim and desolate in appearance. The olive and the almond have now disappeared, and have given place to the more hardy and stalwart walnut, which makes a dark-green fringe to the stream below. Above the walnut fringe terraces have been formed against the precipitous slope, and water conveyed to them with incredible labour. Near these, and generally overlooking them, are the hamlets of the mountaineers, more like small flat mounds of clay stuck against the steep slope than the habitations of men. From the two-hundred-feet line of cultivated terraces upwards there extends the most desolate and precipitous slope of rocky debris that the mind of man can conceive, saddest grey in colour, and without a relieving patch of green or any feature on which the eye can rest with pleasure. We thought we had seen the worst of Atlas scenery in the glen of Titula, but here, if not more forbidding, it was at least more striking in its air of desolation.

As we continue our way, we find the metamorphic rocks more and more smashed and penetrated by intrusive masses of igneous rocks, chiefly diorites and por-

VILLAGE IN THE GLEN OF THE WAD IMINNEN.

phyrites. The walnut becomes more and more rare; the evergreen oak disappears, and not even an arar is to be seen.

After some four hours of stiff travelling, winding along the merest ledges, zigzagging up steep slopes to get past an obstacle, only to zigzag down again on the other side, or splashing up the rocky bed of the torrent, slipping over rocks and floundering into treacherous pools, we turn a corner, and find the course of the glen becoming more easterly, and parallel with the main range which lies in front of us.

In this section we found a considerable series of terraces in the lower zones, though overhead were nothing but tremendous precipices and angular rocks. It seemed incredible that people could live in such a barren repellent region, shut off from the outside world for months together during the winter, and imprisoned in their houses the greater part of that time, during which they have to depend largely on their animals for the necessary warmth. Their persons eloquently tell their tale of extreme hardship and scanty living. I have nowhere seen such wizened, wrinkled faces, bleared eyes, and stunted figures. And yet even here the Sultan's government is the mountaineer's worst foe. Nothing can escape its remorseless exactions. The people speak of a time when even in the Wad Iminnen they were contented and prosperous. Now they show only the poorest remnants of fine flocks of sheep and goats, and exhibit the scanty rags that cover their forms.

These poor people, hearing we were the bearers of Sharifian letters, naturally looked upon us with suspicion as probable instruments of more extortion, and

TASHDIRT WA IMINNEN.

we feared that they would drive us back, as not infrequently happens to the tax-collectors.

We did not give them time to think too much, however, but hurried on at a break-neck speed for the top of the valley. At length, five hours from Asni, we reached our goal for the time being, at a village called Tashdirt, 7560 feet above the level of the sea. Here we halted to hold a council of war. We deemed it wise not to wait till the morrow to make the ascent of the Tizi; but to strike while the iron was hot, and before the natives made up their mind what course to take in regard to us.

Taking only two men and our Asni guide, who had shown himself a capital fellow, we pushed on at once. After crossing the stream, we commenced the ascent. We had not proceeded far before we were compelled to dismount from our mules. For a time we held on to their tails, but even that soon proved to be too much for them, and we had to rely upon our own unassisted efforts. We speedily got above the irrigated lower zone, where a scanty crop of grass helped to tone down the grey desolation of the rocks, and gave some sustenance to a few flocks of sheep and goats, whose melancholy bleats were the sole sounds which told of life. The path to the pass lay up a dry gully which cut through the overhanging cliffs. Fearing to be caught in the darkness, we taxed limb and lung to the uttermost, and struggled persistently upwards. Even in the gully it was impossible to keep straight up, the slope was so steep. At length, by dint of much zigzagging and frequent momentary halts to regain breath, we reached the top of the Tizi-Likumpt, at an elevation of 13,150 feet. Even at that late time of the year we found ourselves among wreaths of snow. The view presented to our gaze well repaid us for our extreme exertion, apart from the fact that, for the second time, we had beaten the record of all previous travellers in the matter of height.

Greatly to our surprise, we found the head-stream of the Wad Urika flowing in a deep glen in front of us, and running parallel with the range in the same fashion as the upper waters of the Nyfis. The opposite side of the Urika glen was formed by a second lower range of mountains, cutting off the view of the wild region of Tifnut, which we had expected to find at our feet. We got a glimpse of it, however, through a notch in the opposing mountains.

Looking westward, we were chiefly struck by the unexpected sight of a magnificently rugged peak towering above the surrounding heights to an elevation of quite 2000 feet above our point of view. This, we were informed, was the Tizi-n-Tamjurt. Taking into consideration the altitude we ourselves had attained, and what still lay above us, we had no hesitation in concluding that the Tizi-n-Tamjurt was the highest elevation in the Atlas—certainly not less than 15,000 feet, and possibly more.

As we looked around and noted the bewildering and awe-inspiring assemblage of snow-streaked elevations, sharp jagged ridges, and deep glens and gorges, and remarked also the geological formation, we felt assured that we were on the oldest part of the range. The predominance of metamorphic and igneous rocks, with their gradual replacement by sedimentary formations to east and west, clearly indicated to my mind that here had been the nucleus of all, and, in a sense, the focus of elevation. When all else had been submerged under water, the highest part, say some five thousand feet, had stood out as an island in a cretaceous sea. Around it had been deposited the limestones, the shales, and the sandstones which now flank it on every hand. Then in a later period had come the great earth movements which had raised the Tizi to its present proud elevation, and tilted and folded the horizontal cretaceous rocks to their position on its sides.

We had little time for reflection, however, and almost as little to look around and fix on our mind the varied aspects of the scene. On the north side of the Tizi-n-Tamjurt we could trace the course of the Wad Tisgi glen leading from the Tizi-n-Tagharot. We were informed that near the Tizi-Nzaowt a mountain tarn called Ifri was situated, in which were large fish. It was said of this lake that if stones were thrown into it great storms of wind immediately arose. A somewhat similar superstition occurs over all the mountains with regard to turning over stones in the higher elevations. After completing our observations for altitude, we hurried back at a break-neck speed to reach camp before dark.

We had reason to congratulate ourselves, on reaching

our tents, on having lost no time in making the ascent. The mountaineers had become suspicious of our strange movements. They had gathered in from all quarters to demand our business there. Had we been at Tashdirt instead of on the top of the mountain, we would have been ordered back at once. As it was, we were boycotted, the mountaineers not allowing any one to sell us food, and letting us clearly understand that we must decamp on the morrow.

The evening was distinguished by an unusually fine after-glow, which decked the stern mountains in the most beautiful colours. We stood watching while pink passed into purple and purple became sepia. Darkness came at last, and then we turned to make the best of our position for the night. We had now to consider what we should do next. That we had to leave Tashdirt was certain, but should we follow Hooker's tracks up the Ait Mesan valley and the Tizi-n-Tagharot? Beyond lay the most tempting district in the whole of the Atlas for the enterprising explorer. There was the highest point, and there the curious mountain lake Ifri. All things considered, we resolved to return to Asni. The deepest loathing of Atlas travelling had taken possession of us for the time being, due for the most part to our eternal wrangling with our men. We had never been able to repose the slightest confidence in them. We had constantly been compelled to enact the part of slave-drivers, while their laziness, cowardice, gluttony, and treachery had driven us nearly frantic. With the

JEWS, ASNI.

Page 465.

natives our experience had been little more agreeable. We were never out of a revolting atmosphere of trickery, lies, treachery, and unutterable meannesses. If we had only had half a dozen more like Shalum, we could have gone almost anywhere in the Atlas and enjoyed the life thoroughly; but as things were, we could stand it no longer, unless we could get back to Mogador and start afresh with a new set of followers.

We accordingly left Tashdirt next morning, after contriving to take one or two photographs. We reached Asni at mid-day, with nothing more striking to chronicle than two narrow escapes which a couple of our mules had of falling over the precipices. The two men we had left behind had been in a great panic while we were away, and had slept up a tree for greater safety.

Next day, the 5th September, we left Asni in the midst of a dense mist which veiled the entire landscape—a matter we greatly regretted, as we had promised ourselves some good views of the mountains from the spur of Gurguri. Our way lay parallel to our former route when crossing this small province. The mist did not clear away till we had left the heights and descended once more to the plain, near where the Wad Nyfis leaves the mountains. Some time after mid-day we re-entered Amsmiz.

Our route now lay west along the base of the mountains, through the provinces of Mzuda, Duerani, and Seksawa.

There was little worth remarking beyond the low elevation of such of the Atlas as we could see (the

2 G

main chain was masked by the lower ranges), and the characteristic monotony of the semi-sterile and almost uninhabitable plain. We hailed with pleasure the sight of an olive grove or a passing wayfarer.

There was one melancholy procession which we viewed with interest. This was a caravan of some forty slave-girls, fresh from their savage homes in the Sudan. A few there were on camel-back, but most of

WINNOWING CORN.

them trudged on foot, their appearance telling of the frightful hardships of the desert route. Hardly a rag covered their swarthy forms. These were the only raw slaves we saw in Morocco. Though they had evidently suffered great privations and hardships, we could not say that they were treated with any unnecessary cruelty.

At places we saw countrymen winnowing corn by the simple process of throwing it up in the air with wooden shovels, and letting the breeze carry off the chaff.

At the Wad Kehira, where we camped on our second march from Amsmiz, our men were thrown into great alarm by the confirmation of a story we had heard at Mzuda, that the province of Mtuga, through which we talked of passing on our way to Mogador, was up in arms and divided into two factions over the appointment of a new Kaid. There had been no end of burning, and murdering, and general chaos. We were not surprised to hear through Shalum, that on the first appearance of an armed force our Mogador men meant to bolt, and not risk their precious lives in our company. Meanwhile we were meditating a little surprise for them.

On the morning of the 8th, two hours from the Wad Kehira, we reached Imintanut, and camped in a grove of olives.

CHAPTER XXXI.

THROUGH SUS TO THE COAST.

At Imintanut lies the main road to Tarudant, the capital of Sus. From the moment we had landed at Tangier, we had heard always the same tale of the dangers and terrors of this wild land. Every one, native or foreigner, had with one accord declared it quite impossible even to enter it. We had made no rash vows to accomplish this so-called "impossible" feat, but the hope of doing so had never left our minds. We had not been able to carry our desires into execution either at Glauwa or at Gindafy, thanks largely to our men; and now, if it had to be done at all, it must be from Imintanut.

We resolved accordingly to make the attempt. Circumstances were unusually unfavourable. The route lay through the very worst of the disturbed districts of Mtuga. Between the death of one Kaid and the assumption of power by another, law and order are suspended, it being a standing rule that no action can be taken on whatever happens in the interval. In the case of Mtuga, a rebel chief had taken advantage of the prevailing anarchy, and had descended upon the more orderly population with fire and sword. If by accident we fell into the clutches of either party, we might expect but scant shrift.

That our men suspected some such enterprise on our part became evident on our way from the Wad Kehira to Imintanut, for again Abdul Kader became grievously ill, and seemed incapable of sitting on his mule. On our arrival in camp, he came to tell me he was going to die. I was at once all sympathy and tenderness, and asked him if it was the same sickness as he had in Morocco. He replied practically that it was "the same, only more so." "Very well," I added, "I have a capital cure for it," and jumping up with an air of great wrath, I made for my hunting-crop. His pains vanished in an instant, and his bent back straightened as he bolted to take shelter behind his companions. Deeming castigation to be unnecessary, I called him forward, and in the most emphatic and deliberate manner warned him and his Mogador companions to be very careful what they did or said here. I let them know that I had learned all their doings at other places, and I swore an oath that if by word or deed they tried again to thwart me, I should not only have them all put in prison, but would deprive them of their four months' wages. Of course there was an outburst of righteous indignation and protestation, to all of which I listened unmoved. From virtuous indignation they passed to the venomous wrath of exposed villains, and yelled and gesticulated like madmen. They cursed the day they had joined us. They threatened to leave us at once. Very unnecessarily they told us that if they had had the three Mogador men we dismissed at Saffi, they would have taught us a lesson.

I listened smilingly to everything they said, and even told them I should not attempt to stop them if they pleased to go away,—only they need never hope to enter Mogador again. By and bye the noisy effervescence of their rage subsided into sullen consultation among themselves. Abdarachman strongly urged the others to desert. Hadj M'Hamad, though not so eager, was willing to join him; but Abdul Kader had more sense, and elected to remain.

This scene over, we set off to interview the Sheik. We could not tell what attitude to assume till we had seen our man. The Sheik himself gave us the cue, for he took it into his head that we were European officers of the Sultan's army on government business. We nursed the idea assiduously, and assumed an arrogant manner appropriate to our character. We ordered him to have guides provided for us in the morning, to conduct us on our way to Sus and Agadir. He received our commands with suitable humility and acquiescence, though he failed not to warn us of the dangerous state of the country. We, however, only shrugged our shoulders, and announced that we knew only Allah and the Sultan's will. What else could we do but go as we had been directed?

To keep up our character we smiled contemptuously at the *mona* laid before us as if we would say, it is fit only for our dogs, but we make allowance for your poverty.

On leaving the Sheik our greatest fear was that our men would discover the character we had assumed on finding it conferred on us, and would undeceive him; but happily they remained in ignorance and occupied themselves with surmises as to what our route was to be on the morrow. I had been careful to warn them that if any trouble whatsoever sprang up here I should place it to their credit and act accordingly. The warning had taken the desired effect.

Owing to the disturbed state of the country we had to be on the alert all night, though we had a large number of guards posted round us by the Sheik.

On the morning of the 9th we were up before daylight. No attack had been made on us by marauders, and nothing had happened to explode the sanguine hopes of the evening before.

As we set out towards the mountains it was with a certain amount of satisfaction that we watched the disgusted and sullen faces of our Mogador scoundrels. The pious Hadj passionately demanded of Allah what great crime he had committed that he should be doomed to expiate it in this fashion. Abdul Kader felt the iron hand of fate lying heavy upon him, and he never ceased muttering "*Allah tif! Allah tif!*" (God help me). Abdarachman, more bitter and malicious, lagged behind as was his wont, whacking his mule as if it had been I who was being castigated, and cursing the animal and its owner—an amusement with which he had frequently before beguiled the tedium of the road.

The Wad Imintanut escapes from the mountains by an exceedingly narrow gorge or cleft, where a thick bed of compact limestone has not yielded so readily to the eroding action of the stream and. rain. Inside this constriction the glen rapidly opens out, dividing a little distance up into three branches, trending respectively east, south, and west. It was the western branch that we chose to follow. An unusually broad and easy road conducted us up the bottom of the small valley.

In the interval of cheering our men with suitable remarks about fate and submission to Allah's decree, I remarked that the glen of the Wad Isserato had been excavated along the line of junction of the metaphoric series with the outer sedimentary rocks. On our left were the irregular mountain masses of the former, and, on our right, forming the opposite side of the glen, was a lower range of the latter, the limestones capping and protruding from its sides like string-courses of masonry. We passed for ten hours through groves of almond trees, from which the natives were gathering the nuts. Here and there a village, and flocks of bleating sheep and goats, gave some slight variety to the features of the scene.

Ten miles from camp we reached the head of the Wad Isserato. We then turned due south round the shoulder of the metamorphic mountains, the series here masked by overlying red sandstones. This brought us into the irregular valley of the Wad Msira, whose red glaring sandstones and shales showed up brightly among the trees and bushes. At the bottom we found a sok in full swing. The disturbed condition of the country was well illustrated by the fact that all the men were armed with knife and gun, and kept in groups according to their villages, ready for fight or flight. Our own position was too precarious to allow of a halt. A malicious cry or a fanatical curse would have been sufficient to rouse an attack. Evidently they did not know what to make of us, but our very boldness in marching through them, and the presence of Zemrani in his Government fez, suggested prudence on their part. Moreover, the two factions who had reduced Mtuga to chaos were here in force, and were fully occupied watching each other. As it was, we had barely left the place when a fight ensued with bloody results. We ourselves had more to fear from parties following and attacking us at some favourable spot, and to avoid this if possible we urged on our animals to their utmost speed, our Mogador men not the least active in pushing forward.

In half an hour we crossed the glen and reached a pass on the opposite side. Here, to our great surprise, at an elevation of only 4750 feet, we found ourselves on the watershed of the range. Before us and trending south lay a glen opening into a broad valley, whose waters undoubtedly drained into the Sus River. In front of us from where we stood we could see no higher range. On our left the mountains attained an estimated elevation of between 6000 and 7000 feet, and on our right of little more than 5000. Westward the eye roved over what was simply a plateau of from 4000 to 5000 feet in height, having almost no marked elevations, and forming the provinces of Mtuga and Haha. As I remarked these facts, I felt assured that here practically was the end of the Atlas as a range.

Our way now lay down the glen. We found that it extended, as in the case of the Isserato, along the line of junction of the metamorphic and the sedimentary rocks, the two sides of the rapidly expanding glen showing their characteristic surface features.

As we continued south, at first over boulder-strewn paths, there began to appear in the haze in front of us the outlines of a range of mountains which were grand in massiveness, height, and ruggedness, so that we could not but conclude that here, after all, was the true continuation of the Atlas. Soon we were able to identify the dark imposing peak due south as the Jebel, or mountain of the Ida Mhamud (*Ida*, like *Ait*, *Beni*, and *Ulad*, means tribe or sons of), while further west, and cut off by a deep depression, lay the less conspicuous mass of Ida Uziki, which, followed westward, could be seen to tail off and become apparently merged in the plateau of Mtuga.

The first part of our way down the glen led us over a very broken country, in which only a few almond-trees found sustenance, the staple support apparently of the inhabitants of a couple of small hamlets. Gradually, however, as the glen opened out the country became more even and less rocky. The argan tree, which we had not seen since we left Shiedma, took the place of the almond. Many curious flat-topped mounds, remnants of former river banks, or it may be of lake debris, protected from destruction by a capping of consolidated gravel, formed striking features in the landscape. These mounds, the huge boulders which lay here and there, the prevalent purple colour of the scene, as well as the general aspect of sterility, gave the whole valley the appearance of an enormous deserted quarry of red rock. On one of these isolated hills we discovered some remarkable ruins, which we found time to examine in spite of the urgent necessity to hurry on. Towards the east the hill presented a steep declivity, surmounted by a cliff, while westward it sloped away irregularly. Along the edge of the crag ran a wall some eight feet thick, forming a large enclosure by taking in all the upper part of the opposite slope. At the southern end the ridge of the hill broadens, and here seem to have been the chief buildings. One chamber we saw was little more than six feet square, and had walls as many feet thick.

From the "Burj Anserrani," as it is called, the valley rapidly widened out and presented a less forbidding aspect. The argans were now more common and of larger growth, there were greater evidences of cultivation, and we passed one or two villages.

Towards sunset we arrived near the base of the Ida Uziki Mountains. These we calculated attained an altitude of over 6000 feet, while those of the Ida

Mhamud rose undoubtedly two or three thousand feet higher.

We chose as our camping-ground a sok, where there were a number of stone-built shed or huts, used by the cobblers, &c., who attend the markets. As we had every reason to fear a night attack we did what we could to fortify the place, and disposed ourselves for defence, though we knew we would have but a poor chance if any onslaught took place.

For about the first time since we started from the coast the Mogador men did not grumble at a lack of food; they were all too anxious to stow themselves so as to be most out of danger in the event of trouble. Not one of them dared keep a look-out, though each kept a sleepless watch over his own particular self—ready to bolt on the first hint of danger. Happily the night passed without any disturbance, and wearied at length with our fifty-mile ride under a burning sun, we fell asleep.

We were on the road again by dawn, our men showing a gratifying alacrity to push on and get out of the troubled district.

Not far from camp the main road to Sus deviates. One branch crosses the Ida Uziki Mountains and the Pass of Bibawan to Tarudant; the other passes into Sus by an easier westerly route. Unaware of this fact, and not apprised by Shalum, on whom we depended, we found ourselves a couple of hours beyond the former route before we knew. Not deeming it of any consequence, we continued our way.

Our way now trended more south-westerly, skirting the base of the rapidly tailing-out range. The escarpment of the Mtuga plateau on our right closed in upon us once more.

Some three hours from camp, the Wad Ait Musa, formed by the united streams of the valley, suddenly turned due south, disappearing in a deep gorge or cleft of the range. We still, however, continued our way along the mountains, as there was no practicable path by the narrow gorge. At this section we could hardly consider ourselves happy, for the Ait Musa were the chief leaders in the Mtuga rebellion. On asking some people at one village who their Kaid was, we were answered that "they were under God," meaning that they had no Kaid. This was not an agreeable state of affairs for us, and we hurried on as rapidly as possible. The low altitude we had now reached was evidenced by the appearance of date-palms, which formed a pleasing element in the scene.

At mid-day we crossed from the basin of the Ait Musa into the smaller one of the Asif Ig, and an hour and a half later we camped, with some feeling of security, at the Zawia or sanctuary of El Batmi, and under the protection of a descendant of the saint.

The morning opened with our men in a delightfully nervous condition—not that we ourselves were quite free of apprehension, for the dreaded region of Sus was now to be entered. For an hour we descended the broken valley of the Azif Ig, whose hilly irregularities gave us glimpses of the great plain and the bounding heights far beyond. From one elevation we even got a distant view of the celebrated town of Tarudant. There is no wilder land in Northern Africa than this province of Sus. For centuries its fanatical Arab tribes have, with more or less success, retained their independence—at no time wholly subdued, as at no time completely free of the Sharifian shackles. Never-ending revolts and petty wars, invasions, and all manner of treacheries, have been its history. Only eight years ago the present Sultan succeeded by force of arms, but chiefly by the grossest treachery, in establishing his authority over the greater part of the province; but ever since there has been a continued series of massacres and murders, and no traveller has left its borders without a new tale of bloodshed.

In no other region either has Mohammedanism shown itself so aggressive and exclusive. "Death to the infidel" is said still to be the favourite cry; and it was deemed an impossibility for a Christian to venture within its borders undisguised.

The same, however, had been said about the greater part of the Atlas, and yet everywhere we had shown ourselves, without serious results, in our customary European clothes.

We resolved not to discard them now, but in our proper characters face the fate in store for us. In such countries as we were travelling in, audacity even to rashness is frequently one's greatest safeguard.

As we descended the Asif Ig, very much on the alert and ready for action, it became evident that we were entering an unusually troubled region. Wayfarers coming suddenly in sight of us invariably halted, and, while they reconnoitred us, grasped their guns like men accustomed to incessant warfare. Some took up positions behind rocks or trees, others disappeared altogether.

These last we liked least of all, for we did not know but that their salute might be a bullet from some inaccessible place on the hill-side. As a rule we, for our part, held straight on, and showed that we at least were peaceably disposed.

Nothing more unpleasant happened in our descent of the glen till coming near the plain we got into parley with a traveller, and heard to our dismay that the powerful Arab tribe called Howara were up in revolt. Only that morning they had swooped down on a caravan camped at the village of Mskorod, half a mile from where we stood, and plundered it of many camels. If they did that to true believers, what would they do to Kaffirs like ourselves? The question was one which did not admit of a pleasing response. We could only cheer ourselves and our men with the remark that "we were in the hands of Allah," and in His name we resolved to go forward. For the moment we thought of pushing on at once to Agadir, but a sight of our mules, and the knowledge that we were still nearly forty miles from that place, made us aware that that was impossible. We therefore decided to seek shelter and protection in the Kasbah of the Kaid of the Msgina, a tribe of the Shellach. This seemed like jumping from the frying-pan into the fire, as the revolt of the Howara was chiefly directed against the Kaid of the Msgina, but we saw no other course to pursue.

We spurred on our jaded animals accordingly, passing over an argan-clad and crust-bound sloping plain resembling Shiedma in its general character. Here and there we saw parties of armed men hurrying about, and we were kept in continual apprehension lest they should fall foul of us.

At length we caught sight of a very unpretentious Kasbah. We could not see a soul about the place, and we began to think that the stories of a contemplated attack on it by the Howara were all nonsense. No sooner, however, had we pulled up our animals near the principal entrance than we found ourselves surrounded by over fifty wild-looking armed men, who seemed to spring from the very ground, so sudden and unexpected was their appearance from their places of concealment.

An ambuscade had clearly been laid for us, and we expected the worst. Bonich for the moment lost all powers of speech, and sat silent till I shouted to him to ask for the Kaid, and announce us as bearers of letters from the Sultan. This he contrived to do in a timid, hesitating manner, which tended very much to rouse my wrath. A few minutes of unpleasant uncertainty ensued, and then the Kaid appeared with a great following of soldiers, with whom the seemingly empty Kasbah was filled. We thought matters looked nasty when he cast only a furtive, suspicious glance at us, and did not even deign to look at the Sultan's letter. At length, in brusque tones he ordered us to come inside; and inside we went, very much as if we were marching to a dungeon or a scaffold. C.-B. and I were shown into a court half filled with soldiers, while the others were conducted elsewhere. Nobody offered to take charge of our horses, and we could not leave them. Minute after minute passed and still nobody came to our assistance. The sun was blazing hot, and the situation was anything but in accord with our dignity and importance. All sorts of unpleasant ideas passed through our heads. For all we knew, we might be prisoners. By and bye, however, we contrived to get away, and, to our unbounded indignation, found Bonich and our men amusing themselves showing the Kaid our rifles. We now found our fears quite groundless, for our entertainment, though rude, was lavish and hospitable.

The Kaid's father had been shot six months before by the Howara, on which occasion he had himself got a bullet through his shirt. The Howara, however, had vowed to do their work properly the next time, and were now collecting to besiege him in his Kasbah. Our reception derived its cordiality from the fact that the unhappy Kaid took us for European officers of the Sultan, and he was anxious to get a medium whereby to convey his troubles to his master.

Under the circumstances, we deemed it foolhardy to think of venturing to Tarudant, and resolved to get out of this dangerous region as quickly as possible. We were kept in the greatest apprehension lest we should be beleaguered in the castle. All night long the garrison remained under arms, but the expected night-attack did not come off. Shortly after daybreak, the Howara not having been seen in the neighbourhood, we left for Agadir, escorted by the Kaid's brother and several soldiers. We retraced our steps to near the foot of the plateau of Mtuga, the Atlas range having ended at the Asif Ig.

Pushing on without molestation, it was delightful to see the returning courage of our men as each half hour took us a couple of miles nearer Agadir and away from the disturbed region.

At mid-day we descried Agadir gleaming like a snow-cap on an isolated precipitous hill with the blue Atlantic beyond. In an hour and a half we were on the glistening yellow sands, delighted to listen once more to the ocean rollers and feel its cool breezes. Here our escort stopped, as their Kaid was not on good terms with the ruler of this southern stronghold of the Moorish empire. In bidding the leader goodbye, Hadj effusively kissed his hands, calling on Allah to bless him and his for what they had done for us. No sooner were their backs turned than his benign expression changing to that of a coward's hatred, he shook his fist at the retreating troop and exclaimed, "May God send you the Sultan," meaning thereby ruin and desolation, for nothing else ever follows the Sharifian path.

Agadir, till the end of last century, was a prosperous port, frequented by numerous vessels and merchants of all nations. To-day it is closed, and only known as a stronghold built by the Portuguese in the days of their ascendancy on the coast, and as a thorn in the side of Sus; not now adding to its wealth and prosperity, but serving as an instrument to carry out the Sharifian policy of grinding down the wild tribes to their proper level. Everybody now leaving or entering Sus must pass over the 120 miles of stony road which runs along the coast from Agadir to Mogador. By this means the Sultan hopes to keep a check on the importation of arms and gunpowder, and on the growth of wealth. This is but one of a hundred striking instances of Moorish imbecility and incapacity for governing. The opening of the port would do more to pacify the ever-bubbling passions of the Sus tribes than the bloodshed and ruin produced by half a dozen such armies as the Sultan can dispatch against them.

After a day's rest to our animals, we pushed on to Mogador on the 13th. In three marches, over country which we need not describe, we reached the Palm-Tree House, where we stayed for the night, and next morning, on the 17th of September, re-entered Mogador.

Our first business was to get rid of our Mogador servants before resuming our way north. We would gladly have put them in prison, but as they admitted having acted badly, and we were not desirous of further worry, we paid them their wages and let them go free.

It was not till the 6th of October that we left Mogador *en route* for Fez by way of Casablanca and Rabat. Our plan was to make the northern capital a centre of exploration for the surrounding region as Maraksh had been for the western part of the Atlas. On the 13th we entered Casablanca. Hardly were we installed once more under the roof of Arturo Pitto before a dispatch was placed in my hands, which at once altered all my plans. An expedition to the relief of Emin Pasha was more to my mind than the exploration of Morocco, and I did not hesitate for a moment in my decision.

Next morning a steamer loaded with grain was leaving for Tangier, and I took passage thither, preparatory to sailing for England. Mr. Crichton-Browne, now a full-fledged traveller, continued overland by way of Mequinez and Fez to Tangier, and so ended our travels in the Atlas and Southern Morocco.

MOORISH GUNS, DAGGERS, AND POWDER-HORNS.

Page 484.

INDEX.

ABDA, province of, 52, 118
Achliz, 446
Adrar-n-Iri, 201, 204
Agadir, 437, 483
Aid el Kebir, 393
Ait Mesan, 456, 457, 464
Ait Humwali, 241
Akermut, 61, 63
Amsmiz, 280
    Jews of, 283
    population of, 283
    return to, 319, 465
    town of, 282
    valley, 285
Anti-Atlas, 211, 234, 236
Antimony, 238
Arabs, 38, 119
Arar, 61, 235
Architecture, Moorish, 18, 25, 346-356
Argan-tree, 61, 92, 97, 475
Art, Moorish, degeneracy of, 376
Asif Adrar-n-Iri, 212, 213
Asif el Mel, 322
Asni, 455
Atlas, elevation of, 205, 207, 234, 236, 243, 301, 344, 462
    first view of, 62
    near aspect of, 139
    panorama of, 123, 172, 189, 342, 430
    termination of, 474, 482
Azamor, 46

BASALT dykes, 137, 141, 143, 162, 179, 455
Berbers, *see* Shellach
Bled Hummel, province of, 118
Boar-hunting, 79-87
Bonich, M., 133
Bread-baking, 185
Burj Anserrani, the, 475

CAFÉ, a Moorish, 5
Calitris, 61
Carpets, Moorish, 38
Casablanca, 32
Caves, 181, 237
Charms, 425
Child-marriages, 159, 254, 284
Children, Moorish, 23
Christians, ancient, *see* Rum
Costume, Jewish, 417, 422
    Moorish, 148
    of mountaineers, 208
    of mountain Jews, 253
    women's, 74, 384
Courtyard, a Kaid's, 54
Crichton-Browne, Mr. Harold, 14, 121, 149, 311, 405

DAISY, blue, 291
Dancing, Moorish, 257-261, 391
Decoration, Moorish, 13, 25, 131, 152, 374
Demnat, approach to, 144
    caves at, 164

INDEX.

Demnat, Jews' quarter of, 157
    Kaid of, 150
    Kaid of, audience with, 151
    Kasbah of, 151, 154
    valley of, 160
    women of, 156
Dukkala, Southern, 51, 52

EL GLAUWI, 220, 225
    attendants of, 229
    interview with, 220
    Kasbah of, 215, 218, 231
Enzel, village of, 197, 198
Escort, rapacity of, 95
    trouble with, 93, 108, 111, 113, 122, 125, 135, 177, 196, 224, 238, 274, 328, 444, 469
Euphorbia resinifera, 168
Exclusiveness, Moorish, 29

FANATICISM, Moorish, 76–78, 266, 404
Feast, a Moorish, 268
Feats on horseback, 410
Fountains, 357
Fundak, 41
Funeral, a Moorish, 24

GADAT, glen of, 197–211
Geology, 277, 300, 307, 322, 323, 448, 457, 463, 472
Gibraltar, 1
Gindafy, province of, 308
    Kaid of, 310
Glaciation, traces of, 210, 276, 279, 319, 326
Glauwa, Kaid of, *see* El Glauwi
    province of, 142
Goats climbing trees, 92
Government, Moorish, 232, 436
    effects of, 228
Great Feast, the, 393
Green, Sir W. Kirby, 16
Gurguri, 279, 465

HAHA, Kasbah of, 93
Hammum, the, 386
Harem, a, 344
Hawking, 59, 232
Holiday, a Moorish, 255
Hooker, Sir Joseph, 14
Houses, 373, 348
House-tops, the, 429
Howara, revolt of, 479
Hunot, Mr., 59, 441

IDA Mhamud mountains, 476
Ida Uziki mountains, 475
Ifri, mountain lake of, 463
Iminifri, natural bridge at, 164
Imintanut, district of, 467, 468
Imintella, 294
Immorality, Moorish, 226
Insect pests, 324
Irghalnsor, ascent of, 170
Iron-mines, exploration of, 104
Iron Mountains, *see* Jebel Hadid
Irrigation, native skill in, 136, 162

JEBEL Asif Sig, 446
    Glauwi, 201, 205
    Hadid, 61, 93, 97
    Hadid, ascent of, 99
    Hadid, camp at, 98
    Hadid, geology of, 106
    Hadid, view from, 100
    Ogdimt, 328–345
    Tezah, 301
Jewish women, 71, 422
Jews, condition of, 414–428
    dress of, *see* costume
    dwellings of, 186
    hospitality of, 425
    mountain, 249
    ophthalmic disease among, 158, 423
    over-crowding among, 424
    of Amsmiz, 283
    of Mogador, 70, 71
    of Tabugumt, 238

INDEX. 487

Jews, past persecution of, 427
    usury of, 418
Justice, Moorish, 412

KASERIA, 361
Kuba, 49, 58
Kuskussu, 56
Kutubia, tower of, 123, 138, 353

LAB EL BARUD, 407-410

MAROSSA, 323
Marren, Asif, 237
Mazagan, 46
Medinah, 68, 421-426
Mellah, 69, 421-426
Metamores, 51
Misfiwa, province of, 137
Mitfires, 51
Mlitsin, 431
Mogador, arrival at, 64
    climate of, 66
    departure from, 90
    description of, 67, 68, 69.
    first view of, 62
    Mellah at, 69
    procession at, 75-78
    sand-dunes of, 91
Mohammedanism, 435
Mona, 51, 55, 129, 446, 453
Morocco, city of, 346
    approach to, 126
    bazaars of, 359
    first impressions of, 130
    first start from, 136
    general sketch of, 130-133
    Kasbah of, 350
    Mellah of, 423
    mosques of, 348, 353
    our quarters at, 127, 373
Morocco, Plain of, 124, 138
    population of, 350
    view of Atlas from, 430
Morocco, empire, government of, 436

Morocco, policy of, 440
    prisons of, 25, 417
    prospects of, 442
Moufflon, 232
Msgina, Kaid of, 480
Mtuga, 93, 468
Mueddin, 10
Mules, sure-footedness of, 199, 206
Mullai Hassan Mountains, 93
Musicians, itinerant, 380

OGDIMT, Jebel, 304, 328-345

PAYTON, Mr., 64, 66, 79, 441
Portuguese remains, 48, 59, 116
Powder-play, 407-413
Prisons, 25, 417

RAHAMNA, mountains of, 119, 124
Ramadan, 224
Ratto, Mr., 66, 79
Reception of Kaids, 400
Religion, Jewish, 426
    Moorish, 226, 434
Religious procession, 72-78
Reraya, 454
Rum, remains of, 169, 182, 187, 229, 237, 291, 293

SAFFI, approach to, 58
    climate of, 116
    departure from, 117
    palace at, 114
    second visit to, 114
Salutations, Moorish, 37
School, a Moorish, 16
Shalum, 134, 167
Shawia, 38, 58
Shellach, characteristics of, 155
    condition of, 228, 460
    costume of, 208
Shellach, dwellings of, 187, 208
    industry of, 208
    villages of, 187, 201, 333, 458
Shiedma, province of, 61, 95
Sidi Aissa, 60, 72

Sidi Buzarktan, 62
    Hamadsha, 72
    Rehal, 138
    Yakub, 63, 102
Slave caravan, a, 466
Snake-charming, 295, 367
Sok, 97, 197, 446
Soldier, a Moorish, 34
Spartel, Cape, 32
Srarna, province of, 142
Stoning at Morocco, 404
Sultan, letter of, 31
Sus, province of, 478

TABIA, 154, 202
Tabugumt, reception at, 238
Tachnowt, 454
Tajen, 56
Takat, 97, 99
Tangier, arrival at, 3
    Kasbah, the, 15
    market-place, the, 21
    Marshan, view from the, 27
    streets, the, 21
Tarudant, 468
Tashdirt, 461, 465
Tasimset, 174
    route to, 179
    waterfall at, 181
    caves at, 181
Taurirt, ascent of, 241
Teluet, caves at, 237
    climate of, 233
    crossing the pass of, 211–214
    Kasbah of, 215, 218
    pass of, 237
    population of, 235
    reception at, 215
    valley of, 212–234
    view from pass, 211
Tensift, river, 60, 124
    fording of, 109

Tetuan, 28
Tezert, 192, 193
Tifnut, 223, 462
Tizi Likumpt, ascent of, 456–467
    Nemiri, 302, 305
    Nslit, 332
    n-Tamjurt, 462

ULAD DLIM, district of, 120
Urika, 137, 444–455
Usury of Jews, 418

VICEROY, the, 396
Villages, ruined, 92, 301

WAD AGANDICE, 313
    Amsmiz, 292
    Dra, 142, 212
    El Mulha, 197
    Gadat, 137, 197
    Iminnen, 456
    Isserato, 472
    Kseb or Diabat, 92
    Misfiwa, 137
    Msira, 473
    Nyfis, 318, 333, 337
    Reraya, 454
    Tedili, 143
    Tensift, 60, 136, 212
    Tessaout, 142, 189
    Urika, 137
Wedding, a Jewish, 7
    a Moorish, 24
Wells, Moorish, 41
Winnowing, 467
Wishdan, Mountains of, 303, 304, 313, 315
Women, Jewish, 71, 157
    Moorish, 23, 131, 378, 382

ZAWIA, 107
    of Bin Mahida, 107
Zarktan, 196, 201

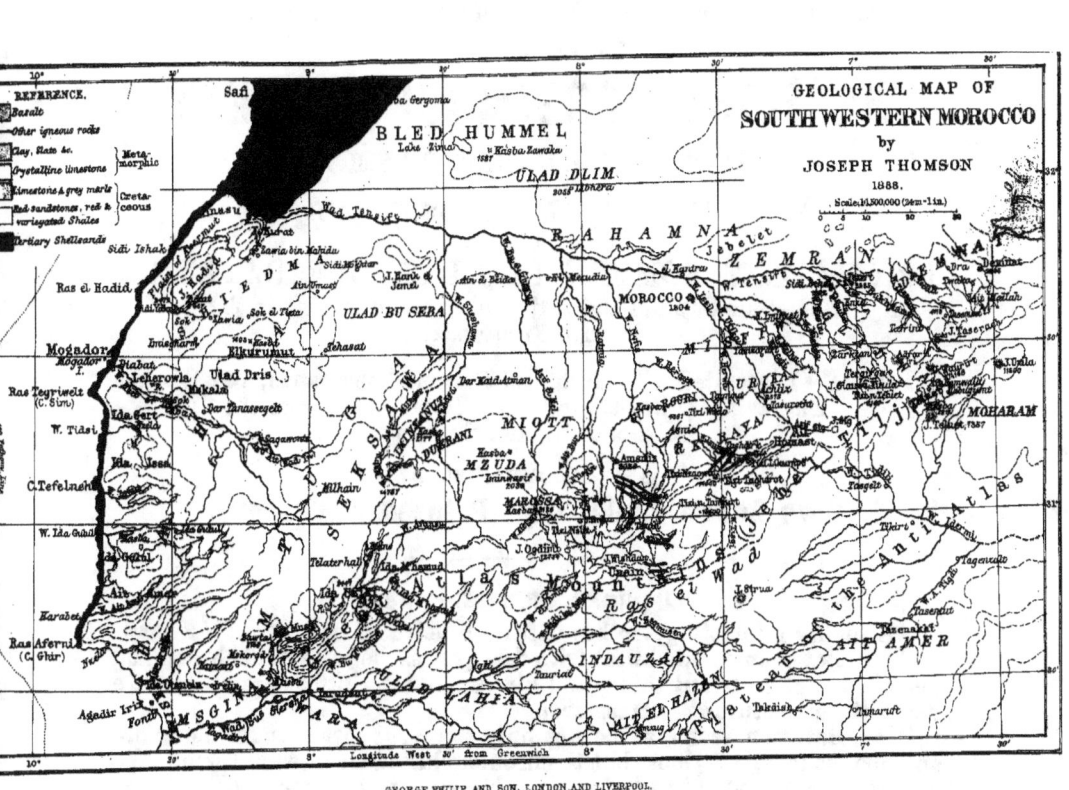

32 FLEET STREET, LONDON,
MAY 1889.

A SELECTED LIST OF WORKS
PUBLISHED BY GEORGE PHILIP & SON.

JUST PUBLISHED,

Medium 8vo, in handsome Illustrated cloth cover, bevelled boards, gilt top, price 21s.

THE FIRST ASCENT OF THE KASAÏ

BEING SOME RECORDS OF SERVICE
UNDER THE LONE STAR.

By CHARLES SOMERVILLE LATROBE BATEMAN,
Sometime Captain and Adjutant of Gendarmerie in the
Congo Free State.

Profusely Illustrated with Etchings, Chromo-lithographs, and Wood Engravings (Fifty-seven in all), Reproduced from the Author's Original Drawings,

AND ACCOMPANIED BY

Two Large Scale Maps Printed in Colours.

OPINIONS OF THE PRESS.

"A highly interesting and beautifully illustrated narrative."—*Times.*

"Mr. Bateman is as skilful with the pen as he is with his brush and pencil; his style is animated, and his verbal descriptions are quite on a par with his pictures."—*Athenæum.*

"Mr. Bateman seems to be not only the right sort of man to explore and civilise savage regions, but to chronicle his adventures in them. We do not know whether to admire most his energy, his indomitable pluck, his practical common sense, his modesty, his rigid sense of duty, or his burning zeal for the regeneration of long-degraded races of his fellowmen."—*Saturday Review.*

"The whole book is well worth reading; it is instructively illustrated, and its pages present an excellent picture of life in a corner of the Congo Free State, and of death too; for in Africa as elsewhere, the foundations even of relatively slight improvements are the lives of men."—*Spectator.*

"Fair in outward seeming this handsome volume makes no vain show. With pen, as with pencil, the author evinces masterly skill in the production of choice specimens of literary and artistic excellence."—*Whitehall Review.*

"His book is of considerable interest. . . . Above all the book is valuable for the light it throws on the influence that is being created by the Congo State."—*Nature.*

JUST PUBLISHED, Medium 8vo.

THE UNKNOWN HORN OF AFRICA.

An Exploration from Berbera to the Leopard River.

By F. L. JAMES, M.A.,
Author of "Wild Tribes of the Soudan."

With Additions by J. GODFREY THRUPP, M.R.C.S.;
the Map by W. D. JAMES and PERCY AYLMER;
the Narrative Illustrations by ROSE HAKE;
and the Drawings of the Fauna by K. KEULEMAN, from Specimens chiefly collected by E. LORT-PHILLIPS.

1. With Illustrations of Fauna beautifully coloured by hand. Price 28s.
2. With Illustrations of Fauna uncoloured. Price 21s.

OPINIONS OF THE PRESS.

"This narrative is of special interest at the present time. . . . Mr. James's expedition was one of unusual hazard, but it was completely successful. . . . The entire get-up of the volume is highly creditable."—*Times.*

"A book to please every one—good to handle, entertaining to peruse, and delightful to look at."—*Whitehall Review.*

"A book done as books should be."—*Spectator.*

"The public owe Mr. James and his companions a distinct debt of gratitude."—*Saturday Review.*

Royal 8vo, cloth, with Portrait and Map, price 16s.

EMIN PASHA IN CENTRAL AFRICA.

Letters and Journals Collected and Annotated

BY

Dr. SCHWEINFURTH, Dr. RATZEL, Dr. G. HARTLAUB,
and Dr. FELKIN.

The only existing Record of Emin Pasha's Life and Work in Central Africa.

"This volume is a record of the highest type of exploring work. Every page abounds with interest."—*Times.*

GEORGE PHILIP & SON, PUBLISHERS, LONDON AND LIVERPOOL.

Large crown 8vo, handsomely bound in cloth, published
at 12s. 6d., offered at 7s. 6d. nett.

ACROSS AFRICA.

BY

VERNEY LOVETT CAMERON, C.B., D.C.L.,

COMMANDER, ROYAL NAVY;

Gold Medallist, Royal Geographical Society, &c.

WITH NUMEROUS ILLUSTRATIONS.

New Edition.

WITH NEW AND ORIGINAL MATTER, AND CORRECTED MAP.

SELECTIONS FROM OPINIONS OF THE PRESS.

"Nothing beyond the mention of the fact will be necessary to secure a favourable reception to the re-issue in a popular form of Commander Cameron's 'Across Africa.' Though much has happened since the story was first written it is not out of date. Into a considerable portion of the Dark Continent traversed by the author no other white man has yet penetrated, and what has occurred has rather tended to give additional interest to all African exploration. In this edition Commander Cameron does justice to the explorations of Mr. Stanley in the Congo Basin, of Mr. Johnston in the Kilimanjaro district, and the Portuguese, Italian, and German travellers. But the most important part of the added matter has reference to the commercial openings now inviting British energy and capital in Africa."—*Daily Telegraph.*

"In a second edition of 'Across Africa,' Commander Cameron summarises the results of exploration in the Dark Continent since his own expedition in 1876, and offers some valuable suggestions as to the future of African travel and commerce. Subsequent discoveries, it is well known, have mainly gone to confirm Commander Cameron's anticipations, notably in the identification of the Lualaba and the Congo. The precise nature of the Lukuga river, or creek, is still, however, a battle-ground between geographers."—*Academy.*

GEORGE PHILIP & SON, PUBLISHERS, LONDON AND LIVERPOOL.

Technical Education, Industry, and Trade.

RECENTLY PUBLISHED,

In Four Volumes (Materials, Production, Distribution, and Competition), Crown 8vo, strongly bound in cloth, price 24s., or separate volumes, price 6s. each.

With Illustrative Maps, Synoptical Charts of the World's Produce, and Tables of Reference for Scientific Purposes.

Manuals of Commerce.

By JOHN YEATS, LL.D., F.G.S., F.S.S.

Vol. I.—The Natural History of the Raw Materials of Commerce.

Their Geology and Geography, with their chief economic uses; also copious Lists of Commercial Products, and their Synonyms in the principal European and Oriental languages; a Glossary, an Index, and an Industrial Map of the World.

Vol. II.—The Technical History of Commerce.

Or the Progress of the Useful Arts, of Discoveries, Inventions, and their Applications. Illustrated by an Industrial Map of the British Isles, and Tables of Alloys.

Vol. III.—The Growth and Vicissitudes of Commerce in all Ages.

An Historical Narrative of the Industry and Intercourse of Civilised Nations. Illustrated with Chart showing the Rise, Progress, Culmination and Decline of Commercial Nations, Maps of the British Empire in 1888, of Caravan Routes, Ancient and Modern, and Appendix and Folio Sheet of Products from the Three Kingdoms of Nature.

Vol. IV.—Recent and Existing Commerce.

A brief review of British industry and trade; a survey of our Colonial and Foreign relations; the Natural Divisions of Commerce, based upon similarity of produce and seasons of shipment; list of upwards of one thousand centres of industry and trade with all the most prominent products of each—its imports, its currency, its nearest seaport, its internal means of communication by railway or canal, and its approximate distance from London; also supplementary Tables, which show at a glance the share obtained by the United Kingdom in the commerce of other countries, with percentages of the rise or fall of our trade in every great market.

SELECTIONS FROM OPINIONS OF THE PRESS.

" . . . A work which must be regarded as a standard authority on the great subject which is so learnedly and exhaustively treated in its pages. The addition of many excellent maps, commercial lists of various kinds carefully arranged and tabulated, and copious indexes, renders these 'Manuals of Commerce' still more worthy the attention of all students of mercantile and manufacturing economics."—*Daily Telegraph.*

" . . . Cannot fail to give an important impetus to the movement in favour of technical instruction."—*Daily News.*

"Dr. Yeats' four volumes are a practical contribution to that scheme of technical, industrial, and trade education which he has so long and so ably advocated. For a long time the British public received with little favour proposals for technical education. . . . But the example of Germany and the near approach of the time when Americans may be expected to compete keenly with us in the foreign markets of the world, have at length convinced most persons who take an interest in the subject that we can no longer depend upon our natural advantages for maintaining our commercial supremacy, and that it is therefore absolutely necessary to give our people sound technical, industrial, and commercial instruction."—*Saturday Review.*

GEORGE PHILIP & SON, PUBLISHERS, LONDON AND LIVERPOOL.

Imperial 8vo, price 7s. 6d.

PICTURES OF NATIVE LIFE IN DISTANT LANDS.

A Series of Twelve Illustrations (size 15 by 12½ inches), drawn and designed by H. LEUTEMANN, and beautifully printed in colours, affording life-like representations of the most striking features of the Life of the Principal Races of Mankind.

Each Plate is accompanied by interesting and instructive explanatory letterpress, translated from the German of Professor A. KIRCHHOFF, Professor of Geography at Halle University, by GEORGE PHILIP, Junr.

The following Races are illustrated and described:—1. THE ABORIGINES OF AUSTRALIA.—2. THE PAPUAS.—3. THE POLYNESIANS.—4. THE ESKIMOS.—5. THE AMERICAN INDIANS.—6. THE HOTTENTOTS AND BUSHMEN.—7. THE NEGROES.—8. THE NUBIANS.—9. THE ARABS.—10. THE HINDOOS.—11. THE CHINESE.—12. THE JAPANESE.

An extraordinary amount of Ethnographical Information is embodied in this work.

"A book calculated to engage the deep interest of young readers."—*Daily Telegraph.*

"A capital book, from which young and old alike may learn much that is both interesting and instructive about the less known inhabitants of the globe."—*Army and Navy Gazette.*

"The boy or girl who becomes familiar with Herr Leutemann's carefully executed pictures will have acquired a firm foundation on which to rest the knowledge to be thereafter acquired from books of travel."—*Morning Post.*

"These graphic pictures, well drawn and coloured, illustrate the typical races of mankind."—*Spectator.*

"The volume deserves to meet with great success."—*Daily Chronicle.*

"I also advise you to look at 'Graphic Pictures of Native Life in Distant Lands.'"—*Truth.*

A New Aid to the Study of the Stars. Just Published, Printed in Colours.

PHILIPS' REVOLVING PLANISPHERE.

Showing the Principal Stars visible for every Hour in the Year. Price 2s. net.

This novel Planisphere consists of a circular disc on which the principal Stars visible from our latitude are clearly indicated. By means of an exceedingly simple arrangement the disc may be made to revolve in such a way as to show only those stars visible at any given time. In addition to this may be shown the varying time of sunrise and sunset during the whole year. The Stars are clearly shown in white on a dark ground. The Publishers invite the attention of all interested in Astronomy to this *unique* and *cheap* publication, which, it is hoped, will tend to popularise and simplify the study of the Heavens.

EDITION FOR THE SOUTHERN HEMISPHERE.

THE extraordinary success of the English Edition of this useful little instrument has induced the publishers to produce another of precisely similar construction for use in the Southern Hemisphere. It is specially arranged for latitudes 35° to 40° S., but for practical purposes it may be used in all the English-speaking countries S. of the Equator. Price 2s. 6d. nett.

"Messrs. George Philip & Son send us a 'Revolving Planisphere,' which by a simple contrivance indicates the stars visible in and near London for every hour in which absence of daylight and clearness of sky enable them to be so. The principal stars round the north pole as a centre, and extending to 28° S. declination, are mapped in white on a dark ground; over this is a disc with an elliptic aperture easily turned by handles, and round it the twenty-four hours are marked, whilst on the circumference of the star-map are marked the months and days of the year. By turning the disc till the hour coincides with any particular day, that portion of the heavens is uncovered which is visible on that day at the hour in question. The arrangement is useful for those who desire to learn the principal stars and constellations, and handy also for amateur astronomers, who may often wish to ascertain at a glance what part of the stellar sky is visible at an hour when they purpose to look for some special celestial object."—*Athenæum.*

GEORGE PHILIP & SON, PUBLISHERS, LONDON AND LIVERPOOL.

A NEW DESK AND POCKET ATLAS.

Handsomely bound in cloth, size 5¾ by 3½ inches, rounded corners, price 3s. 6d.; or in French morocco, gilt edges, price 5s.

PHILIPS'
HANDY-VOLUME ATLAS OF THE WORLD.

A Series of Sixty-four Plates, containing One Hundred and Ten Maps and Plans, embodying the most recent Geographical Information, and beautifully printed in colours.

Accompanied by a Complete Consulting Index of over 12,000 Places, with Geographical and Statistical Notes to each Map.

By J. FRANCON WILLIAMS, F.R.G.S.

Dedicated to the Right Hon. LORD ABERDARE, G.C.B., F.R.S., President of the Royal Geographical Society.

AND HAS BEEN ACCEPTED BY

Her Most Gracious Majesty the Queen, and
His Majesty the King of the Belgians.

PRESS NOTICES.

"Philips' 'Handy-Volume Atlas' is about the right size. 'The World,' it is often said, 'is a small place;' but for all that, it does not go so easily in a tail-coat pocket, where Mr. Philip's Atlas can be conveniently carried. It is an invaluable companion for everyday newspaper reading. *Happy thought* for travellers, to whom this little volume is recommended, 'Philip on his way through the World.'"—*Punch.*

"It is a pleasure to handle this delightful little volume.... Within its small compass it comprises a series of no less than 64 plates, containing 110 maps and plans of the different parts of the earth. Prefixed to each plate is given, in a concise form, a complete geographical description of the different countries and places represented, together with a large amount of statistical and other useful information, which could only be included by the most judicious and ingenious economy of space. The maps, though full, are remarkably clear and well-defined, and, to crown all, there is a complete index. A more charming, handy, and useful little volume could hardly be devised."—*Bookseller.*

"... A useful and convenient book ... not only an atlas but also a geography. It is compiled and edited by J. Francon Williams, F.R.G.S., who dedicates it to the President of the Royal Geographical Society."—*Morning Post.*

"It has been a long recognised need of journalists, politicians, and others, to have a set of handy volumes of this kind, with good indexes for easy references."—*Literary World.*

"We have carefully tested this atlas ... seems excellent."—*Athenæum.*

GEORGE PHILIP & SON, PUBLISHERS, LONDON AND LIVERPOOL.

A NEW COLONIAL POCKET-ATLAS.

Handsomely bound in cloth, size 5¾ by 3½ inches, rounded corners, price 3s. 6d.; or in French morocco, gilt edges, price 5s.

PHILIPS'
HANDY-VOLUME ATLAS OF THE BRITISH EMPIRE.

A Series of Sixty-four Plates, containing One Hundred and Twenty Maps and Plans of the United Kingdom, and British Colonies and Dependencies throughout the World.

Accompanied with a Complete Consulting Index of over 10,000 Places, with Geographical, Statistical, and Historical Notes to each Map.

By J. FRANCON WILLIAMS, F.R.G.S.

PRESS NOTICES.

"A delightful little volume of which every one should possess himself. The maps are reliable, and the statistical information of a really useful kind. There is, moreover, a comprehensive index."—*Pall Mall Gazette.*

"A compendious and useful book of reference."—*Morning Post.*

"A charming little book . . . portable, and can accompany a traveller everywhere."—*Anglo-American Times.*

"For neatness, conciseness, and general accuracy, 'Philips' Handy-Volume Atlas of the British Empire' leaves little to be desired. . . . A dainty little volume that can be easily carried in the pocket . . . a veritable miniature cyclopædia of the British Empire."—*School Guardian.*

"A boon to the public."—*Home and Colonial Mail.*

"Charming little pocket atlas. . . . It is long since we have seen a book which combines in an equal degree neatness, clearness, accuracy, and cheapness."—*Journal of Education.*

"We have but little doubt that the volume will prove serviceable to the ever increasing number of those who are interested in the development of our Colonial and Imperial resources."—*European Mail.*

"In the handy compass of a volume that can easily be carried in the breast pocket, this dainty little book contains no less than 120 maps illustrative of every corner of Her Majesty's dominions. . . . Messrs. Philip have provided a book that is the beau ideal of a student's manual which cannot be surpassed."—*The Teachers' Aid.*

"Messrs. Philip, in publishing this atlas, have taken a step in the right direction. . . . The statistical tables given appear to have been very carefully compiled, and contain a large amount of useful information."—*The Field.*

GEORGE PHILIP & SON, PUBLISHERS, LONDON AND LIVERPOOL.

Demy 8vo, cloth, price 18s.

THE GEOLOGY OF ENGLAND AND WALES,

WITH

NOTES ON THE PHYSICAL FEATURES OF THE COUNTRY.

By HORACE B. WOODWARD, F.G.S.

(Of the Geological Survey of England and Wales.)

Second Edition.

With Large Geological Map printed in colours (size 22 inches by 27 inches), Autotype Frontispiece, 104 Sections and Pictorial Illustrations, and numerous Tables, showing the classification and correlation of the Strata.

OPINIONS OF THE PRESS.

"During the ten years which have elapsed since the first appearance of this work, the progress of geological observation in this country has been so great that Mr. Woodward has found it necessary to amplify and almost re-write every chapter. The present volume may, therefore, be regarded not so much as a new edition as a new work. . . . A praiseworthy feature of this new issue of the work is the copious references which it offers in the form of foot-notes. By thus referring the reader to original papers the book has come to be a valuable repertory of information; it is, in fine, a book which every English geologist must have at his elbow."—*Athenæum.*

"The student, at a certain stage in his education, is often bewildered by being invited to survey too wide a field, to contemplate at one glance too many variations. Hence a work of this kind has a distinct educational value, besides its utility for purposes of reference. . . . Not the least noticeable enlargement of the present volume is in the appended geological map. The scale of the former one was too small to be of much use; this has now been doubled, with the result of producing a really serviceable map. . . . The result is a volume which for some years will be an essential to every student of British geology, and will save even the most advanced worker many an hour of weary hunting through the pages of scientific periodicals—a task not seldom as arid and unprofitable as the proverbial search for the grain of wheat in a bushel of chaff."—*Saturday Review.*

GEORGE PHILIP & SON, PUBLISHERS, LONDON AND LIVERPOOL.